How to Interpret Literature

How to Interpret Literature

Critical Theory for Literary and Cultural Studies

Fourth Edition

Robert Dale Parker
University of Illinois at Urbana-Champaign

New York   Oxford
OXFORD UNIVERSITY PRESS

Oxford University Press is a department of the University of Oxford.
It furthers the University's objective of excellence in research, scholarship,
and education by publishing worldwide. Oxford is a registered trade mark of
Oxford University Press in the UK and certain other countries.

Published in the United States of America by Oxford University Press 198 Madison Avenue, New
York, NY 10016, United States of America.

For titles covered by Section 112 of the US Higher Education
Opportunity Act, please visit www.oup.com/us/he for the latest
information about pricing and alternate formats.

Library of Congress Cataloging-in-Publication Data
Names: Parker, Robert Dale, 1953- author.
Title: How to interpret literature : critical theory for literary and cultural studies / Robert Parker.
Description: Fourth edition. | New York : Oxford University Press, 2019. | Includes bibliographical
references and index. | Summary: "Distinguished in the market by its ability to mesh
accessibility and intellectual rigor, How to Interpret Literature offers a current, concise, and
broad historicist survey of contemporary thinking in critical theory. Ideal for upper-level
undergraduate courses in literary and critical theory, this is the only book of its kind that
thoroughly merges literary studies with cultural studies, including film. Robert Dale Parker
provides a critical look at the major movements in literary studies since the 1930s, including
those often omitted from other texts. He includes chapters on New Criticism, Structuralism,
Deconstruction, Psychoanalysis, Feminism, Queer Studies, Marxism, Historicism and Cultural
Studies, Postcolonial and Race Studies, and Reader Response. Parker weaves connections
among chapters, showing how these different ways of thinking respond to and build upon each
other. Through these exchanges, he prepares students to join contemporary dialogues in literary
and cultural studies. The text is enhanced by charts, text boxes that address frequently asked
questions, photos, and a bibliography"—Provided by publisher.
Identifiers: LCCN 2019021363 (print) | LCCN 2019980803 (ebook) | ISBN 9780190855697
(paperback) | ISBN 9780190855703 (ebook other) | ISBN 9780190074722 (ebook other)
Subjects: LCSH: Criticism—History—20th century. | Criticism—History—21st century.
Classification: LCC PN94 .P37 2019 (print) | LCC PN94 (ebook) | DDC 801/.950904—dc23
LC record available at https://lccn.loc.gov/2019021363
LC ebook record available at https://lccn.loc.gov/2019980803

Printing number: 9 8 7 6 5 4 3 2 1
Printed by LSC Communications, Inc., United States of America

Contents

⚛ Preface ⚛

I wrote this book because my students needed it and asked for it. As college and university literature and cultural studies courses have raised our expectations for teaching critical theory, the number of surveys and introductory theory books has grown. Some of those books have proven valuable. But based on my experience as a teacher, it seemed to me that we still needed a book that approaches critical theory more historically, showing how different movements in critical theory respond to and build on each other, and a book that goes beyond cautious textbook summaries to cover a good many issues, debates, and controversies that I did not see adequately addressed in other books on the topic. To name only a few out of many possible examples, as a teacher I wanted a book that did more than other such books to introduce narrative theory, because most students take a particular interest in novels and stories. I wanted a book that introduces the dialogues among different kinds of feminist criticism and a book that introduces queer studies, the debates over essentialism and the construction of race, the dialogues among critical race studies, postcolonial studies, and international indigenous studies, and newer movements of enormous consequence, such as disability studies and environmental studies. I also wanted a book that would take formalism seriously while at the same time taking history and cultural interpretation seriously. In that sense, I set out to write a critical theory survey committed to the interpretation of literature—including film—and at the same time committed to cultural studies and the interpretation of culture at large.

This book sets out to do all those things and to do them in readable language that does not assume previous knowledge of the material, yet also in language that takes students seriously and respects their curiosity and ability. In that spirit, I welcome feedback from students, teachers, and other readers.

The primary though not the only audience for this book is the critical theory survey course now routinely offered in college and university English and literature departments. I have tried to present the material in a format flexible enough to go along with the ways that different teachers approach a wide range of courses. Teachers, for example, may choose to use this book with a variety of other materials, depending on the course. The book may hover in the background as a supplement to the study of Shakespeare, the modern novel, film noir, and so on, or it may anchor a course in critical theory. For courses in critical theory, some teachers may choose to have this book carry the course, while others may combine it with readings from critical theorists. Interested instructors will find a concise selection of such readings in the companion volume to this book, *Critical Theory: A Reader for Literary and Cultural Studies*. They may also choose to combine this book with works of criticism and with works of literature and film. Some teachers will want to return to the same works of literature or film across a large part of the course, but different courses and populations of students will lead instructors to choose different works and strategies, sometimes changing from semester to semester, so I have opted to leave those decisions to instructors rather than to lock this book and its readers into relying on the same works over and over.

Now and then, I offer anecdotes from my own classroom experience. I have found that students appreciate and learn from such anecdotes, and I hope that readers beyond my classroom will find them helpful as well. I do not include samples of student writing, because many instructors find that such samples are not a good match for their own students and lead students to think too imitatively. Instructors who find student examples useful can probably find the best examples for their own students from previous students at their own institutions. Throughout the book, however, I provide examples of how to interpret literature and culture in dialogue with the movements in critical theory that this book presents. I have tried to write those examples to encourage, rather than to interfere with, teachers' and students' readiness to develop their own examples.

In many ways, Terry Eagleton's now dated classic *Literary Theory: An Introduction* (1983) inspired this book, more than the various other books that arose in its wake. Though this book differs greatly from Eagleton's, for I bring fewer skills to the task and bring different limits and resources, I hope it can honor Eagleton's legacy, even while I speak from the perspective of a later generation and a different intellectual history. I hope, as well, that this book can lead students to continue thinking about the issues that it puts forward as they move on to other courses and, beyond course work, as they live their daily lives.

WHAT'S NEW IN THE FOURTH EDITION

I am grateful for the enthusiastic response to the first three editions. The fourth edition continues what people liked in the earlier editions and makes many improvements. While it was not possible to follow every suggestion I received, I am grateful to the many scholars and teachers who shared their ideas, and I look forward to hearing responses to this new edition.

The new edition does not attempt to address every latest idea in current conversations around critical theory. Some additions seemed called for, but I have also tried to retain the book's focus and shape while telling a larger story. For the new edition I reviewed every page in every chapter many times, sharpening, condensing, expanding, changing or adding examples, and updating. Roughly half of the pages include at least a little revision, and many include extensive revision. The new edition uses subheadings more consistently across the various chapters, clarifying and highlighting the progression of ideas. I will list the larger revisions here, while recognizing that such a list masks the frequency of smaller but consequential revisions across the book.

- Chapter 3 now includes a review of Charles Sanders Peirce's theory of the sign, modestly expands the reading of sitcoms, and expands the ending of the reading of detective novels.
- Chapter 4 adds a box on common misunderstandings.
- Chapter 5 modestly expands its brief discussion of the mirror stage.
- For Chapter 6, I added a paragraph on how there are many different ways to be a feminist; expanded the discussion of sex and gender to take into account intersex and transgender identities; added remarks on the claim that feminism is a western export imposed on the rest of the world; clarified the discussion of Mulvey's argument about visual pleasure, including a short paragraph on the term "male gaze"; added a paragraph on bell hooks's critique of Mulvey, including hooks's concept of the oppositional gaze; and added a box on the claims that we have now reached a fourth-wave feminism.

- Chapter 7 now includes more about transgender identities; reviews the evolving vocabulary around queer identities; expands the section on Foucault's *The History of Sexuality, Volume I*; adds Muñoz's concept of disidentification; and adds a section on the anti-social turn and queer time.
- Chapter 8 better highlights the connection between Althusser's understanding of ideology and Lacan's concept of misrecognition.
- Chapter 9 adds a box on the status of facts; adds a section on biopower; connects cultural studies to interpreting the resurgence of far-right politics; adds a section on Raymond Williams's terms dominant, residual, and emergent; and adds a short paragraph on the relation between cultural studies and aesthetics.
- Chapter 10 adds more on migration and Stuart Hall's discussion of hybridity; adds more about Fanon and racial labeling; further clarifies the discussion of Spivak's "Can the Subaltern Speak?"; adds a discussion of race, representation, and form; describes how indigenous identities are not the same as racial identities; sharpens the discussion of critical race theory, including the concepts of implicit bias, disparate impact, and white privilege; adds a section on racial appropriation; briefly brings in the debate between George S. Schuyler and Langston Hughes as well as Spillers's "Mama's Baby, Papa's Maybe," Hurston's "Characteristics of Negro Expression," and Beyoncé and Jay-Z's *Apes**t*; and adds a reading of Nella Larsen's *Passing*.
- Chapter 11 now includes distant reading.
- Chapter 12 adds a section on the nonhuman, brings in the relation between feminism and disability studies, better highlights invisible disabilities, and expands the discussion of the critique of disabilities stereotypes.
- The back of the book now also includes a concise glossary of terms for poetic form, which can complement the account of narrative theory in Chapter 3.

Acknowledgments

For a book like this, it is more than mere formula when I say that no one besides myself is responsible for my mistakes, oversights, and misjudgments. Nevertheless, I am grateful to many people for encouraging this book and helping to improve it. Over years of studying literature, literary criticism, and critical theory, I have learned so much related to this book from so many different people that the task of trying to name them all is too daunting to dare. I would inevitably leave out many people by oversight and for lack of space.

But some people cannot go unmentioned. I want to thank my students. They provoked me to think about the issues this book confronts and taught me to ask many of the questions it depends on. They made this book worth writing. More than that, they compelled me to write it. An extra thank-you goes out to the student—I wish I could remember who it was—who said something like "This course should be called 'How to Interpret Literature.' Then students who don't get it would realize how interesting this stuff is and realize that they need to learn it."

I would also like to thank Brian McHale for insisting, from early on, that there was more out there in criticism and theory than I had usually been led to believe, and Zohreh T. Sullivan for helping to convince me, long ago, that literary and critical theory had found ways to reach beyond the formalisms that I cherished but found confining. With pleasure and appreciation, I also thank the long list of challenging and dedicated friends and colleagues who have made it a privilege to work in the Department of English, the Unit for Criticism and Interpretive Theory, and the Program in American Indian Studies at the University of Illinois at Urbana-Champaign. They continually expand my sense of what there is to know and make me question my own thinking. I am especially grateful to Janet M. Beatty, my original editor at Oxford University Press, for her receptive interest in this book, her canny ability to point me in helpful directions, and her diligence in getting useful responses from the following readers of the manuscript for the first edition: Nathan A. Breen, DePaul University; Michael Calabrese, California State University, Los Angeles; Lynn A. Casmier-Paz, University of Central Florida; Barry J. Faulk, Florida State University; James Ford, University of Nebraska, Lincoln; George Hahn, Towson University; Brady Harrison, University of Montana; Susan Howard, Duquesne University; Cy Knoblauch, University of North Carolina at Charlotte; Ira Livingston, Pratt Institute; Alan S. Loxterman, University of Richmond; Elsie B. Michie, Louisiana State University; Harry Rusche, Emory University; and Douglass H. Thomson, Georgia Southern University. To those readers, as well, I am immensely grateful.

Thanks as well to the readers for the second edition: John Alberti, Northern Kentucky University; Jen Camden, University of Indianapolis; James Campbell, University of Central Florida; Wendy Carse, Indiana University of Pennsylvania; John Dudley, University of South Dakota; Tiffany Gilbert, University of North Carolina Wilmington; David Greven, Connecticut College; Christopher Hogarth, Wagner College; Paul Klemp, University of Wisconsin Oshkosh; Peggy Kulesz, University of Texas at Arlington; Chad Luck, California State University Santa Barbara; Christian Moraru, University of North Carolina at Greensboro; and Vicki Smith, Texas State University. I am also grateful to those who reviewed the second and third editions to advise about the possibility of a new edition: Kenneth Asher, SUNY Geneseo; Noelle Bowles, Kent State University at Trumbull; Tiffany Gilbert, University of North Carolina Wilmington; Evan Gottlieb, Oregon State University; David Greven, University of South Carolina; Paul Klemp, University of Wisconsin Oshkosh; Christine Kozikowski, University of New Mexico; Tracy Montgomery, Idaho State University; Richard Zumkhawala-Cook, Shippensburg University; Matthew Biberman, University of Louisville; Kirsti Cole, Minnesota State University; Jaime Goodrich, Wayne State University; Anthony Grajeda, University of Central Florida; Holly Henry, California State University, San Bernardino; Kathryn Ledbetter, Texas State University; Nowell Marshall, Rider University; Kevin Swafford, Bradley University; Jeffrey W. Timmons, Arizona State University-West; and Kelli D. Zaytoun, Wright State University.

I am grateful as well to Stacy Alaimo, J. B. Capino, Meghan Dykema, Trish Loughran, Brian McHale, Laura Mielke, Michael Rothberg, Dustin Tahmahkera, and Patrick Walker for suggestions or conversations that helped with the revised editions.

I have continued to be fortunate in my editors at Oxford University Press. For their work on the second edition, I remain grateful to Janet M. Beatty and her assistant Cory Schneider. My next editor, Frederick Speers, supported this book through its second and third editions with commitment and insightful suggestions. Thank you to him and to his assistants Talia Benamy and Kristina Nocerino. In a time of editorial turnover, I lucked out in the editor for the fourth edition, Steve Helba, who has been a model of sharp-minded, easy-to-work-with profession-alism. Thank you to Steve, to his assistant Kora Fillet, and to Patricia Berube, who oversaw the production. And as always, and yet again, at the beginning, the middle, the end, and beyond, thank you to Janice N. Harrington.

❊ 1 ❊

Introduction

This book sets out to invite its readers into contemporary conversations about how to interpret literature, culture, and critical theory. It surveys the most influential patterns of thought in critical theory from the 1930s to the present, with a special interest in the role of critical theory for interpreting literature and culture. The study of critical theory has changed rapidly over the last few decades, and though teaching has changed more slowly than scholarship, teaching has now caught up. For many years, I felt impatient with my own field of English because of its attitude toward theory in the classroom. Since the mid-1970s, when I was an undergraduate, and arguably still today, "theory" has been at the center of what English professors do, but at the same time, many English professors worked by the unspoken principle that this thing at the center of what we do had better be kept a privileged secret. The idea was, go ahead and learn all the critical and literary theory that we can, and let it drive everything we do as professors of literature, but *don't tell the students.*

Don't tell the students, because it will scare them. Don't tell the students, because they can't handle it. They're not smart enough.

Fortunately, the fear of teaching theory in the classroom has mostly faded away, and at many schools it is already buried. When students read this book for a class, then, their teacher and perhaps the department their teacher belongs to are part of that change. Indeed, I have written this book because I join with the many critics—perhaps we are now a majority—who think that the idea that students cannot learn critical theory is nonsense. Theory will scare students if we do

1

it in a scary way, and I will admit that many professors discuss theory in ways that can scare off the uninitiated. But we do not have to discuss it that way.

Devotees of theory sometimes like to claim a privileged territory that they can paint as terribly difficult for everyone else, but it is not usually difficult unless we make it difficult, trying to make it sound sophisticated so that we can tell ourselves, and others, that we are sophisticated. In fact, most students are already sophisticated theorists. They just don't use the same vocabulary of theory that English professors use. While students may not know English professors' vocabulary, they have their own specialized vocabularies that most English professors do not know, and many of them theorize with their specialized languages enthusiastically. Does that mean that English professors are not smart enough to understand them? It only means, of course, that people who do not know a given vocabulary cannot speak the language that uses that vocabulary. And theory is a language with its own vocabulary of words and ideas, whether in the latest mix of music, technology, and social networking or in the scholarly, college, and university dialects of "literary theory," "critical theory," and "cultural criticism."

Since the early 1970s, the growth of "critical theory" (the broader category) and "literary theory" (the narrower category) has revolutionized literary criticism and cultural criticism. For a time, the swiftly accumulating changes came wrapped in scandal. How dare they contaminate—or even replace—the study of literature with "theory," opponents asked. In the late 1970s, many English and other literature departments splintered into pro- and antitheory factions. It was partly a generational difference, for to some people, theory seemed like the newfangled fad of the young. But the younger generations were learning the theory from older generations, and in its broadest sense theory goes back at least as far as the ancient storytellers and philosophers, so it was never just a matter of people's age. Eventually the sense of scandal disappeared, for no one asks theory to replace literature. And it is hard to argue convincingly that theory is bad, because by saying so, opponents of theory end up proposing another theory—the theory that theory is bad—so that they end up endorsing what they thought they were objecting to. Gradually, from the late 1970s and into the 1990s, the theory wars died out and theory went mainstream, sometimes over the objections of theorists themselves, who often fancy their role as troublemakers or gadflies.

Though the varieties of theory described in this book hit their first big threshold in the debates of English and literature departments, they also drew on and then came back to influence ways of thinking in philosophy (which of course was always theoretical), linguistics, political science, history, communications, anthropology, film studies, sociology, and many other fields. Eventually, the growth of critical theory generated a common language that allowed people in different fields, and in widely varying precincts of the same fields, to talk with, understand, and learn from each other across their differing backgrounds and interests. Students and faculty from political science, for example, found that they could talk about their interests with students and faculty in English in ways that they rarely could before.

That helps give the lie to the complaint, still occasionally heard, that theory is so arcane that it makes literary study irrelevant at a time when relevance and connection to the troubled, practical world have a desperate urgency. In fact, and as we will see as this book moves along, theory is about nothing if it is not about the interweaving of literary study, critical study, and the everyday world where all of us live. This book—and the ideas it presents and discusses—sets out not to make literary study less meaningful in our daily lives, but to make it more meaningful. So much so that as you read this book, you might start to find connections between what this book discusses and a great many other things you care about, such as politics, art and beauty, the environment, music, movies, social policy, identity, and on and on, including, for students, a wide range of classes in literary studies and other fields. Literature connects to and is part of everything else around us, and literary criticism, critical theory, and the study of literature also connect to and are part of everything else. This book sets out to bring all those things together: literature, criticism, theory, cultural studies, and everything around us. In short, this is a book about how, every day, we interpret—and can enjoy interpreting—the dialogue between art and daily life.

Criticism, theory, literature. Students sometimes ask what we mean when we refer to *criticism*, because criticism does not usually carry the same meaning in literary and cultural studies as it carries in casual conversation. When we use the term *criticism* in casual conversation, it refers to saying what we dislike. But that is not what the term means in this book, and it is not what the term typically means in critical writing or in college and university literature, film, and cultural studies classes. Instead, as this book uses the term, and as cultural, film, and literary critics typically use the term, it refers to interpretation and insightful commentary. While film and book reviewers see their role as judging whether a film or book is good or not-so-good, critical writing focuses far more on interpreting and usually lets judgments about a work's value remain implicit or peripheral.

Even so, there is a difference between *criticism* and *theory*. Criticism tends to focus on interpreting a cultural practice, such as a movie, a music video, a trend in fashion or social networking, a novel, a play, or a poem. Theory tends to focus, by contrast, on proposing or interpreting models for how to do criticism. Nevertheless, theory and criticism overlap, because theory includes criticism and criticism draws, at least implicitly, on theory. Still more, as I discuss later, theory and criticism depend on each other and can even merge into each other.

Some criticism, however, focuses less on theory. And some ways of thinking about models for criticism do not usually find room under the umbrella of critical theory and thus are not included in this book. For example, while readers will find an appendix of terms for discussing poetic form at the back of the book, this book does not focus on poetic form (*prosody*) or offer suggestions about how to craft a critical essay. Such concerns can influence how we think about, understand, and write criticism; but other, easily found books already address those concerns well, so this book concentrates more on the topics typically associated with critical theory.

It can probably help, as well, to ask what we mean by the term *literature*. The truth is, there is no exact, definitive, and widely agreed-on meaning for the term *literature*. For the purposes of this book, literature is simply those things we refer to by the word *literature*. For more traditional critics, literature refers to poetry, drama, and fiction and perhaps sometimes to more self-consciously artful essays or autobiography. In recent years, however, as we will see through the course of this book, the term has opened up considerably. It can include any writing that people wish to study with the same critical intensity and appreciation that critics traditionally bring to poetry, drama, and fiction, and not only writing, but also film. More broadly still, especially under the influence of cultural studies, critics increasingly see the textuality of literature as overlapping with the textuality of all language and with the textuality, loosely speaking, of popular culture and other forms of communication, whether written (a magazine article, a poem), aural (music, speech), visual (photography, painting), kinetic (sports, dance), or some combination of those (film, new media). While in the narrow sense of the term, literature often continues to refer to poetry, drama, fiction, and perhaps essays and autobiography, critics seem comfortable moving back and forth between narrower and broader uses of the term, without worrying over definitions and flexible categories. In that way, then, this book takes heed of film and popular culture as well as poetry, drama, and fiction.

The shape of this book. Some instructors may choose to assign the chapters of this book in a different order. For example, while many instructors have praised the sequence of chapters, some have chosen to assign Marxism or reader response earlier in the sequence, or to separate postcolonial studies and race studies, or to combine queer studies and feminism under the category of gender studies. While the book can accommodate such strategies and others like them, the progression of chapters follows a shape that it may help to lay out explicitly at the beginning.

For the most part, the book follows a chronological sequence, and in a sense it is also circular. If you look at the table of contents, you might think that it does not look chronological, because even readers who do not yet know much about the ways of thinking referred to in the table of contents will sometimes know, for example, that psychoanalysis began before structuralism or deconstruction, that feminism began before psychoanalysis, or that Marxism began before queer studies. But rather than organizing the chapters in a sequence according to when each way of thinking began, I have put them in a sequence that roughly follows when each way of thinking reached its threshold in the history of literary criticism and theory. There are two exceptions. The chapter on queer studies comes a little early in the sequence, right after the chapter on feminism, because queer studies builds closely on feminism. Many critics, as we have already seen, even group them together as movements in gender studies. And the chapter on reader-response criticism comes near the end, before the recent and emerging developments, simply because it refers to issues from other chapters in ways that will grow clearer if it comes after those other chapters. In the process, the chapter on reader response can help review the earlier parts of the book. Apart from those two exceptions, I have chosen the roughly chronological sequence not out of some sterile notion of counting the years, but because it tells a story across the book.

That is to say, each movement in criticism and theory draws on and responds to the movements that preceded it, and so to understand each movement, it helps to have studied the movements that came before it. For that reason also, as we move forward in the book, our patterns of thought will build on each other and make the discussion cumulative. Beginning especially with Chapter 4, on deconstruction, as we work with each new movement we will use the movements that preceded it. Deconstruction, as we will see in Chapter 4, is partly a response to structuralism, from Chapter 3. And structuralism (not in its roots, but in its use by literary critics, especially in the United States) is partly a response to new criticism, from Chapter 2. Psychoanalysis began with Freud's work before new criticism, structuralism, and deconstruction, but it did not grab powerful hold of literary criticism until after it had structuralism and deconstruction to work with. Feminist criticism, then, responded profoundly to psychoanalysis, and so on through the rest of the book. In that way, the book tells a story. But also in that way, the chapter boundaries are not as firm as the table of contents might suggest, because when we study any one method, we will continue to study the methods before it.

As we study the earlier ways of thinking, I will risk making things a little more difficult, now and then, by peeking forward to begin (just briefly) making comparisons to ways of thinking that came later. While in the short run that risks confusing readers, in the long run it makes things easier and clearer, because it would be artificial to pretend, while studying a set of ideas from the past, that other ideas from later on have not influenced the way we can understand the older ideas. In discussing new criticism, for example, I will draw (a little) on historicism, because now that critics have developed a new range of skills for reading historically, it would be false to pretend that historicist insights cannot help us read new criticism, even though the new critics themselves (as we will see) were not especially historicist. Similarly, it would be false, and even damaging, to rule out references to feminism before we reach the chapter that specifically focuses on feminism. Whatever readers know or do not know about feminism, it will be on many readers' minds from the beginning of the book, and that is a good thing, not a problem.

At the same time that the sequence of chapters has a chronological shape, in another sense it has a circular shape. That is to say, at the end we will return to where we began. The new critics whom we will begin with wanted to make criticism more formalist (we will see what that means soon, in Chapter 2), and in making it more formalist they tended to make it less cultural and historical. The structuralists and deconstructionists, then, whatever their differences from the new critics and from each other, extended that interest in formalism. Then eventually, as we will see, many critics reacted against formalism and sought to take criticism back to a focus on the cultural and historical. In that sense, the story this book tells is circular. But when critics returned to the cultural and historical, they returned in the light of the intense developments in formalist criticism under the new critics, structuralists, and deconstructionists, which meant that in their hands, cultural and historical criticism looked dramatically different from how it looked several generations earlier, before the new critics. That is the story that this book will tell.

Along the way, the book will introduce a great deal of vocabulary, because, as we have already suggested, studying critical theory is not only *like* studying a language, it *is* studying a language. And so this book will go a good distance toward introducing the language of critical theory. Sometimes the terms are specialized and stuffy, and other times they are lively and provocative. Either way, the terms have a momentum behind them, and so learning them can at the least help us follow other people's use of them. At the most, the terms can help us learn and use the concepts of criticism. Each term provides a handle that helps us grasp the idea it represents and that may help us turn that idea to use, whether we respond to the idea skeptically or enthusiastically. (Key terms appear in **bold** when they are introduced and explained, usually the first time they appear in the book. In the index, those terms are also bolded, along with the numbers for pages that introduce and explain them. After finishing the book, some readers may find it helpful to go back over the concepts by reviewing the bolded terms in the index.) Along the way, as well, the approach of the book will change a little after the first few chapters. Chapters 2 and 3 run longer, not because new criticism and structuralism are more important than the topics in later chapters, but because, besides introducing new criticism and structuralism, those chapters also introduce the overall book. Later chapters can sometimes be shorter, because the earlier chapters will already have introduced many of the key concepts and terms that later methods of criticism rely on.

In the process, this book attempts to include two different approaches. Some scholars, teachers, and students of critical and literary theory favor an approach that studies theory for the sake of theorizing, while other scholars, teachers, and possibly a majority of students favor an approach that addresses theory for the sake of interpretation, such as the interpretation of literature or film. Rather than leaning in one direction or the other, this book respects both impulses and is willing, at any given point, to favor one or the other, if that helps get across a concept. I see the opposition between theory and interpretation as a false dichotomy, what deconstructionists call a *false binary*. Without trying either to balance them or to lean in either direction, this book welcomes the conflict between theory and interpretation as a fruitful provocation. I try to speak in practical, accessible, and provocative ways both to theory itself and to the interpretive "application" or "use" of theory without the skepticism that each of these interests sometimes brings to the other, for I see theory and interpretation as versions of each other, two faces of the same coin.

Readers will get the most from this book if, when possible, they read the written literature or watch the films that the book takes as examples for detailed discussion. Even so, I provide enough quotation or context to help readers unfamiliar with the works. And for longer texts, such as films, plays, and novels, I have kept in mind that readers who do not already know the works may not find it convenient to read them or watch them while reading this book. But many of the sample texts are so short that they are included within the book or are easy to find and read, because they are readily available online and in libraries.

Thus, at the appropriate point in the course, instructors might assign (or students might read on their own initiative) John Donne's "The Canonization," Emily Dickinson's "Further in summer than the birds," Walt Whitman's "Beat! Beat! Drums!," Wallace Stevens's "Anecdote of a Jar," Section 11 of Whitman's "Song of Myself," Ezra Pound's "In a Station of the Metro," Arthur Conan Doyle's "The Adventure of Charles Augustus Milverton," Elizabeth Bishop's "First Death in Nova Scotia," Ernest Hemingway's "Cat in the Rain," Bharati Mukherjee's "Jasmine," Dorothy Parker's "A Telephone Call," Gwendolyn Brooks's "We Real Cool," Edwin Arlington Robinson's "Richard Cory," Kate Chopin's "The Story of an Hour," William Wordsworth's "Lines Composed a Few Miles above Tintern Abbey," Shakespeare's Sonnet 130, and Robert Frost's "Design." Films and videos discussed in at least a little detail include *The Descent, Salt, Top Gun, A Single Man, Apes**t,* and especially *The Crying Game, Brokeback Mountain, Dirty Pretty Things,* and *Avatar.* While *Get Out* is mentioned only briefly, it can go well with Chapter 10's discussion of racial appropriation.

With these works and the many others that the book discusses or mentions, I have tried to choose a variety of examples. A few instructors have asked me to scrap most of the earlier materials and focus only on contemporary writing and on film from the last few years, or focus much more on the time period that the instructor specializes in, but that would go against most other instructors' interests and goals. Still more, it would pass up the chance to model the possibility and the pleasure of reading and viewing across a wide range of film, TV, and literary history. In that spirit, this book works with all periods of English-language literature, including both older and more recent writing, film, and TV. It also works with both longer and shorter literature and with a variety of genres, including poems, short stories, films, novels, TV shows, and plays. As most of the book's readers come from English departments, the literary examples draw mostly on English-language literature. I am encouraged, nevertheless, that readers interested—as I hope we all are—in a wide range of languages and literatures have found the book useful.

One caution, and one word to the wise: First, the caution. As readers new to the material get excited about how the new ideas influence their thinking, they can find themselves reading on eagerly and quickly. While such eagerness is appealing, most readers will learn more if they pace their reading. Instead of reading multiple chapters in quick succession or even reading an entire chapter at once, most readers will find it helpful to break up a chapter into two or more episodes of reading, giving them time to contemplate the material and begin getting used to each method's patterns of thinking before they read onward. The structuralism chapter, especially, introduces a large number of concepts, making it helpful to read on the installment plan and focus, at first, on getting the key general ideas. Readers can always go back and review the particulars later. After finishing a chapter, many readers find it helpful to reread the passages that offer interpretations of particular texts (which often but not always come in the "How to Interpret" sections). Rereading those passages from the perspective gained by finishing a chapter can help readers develop a feeling for the questions, assumptions, and patterns of thinking that characterize each body of thought.

Now, the word to the wise: Most critical and literary theory after the new criticism comes from the political left, and most of it is secular. I say this up front not to scare off readers who may not come from a left or secular perspective, but instead to welcome them to the conversation. I believe that it is better to make that explicit than to try to sneak it in. Most people who teach and write about the material discussed in this book approach it as if all their readers and students will share their left and secular perspectives. While I recognize that many readers of this book will share those perspectives, either more or less, I do not assume that all students, teachers, and other readers will join me in such views. I also believe that left and secular positions need have no monopoly on the ideas and debates discussed in this book. Even Marxist strategies of interpretation (if not Marxist goals) seem to me mostly adaptable to right-wing thinking. In many respects, the ideas in this book can be debated, endorsed, or applied by readers on the right just as well as by readers on the left. It would be healthy for critical theory to have the right and left join in more dialogue, and more mutually informed dialogue, about the debates that this book reviews.

I have written this book in part because I find that the courses I teach that evolved into this book make more difference to students than any other courses I teach. They make so much difference because learning about critical theory helps us think about everything else we do, and it often helps us think about those things in dramatically new and exciting ways. While this book sets out to help its readers think and write about literature, including film, it also assumes a give-and-take relation between literature and everything else, so that it tries to help readers discover ways to build what they can do as critical thinkers in general. That, in turn, can feed back into our thinking about literature, which then can feed our other thinking all the more, which comes back yet again to energize our thinking about literature, and so on in a cycle that can inspire our commitment to and pleasure in literary and cultural interpretation.

⁕ 2 ⁕

New Criticism

The new criticism is now the old criticism and the bogeyman that every later critical method defines itself against, but when the new criticism emerged in the 1930s and 1940s, it seemed revolutionary. It radically changed critical practice, especially in the United States. Though it is far out of fashion now, the new criticism continues to wield enormous influence, even on many critics and teachers who reject it.

When I introduce students to new criticism, I like to ask how many of them, in their previous experience in literature classes, have heard any of the following phrases, which all come from new criticism: close reading, evidence from the text, pay attention to the text itself, pay attention to the words on the page, unpack the words. Every time I ask that question, sometimes to classes as large as seventy students, every single student raises a hand, even students from continents far beyond the United States. It has a powerful effect when students look around the room and see that every one of them shares that experience. Then I ask how many of them have heard of new criticism? Suddenly, all but a few hands drop. Sometimes I ask if the few people whose hands have not dropped think they might be able to define new criticism (telling them, of course, that I won't actually put them on the spot and ask them to define it), and usually their hands drop too, or if they don't drop, they wobble.

In short, across an enormous range of different schools, in colleges and high schools, many English teachers have taught students these principles but not told them about the larger set of ideas that the principles come from. I want to take the opposite approach here. This book sets out to bring students behind the curtain and invite them to join the sometimes-hidden discussions about critical theory that drive the study of English.

Methods of interpretation. In fact, though some teachers do not tell students this, everything the students have done in their English classes over the years has followed, and owes its ideas to, a selection of specific *methods of interpretation.* By keeping quiet about those methods in front of students, teachers make it harder for students to question what we do in English classes and also make it harder for students to learn what their teachers are doing and to figure out ways to do it themselves. By contrast, if we make the methods visible, then students can evaluate those methods (and how the teachers use them). That might make it harder for teachers, if the teachers do not want their students to think critically about what the teachers do, but to my mind getting students to think critically about what their teachers do is a good thing. And in the process, for most students, the study of critical method—of critical theory—will make English easier, and far more interesting, and even more *fun.* In that way, this book sets itself against the view that critical theory is too difficult for students. We make literary study too difficult if we cloak its premises in mystifying secrecy, but we make it more accessible—and more honest—if we yank open the curtain to reveal the squeaky machinery behind it.

Students may find it helpful, as they read this book or after reading it, to use what they read about here to help themselves ask, in every class (not just English classes), what methods of criticism (or thinking, or experiment, or research, and so on) the class is using. What are the specific characteristics of those methods? Why would people choose those methods, or not choose them? Why would other people choose other methods, and what other methods might they choose? How would different methods produce different results? How have the methods changed over time, and why? If it were up to you, what methods would you choose? These are the questions we will ask about literary and cultural criticism in this book. The assumption is that readers will get far more out of their interests in literature and criticism and their interests in artistic and cultural expression in general (movies, music, paintings, websites, politics, sports, and so on) if they step back and think about the methods at stake when they think about literature, art, and culture. Critical theory, in short, is simply thinking about thinking. We can think more expansively—and enjoyably—if in the process of thinking we also think about thinking.

The new critics were the first modern Anglo-American critics to set up a programmatic, deliberate method for interpreting literature, and in that sense they begin the story that this book tells. Moreover, since everything we will study later in this book defines itself, in part, as an alternative and response to new criticism, we can better understand more recent ways of thinking about how to interpret literature and culture if we first get a good grounding in new criticism.

BEFORE NEW CRITICISM

While for the most part this book begins with new criticism, we can better understand new criticism and today's criticism if we look briefly at the state of things before new criticism, at the practices that the new critics invented new criticism to replace. New criticism succeeded so widely in taking over the critical landscape that even now, when every later critical method sets itself against it, new criticism has come to seem so natural that students often find it hard to imagine alternatives to new criticism or to understand how it seemed new from the 1930s to the 1950s. New—as opposed to what?

Before the new critics, the classroom study of English literature routinely focused on history, on what the new critics sneered at as "impressionistic" responses to literature, on moralizing, and on reading aloud. The new critics set up their ways of reading literature in direct opposition to each of these previous routines.

History. Teachers and critics who focused the study of literature on history often concentrated on the writer's biography. Sometimes they focused on the writer's "milieu," meaning the writer's circle of friends and of other writers and artists. Many historical critics gave special attention to studying a writer's influences and sources. For example, they might note that the British Victorian poet Alfred, Lord Tennyson, uses lyrical language that often echoes the lyrical language of his predecessor, the British Romantic poet John Keats. Sometimes they would go to great lengths to trace individual words or phrases, pointing out that Tennyson echoes or repeats words and phrases from Keats or perhaps from an earlier poet, such as Edmund Spenser. Beginning with the new criticism, this kind of source and influence study came to seem arcane or dry. Despite a gossipy exception here and there, it does not usually hold students' interest for long. Biography continues to interest readers, but many critics, influenced by the new critics, believe that biography tends to stray from the point, for they believe that the point is the literature itself, in the "text" that new critics ask us to read "closely." (We will address biography again later in this chapter, when we talk about the *intentional fallacy*.)

Sometimes, especially at the graduate level, the historical study of literature focused on "philology," that is, on the history of the language (in this case, English). Scholars of philology and literature study how literature shows the way languages have changed over time. To the new critics, such study offered scholarship but not much of the criticism and interpretation that they saw as crucial for literary study.

Impressionism. The new critics wanted a rigorous, systematic, theorized approach to literature. They looked down on more casual approaches, which they dubbed mere impressionism. To say that Tennyson's "Marianna" is the saddest poem in the English language or that the humor of Shakespeare's Falstaff or the suspense of Jane Austen's *Pride and Prejudice* can warm troubled hearts would seem anti-intellectual to the new critics. They saw remarks like that as mere fluff that we need to replace with concrete methods of criticism.

To some readers, the new critics suffered from what we might call "science envy," and we can understand why. Literary studies and science both held considerable prestige, but they did not hold the same prestige. In the university environment of the first half of the twentieth century, the hard or social sciences might seem more established than English. They had methods, and their methods gave them an identity. If professors taught or wrote about sociology, they were sociologists. If they taught or wrote about botany, physics, or chemistry, they were botanists, physicists, or chemists. But if you crossed the university lawn to the professors who taught or wrote about English literature, what would you call them? There was no term for it and no concrete sense of what they actually did as scholars or teachers. The new critics, who sometimes wrote anxiously about the relation between science and literary study, sought to change that fuzziness of definition by proclaiming that the work of literary study is criticism and that criticism has its own methods, just like chemistry or sociology. To the new critics, criticism was not about vague impressions or feelings. It was about methodical interpretation.

Moralizing. In that context, moralizing had no place in criticism, the new critics thought. The point of studying William Wordsworth's "I wandered lonely as a cloud" is not to teach us how to behave better. We do not—or should not—read Emily Dickinson's "Further in summer than the birds" for the purpose of learning to appreciate the environmental value of crickets or even to gain a profounder understanding of loneliness. The point of Austen's novels is not to teach us when to speak out and when to hold our tongue, and the point of Nathaniel Hawthorne's *The Scarlet Letter*, for a new critic, is not to teach us the danger of adultery or to instruct us in sympathy for our neighbors. To new critics, criticism should look for the art or artistic form of the story, not for the moral of the story.

It would get hard for new critics to insist on that distinction for literary works explicitly devoted to moral or ethical causes, such as Harriet Beecher Stowe's *Uncle Tom's Cabin* or Upton Sinclair's *The Jungle*, but they would happily escape that bind by seeing such works as propaganda and not as great art fit for serious critical analysis. To be sure, not everyone agrees about that distinction between propaganda and art, especially for more self-consciously literary works that still speak directly to politics, such as Charles Dickens's *Hard Times*, Richard Wright's *Native Son*, Joy Kogawa's *Obasan*, Margaret Atwood's *The Handmaid's Tale* and its film and TV adaptations, or Pat Barker's *Regeneration* trilogy. But new critics would avoid such examples, or they would see the combination of art and political commitment in such books as coincidental, with the politics not illuminating the art. Such examples can start to show the theoretical rectitude that often attracted people to new criticism and that also made many people skeptical of an aesthetic fastidiousness and social aloofness in the new critics. Readers may continue to see both sides of that dilemma as this chapter goes along.

Reading aloud. Before the new critics, many literature classrooms took no interest in the goals of criticism as the new critics understood those goals. Teachers and students cared more about the appreciation and the performance of literature than about the criticism of it. That pattern continues in some classrooms, especially in the lower grades or, at some colleges, in general education courses for nonmajors. In that vein, and especially before the new critics, many classes gave little or no heed to criticism and concentrated on reading the literature out loud. New critics might not object to reading aloud, but they would see it as just a beginning, as incidental to their critical goals, rather than see reading aloud itself as the goal.

Let me give an example. Once long ago I heard Maynard Mack, a distinguished and by then elderly critic of Shakespeare and eighteenth-century British literature, tell a story about what college classes in English literature were like before the new critics, based on his recollection of his time as a student. (He graduated from Yale University in 1932.) He said that a Shakespeare class on *Romeo and Juliet* might begin with the professor asking the students to write an account of how they once felt the way that Romeo feels. (At Yale in those days, all the students were male. I wonder how things might have gone if they were asked to recall a time when they felt the way Juliet feels or if they were given a choice between Romeo and Juliet.) A class like that usually strikes today's college students, when I tell that story, as far from what they would expect at the college level in our own time, and in that way it gives us a feeling for the impressionism that the new critics rebelled against and for how dramatic a change they brought to the study of literature.

HOW TO INTERPRET: KEY CONCEPTS FOR NEW CRITICAL INTERPRETATION

Interpretation, close reading, and unity. Instead of history, impressionism, moralism, or reading out loud, the new critics called for the study of literature to focus on rigorous, systematic *interpretation*. For the new critics, the best response to a literary text is an interpretation of that text. And the best way to develop interpretation, according to the new critics, is through **close reading,** which means detailed, careful attention to evidence from the text itself, to the words on the page.

The study of history, philosophy, religion, and politics, they believed, is acceptable for background, but it is no substitute for close study of the text itself. After all, they reasoned, we can explain nonliterary writing by studying its history, ideas, beliefs, and politics, but literary writing (poems, plays, stories, and novels) differs from other writing—and to the new critics, literary writing was its own special category. They saw literary writing as primarily about literary art and only secondarily about ideas and beliefs. The art, they insisted, rests in the literary form, in the way that literary texts use words, as opposed to resting in the ideas that the words express. They dismissed literary commentary that focuses on history and culture as **extrinsic criticism,** as not really literary criticism, because it concentrates on matters they saw as outside (extrinsic to) the literary text. They called instead for **intrinsic criticism,** criticism that focuses on the text itself.

They also believed that good literature is unified. The new critics were not the first to exalt unity in literature or art. In Plato's *Phaedrus* (c. 370 BCE) Socrates argues "that every discourse ought to be a living creature, having a body of its own and a head and feet; there should be a middle, beginning, and end, adapted to one another and to the whole" (Plato 3: 172–173). Similarly, in his *Poetics* (c. 350 BCE) Plato's student Aristotle argues that "tragedy is an imitation of an action that is complete, and whole. . . . A whole is that which has a begin-ning, a middle, and an end . . . , the structural union of the parts being such that, if any one of them is displaced or removed, the whole will be disjointed and disturbed" (Aristotle 65, 67). While such ideas have long been commonplace, the new critics intensified the focus on unity as a defining feature of great art. They often grounded their thinking in what they called **organic unity,** the belief that an admi-rable literary work forms an **organic whole.** The term *whole* suggests completeness and self-sufficiency, as if, to interpret a work of litera-ture that forms an organic whole, we need to read only the work of literature itself. The term *organic* (referring to living organisms, such as plants and animals) suggests that the unity is natural and complete and that an admirable work of literature, like a plant, grows naturally into its full expression and beauty, with each of its parts unified with each other part. As Samuel Taylor Coleridge, the Romantic poet and critic, famously put it, "a *legitimate* poem . . . must be one, the parts of which mutually support and explain each other; all in their pro-portion harmonizing with, and supporting the purpose and known influences of metrical arrangement" (Coleridge 2: 13).

By now, that view of unity is embedded in our typical cultural assumptions about art and the value of art. Most readers can prob-ably remember conversations about a movie when someone said that he or she liked the way one part of the movie went with another part, maybe through foreshadowing, or echoing, or simple repetition or consistency. Readers can probably also remember conversations when someone said that she or he did not like a movie because part of it did not fit with another part. Perhaps the movie's ending clashed with something in the middle, or viewers saw a troubling inconsis-tency in character, plot, mood, or cinematography. In cases like that, viewers judge by a principle that privileges unity. They assume that if a work of art is unified, that is good, and if it is not unified, that is bad.

Most readers can probably remember similar discussions in litera-ture classrooms, when students or the teacher pointed out unities or disunities, working from the assumption that unity is good and dis-unity is bad. Many an English class takes the form of students arguing about, or students or the teacher pointing out, how different features of a literary text fit together or explain each other, working from a taken-for-granted assumption that unity is good and that pointing out unity in a work of literature might convince skeptical students to appreciate and enjoy the work as literary art. Eventually, we will see ways to question the assumption that a literary text should be unified and to question the assumption that our purpose as critics is to find the unity in a good text (or the disunity in a not-so-good text). But for now, the point is simply to underline the focus on unity or organic unity as a new critical assumption that grew so **naturalized** (so taken for granted, as if it were simply natural) that we do not usually even recognize it as an assumption.

Paradox, ambiguity, tension, and irony. The new critics' commitment to interpretation revolutionized the study of literature. In the process of pursuing interpretation and arguing for a systematic approach to literature, they popularized four key overlapping concepts—paradox, ambiguity, tension, and irony—along with intense attention to patterns and symbols. These terms and concepts have grown so familiar that most students have no idea that we owe much of their routine use in literary interpretation to the new critics.

Paradox, ambiguity, tension, and irony, for the new critics, typify the connotative art of literary writing, as opposed to what they saw as the denotative straitjacket of scientific writing. A **paradox** refers to an expression that combines opposite ideas, such as when Shakespeare's witches tell Macbeth that "Fair is foul, and foul is fair." Similarly, Shakespeare's Sonnet 138 proclaims, "I do believe her, though I know she lies" (Shakespeare 1360, 1868), and Wordsworth tells us, in "My Heart Leaps Up," that "The Child is father of the Man" (Wordsworth 62). Sometimes paradoxes are witty, such as in the poems of John Donne (a new critical favorite). In "The Canonization," Donne wittily and paradoxically merges religious and erotic language. He argues that the love between his lover and himself can "canonize" them (make them into saints), saying (in a punning paradox on the Renaissance notion of orgasm as a little death) that "Wee can dye by it, if not live by love."

Ambiguity, similarly to paradox, refers to suggestively multiple and unsettled meanings. The end of Zora Neale Hurston's story "Sweat," for example, leaves the blame for Sykes's death ambiguous. His battered wife, Delia, could have prevented it, but readers might want to blame Sykes for Delia's inability or, ambiguously, her unwillingness to prevent his grisly demise. "The Canonization" leaves it ambiguous whether Donne exalts or spoofs religion by comparing it to sexual love, and ambiguous whether he exalts or spoofs sexual love by comparing it to religion.

Tension refers to ideas that stay connected and yet at the same time also pull away from each other without reaching resolution. The term *tension* often confuses students who are new to its use this way, as a term about language or literature. It does not refer to tension as in "My roommate's crazy habits make me really tense" or "This critical theory stuff makes me tense." It is not an emotional tension, though sometimes it includes emotional tension. Instead, it is a suspended set of conflicting possibilities that will not settle into resolution, as in Emily Dickinson's paradoxical insistence that "Much Madness is divinest Sense" (Dickinson 278). "The Canonization" evokes a tension between religious exaltation and erotic exaltation, especially in such lines as "Wee can dye by it, if not live by love" and "all shall approve / Us Canoniz'd for Love" (Donne 11–12), where the off-rhyme between "love" and "approve" can evoke an ambiguous blend of assertiveness with modesty or hesitation. To take one more example and bring several strands together, we can see an ambiguous paradox in the tension between opposed meanings of the scarlet letter in Hawthorne's novel about Hester Prynne, who wears an "A" on her breast, a scarlet letter that over the course of the novel comes to stand for many possibilities, ranging from adultery to angel and even—it might seem for a new critic—to ambiguity itself.

To most readers, **irony** is probably a more familiar term. Though deeply linked with new criticism, it has a life of its own before and after new criticism and remains too common a term for the new critics to have it to themselves. *Irony* is notoriously slippery and hard to define, but we can approximate a definition by saying that it refers to an expression or event that means something different connotatively from what it means denotatively. The same words can easily gain or lose irony, depending on the context and on the way we read them or speak them. Is Donne's "The Canonization" ironic? A new critic might say that the poem's paradoxes set up a linguistic tension that makes it ambiguous whether the connection between sex and religion is ironic or straightforward. But often we know irony when we see it. We see irony in Charles Dickens's *Great Expectations* when we learn the secret that Pip's mysterious benefactor is the last person Pip would otherwise feel beholden to. Or we might find it ironic in William Faulkner's *Absalom, Absalom!* that Charles Bon, the very man who offers the possibility of fulfilling Sutpen's dreams, also threatens to destroy those dreams. (We might also find it ironic that Bon threatens to expose the tragic way that Sutpen founds his ambition on horrendous misconceptions about class, race, and men's abuse of women. But that would take us into critiquing social structures, which, as we will soon see, the new critics tended to shy away from critiquing.)

Key New Critical Concepts

Close reading of a literary text, through the study of:

- paradox, ambiguity, tension, irony
- patterns, symbols
- unity (organic unity, balance)

By this point in the description of new criticism, some readers might smell a rat. How can the new critics believe that the same poem, novel, story, or play they describe as fraught with paradox, ambiguity, tension, and irony is also unified? That paradox in new criticism dramatizes a key issue for the new critics, an apparent contradiction that threatened to topple their entire system, because paradox, ambiguity, tension, and irony might seem to make the literary text a seething stew of conflicts, which sounds like the opposite of unity. But the new critics managed to make that apparent contradiction integral to their system.

They proposed that eventually, at least in great literature, the paradoxes, ambiguities, tensions, and ironies all balance each other out, suspending the competing energies in a unifying harmony. That way of reading takes what might seem like a fatal contradiction between unity, on the one hand, and paradox, ambiguity, tension, and irony, on the other hand, and turns the apparent contradiction into a unity-making machine, into the very definition of great literature. It also takes the work of finding that balance and turns it into the purpose and goal of literary criticism.

Even readers learning here about new criticism for the first time have probably seen and heard criticism work according to that new critical model many times, in the classroom, in criticism they may have read, and perhaps even in papers they have written (or papers they may have seen by other students). The usual pattern is pretty standard now, but the new critics invented it. First the critic, whether a professional critic or a student writing a paper, finds a problem. For the new critics, the problem, as we have seen, often took the form of a paradox, ambiguity, tension, irony, or a combination of those overlapping categories. Then the critic traces the pattern of that problem as it repeats itself across the text. For example, we might find a series of moments in Donne's "The Canonization" that suggest a paradoxical, ambiguous, potentially ironic tension between the language of religion, or love of God, and the language of eroticism and earthly love. (This is exactly what Cleanth Brooks, one of the founding new critics, did in an influential discussion of Donne's poem called "The Language of Paradox.") Then, at the last possible moment, just when the text seems ready to crash into unresolvable chaos and the new critical method seems ready to collapse, the new critic rescues the critical method, and the text itself (and maybe the student critic's grade on a paper), by brilliantly pointing out how the balanced suspension of competing possibilities makes a larger argument about the relation between, in this case, two different kinds of love, or the mysteries and multiple possibilities of literary language, and perhaps even about poetry itself (or about fiction or drama or whatever genre of literature the critic is writing about). In this way, the new critics offered a systematic critical method, interpretations of individual texts, and also a claim that literary language itself depended on a balanced tension of ambiguity, irony, and paradox.

Patterns and symbols. In the process, two other characteristic strategies of new criticism emerged that later commentators have not called attention to as much as they have to paradox, ambiguity, tension, and irony, namely, the new critical preoccupations with **patterns** and symbols. We have already begun to see the new critical interest in patterns through the way that the new critics traced patterns of paradox, ambiguity, tension, and irony and discussed how the various conflicts balanced each other to form a unity. That interest drew on and contributed to a broader interest in literary patterns at large. Repetition makes patterns, whether for a predictable category like description (a color, perhaps), language (a favorite word or image), an event (such as scenes at a window or two characters repeatedly meeting), a habit (such as a character's repeated gesture), or a structural feature (such as chapters or scenes that begin in a similar way), and so on with endless possible variations. Most students and teachers of English have read or written literary criticism or sat through a class that traces a pattern across a work of literature. But the point is not just to say that the pattern is there; the point is to interpret the pattern. The interpretations vary as widely as the interpretive methods discussed throughout this book, but the habit of looking for patterns and treating them as evidence gained enormous momentum from new critical practice and from the new critical assumption that a repeating pattern indicated a unified artistic vision across the breadth of a literary text.

The new critics have no monopoly on **symbols,** but new critical practice fit snugly with an interest in symbols and helped expand that interest to the point that symbols became almost definitional of what many people think they are supposed to find in a literary text and what they expect to hear about from English classes and English teachers. The concept of symbols seems ready-made for new criticism because a repeated symbol (Hawthorne's scarlet letter, Herman Melville's great white whale, Samuel Beckett's Godot) makes a pattern and because patterns and symbols lend themselves to the new critics' commitment to interpretation. It has reached the point where we might say, without much fear of exaggeration, that generations of high school students and beginning college students terrified of their English classes have learned that the safe path through the gauntlet of interpretation is to play a game of *find the symbol.* If they fear their English class, they only need to find a symbol, and then everything will turn out O.K. We can often hear the pride in achievement when beginning students start to talk about symbols, and they deserve credit for learning the lesson that English teachers have taught them. But by the time students get to college—or beyond (for the symbol treasure hunt sometimes continues into graduate school and professional criticism)—they owe it to themselves to set a more challenging goal. The best criticism has little to do with that kind of symbol chasing, so it is now long past time for teachers to tell their students, at least once they get past high school, that the resort to symbols as a crank that they can turn to produce an interpretation has come to seem like a parody of literary criticism more than an enactment of literary criticism.

The problem comes in the assumption that a symbol bears a one-to-one relation to a meaning that it symbolizes. As it happens, such famous symbols as the scarlet letter and the great white whale bear anything but a one-to-one relation to their meaning, for in many ways the whole point of *The Scarlet Letter, Moby-Dick,* or *Waiting for Godot* is that readers cannot determine the meaning of the symbol, that it defies any one meaning. Moreover, it was exactly that ambiguity, that tension between competing meanings, that excited the new critics. The usual use of symbols in new critical writing, however, or perhaps even more in the imitators of new criticism, including the classroom discussions and the papers of generations of English classes, implies that a symbol expresses a single meaning that rescues us from the seething uncertainty of literary language, and in that way the usual search for symbols seems far too simple. Symbol hunting is a travesty of the mysteries of literary meaning and even, arguably, an oversimplifying travesty of new criticism. The way most people use the word *symbol* seems to suggest that they think they have solved and done away with the mystery of a text, instead of helping us see and participate in its mystery.

HISTORICIZING THE NEW CRITICISM: RETHINKING LITERARY UNITY

Some of the new critics were friends, but they were not a set group or organized movement. They were mostly Americans and often Southerners, though the new criticism has loose analogues in other traditions, including French *explication de texte* and Russian formalism (discussed in Chapter 3).

Several influential British critics associated with Cambridge University, I. A. Richards, William Empson, and F. R. Leavis, often attract comparison to the new critics. Richards's *Principles of Literary Criticism* (1924) and *Practical Criticism* (1929) influenced many new critical ideas. In *Practical Criticism*, Richards experimented with showing readers poems without the poets' names on them and then interpreting the readers' responses, a project that relates roughly to the new critical interest in focusing on the text itself more than on its cultural, historical, and biographical context. Empson's quirky *Seven Types of Ambiguity* (1930), written while he was an undergraduate, influenced the new critics' sense of complex literary language. F. R. Leavis, working closely with Q. D. Leavis, called for a close scrutiny of literary works that in some ways parallels the new critics' interest in close reading. But F. R. Leavis was more concerned with the social role of literature than the new critics were, and his critical writing, rather than providing the close reading that the new critics called for, favored broadly impressionistic evaluations about which writers and works of literature are "great" and which are not great.

The best-known figures more directly associated with the new criticism include R. P. Blackmur, John Crowe Ransom, and Allen Tate, as well as René Wellek and Austin Warren in a book called *Theory of Literature* (1949) that was often required or expected reading for English graduate students, though it gets little attention today. The term *new criticism* comes from the title of a 1941 book by Ransom. To my mind, however, the most influential new critics, through their critical, theoretical, and textbook writing, were Cleanth Brooks and Robert Penn Warren (see Figure 2.1).

Figure 2.1 Cleanth Brooks (1906–1994) (left) and Robert Penn Warren (1905–1989), about 1980.

In 1938, Brooks and Warren published a revolutionary new critical textbook called *Understanding Poetry*, which went through many editions, and which they soon followed with *Understanding Fiction* (1943) and *Understanding Drama* (by Brooks and Robert B. Heilman, 1945). In later years, Warren would become the only writer to win Pulitzer prizes for both fiction and poetry, and he would serve as the first poet laureate of the United States. *Understanding Poetry* revolutionized the teaching of introductory poetry courses, but at first it met outraged resistance. Determined to teach the skills of close reading, Brooks and Warren organized their book according to principles of interpretation and poetic form, instead of according to the historical sequence of the poems and poets. To their detractors, they took the life out of literature by dehistoricizing it. To their advocates, they cut back the drab recitation of secondary background information and focused instead on the glories of the poems themselves and of the interpretation of poems. Their method came to represent the cutting edge of new criticism and gradually became the norm. For a generation or more, students trained through the *Understanding* books became the teachers of high school and college students and future generations of teachers. Brooks also contributed two key books of new critical interpretation and theory, *Modern Poetry and the Tradition* (1939) and *The Well Wrought Urn: Studies in the Structure of Poetry* (1947), which included his widely read essay on Donne's "The Canonization." Brooks's book takes its title from a phrase in "The Canonization" and perfectly expresses the characteristic new critical confidence in the polished completeness and unity of the works that new critics saw as great literature.

In seeing works of literature as complete, unified, and ripe for interpretation through close reading of the words on the page, through what they sometimes called "unpacking" the figurative language of paradox, ambiguity, tension, and irony, and through image patterns and symbols (see the list of key new critical concepts on p. 00), the new critics replaced predominantly historical criticism with what we call **formal** criticism or **formalism,** terms that sometimes confuse beginning students. To call new criticism formal does not mean that it is stuffy or wears an evening gown or a tux. It simply means that it focuses on the form of literary works, that is, on such matters as the literary structure and language. For the new critics, the focus on form meant a declining focus on history, cultural context, biography, and politics. The turn from history and culture is a lightning rod for the opponents of new criticism, who often misrepresent how the new critics actually understood the relation between literary interpretation and history and culture.

As readers will soon see, I can be highly critical of new criticism, but the common idea that new critics reject history and reject the study of the culture that literature comes from is so exaggerated that it is fair to say it is just plain wrong. They were extremely knowledgeable about history, and they often drew on literary and cultural history as background to their interpretations of literature. But they asked for criticism not to *focus* on history and culture. They asked for criticism to focus, instead, on the literature itself (those words on the page). In focusing on literature itself instead of on history or cultural context, they implied that literature has a relatively independent existence apart from its culture. In the wake of new criticism, for many critics an interest in formalism came to seem opposed to an interest in history and culture, an oversimplification as unfortunate as the mistaken idea that the new critics rejected history and culture. In any case, the turn away from history and culture, partial though it was, has stuck out notoriously for later generations of critics.

Indeed, from the perspective of a later time (a time that Brooks and Warren lived long enough to see), a time far more interested in reading historically and culturally (as we will see later in this book), we can understand the new critics by reading them with the resources of an interest in history and culture. If we read them historically, we can see a relation between the new critics' interest in form and unity and their relative lack of interest in the relation between history or politics and literature. That requires characterizing the most influential new critics.

The most influential new critics, including Brooks, Warren, and Ransom, emerged out of a group of conservative American Southern, white male writers and cultural commentators at Vanderbilt University called the Fugitives (after their magazine, *The Fugitive*), who evolved into a group known as the Agrarians. In 1930, the Agrarians published *I'll Take My Stand* (Brooks was not a contributor, though he was close to the Agrarians), which attacked modernism and industrialism and called nostalgically for a return to the lost sense of community and harmony in the preindustrial, agrarian South.

This nostalgic view of the old South should, I think, give us pause. The old South romanticized by the Agrarians was not the long-standing center of Western humanism, harmony, and community that they imagined. Their imaginary vision drew on the wave of turn-of-the-century novels romanticizing the old South (soon to culminate in the novel and movie *Gone with the Wind*). But the old South was a land teetering on the edge of slave resistance and class conflict. The unsteady profits wreaked from that land, as the economy swung back and forth between frenzies of boom and bust, depended on the forced, unpaid labor of enslaved black people. And for much of the South (especially in North Carolina, Georgia, Alabama, and Mississippi), far more than most Americans realize, that economy fed off agricultural improvements made by American Indians and by black people held by Indians in slavery. Whites stole the Indian-owned farms while pressing the federal government to drive Indian people from their land. The old South was not the idyll of humanistic letters celebrated by the Agrarians. It was not, as they supposed, isolated from the market economy. Instead, it was a place of riotous land speculation where most people, black, white, and red, suffered horrendous poverty and had little or no access to books, and where an environmentally exploitive, revolving class of coastal entrepreneurs, who desperately painted themselves as patricians, and a newer set of inland upstarts eventually cobbled together a generation of shaky prosperity before the Civil War. The Agrarian movement, in short, was founded in self-serving delusion and denial.

In the community of shared values that the proto-new critical Agrarians imagined, people always knew their place and accepted their place, but when I look around at my students or family, I see hardly anyone whose ancestors fit into the imaginary world of the Agrarians. In short, scandalized by the social disunity they saw around them, they feared the dangers and excitements of modernity. The Agrarians called for us to return to a phony, fantasy past where people always knew and accepted their place, but where, in fact, only people like the Agrarians themselves might want to go. From there it appears that they projected their deluded vision of social unity, and of escape from the strife of contemporary culture, onto a model of literature and literary criticism that sought to prop up their ideal of harmonious unity and divorce it from the cultural and historical conflicts that threatened their privilege.

And so when the new critics see unity in the literary text, whose unity do they see? By choosing not to give weight to social issues, they deny—or we might even say suppress—the role of social conflict in literature, as if the symbols and patterns, the paradoxes, ambiguities, tensions, and ironies, were all about language in a tunnel-visioned way that isolates language from history and culture. On the contrary, the language and literary form that the new critics so lovingly caressed have everything to do with ideas and social meanings that the words in that language and form represent. And ideas and social meanings have everything to do with language, which we use partly to express them, including literary language. Readers and critics can choose to pay less attention to social meaning, but they cannot fence it into the mere background of literature. Even the new critics' effort to exile social meaning carries (ironically) a social meaning, for it suggests their fear of the changing social world, of conflicts across race, gender, and class. Their vision of unity has no place, literarily or socially, for most of the rest of us.

We might go so far as to question the cherished notion of literary unity altogether. Unity is not something *in* a text, intrinsic to a text, but something we project onto a text if we follow a method of reading, like the new critics' method, that seeks unity. Readers can find unity in any text, if they want to. Even if it is disunified, that is a kind of unity. Readers can always find some connection between different parts of a text, if they want to see them connected. After all, the new critics' almost-audible sighs of relief when they marshal the panoply of paradoxes, ambiguities, tensions, and ironies into an orderly balance to prop up organic unity should tell us just how precarious that balance can look from another critical perspective. It might not look like balance at all. It might look like chaos—exactly what the new critics feared and sought to exile from the works they were willing to see as great art, as well as from their agrarian social fantasy.

When we see disunity in a work that someone else reads as unified, that disunity might come from a paradox, ambiguity, tension, or irony, or from a social conflict or a conflict of ideas, or from variations in form. Here, for example, a stanza of poetry rhymes, and there it doesn't rhyme. Here a line of poetry follows a perfect iambic rhythm, and there another line varies the rhythm. In one place a story relies on a character's perspective, but in another place it relies on an exterior narrator's perspective or the perspective of a dramatically different character. Here a play or a movie proceeds at a pace that makes the time on the stage or screen match the amount of time it portrays, but there it suddenly skips ten years. In one scene the cast faces the audience or the camera and the set shines with yellow light, but in another scene they face each other or the lighting bathes them in blue. Here a work uses colloquial language, and there it uses decorous, stately language, and somewhere else it mixes the colloquial and the stately, perhaps spicing them with shifts between italic and roman fonts, or shifting between dialogue and description, or jumbling together French and English. The possibilities that we can read as disunity are endless. And one instance of disunity will trump a pattern of unity, because as soon as we find one disunity, then we no longer have unity.

As readers, we can choose to put more weight on the unities than on the disunities, perhaps choosing to look at connections between different characteristics of a text more than we look at the disconnections, but that is a choice we make as readers. It is not an inherent, intrinsic property we discover in the text, but a preference we project onto a text.

Why care about the new critical infatuation with unity? Because the cultural habit of supposing that one goal of critical discussion must be to find the unity (like finding the symbol) hugely limits the possibilities for criticism, as we will see again when we get to deconstruction in Chapter 4. The critique of unity will also help prepare us to study deconstruction. (Indeed, readers experienced with later methods of criticism or readers who have skipped around in this book may hear the influence of reader-response criticism or deconstruction in this critique of the new critical notion of unity. While readers do not need experience with those later methods to follow this discussion, the critique of new criticism here gives a hint of things to come.)

In these ways, the critique of aesthetic unity goes hand in glove with the critique of the new critics' turn away from history and culture. To most contemporary critics, the new critical turn from history and culture did great damage to our sense of critical possibilities and even our sense of what literature we might read. The new critics could only sustain their notion of unity if they focused on literary works that allowed them to deny the social conflicts seething around them. That made it possible for them to sustain the historical preference of most white men of their time, education, and class for writing by other white men, to the exclusion of writing by the rest of the world. As the study of English has moved beyond new criticism, so also, in recent decades, has it vastly expanded the social range of the writers whose work critics and English classes read and study.

In the 1930s, when the new criticism emerged amidst the Great Depression and a fervor of political activity from both the left and the right, there was a burgeoning new interest in writing from beyond the traditional boundaries of race and class that had come to typify college reading lists. The new critics' narrower sense of what might make great literature helped put the brakes on that emerging receptiveness until the 1970s and 1980s. Meanwhile, their resistance to political interpretation, especially to Marxist or leftist interpretation, had a quietist, antipolitical cast that fit well with the conservative, anti-Communist America of the Cold War 1950s. That itself carries a certain irony, since the new critics' fantasy of a retreat from modernist industrialism and back to a lost idyll of agrarian harmony was anticapitalist, and the new critics might even seem like the intellectual outsiders that 1950s anti-Communist McCarthyites scorned. Still, by separating the study of literature from the unruly politics that readers often found in plays, novels, stories, and poems, the new critics managed to contain (in the Cold War sense of the term, meaning to contain or limit Communism) ideas about art, literature, and literary criticism that might disrupt conservative Cold War pieties. But as American politics changed with the rise of the civil rights movement, with the resistance to the war in Vietnam, and with the growth of feminism, students, teachers, and critics increasingly rejected the new critical impulse to separate literature from its social meaning.

We might wonder, in these contexts, whether the new criticism has grown so maligned that a book like this may no longer need a chapter on it; indeed, this chapter differs from the following chapters in that it explains a method of criticism that most college students and other readers of this book will in many ways already know, even if they do not know that they know it. The later chapters, by contrast, will introduce methods of criticism that perhaps, with the partial exception of feminist criticism, are far less familiar to most readers. Because the new criticism now seems dated, I used to have a student or two in most critical theory classes suggest that we skip it to make more time for studying the later methods. Eventually I tried skipping it, and then many students complained that they missed it, because they saw how other methods defined themselves against the new criticism, and they believed—wisely, I think—that they would understand those later methods better if they also understood new criticism. As much as new criticism seems part of our past, therefore, it also has a way of hanging on and defining our present.

THE INTENTIONAL FALLACY AND THE AFFECTIVE FALLACY

Two additional concepts from new criticism, **the intentional fallacy** and **the affective fallacy,** attracted great interest, and both help us understand new critical assumptions. The critic William K. Wimsatt, a colleague of Brooks and Warren at Yale University, which became the hotbed of new criticism, and the philosopher of art Monroe C. Beardsley introduced these concepts in articles reprinted in Wimsatt's book *The Verbal Icon* (1954), a term that, like "the well-wrought urn," perfectly expresses the new critics' sense of the literary text or any other object of art as a self-sustaining artifact almost complete unto itself.

A fallacy is a mistaken (fallacious, false) idea or belief, or an error in reasoning. (If it helps, you can translate *fallacy* simply as "mistake.") The idea, once widely advertised, that smoking is good for our health is a fallacy, and it is fallacious to believe that if Jean is intelligent and good-looking and Terry is also good-looking, therefore Terry must also be intelligent. (Terry might be intelligent, but we would need something else to prove it.) *Affect* refers to emotions. (The word *affect* should not be confused with the word *effect*.) Wimsatt and Beardsley coined the term *the affective fallacy* to refer to what they saw as a logical error or mistaken belief about how we determine literary meaning. They argued that critics should not let their claims for the meaning of a literary text or other artistic object be determined by their emotions. As intrinsic critics, they believed that a text's meaning lies within the text itself, not in our response to it.

This is the opposite of the later approach sometimes called *reader-response criticism*, which assumes that we know a text only through our response to it. (See Chapter 11.) Whether or not a text exists apart from our response to it (a separate philosophical question), we never experience the text as an intrinsic object independent of our response to it. Emotions (affects) are inevitably part of our response. For that reason, later critics usually reject the idea that an affect- or emotion-influenced response must be fallacious. They do not believe that we can respond to literature without including emotions in our response.

While the critique of the affective fallacy receives little if any support today, the critique of the intentional fallacy continues to wield a vast influence. Like most contemporary critics who feel a deep skepticism about the new critics, I nevertheless agree with their critique of the intentional fallacy. But for many students it remains a confusing idea, and so it will merit extended consideration here. Traditionally, critics simply took it for granted that one route to interpretation was to determine what the author of a text intended, and they took it for granted that there was a perfectly reciprocal link between the author's intention and the best interpretation. If we knew the best interpretation, then we could say that it expressed what the author intended. If we knew what the author intended, then we knew the best interpretation. Nobody questioned it, not even the early new critics.

But Wimsatt and Beardsley, drawing out the implications of the new critics' belief in the text as a verbal icon, and thus seeking an intrinsic criticism that relied on the text by itself, argued that it was fallacious to suppose that the author's intention and a good interpretation of the text are necessarily the same. While they did not object to critics considering what the author may have intended, as a way to raise possible interpretations that critics might not think of themselves, they still believed that any argument for an interpretation must come from the text itself.

Though not every critic has agreed that it is a fallacy to base a critical interpretation on what an author intended, the predominant movements in critical theory after the new criticism all agree that basing an interpretation on an author's intent is indeed a fallacy, even though they disagree about many other issues. To put it in a nutshell, they agree that what we think the author intended should not govern our interpretation of a literary text.

Putting the principle that way allows a certain nuance. It allows us to consider what we think the author intended as an aid to interpretation but not as a determinant of interpretation. It also hedges a key issue by saying "what we think the author intended," as opposed to saying, simply, "what the author intended," and that is because we can never truly know what the author intended.

That argument leads us to some glimpses ahead to methods of criticism addressed in the later chapters of this book. While the methods described later in this book differ in a great variety of ways, they do not reach different conclusions about the intentional fallacy, even though they have a wide variety of reasons for continuing to believe that what we might think an author intended should not govern our interpretation.

The structuralists turned away from the traditional interest in individual authors and called for us to pay more attention to broader structures of language and culture, which have patterns and directions but do not have "intentions." The deconstructionists, who focus on multiplicity, would not grant the idea that an author has one particular intention, free of internal contradictions that might undermine any one intention with competing impulses in multiple directions. Like the new critics, the structuralists and deconstructionists advocate a formalism that calls for us to interpret the text itself, not the biography of its author.

Psychoanalytic criticism, with its belief in what it calls *the unconscious*, argues that a great many forces swirl through any given mind, including the mind of an author, including unconscious intentions that may differ dramatically from conscious intentions. In that context, what authors say, write, or even believe about their intentions may not accurately describe the most powerful impulses that direct their actions. And especially as psychoanalytic critics begin to combine psychoanalytic thinking with deconstruction, they may come to believe that intentions are often too multiple and contradictory to allow us to say, convincingly, that the authors' intentions were any one particular thing, let alone something conscious and visible to literary critics.

Feminist, queer studies, and Marxist critics as well as historical and cultural studies critics may point out ways that cultural assumptions influence writers' ideas independently of or even against what writers suppose they intend. According to all these methods, then, we often do not know what writers intend, and it often oversimplifies writers to believe that they have specific and complete intentions for every question we might ask about the works they write.

Sometimes it seems clear enough. We can probably agree that Emily Dickinson's intentions did not include flying to the moon. We can probably agree (though not everyone does) that she intended to write poems. We can probably agree that she sometimes intended to

write emotionally intense poems, and funny poems, and philosophical poems, as well as poems in ballad form (lines in iambic tetrameter
alternating with lines in iambic trimeter), like the hymns that she
grew up with. But sometimes it is not clear at all. It is much harder to
say, with assurance, that she wrote "Further in summer than the birds"
to teach her readers a reverence for nature. We might argue more successfully that the poem itself teaches such reverence, based on the
new critical principle of evidence from the words on the page, with
or without using later methods of criticism, as opposed to supposing
that we can tell what Dickinson was thinking outside the poem, that
those thoughts equal her intentions for the poem, and that the poem
succeeds in fulfilling those intentions. Criticism based on what we
suppose the author intended can end up looking more like biography
than like literary criticism. Biography has its own value, and it can
overlap with literary criticism, but it is not literary criticism.

Nevertheless, the cultural habit of supposing that we can know,
and usually do know, what authors intend and that their intentions
should govern our interpretation of their writing is so strong, has
come to seem so intuitive, that the critique of the intentional fallacy
usually takes a lot of getting used to. And the truth is that it takes
a lot of getting used to for professional critics as well as for students.
Many professional critics slide easily into the habit of taking the intentional fallacy for granted, even when they do not mean to. Even
the early new critics, before Wimsatt and Beardsley, routinely referred
to the author's intention, without thinking about it or realizing that
such references might undermine their notion of concentrating on
the text itself. Even when we say something like "Hemingway sim-
plifies his language to" do this or that, the phrase "to . . . " suggests
that we know the author's intention and that the author's intention
can determine our interpretation.

Let me give an example from my own teaching that can help illustrate ways to think about authorial intention. One morning, I was
teaching Walt Whitman's "Beat! Beat! Drums!" for a survey class in
early American literature. I knew my stuff—or so I thought. I knew
the poem, the history around it, the biography around it. I knew that
Whitman wrote it in 1861 as a call to arms at the beginning of the
Civil War. In today's lingo, we might call it a pro-war poem. Here is
how the poem begins (and it continues on in the same vein):

Beat! beat! drums!—blow! bugles! blow!
Through the windows—through doors—burst like a ruthless force,
Into the solemn church, and scatter the congregation,

Into the school where the scholar is studying;
Leave not the bridegroom quiet—no happiness must he have now with
     his bride,
Nor the peaceful farmer any peace, ploughing his field or gathering his
     grain,
So fierce you whirr and pound you drums—so shrill you bugles blow.
                                                              (Whitman 419)

One of the students started discussing the poem as an antiwar poem.
I knew it was not an antiwar poem. I knew that in 1861 Whitman fervently supported the war, and so I knew that the student was wrong.
I didn't want to say, "You are wrong," fearing that that would hurt the
student and frighten the other students, so I asked, "What do other
people think?" I was confident that another student would have the
right answer and correct the first student. The next student chimed in
with enthusiasm, but to my astonishment the second student agreed
with the first student, and then a third student, and then a fourth. By
this point, I knew I was in trouble, especially because each student came
up with specific evidence from the poem itself. With new criticism in
the back of my mind, I had tried to teach the value of close reading
with evidence from the text, and the students had learned their lesson
well. Look at the terrible things that the war is doing in the poem, they
noted. It bursts. It is ruthless and forceful. It disrupts the church and
the congregants. It disrupts the school and robs happiness from a new
marriage, and so on. All these are terrible things, the students argued,
with perfect plausibility, and so the poem must be protesting the war.

To my mind, the students' post-Vietnam War way of thinking kept
them from seeing that Whitman was saying that all these seemingly
terrible things were actually good because they gave us a noble and
needed war that he thought the United States would win in a few
glorious weeks. I found myself wanting to tell the students that they
were wrong and that I knew they were wrong because I knew what
Whitman intended, but I also knew that that was a feeble argument
against the excellent evidence that students had offered. I didn't
know what to do, and to tell the truth I cannot remember what I did.
But whatever it was, it went badly, and I let the students down.

Since then, I have thought a lot about that bad day in the classroom, and the picture has grown more complicated and interesting
than a mere story of shoddy teaching. Whitman first published this
poem in an 1861 newspaper. Later, as the war continued, he kept writing war poems, and they changed a great deal in mood and manner as
the war's brutality deepened and dragged on and as Whitman saw the

war's devastation up close, working intimately to nurse the wounded and dying. After the war, in 1865, he gathered his war poems into a volume called *Drum-Taps*, and he put "Beat! Beat! Drums!," his first war poem, written as a pro-war poem, near the beginning of the volume.

"Beat! Beat! Drums!" can thus challenge any confidence in the traditional idea that we can say what an author intended and use that intention to govern our interpretation of a text. For it seems that Whitman published the poem in 1861 with one intention and then published it again in 1865 with another, opposite intention. After the horrors of the Civil War, which his poems evoke so movingly, the textual details that my students called attention to take on a different meaning from the one that I had seen in the poem or that Whitman seems to have seen in 1861. It seems that in 1861, his poem anticipated possibilities for the meaning of its language beyond those meanings he seems to have been conscious of. In short, Whitman seems to have had more than one intention for "Beat! Beat! Drums!" He not only had different intentions at different times, but in some sense he seems also to have had different intentions at the same time, including latent antiwar impulses in 1861 and a willingness in 1865 to look back at his pro-war intentions and expose them to the scrutiny of his later understanding.

In this way, Whitman's poem, my students' insights, and my sorry effort to teach the poem can suggest the oversimplification inherent in the usual confidence that we can identify a specific authorial intention and then use that intention to determine our interpretation of a literary text. Intentions often come in such multiple and self-contradictory ways that they give the lie to any one overall notion of "authorial intention," and they may or may not match what a text actually produces, which is likely to be as multiple and as susceptible to contradictory readings as the intentions that may or may not lie behind them. As it turns out, most of the time when critics slip into reasoning from authorial intention, they simply take an interpretation they like, suppose that it matches what the author intended, and then use the supposition about intention as evidence to back up the interpretation. That slippery series of suppositions can deter them from coming up with actual evidence for their interpretation.

When students first encounter the critique of basing interpretations on authorial intentions, they often feel at a loss. What is literature about, if it is not about determining what the author intended? How can we find evidence, if the author's intentions do not qualify as evidence? Those questions are not so hard to answer, once we think about them. Literature may relate to its writer's personal history, but it is not the same as the personal history. So the evidence must come from the literature. Perhaps it need not come from the literature all by itself. It may come from the literature in relation to the writer's life story (as we have seen with Whitman) and in relation to many of the other things that we will study later in this book (gender, history, economics, and so on), but we still need evidence from the literature if we want to back up a claim about the literature.

It can help if we shift one of the usual questions that students ask (and that critics and teachers ask). The question often goes like this: What was she or he (the author) trying to do? For example, what was William Faulkner trying to do by telling the beginning of *The Sound and the Fury* through the mind of a so-called idiot, an adult whose intelligence has not grown beyond that of a small child? Or what was Gertrude Stein trying to do by repeating the same phrases so many times? Why did Chaucer use talking animals to tell "The Nun's Priest's Tale," or why did e. e. cummings splatter his lines of poetry in fragments across the page? When students ask what the author was trying to do, they usually hit a wall. They feel stumped, or they leap to claims that they cannot back up, and then they feel defeated. I propose that instead of asking why the author did this or that, we ask *what is the effect of* this or that. Students who feel defeated by the question about intentions usually come up with a flood of insight, interpretation, and evidence as soon as we shift the question from what the author was trying to do to what is the effect of what the author (or text) actually does.

The debate over the intentional fallacy has exerted considerable influence in areas outside literary studies. Legal theorists often ask what the writers of the United States Constitution, or the writers of a particular piece of legislation, intended. They debate whether we can know that intention and whether what we suppose we know about their intention should influence how we interpret the laws they wrote. Should we confine ourselves to the meanings the Constitution had in 1789, when in most states only propertied white men could vote, or should the words carry different meanings in the changed world we read them from today? If the meaning can change, then how do we determine the changing meaning? Similarly, we often ask how we can interpret each other's actions. If someone hurts someone else but we believe that that person did not intend to hurt anyone, then should we still condemn, either legally or ethically, the person who hurt someone else? Should we forgive? Should we blame? The study of critical theory can help us ask these difficult questions and think through our answers, even when we disagree.

Common Misunderstandings

- It is often said that the new critics believed that literary criticism should not address history, culture, politics, and so on. But the new critics never said that and resented being criticized for saying it. They were deeply knowledgeable about and interested in history, culture, and politics, and they often addressed such topics as part of the *background* for literary criticism, but they did not believe that such topics should be a *focus* for literary criticism.

- It is sometimes said that the new critics wrote mostly about poetry and took little interest in fiction or drama. While most of the early new critical writing focused on poetry and often on the close study of language that we associate with studies of poetry, the new criticism grew so standard that it came to dominate the criticism of fiction and drama as well, though new critics used language-focused terms like *paradox* and *tension* less often when they wrote about fiction and drama and focused more on patterns of character.

- It is often said that the new critics believed there is only one correct interpretation. While, like other critics, they worked hard to back up their own interpretations, and they believed that their method of interpretation was the best method, they did not banish other views of individual works of literature, and indeed their focus on ambiguity can encourage competing interpretations.

HOW TO INTERPRET: A NEW CRITICAL EXAMPLE

Let us look at a more extended example of how new critics might read. A new critic would likely see an abundance of paradox, ambiguity, tension, and possibly irony in Wallace Stevens's "Anecdote of the Jar" (1919):

> I placed a jar in Tennessee,
> And round it was, upon a hill.
> It made the slovenly wilderness
> Surround that hill.

> The wilderness rose up to it,
> And sprawled around, no longer wild.
> The jar was round upon the ground
> And tall and of a port in air.
>
> It took dominion everywhere.
> The jar was grey and bare.
> It did not give of bird or bush,
> Like nothing else in Tennessee.
>   (Stevens 76)

A new critic might ponder the ambiguity of "in Tennessee." Typically, we place a jar *on* something, perhaps on a table, a counter, or a shelf. If we place it *in* something, then we place it in something like a pantry or a refrigerator. But Tennessee seems almost paradoxically too broad and unspecified a space for an act as concrete, mundane, and small as placing a jar. The jar emerges as a symbol. It changes the world around it, imposing order on the "wild" and "slovenly wilderness." It seems crafted. As a synthetic object, then, it can symbolize art. The ambiguous little jar grows into something paradoxically, even ironically, grand, perhaps so grand that it is "like nothing else in Tennessee," a state not terribly associated with the history and lore of the fine arts. Ringing with the echoing sound of extended, lengthy syllables in "round," "surround," and "ground," the jar looms "tall and"—in a strangely exalted locution—"of a port in air," so much that "It took dominion everywhere." Yet as a mundane object, "grey and bare" in "the wilderness," this out-of-place synthetic intruder can also suggest something more ordinary. Even the line that speaks of it as "grey and bare" enacts the spareness that it describes by squeezing its thoughts into one-syllable words (like only two other lines in the poem) and ending abruptly, metrically after only three iambic feet, when all but one of the other lines have four feet.

On the one hand, then, the jar symbolizes the exalted grandeur of art, and on the other hand, it suggests trash, even litter. As litter, it cannot "give of," or seems frighteningly dissociated from yet still in the midst of, the surrounding natural world of "bird or bush." A sustained tension between these two opposite possibilities suspends the poem in a lyrically balanced evocation of opposite poles in the human imagination, perhaps suggesting or even symbolizing the vulnerability of art and the potential beauty and grandeur of ordinary things.

In proposing such a reading, I have not asked what we think Stevens might have intended. Nor have I gone much into history, apart from noticing, at the risk of snobbery, a little about the reputation of Tennessee. I certainly have not crossed the line into seeing the suggestion of litter as leading the poem into environmentalist critique, even though the ecocritic within me would like to do that. Nor have I rolled the jar, or the anecdote, around looking for cracks in the poem's unity. I did not risk suggesting, for example, that the poem's sometimes oddly exalted language seems evocatively out of place with its setting or its ironic reveling in bric-a-brac. Instead, our sample new critical reading concentrates on how the form of the poem relates to its meaning and expresses an attitude toward art itself.

THE INFLUENCE OF NEW CRITICISM

The new criticism was a brilliant innovation in the history of reading, understanding, interpreting, and enjoying literature. It gave critics a concrete set of goals, and, gradually, in the 1950s, it grew into the dominant way of reading literature in published criticism and in college literature and creative writing classrooms and, eventually, often in high school classrooms. New criticism grew dominant in part because it offered a concrete method for teaching English classes and publishing literary criticism. If students could read and interpret literature based on close reading, on the words on the page more than on historical knowledge, that gave teachers and students a concrete goal for what to accomplish in the classroom, and in many people's eyes it made the classroom more democratic. The teachers' greater knowledge of history no longer gave them such an advantage over their students. If all the students could have the text in front of them at the same time, then the students who had a better previous education and the students who had read more or who knew more history or literature had less advantage over other students who had the same words in front of them. After World War II, when American college classrooms grew crowded with students on the federal GI Bill, which funded college educations for veterans who often would not have gone to college in earlier times, a more democratic classroom method held great appeal for American English professors looking for a new way to teach a changed population of students.

Meanwhile, the new criticism also changed English professors' research. English research, as we have noted, was typically historical. But with the new criticism, instead of publishing historical research about literature (which took time and library resources that many professors did not have), they could publish interpretations of literature, which did not necessarily take much more research than went into reading the words on the page and perhaps other works by the same writer or the writer's friends. Professors realized that they could publish the interpretations they developed for their classes. Gradually, the pace of publication for literary criticism accelerated. Literature professors could finally compete with the publication records of scientists. In research universities, the new criticism gave English professors a way to meet the emerging expectation that they "publish or perish"—that is, publish research or lose their jobs. A vast apparatus grew up to turn the publishing of literary criticism into a full-scale industry, and for research universities and some colleges, publishing literary criticism came partly to define what was expected from English professors. Propelled by the rapidly expanding economy of the 1950s and 1960s, new books and journals of literary criticism sprouted like dandelions.

The enormous commitment to research had consequences for teaching. Many college English teachers cared more about their research (usually consisting of interpretation, whether it involved much actual research or not) than about their teaching, and their teaching suffered. On the other hand, many teachers found that their research inspired their teaching. It certainly changed what they taught, because as the new critical focus on teaching interpretation changed criticism, so, in return, criticism's focus on interpretation changed teaching, in an accelerating cycle. The hyped-up spiral of critical interpretation, combined with the pressure to professionalize, launched an entire institution of modern "English," with parallel planets in the various departments of modern languages.

But eventually, the very systematicity of the new criticism that gave it such power also started to undermine it from within, because it grew formulaic and predictable. Experienced critics and teachers got to the point where they could crank out uninspired interpretations that drained the pleasure out of reading instead of generating the excitement that many readers felt when the new criticism really was new. They could also predict what other critics might say about a text, before they even read what other critics actually said. Graduate students looking for something new and professors exhausted with the old sought out alternatives to new criticism and developed a distance from new criticism that enabled them to look at it skeptically, with the same intense scrutiny that they had grown accustomed to bringing to literary texts. It took time for alternatives to the new criticism to coalesce, but new developments in linguistics, anthropology, and philosophy began to reach literary criticism, and in the

1970s literary critics began to transform those developments into new visions of literature and literary criticism. That is the story told in the later chapters of this book.

As readers move through the later chapters of this book, the new criticism may continue to present a challenge, even if it seems like a dated challenge, for new criticism retains enormous power. In many ways it has come to define criticism itself, sometimes making it hard to get beyond new criticism even if we want to. Even when we work with more recent methods of criticism, many readers, still under the sway of new criticism, will see only the new critical dimensions of the criticism we write. I myself would almost never use such terms as *paradox, ambiguity,* and *tension* in my own criticism, because they would suggest new criticism, even if I used them in a non-new critical way. And just as readers tend to project new criticism onto other, more recent styles of criticism, contemporary students and critics sometimes slide into new criticism even when they set out to do something different. Without realizing it, they repeat new critical strategies and assumptions, merely dressing them up in the vocabulary of more current ideas.

In recent years some critics, fearful that the later methods of criticism discussed in this book leave formalism behind, have called for a "new formalism." A new formalism, presumably, would combine the methods reviewed later in this book with the formalism encouraged by the new critics or perhaps by structuralists or deconstructionists. In the wake of post-new critical questions, the new formalism would look different from the formalism of the new critics. Other contemporary critics look warily on the idea of a *new* formalism. Some of them fear it opens the door to a resurgence of new criticism, while others argue that there is nothing new about it, because much of the best recent criticism already combines formalism with an interest in the social world. Caroline Levine has called for new ways of understanding literary form in a broader dialogue with social and political form, instead of merely returning to the understandings of form in earlier modes of criticism. Thus, critics debate whether the new formalism and its offshoots merely reheat the old new criticism and spice it up in contemporary language or manage to rethink formalism in dialogue with the interests, issues, and methods discussed in the rest of this book. Probably, the answer varies from one formalist critic to another.

In short, we might ask ourselves, as we attempt to draw on post-new critical methods of literary and cultural criticism, how much we want to go beyond the new criticism, whether we want to bring any of the new criticism with us, and whether it is possible to hold on to certain features of new criticism and still reject others. Do we continue to believe in close reading? Do we continue to believe in evidence from the text? How much weight should we put on the unity of a literary text? Can we cherry-pick from the array of new critical ideas, continuing such practices as close reading, without continuing the new critical politics that most readers of later generations find disturbing? I hope readers will keep asking these questions as we move through the remainder of this book.

FURTHER READING

Brooks, Cleanth. "The Language of Paradox." In *The Well Wrought Urn.* New York: Reynal & Hitchcock, 1947: 3–21.

———. *Modern Poetry and the Tradition.* Chapel Hill: University of North Carolina Press, 1939.

———. *The Well Wrought Urn: Studies in the Structure of Poetry.* New York: Reynal & Hitchcock, 1947.

———, and Robert B. Heilman. *Understanding Drama.* New York: H. Holt, 1945.

———, and Robert Penn Warren. *Understanding Fiction.* New York: F. S. Crofts, 1943.

———, and Robert Penn Warren. *Understanding Poetry: An Anthology for College Students.* New York: H. Holt, 1938.

Empson, William. *Seven Types of Ambiguity.* London: Chatto and Windus, 1930.

Hickman, Miranda B. and John D. McIntyre. *Rereading the New Criticism.* Columbus: Ohio State University Press, 2012.

Jancovich, Mark. *The Cultural Politics of the New Criticism.* Cambridge: Cambridge University Press, 1993.

Levine, Caroline. *Forms: Whole, Rhythm, Hierarchy, Network.* Princeton: Princeton University Press, 2015.

Ransom, John Crowe. *The New Criticism.* Norfolk, CT: New Directions, 1941.

———. *The World's Body.* New York: Charles Scribner's Sons, 1938.

Richards, I. A. *Practical Criticism: A Study of Literary Judgment.* London: K. Paul, Trench, Trubner, 1929.

———. *Principles of Literary Criticism.* London: K. Paul, Trench, Trubner, 1925.

Wellek, René, and Austin Warren. *Theory of Literature.* New York: Harcourt, Brace, 1949.

Wimsatt, William K., with Monroe C. Beardsley. *The Verbal Icon: Studies in the Meaning of Poetry.* Lexington: University of Kentucky Press, 1954.

❋ 3 ❋

Structuralism

Structuralist criticism was the first wave in the flood of change that revolutionized literary criticism in reaction against the earlier revolution of new criticism. English-language literary critics began drawing on structuralist linguistics and anthropology in the 1970s. Now, in the twenty-first century, hardly any critics still call themselves structuralists, so that structuralist criticism, like new criticism, can seem out of date. But as the first wave in a torrent, structuralism set up the model for later ways of thinking. Those ways of thinking frequently respond to and draw on structuralism's most provocative ideas, making a familiarity with structuralism crucial for understanding what comes after it.

Indeed, it is often hard to tell where structuralism ends and many of the later methods begin. For that reason, in introducing structuralism we will also begin to introduce the later methods of critical thinking that both changed structuralism and absorbed it. Because of those changes over time, we cannot say that structuralism is any one thing, but we can summarize its history, describe its general principles and many of its practical strategies, and take into account how it evolved from what I will call early or classical structuralism into structuralism as later thinkers reshaped it and made it their own.

After a general review of structuralism in the first sections of this chapter, the later sections introduce the structuralist study of narrative. Most readers will do best to pause before going on to the study of narrative. It can help to review the first sections and let some time pass while you get used to the general concepts. For as structuralism in general introduces a challenging array of abstract concepts, the structuralist study of narrative introduces a challenging array of specific concepts and terms. Because most readers enjoy stories, they look forward to reading about narrative, but this chapter gets easier to process if you do not try to take it all in at once.

KEY CONCEPTS IN STRUCTURALISM

If we boil structuralism down to one idea, it is about understanding concepts through their relation to other concepts, rather than understanding them as intrinsic, in isolation from each other. Already that tells us how structuralism and structuralist criticism differ from new criticism, which sought to interpret literary texts intrinsically as objects without focusing on their relation to the world around them. In that sense, structuralism is always comparative. For structuralists, we understand everything by seeing its **difference** from something else. We interpret the world by juxtaposing different concepts against each other in what structuralists call **binary oppositions.**

For example, we understand hot and cold in relation to each other, by their difference from each other, in binary opposition to each other. We cannot see meaning in either hot or cold except through such comparisons. To structuralists, hot versus cold is only one of an infinite number of oppositions that structure our perception and thought, including north versus south, left versus right, up versus down, inside versus outside, on versus off, and so on endlessly.

Saussure. The principle of binary oppositions comes from the Swiss linguist Ferdinand de Saussure (Figure 3.1), the founder of structuralist linguistics, as part of his broader description of the overall system of language. Saussure died in 1913 without publishing the ideas that would later make him famous. His colleagues, however, drew on students' notes to publish a version of his lectures, uninspiringly titled *Course in General Linguistics* (1916). Later, when the French Jewish anthropologist Claude Lévi-Strauss fled the Nazi occupation of France in World War II, he escaped to New York City. There he met Roman Jakobson (pronounced Yockobson), an influential Russian formalist and linguist. Jakobson, who would emerge as a key figure for structuralism, had also fled from the Nazis, and he introduced Lévi-Strauss to Saussure's ideas. Lévi-Strauss then used

Figure 3.1 Ferdinand de Saussure (1857–1913).

Saussurean linguistics to shape his studies of Brazilian Indians and of kinship structures, inaugurating what came to be known as *structuralist anthropology*. The French writer Roland Barthes then developed an interest in Saussure's ideas through reading Lévi-Strauss. Together Lévi-Strauss and Barthes, along with Eastern European émigré linguists led by Jakobson, propelled the broader intellectual movement that came to be known as structuralism, which had enormous influence in linguistics, anthropology, and literary and cultural criticism.

Instead of describing particular languages or particular uses of language, like previous linguists, Saussure set out to describe the overall system of language. He drew a binary opposition between **langue,** French for "language," and **parole,** French for "speech" (Table 3.1). For Saussure, *langue* refers to the overall system of language, such as the rules of grammar, while *parole* refers to an utterance, an individual instance of language, such as a sentence, a news bulletin, or a poem. Since structuralists, sometimes under the rubric of what they called *semiology* or *semiotics*, would take Saussure's theory of language as a general model for understanding the overall system of culture, I will draw on examples that go beyond language in the narrow sense

Semiology and Semiotics: Peirce's Theory of the Sign as Icon, Index, and Symbol

The terms *structuralism*, *semiology*, and *semiotics* have different histories, but they are sometimes used interchangeably. **Semiology, or semiotics,** tends to refer to the structuralist study of culture apart from linguistics or literature.

Semiology is especially associated with the philosopher Charles Sanders Peirce (pronounced Purse), who distinguished among three kinds of signs, which he called an icon, an index, and a symbol.

- An **icon** represents an object through a resemblance or likeness to the object, as a drawing or photo of you resembles you, or as a road sign with a curving line represents a curving road ahead.
- An **index** represents an object through a factual connection to the object, as smoke represents a fire or paw tracks represent Rover or Kitty.
- A **symbol** represents an object through a habit or culturally agreed-on rule that makes that symbol represent that object, as we have agreed that a red light means stop and a green light means go.

The difference between categories is not always absolute. The same sign may take on qualities of more than one kind, depending how we understand it. Peirce's distinction among icon, index, and symbol has had more influence in visual studies than in literary studies. But literature and film are crowded with icons, indices, and symbols as Peirce understands them, and his description of the sign, especially his concept of the symbol, bears comparison to Saussure's structuralist theory of the sign as described here.

of the term. The rules of chess or football or dating, for example, are the *langue* of chess or football or dating, but any given move or game of chess, football, or dating is an example of *parole*. Similarly, the instructions for setting up a Facebook page are the *langue* of Facebook. But your own page, or your friend's page, is a *parole*—an individual instance—of Facebook. In setting out to describe the overall system of language, the *langue*, Saussure began a model of systematic study which, as we will see, came to define structuralism. (The term *structural* can refer to any structure, such as an engineer's design or a bridge, but the term *structuralist* refers to the tradition of study that emerged from Saussurean linguistics, as described in this chapter.)

For Saussure, language is not, as we usually suppose, a list of words applied to objects. Instead, he saw language as a system of signs, with each **sign** consisting of a sound-image, which he called a **signifier,** and a concept that the sound-image represents, which he called a **signified.** For example, the signifier *cat* represents the concept of a cat. (The signified is the concept of a cat. It is not the physical cat, which Saussure calls the *referent.* Saussure's lack of concern for the referent may seem difficult to understand at first, and readers do not necessarily need to worry about it, but the explanation is that he describes language as a process in the human mind, which generates sound-images and concepts but does not generate referents, physical objects like cats, rocks, or trees.) Saussure saw a firm link between the signifier and the signified, so that any given sign is not merely the concept it represents (the signified) or its representation (the signifier), but the two bonded together like two sides of a coin or a piece of paper (see Figure 3.2).

The link between the signified and the signifier is **arbitrary.** We can notice the arbitrariness when we observe that different languages have different signifiers for the same signified. In English, the signifier *c-a-t* has grown so familiar that we overlook its arbitrariness and tend to suppose that it inherently evokes the signified concept of cat. But it only seems to do so because we have naturalized the convention of attaching the signifier *cat* to its signified. To signify the concept of cat, English speakers could just as well have chosen the signifier *dog.* Or we could have called it *pizza.* Then over time the convention of referring to the signified concept of cat with the

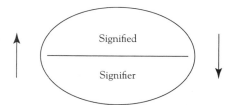

Figure 3.2 Saussure's model of the sign (signified and signifier).

signifier *pizza* would have grown so naturalized that we would lose our awareness of its arbitrariness, and *pizza* would evoke catness as *cat* does now. But the structure of the sign would still depend on an arbitrary, conventional bond (represented in Saussure's drawing by a bar) between the signified and the signifier, rather than on an inherent, natural connection. (Onomatopoeia is a partial exception to the notion that the link between the signifier and the signified is arbitrary, but even for onomatopoeia different languages use different words to represent the same concept. While a rooster crows *cockadoodledoo* in English, in Spanish it crows *kikiriki*, and in Japanese it greets the rising sun with *kokikoko*.)

We only recognize a signifier, such as *cat*, Saussure continued, by processing its **difference** from other, potentially similar signifiers. We recognize the word *cat* because it differs from *bat* and *cut* and *cab* and so on, not because it has an inherent connection to the particular signified that convention has attached it to. Each language has a limited set of sounds, which linguists call **phonemes,** that its speakers—people who know its *langue*—hear as marking meaningful differences. English has about forty phonemes, linguists tell us, varying with the speaker and dialect, but speakers of English have grown so accustomed to those phonemes that they are not conscious of them. It could have worked out differently, such that we did not hear a meaningful difference between the sound *cat* and the sound *cut* or between *cat* and *cad* or *kit*. We apprehend the difference between signifiers, then, by a conventional distribution of phonemes that could have turned out differently and that to some extent has turned out differently in different versions of English. Some English speakers, such as Shakespearean actors, roll an *r* sound, but that causes no confusion because in English speech we recognize two notably different sounds, the rolled and the unrolled *r*, as the same phoneme. But in another language, such as Spanish, they could represent different phonemes, making a word with a rolled *r* (such as *perro*, meaning *dog*) signify something different from an otherwise-identical sound with an unrolled *r* (such as *pero*, meaning *but*).

Writing, Saussure notes, works the same way. Two people may not write the letter *r* exactly the same way, but if we recognize it as the letter *r*, then they both write it within the range of possibilities that readers of English conventionally recognize as signifying the same concept. The writing system could have been constructed differently, such that the differing ways that two different people write *r* could have signified two different letters. We thus come to recognize signifiers, not because of an inherent quality within them, but by their position in a system of differences from other signifiers.

To Saussure, then, **difference**—a system of comparisons and relations—produces meaning. Meaning is not inherent in the signifier. On the contrary, it comes from an arbitrary system of conventions that distributes the differences among signifiers. "In language," for Saussure, "there are only differences," so that "language is a form and not a substance" (Saussure 120, 122).

Construction. Building on Saussure's linguistic model, structuralists contend that we understand something by comparing it to other things, by its difference from other things in a system of structures like the system of language, as opposed to understanding things as essences sufficient unto themselves. Therefore, for structuralists, language itself, in a broad sense of the term that includes all systems of representation and not just words, constructs the things that we use it to describe. Language is not merely layered on top of something more important, like frosting on a cake or the cover on a book. Structuralists thus see reality as **constructed,** not as made up of underlying **essences** that language merely coats over or labels. This concept can take getting used to, because it can seem counterintuitive, since most of us are trained culturally to believe in an underlying reality, an essence, a pure signified independent of and separate from any signifier, independent of and separate from language.

In structuralist thinking, by contrast, the world is not something that we discover. It is something that we produce, that we construct, through language. That is why in learning a new language we also learn a new way of seeing and understanding. The structures we apprehend in the world depend on the way the human mind imposes structure.

To Lévi-Strauss, people across all cultures and times share a set of conceptual patterns or structures that guide human understanding of kinship, of "myth" or storytelling, and of all human culture. Each culture's kinship relations (who it calls an aunt or uncle or cousin, for example, or who it calls by a kinship term that may have no close analogue in English) or myths (stories) represent a **surface structure,** or *parole,* or individual instance of a broader **deep structure,** an overall *langue* or system of kinship relations or stories that all cultures share, and those structures are organized like language through a system of differences and binary oppositions.

Lévi-Strauss's ideas were vastly influential, but structuralism has changed a good deal since Lévi-Strauss. Rarely do structuralist-influenced thinkers continue to say that all people share a common, underlying human consciousness. Over the years, the interest in structure and difference that Saussure and Lévi-Strauss proposed gradually took on so much momentum that it overwhelmed the sense of a universal human deep structure in favor of a continually multiplying array of differences. Eventually, the sense of proliferating differences began to undermine the sense of stable systems at the base of structuralism. As the systems wobbled and then toppled in favor of more interest in differences, partly in response to the social disruptions of the late 1960s and early 1970s (the student and worker strikes in France in 1968, the war in Vietnam), structuralism evolved into deconstruction, the topic of the next chapter. The sometimes blurry line between structuralism and deconstruction can confuse people new to these topics, because deconstruction, though it reacted against structuralism, nevertheless continued to use many of its concepts and terms. In a nutshell, structuralists believe in systems structured by difference, while deconstructionists believe that the differences multiply so vastly that the systems unravel and leave only differences, without any systems stable enough to preserve order. It would be easy to continue to describe structuralism without peeking ahead to deconstruction, but by glancing at what follows structuralism, we can better understand structuralism's limits and how it developed, and we can prepare to follow its momentum into deconstruction.

People who do not "get" structuralism sometimes suppose that the structuralist notion that the human mind produces the world we see means that for structuralism there is no reality. On the contrary, the structuralist idea is that reality is linguistic and structured, not that there is no reality but that we construct it, so that there is no reality independent of the language, the **discourse** that we use to construct it. Here *language*, or *discourse*, refers not only to words and grammars but also, more broadly, to all structures of perception, which, to a structuralist, we represent through words and grammars, through systems of representation. For structuralists, everything is **discursive;** everything is constructed. If you believe in a reality independent of and prior to language, then you believe in a **prediscursive** essence (which makes you an **essentialist**). You cannot back up that belief by offering an example, because as soon as you offer an example, you are using language and discourse. As we have suggested, it is not that there is a set of objects, a reality, and then language comes along afterward and gets spread on top like frosting on a cake. It is that reality is *always* linguistic, or, as the expression often goes, to get at basic assumptions of this sort, that everything is **always already** discursive, always already constructed and **mediated** by language.

Because this notion differs radically from the usual way most people think, students often have difficulty appreciating its implications unless they question it vigorously. Readers may choose not to accept this notion of language and discourse, but I suspect that they cannot disprove it. Some people dodge the debate about whether there is or is not a prediscursive reality by suggesting that if we cannot give an example of it, then it does not matter whether it is there or not. Regardless, it matters a great deal if everything is always linguistic and language is organized by a system of differences or, as deconstructionists might say, more disruptively, by a play of differences. How it matters will come across in a great variety of ways over the remainder of this book, with each later method following through the implications of this basic structuralist argument in different but often complementary ways.

For the time being, we can start to glimpse how it matters if we think about different ways that people use language to describe what might otherwise seem like the same thing and how the different language makes that "same" thing come out differently. For example, if I say that when a reader interprets a poem, he pays close attention to the words, many people would think that my use of the masculine pronoun *he* to refer to all readers has social consequences, that it pays more respect to male readers than to female readers. A similar principle would apply if I use an expression such as "CEOs and their wives" or say that it is time for men to recognize that we need to resolve international disputes through peaceful negotiation. When one teacher explains an abstruse idea to students in language they understand and another teacher, across the hall, explains the same idea by using Latin expressions, phrases like "as you know," and a vocabulary that students do not recognize, the different styles of teaching influence students' understanding of the ideas. That has social consequences if one style does more to reinforce a social system divided between those in the know and those not in the know. The different language for the same ideas has such different effects that the ideas are not finally the same. In short, language not only describes our world; it also produces the world it describes.

HOW TO INTERPRET: STRUCTURALISM IN CULTURAL AND LITERARY STUDIES

We are now ready to look at the implications of structuralism for cultural and literary studies. While structuralist literary critics paid close attention to literary form, leading some skeptics who knew little about structuralism to say that they were not so different from new critics, in fact they proposed a sharply different set of goals from the new critics, so different that the critical world, accustomed to new critical assumptions, had a tough time recognizing and processing the radical shift of structuralist thinking.

For new critics, the goal is to interpret the individual text. For structuralists, by contrast, the goal is to describe or interpret the larger system. Often, they simply describe the system. At their most ambitious they propose a theory of the system and interpret the system. Indeed, though the founding new critics wrote a good deal of literary theory, structuralist theorists popularized the movement from literary criticism and literary interpretation to literary theory, a dramatically different enterprise from the usual new critical "reading" of an individual text.

To understand what it means to describe or propose a theory of the system, it can help to return to Saussure's binary opposition between the *langue* and the *parole*. Table 3.1 (structuralists love charts and graphs) may help us follow a series of terms for roughly the same binary opposition. We can translate Saussure's *langue* and *parole* into English as *system* and *instance*. Linguistically, a parallel pair of terms is the *grammar* and the *sentence* (where *grammar* refers, as linguists say, to the rules that allow speakers of a given language to make sentences that other speakers of that language can understand). Drawing on the terminology of the linguist Noam Chomsky, Jonathan Culler—whose *Structuralist Poetics* (1974) is the most thorough and influential account of structuralism for English-language literary critics—added the terms *competence* and *performance*, where *competence* describes the ability to process or produce language and *performance* describes the particular language we produce, such as a poem or a text message. Similarly, structuralist critics such as Tzvetan Todorov described their task as uncovering a *grammar of literature*, as opposed to the new critic's task of interpreting an *individual literary text*, or as uncovering a *poetics* of literature, where *poetics* refers not necessarily to poetry itself but to a general theory, a theory of literature or of any other system. At the broadest level, then, structuralists can propose a theory of texts and of textuality itself.

Table 3.1 *Langue* versus *Parole*

LANGUE/LANGUAGE	PAROLE/SPEECH
system	instance
competence	performance
grammar (of language)	individual sentence
deep structure	surface structure
grammar (of literature)	individual text
poetics	poem (or other individual text)
theory of texts and textuality	interpretation of individual text

But they do not always or even usually work at that broad a level, for they also take an interest in subsets of literature and in a vast range of cultural practices. For example, they might write about the grammar (or poetics or system, etc.) of poetry, a subset or genre of literature, rather than of literature at large. Or they might study or write about other categories, about genres smaller than or just different from "literature" or "poetry," such as sonnets, novels, comic books, wedding ceremonies, Gothic novels, buddy movies, chick lit, high school movies, vampire or horror novels or movies, slasher movies, Shakespearean comedies or tragedies, clothing styles, advertisements, zombie movies, political speeches, detective novels or movies, reality TV shows, baseball games, Halloween costumes, screwball comedies, professional wrestling matches, villanelles, restaurant menus, local newscasts, tweets, text messages, haiku, romance novels, film noir, first dates, teen magazines, epic poems, college English classes, and so on through endless possibilities across culture. Whatever genre structuralists study, they will try to reveal its grammar, or, as structuralists often say, its codes and conventions. And as structuralism increasingly takes on the broader task of interpreting culture at large, they may often think of those codes and conventions as cultural codes and conventions.

In the same way, the website tvtropes.org charts a vast and often more-or-less structuralist collection of codes and conventions in TV, fiction, and film. The point is not to look down on repetitive patterns but instead to find the pleasure and understanding that come from observing the dialogue between repetition and variation, and from seeing how we recognize and respond to repetition and variation because they are structured by a system of differences.

For examples of structuralist interpretation in these modes, let us look at TV shows, beginning with sitcoms ("situation comedies"). The preeminent classic sitcom is *I Love Lucy* from the 1950s, an era of sanitized feel-good family TV. Since then, the genre has added a host of variations, from *The Jeffersons* to *M*A*S*H, Seinfeld, Roseanne, Parks and Recreation, Modern Family, Unbreakable Kimmy Schmidt*, and many others. Some shows, notably *The Simpsons*, routinely spoof the form, which requires knowledge of the form—of its poetics. *I Love Lucy* was so popular and such a staple of reruns that even this many years later, most of this book's readers may know its poetics intimately, whether they stop to realize it or not, even if they have not seen the reruns. We can uncover that knowledge, with its codes and conventions, and start to generate a poetics of the classic sitcom by teasing at the edges of the genre. Suppose that a long-lost episode of *I Love Lucy* was just discovered. We start to watch it, full of suspense, and then, at the commercial break, Lucy gets lost. What will happen next? The answer is easy. Someone will find her, or she'll find her own way back. In short, each episode stages a problem before the midpoint commercial and then resolves the problem before the half hour ends. We know the form so well that we do not have to think about it, but thinking about it might help us come to know it better.

Now let's vary the scenario. In this version, just before we hit the commercial break, all of a sudden Lucy dies. When I say that in the classroom, students typically react with a burst of uneasy surprise and a murmur of nervous chuckles. They have an adept competence as readers of the sitcom form, and so they know that Lucy cannot die. It's not in the form. It's not part of the poetics. If she did die, then it would turn out that she had not really died, that she was only playing dead, or that some other character had made a terrible mistake in thinking she had died. But the poetics, the conventions of the form, will not allow even that much. Playing with possibilities around the edge of the system helps uncover a poetics and set of conventions that we did not know we knew.

Or let's say that right before we hit the commercial, Lucy has an abortion. Not possible, my students insist. Not imaginable—this is TV in the Eisenhower 1950s. Of course, women had abortions in the Eisenhower 1950s, but not TV characters, not national idol TV characters, and certainly not national idol TV sitcom characters, not Lucy. When star actress Lucille Ball got pregnant, her show broke precedent by portraying her character Lucy's pregnancy. But even then they could not call her "pregnant." She was "expecting."

The form's conventions dictate that certain things can happen in a classic sitcom and certain things cannot happen. For example, unlike in contemporary TV, no problem can arise that cannot be resolved at the end of the half hour. And there are unspoken rules or codes of social decorum or censorship. If we tried to list those rules, we could learn a good deal about the sitcom form and the culture that it both represses and expresses.

Thus, despite the ongoing changes in the sitcom form, abortion remains almost taboo. Or so I gather. Of course, I have not seen every episode of every sitcom. Far from it. But we see enough instances to establish a pattern, and then we extrapolate from that pattern to propose a larger system, a poetics, that describes both the instances of sitcoms that we have seen and, we suppose, those we have not seen. When a network show tests the borders of the system by making a sitcom character refer to an abortion in the past, many viewers protest and the networks crack down on the show. (Meanwhile, beyond sitcoms, television—with its growing number and variety of channels and streaming services—has gradually portrayed abortions more frequently. [See Sisson and Kimport.]) The satirical fake-news review *The Onion* has even spoofed the reluctance of sitcoms to address abortion, offering a made-up sitcom with an episode that treats abortion casually by paralleling an abortion storyline with another storyline about eating a meatball sandwich ("Actress' Abortion"). The humor rides on the way that casual sitcom treatments of abortion remain almost unimaginable, so that a pretend version comes across as edgily funny. The off-color jokesters at *The Onion* understand the poetics of sitcoms and know that their readers share the same understanding. Only a knowledge of the poetics makes it possible for a tasteless deviation from the poetics to come across as enjoyably, if offensively, funny.

Apart from abortion, which continues to define the boundaries of the genre, later sitcoms, then, beginning with *All in the Family* in the 1970s, defined themselves by including what the earlier, classic sitcoms excluded. Each new wave of sitcoms, then, defines itself in relation to the previous wave. After *All in the Family*, things that were unimaginable in *I Love Lucy*—many of the same crises of social, political, and cultural strife that fill the daily news—shape the routine plots of many sitcoms while still speaking back to a form inherited from *I Love Lucy* and its descendants. The dialogue between earlier and later sitcoms (structuralists might call it **intertextuality,** meaning writing or reading one text in relation to another) allows us to distinguish, for example, between two different subsets or poetics of sitcoms, between shows that must resolve their problems in a half-hour frame and never refer back to the same problems in a later episode and other shows, like *The Big Bang Theory*, that continue to joke about the same story arcs across multiple episodes or seasons.

Similarly, if we go a little outside the sitcom to, for example, the original *Star Trek* or, later, to old-style, male-centric private-eye shows like *Magnum, P.I.*, what will happen if Captain Kirk or Magnum falls in love? In a pattern that has faded in contemporary, more sexualized TV, even viewers who had never seen the episode before but had seen other episodes in the series or other series like these knew the system and its conventions well enough to anticipate that the "love interest" (itself a structuralist category) would get killed off or sent away, because a rule in the poetics of the genre said that the hero had to stay single. In the same way, if Captain Kirk or, say, his later variant Captain Mal Reynolds of *Firefly* is captured by evil aliens, viewers knew that somehow he would escape, and the episode plays off their knowledge of the genre to structure its suspense. They knew he would escape, but still they wanted to know how he would escape.

A show like *Game of Thrones*, *The 100*, or *The Walking Dead* plays off the poetics of earlier shows that have charismatic stars living on from episode to episode and season to season. In *The Walking Dead*, any character can get bitten or die (or "die") at any moment and suddenly transform into a zombie, a "walker." The vulnerability of the characters makes viewers want to find out which characters will survive. In that way, *Game of Thrones*, *The 100*, *The Walking Dead* and other zombie shows and films use viewers' knowledge of a show's poetics, in relation to the poetics of other shows, to lock in an audience and tighten the screw of suspense.

Thus, viewers' ability to anticipate the ending of traditional TV plots, their sense of the stories' closure and completion, defines one group of TV shows, in contrast to the currently more popular group that plays against expectations of weekly closure, replacing neat endings with cliffhanger endings, ongoing plots, and ensemble casts, for example, in a hospital or ad agency, like *Grey's Anatomy* and *Mad Men*, or in fantasy remakes of daily life, like *True Blood*, *Game of Thrones*, *The Walking Dead*, and *Luke Cage*. While individual genres define themselves, intertextually, in relation to other individual genres, setting hospital shows against vampire shows against police shows, they also define themselves, intertextually, in relation to other groups of genres, setting binge-worthy, multi-episode shows with on-going plots against single-episode movies and against the older pattern of TV shows with stable casts and plots that wrap up every week in a tidy conclusion.

Several principles stand out from these examples. Students often ask how we can study the system without—like a new critic—studying the instances. Actually, even a structuralist has to study the instances to study the system. Here we can draw on a classic, prestructuralist philosophical principle called the **hermeneutic circle,** which says that to understand the part, we have to understand the whole, and to understand the whole, we have to understand the part. To describe the poetics of sonnets, for example, we need to consider individual sonnets, but to understand individual sonnets, we will also need to consider sonnets in general. Some critics will choose to study instances more, and others will choose to study the system more. We can turn structuralism to something like new critical purposes, if we want, by harnessing our study of the overall system (of sonnets or first dates or film noir or whatever) to the goal of interpreting the individual instance. And, as it turns out, that is exactly the more traditional option that many literary critics have chosen, retaining the fascination with readings of individual texts that the new critics provoked. On the other hand, the more we make the goal an interpretation of the larger system, then the more structuralist our project and the farther we can get beyond new criticism. In this way, structuralism provides an alternative to new criticism or an expansion of new criticism, depending on how we work with structuralism.

Students often ask how a structuralist can know whether a given instance fits into the system at all. If we find a long-lost episode where Lucy dies or has an abortion, then is it still really part of the *I Love Lucy* show, and is it still really a sitcom? If a zombie show turns funny, like *iZombie* or *Z Nation*, then is it still really a zombie show? Or does it change our idea of how to define a zombie show? Maybe, as some people say, it's a zom com, or a zomedy? And if we can't tell where to draw the line around a system or a genre, students often wonder, then could that defeat the concept of a structuralist poetics? Rather than feeling defeated by the problem of odd or borderline examples, however, structuralists relish them, because the odd examples help us figure out the system's structure and boundaries, help us decide where one genre ends and another genre or subgenre begins. When we find an odd example, then we can enlarge the circumference of the system

to include the anomalous case, or we can draw a boundary that defines the system by determining what conventions fit into it and what
conventions do not fit into it.

THE DEATH OF THE AUTHOR

In a sense, structuralists might say, the conventions, not the author,
write the work. One episode of *I Love Lucy* or *Modern Family* is pretty
much like another episode of *I Love Lucy* or *Modern Family*. The
structuralist provocateur Roland Barthes (who gradually evolved into
a poststructuralist) went so far as to write an article titled "The Death
of the Author" (1968), playing off Friedrich Nietzsche's provocative
phrase "the death of god" and arguing that we would do better not to
romanticize individual authorship. For Barthes (who, skeptics might
note, signed his article with his name), literature is written by the
overall system of writing, not by individual authors. While humorless
authors were not amused, and while some critics would say Barthes
exaggerated to make his point, the point bears taking seriously.

No writers make up, all by themselves, the system of writing—or
of novels, plays, poems, or sitcoms. They inherit a repertoire of vocabulary, grammar, syntax, genre, and convention, and we might say
that they do little more than rearrange the materials that they find
around them. But as Barthes puts it: "The image of literature to be
found in ordinary culture is tyrannically centered on the author, his
person, his life, his tastes, his passions, while criticism still consists
for the most part in saying that Baudelaire's work is the failure of
Baudelaire the man, Van Gogh's his madness, Tchaikovsky's his vice.
The *explanation* of a work is always sought in the man or woman who
produced it, as if it were always in the end, through the more or less
transparent allegory of the fiction, the voice of a single person, the
author 'confiding' in us" (Barthes 143). As part of our larger romanti-
cization of individuality, we romanticize authorship partly to conceal
from ourselves how much different authors repeat each other's writing and follow the same formulas. But for Barthes, once the words are
written, they take on a momentum of their own and take over from
the now irrelevant author. "Writing," Barthes says, "is the destruction
of every voice, of every point of origin. Writing is that neutral, composite, oblique space where our subject [that is, the author] slips away,
the negative where all identity is lost, starting with the very identity
of the body writing" (Barthes 142). Drawing on Marxism as well as
structuralism, Barthes saw the fascination with individual agents as

a way of concealing the overall economic system's powerful ability to reproduce itself. In the wake of Barthes's argument, criticism has often focused less on individual authors—or, to put it less romantically, on individual writers—and more on the social forces engaged in many writers' production of literature.

Readers who dismiss Barthes's notion of the death of the author might look at it differently if they think about how students in class discussions often refer to the author, not by name or as *she* or *he*, but as *they*. The habit of referring to the author as *they* can irk teachers. Since teachers often know more than students about the author's life and writings, teachers usually have more sense of who the author was than students have. But students who refer to the author as *they* are on to something nevertheless. They sense that authors do not write by themselves, that the production of literature is collaborative and social. In that way, a work of literature represents not only a single personality but also a cultural world.

HOW TO INTERPRET: THE DETECTIVE NOVEL

I like to invite students—and here I will invite readers—into one more extended example: the detective novel. Before you read past this paragraph, I invite you to pretend that you have just read a hundred detective novels. Based on your (imaginary) sample, jot down a few characteristics you would find in more or less all one hundred novels (or detective TV shows or movies). Do not worry about odd or uncharacteristic examples. We will get to the odd examples later.

First (now that you have jotted down your list of characteristics— and if you haven't, then if you stop to do that now you will get more from what follows), let us complicate the task by drawing on another structuralist binary to organize our poetics, or grammar, of the detective novel. Following a binary opposition described by Saussure, structuralists distinguish between the **synchronic** and the **diachronic.** Technically, a synchronic approach considers a language, or some other system, at one time (as suggested by the combination of "syn" and "chronic"), whereas a diachronic approach works chronologically and so considers how a language, or some other system, changes over time.

In practice, however, I find it more useful to think of a synchronic approach, more radically, as proceeding without regard to time, versus a diachronic approach, which works chronologically and so depends on time. For example, if I say, "I eat too much candy and junk food," then I am providing a synchronic description, because I am not addressing when I eat them or in what sequence of events I do the eating. But if I say, "Yesterday I had a couple candy bars before dinner and then crunched down a bag of potato chips before I went to sleep, but today the only thing I've eaten between meals is fresh fruit," then I have offered a diachronic description. In the same way, we might describe a novel synchronically by saying that it has three major characters from three different walks of life, with witty dialogue and lyrical description, whereas we might describe the same novel diachronically by saying that it begins with a romantic court-ship that then gets broken up by a secretive stranger, who later turns out to be the long-lost mother of the heroine, but after the stranger is forced to leave, the heroine returns to her earlier love, only to find . . . , and so on. Our poetics of the detective novel can help sharpen the distinction between synchronic and diachronic. Now try sorting your list of characteristics of the detective novel into syn-chronic characteristics and diachronic characteristics.

Let us begin with the synchronic, with features of the detective novel that are not related to time. Of course, we need a detective. We also need a dead body (or at least a crime, but in a detective novel the typical crime is a murder, which produces a dead body). We also need suspects, a murderer, clues, false clues (also called *feints* or *unreliable clues*), a motive, and a weapon. (Think of the board game "Clue.") If your list includes a *femme fatale*, then you were thinking of hard-boiled detective novels, a classic American genre; if it includes a country house, then you were thinking of clas-sic British detective novels. Each of those categories then becomes a subset within the larger category of detective novels. The same ap-plies if you said that the detective novel has a Watson figure (after Dr. Watson, who recounts the adventures of his friend Sherlock Holmes). And Watson figures themselves come in a trackable array of varia-tions. Thus, one recent Sherlock Holmes TV show, *Elementary*, has a Chinese American female Dr. Watson. Another, *Sherlock*, adds the twist that Watson publishes his stories about Holmes on a blog.

While some detective novels have a Watson figure, most don't, so again we can see Watson-narrated novels as a subset of detective stories at large, which pretty much always have the items on our main list, with whatever variations. Already, as we sort what belongs on the main list and what does not belong on it, we are using compari-sons to refine and expand our poetics, drawing circles within circles and producing a series of branches in the tree of possibilities. On the other hand, if you said that we discover the murderer at the end, then by saying *when* we discover the murderer you have introduced a diachronic feature.

For a single novel, it is easy enough to say, diachronically, that this happens and then that happens later. But for an entire genre of novels, describing the diachronic features gets more complicated. We might hypothesize that we find the body before we resolve who is the murderer, with the term *before* bringing in diachrony. If readers object to this hypothesis by noting that in a few novels we learn who the murderer is before we find the body, then I will grant those exceptions, but note, again, that we will hold off on uncharacteristic examples until later.

Having made the initial observation, however, that we ordinarily find the victim before we find the perp, we are ready to move on to exceptions, which will show why quirky examples, instead of frustrating the project, as beginners often suspect, can advance the project by helping us elaborate our poetics. Since our interest in a novel that reveals the murderer before it reveals the murder comes partly through the way that it plays off the standard expectation, we can see that part of the interest in reading a detective novel depends on our competence in the poetics, conscious or not, which intensifies the interest in making that poetics, or grammar, explicit. Novels that reveal the murderer before they reveal the murderee, then, form a secondary subset of the poetics, like novels with a femme fatale, a country house, or a Watson-model narrator. Pursuing the diachronic characteristics further, we can suggest that if we get the murderer earlier, then we typically get the methods of murder later. Reciprocally, if we learn the methods earlier, then we typically learn the murderer later. Either way, the reciprocal ratio between fingering the murderer and fingering the methods of murder allows a novel to draw out its mystery and sharpen the suspense.

Then suppose that we read a 101st novel, and it violates the grammar. That leaves us a choice. We can decide that it is not a detective novel, or we can revise our grammar of the detective novel. Perhaps, in the 101st novel, we never learn who the murderer is, or never learn for certain. Or suddenly the victim stands up and talks, proving that he or she was not a dead body after all, but only seemed dead, like Falstaff in Shakespeare's *Henry IV*. Then we can refine our grammar. We might even say that instead of requiring a dead body, a detective novel needs a seemingly dead body. We can write a branch in the grammar, distinguishing between seemingly dead bodies that stay dead and seemingly dead bodies that pop back up and turn out to be alive. The popper-uppers themselves might branch into different categories, such as fakers versus sleepers. Each branch has the potential to define the distinguishing characteristics of a particular novel or subset of novels and to provoke additional novels that talk back to it intertextually. Beginning, for example, with Sara Paretsky and Sue Grafton's private-eye mysteries, for example, novels with a tough-talking female detective talk back to the novels with shallow *femmes fatales* and tough-talking male detectives.

But if we reach a point where the branch takes so abrupt a twist that it no longer seems to belong to the same tree, then it has at least helped us decide where to draw the borders of the genre. Perhaps it takes us outside the detective novel, the whodunit, and to one of its cousins, the crime novel or the thriller. Or perhaps it turns out so differently that we end up placing it among more distant relatives, such as science fiction novels or historical novels or so-called literary fiction. Or it may take us to that kind of novel that works in more than one genre at the same time.

For all these reasons, when we chart a poetics, we often take special interest in borderline examples. They help tell us what defines the categories on each side of the border; and because they speak back to the genre and its poetics with intertextual gumption, we enjoy them. When a detective novelist came up with a narrator who turned out, at the end, to be the murderer, there was an uproar. (I won't name the novel, because I don't want to spoil it for people who haven't read it.) While some readers felt cheated, others realized that the novelist had talked back to the genre and revealed something about it that readers had not realized they already knew, namely, that the grammar that calls for a detective novel to have a murderer or the grammar that says that a subset of detective novels have a character-narrator should actually say a murderer who is not the narrator and a character-narrator who is not the murderer. The exception reveals the rule, and so, rather than toppling the system, exceptions hold special interest for the way they reveal the system.

While many readers find a poetics like this fun, thought-provoking, and illuminating about the detective novel and about the structure of novels and of literature in general, many readers—including some of the same people—find such structuralist descriptions limited for their lack of address to social concerns. Like the new critics, the structuralists have attracted criticism for a formalism that can seem isolated from the social world. But the history of structuralism is far more complicated, and Barthes's work, especially, often had much to say about the social world and popular culture. As anthropologists, Lévi-Strauss and his followers wrote directly about the social world on a large scale. The early literary structuralists, nevertheless, with their charts and graphs and neomathematical formulas, often produced work that many readers found arid and sterile. Binary oppositions like north versus south, left versus right, up versus down, inside versus outside do not seem to matter much to the problems and pleasures that energize our daily lives. Even so, the dry literary structuralism that did little to address the social world was a brief phase confined mainly to a few innovators and their followers in the late 1960s and early 1970s, a phase that we might call *classical* structuralism.

As structuralism evolved, however, it usually merged with the methods discussed later in this book. When later cultural and literary critics think of binary oppositions, for example, they more often choose culturally loaded examples, sometimes including binaries that change over time, or that we might want to change, or binaries that we disagree over how to interpret, such as feminine and masculine, wealthy and poor, more powerful and less powerful, queer and straight, and colonizer and colonized. In that light, such binaries as inside versus outside, north versus south, or east versus west no longer refer merely to abstract structures of opposition. Inside versus outside can carry suggestions about gender, while north versus south or east versus west can evoke geographical and cultural conflicts. Binaries no longer look simply like abstract facts. Instead, they are loaded cultural codes that people contest and seek to stabilize or change.

The poetics of the detective novel would shift if we asked a different set of questions from those that structuralists asked or if we combined structuralist questions with questions driven by social or psychological inquiries. To start thinking about alternative questions—even without having much space here to answer them—we might ask, for example, are the typical murder victims in detective novels from the same walks of life as typical murder victims in the culture at large? In the United States, murder victims are disproportionately urban, poor, juveniles, and people of color. That hardly seems true of murder victims in American detective novels. Perhaps detective novels then, obsessed though they seem to be with uncovering facts, are also dedicated, without realizing it, to covering up other facts. How might such a pattern have developed, and how has it changed or stayed the same over time as the demography of detective novel writers and readers has changed?

Detective novels seem preoccupied with guilt, law, transgression, deception, punishment, escape, and curiosity. They also seem preoccupied with the value of individual life and the blame of individual murderers, for in detective novels the victims are individuals, not the broad swathes of the population killed by tobacco, by drunken driving, by unequal access to healthcare, by pollution or war, and the blame falls on individual murderers, as opposed to seeing the murderers themselves as victims of a social process. What do these preoccupations tell us? (What list of preoccupations might you come up with for another genre that interests you, such as science fiction, romance novels, or slasher or zombie films, and what would that list tell us?) As many readers have noticed, detective novels also seem obsessed with voyeurism, as in the very term *private eye*. Through that obsession, they release an abusive, antisocial desire, implying a likeness or connection among the impulses to look, to watch, and to kill. Arguably, they also constrain that desire. A Marxist critic might argue that the detective novel fits snugly into capitalist ideology by condensing blame onto bad individuals instead of distributing it to social and economic causes.

While socially driven questions like that range outside the usual reach of narrowly structuralist literary criticism, they nevertheless lend themselves to structuralist-inspired critical thinking about patterns, codes, and conventions, and to critical thinking about variations on those patterns, codes, and conventions. Structuralists, for example, could get at such issues by asking questions about their underlying binary oppositions, including urban settings versus rural settings, wealthy victims or murderers versus poor victims or murderers, isolated private detectives versus police who work collectively, and traditional, urban, white-male detectives versus less traditional detectives who break that pattern in gender, sexual orientation, race, and/or region.

STRUCTURALISM, FORMALISM, AND LITERARY HISTORY

In the same way that the early, classical structuralist literary critics were accused of slighting social meanings, they were also accused of slighting diachrony and history. In several respects, that accusation seems distorted. While Saussure's lectures focused on the synchronic rather than the diachronic and historical, his critics usually neglect that Saussure's colleagues never published his lectures on historical linguistics, which probably had more to say about diachrony. In any case, structuralism can work historically and diachronically as well as synchronically. We have already seen ways to gain insight into the structure of detective novels by noting their diachronic features, and we have seen how studying the conventions of the sitcom can show how later sitcoms speak back to earlier sitcoms intertextually, in the same way that later detective novels speak back to earlier detective novels. Similarly, the Russian formalists provided models for thinking in structuralist terms about history, and an active subset of structuralism has focused on studying narrative, which, by recounting an onward-moving series of events, has everything to do with diachrony.

Roughly, the Russian formalists offered an analogue to the Anglo-American new critics, in the limited sense that they shared an interest in formalist ways to read. But the new critics did not know about the formalists, who came to prominence two or three decades earlier yet long remained little known beyond Russian-reading audiences. Eventually, the Russian formalists and their intellectual descendants helped bring Saussure and structuralism to a wider audience (as when Jakobson introduced Lévi-Strauss to Saussure).

Perhaps the most famous Russian formalist idea is Victor Shklovsky's notion of **defamiliarization** (*ostranenie* in Russian, sometimes translated more literally as "estrangement"). Defamiliarization refers to the way that literature, especially realist or satirical literature, can take familiar things and refresh our perspective on them. For example, when Emily Dickinson describes a bat as "a small Umbrella quaintly halved" (Dickinson 536), she helps us see familiar things—a bat, an umbrella—in a fresh way that recovers a sense of their strangeness. Similarly, in Susan Glaspell's play *Trifles*, the male investigators see no meaning in the commonplace domestic details of Minnie Wright's life, but when women see the same details, they find them rife with meaning, defamiliarizing the disarray of Minnie's housekeeping to uncover the story of her marriage and her reasons for killing her husband. For Shklovsky, defamiliarization exposes the formalist technique of literature, "baring the device" (the form) and making us more aware of what the literature represents and of the literariness in literary writing.

Shklovsky also proposed a formalist method for writing literary history. He argued that the system of literature changes over time by absorbing what may seem out of fashion and making it the new fashion. Shklovsky's model works from the classical structuralist notion that a structure is a closed system, changing by realigning its parts rather than by introducing something new from outside the system. In that sense a structure works like a terrarium or, on a larger scale, the classic model of an ecosystem. Jakobson later described a similar process as a "change of dominant," meaning that the going trend shifts from one dominant to another. The less dominant characteristics do not disappear but instead, as in Shklovsky's model, shift back and forth between times of increased dominance and times of decreased dominance. We might illustrate Shklovsky's hypothesis by the history of English-language poetic style and—to see more than one kind of text and system—by the history of women's hemlines.

Let us start with eighteenth-century neoclassical poetry, typically represented by the poetry of Alexander Pope. Pope's language was elite, learned, conspicuously witty, and ornate. William Wordsworth, the great Romantic poet, reacted against the style that Pope typified, seeking instead a plain language of ordinary speech. Then the Victorians, such as Alfred, Lord Tennyson and Dante Gabriel Rossetti, returned to an elite language, more lyrical and less witty than Pope's language but still, like Pope's, conspicuously ornate and poetic. Then the Imagists continued the pattern by reacting against what they saw as the falsity of poetic language and paring their poetry down to its barest bones. Soon after the Imagists, such high modernist poets as T. S. Eliot and the later Ezra Pound again made poetic language elaborate and arcane. And after modernism, in our postmodern time, the pendulum of history that Shklovsky and Jakobson describe played out another variation, rejecting the by-then-predictable movement back and forth in favor of a postmodern eclecticism that courts many styles at once. The story of hemlines looks much the same. Over the twentieth century, they repeatedly bounced up and then down, and now they go every which way (at least when women wear skirts or dresses at all).

History of English-Language Poetic Style

Pope ⟶ Wordsworth ⟶ Tennyson, Rossetti ⟶ Imagism ⟶ Eliot ⟶ postmodernism

neoclassical ⟶ Romantic ⟶ Victorian ⟶ Imagist ⟶ high modernist ⟶ postmodernist

Whether for poetry or skirts, the pendulum theory of how systems operate tells a good story and offers helpful historical insight. Even so, the formalist and structuralist model of history's swings back and forth has notable limits. No system is ever closed from the world or free to operate independently. Hemlines yo-yoed up and down not simply because of a law requiring them to reverse the dominant. They rose during World Wars I and II because so much cloth went into uniforms that there wasn't as much for skirts. Historically, then, the structuralist sense of an isolated system responding to internal, merely formalist laws can help describe the system but is not sufficient to describe it, for the social world has a way of cracking the boundaries of the system.

This tie to history does not mean that we have to throw out the structuralist model, but it complicates the model. At the least, we need to enlarge the system to accommodate social history, which may prove harder to describe by a predictably repeating set of rules. Similarly, the neat story of changing poetic diction over the centuries, taught to generations of students and regularly updated as the generations march onward, tells a reasonably accurate story of canonical poetry by men but not so accurate a story of poetry at large. Now that critics are rewriting literary history to include the poetry of women and nonelite, working-class poets, the old story no longer holds up for so broad a field as the history of English-language poetry, where multiple styles have always coexisted, long before the self-conscious eclecticism of postmodernism. Structuralism can help us historicize, then, but in the process we need to keep the structuralism flexible, need to keep it as hard to predict as history itself.

THE STRUCTURALIST STUDY OF NARRATIVE: NARRATOLOGY

The structuralist study of narrative is called **narratology.** While narratology can lead to insight into individual narratives, and we may choose to use it that way, most narratologists, as structuralists, concentrate their attention on producing broader descriptions of a system. They describe the ways that narratives work in general or the ways that certain kinds of narratives work (the detective novel, for instance). They have two particular focuses: (1) what I will call **the tale and the telling** and (2) what is often called narration.

The tale and the telling. The tale is the sequence of events in the order they take place, and the telling is the sequence of events in the order they are told. In a story, the telling often follows a different sequence from the tale, because storytellers do not always begin at the beginning or end at the ending. Instead, a telling flashes back and flashes forward. The tale includes all the events, but a telling must leave some things out, producing gaps (also called *ellipses* or *lacunae*). Wherever we can find a difference between the tale and the telling, we can ask how it matters for the story, for its art and its meaning, that the telling follows its own sequence instead of the sequence of the tale or some other sequence, a question that can give us a powerful way to interpret a story. In any story, the sequence of the telling is loaded with cultural codes and assumptions.

Jane Austen's novel *Pride and Prejudice* begins with a sentence pronouncing, "It is a truth universally acknowledged, that a single man in possession of a good fortune, must be in want of a wife" and then

---

A Tale of Terms

Different critics often choose different terms for what I am calling the tale and the telling, and the differences lead to confusion. Most readers will not need to know the other terms, but some readers, especially those who may continue to read structuralist criticism and theory, will come across the other terms, so for those readers it may be worth mentioning, briefly, the best-known variations. Like many structuralist ideas, the binary opposition between the tale and the telling takes its inspiration from the Russian formalists. Shklovsky and Boris Tomashevsky proposed a distinction between what they called, in Russian, the *fabula* and the *sjuzet*, terms that are sometimes used in English-language writing and that are rendered in English as *story* and *plot*. Those terms cause confusion, however, since story and plot seem similar. The linguist Émile Benveniste, and later the narratologist Seymour Chatman, proposed the much easier-to-follow terms *story* and *discourse*, while the eminent narratologist Gérard Genette called the same ideas *story* and *narrative*. I propose the terms *tale* and *telling* because they flow more easily across an English-speaking tongue and have a noticeable logic that makes them easier to remember.

swiftly moves to dialogue: " 'My dear Mr. Bennet,' said his lady to him one day, 'have you heard that Netherfield Park is let at last?' " (Austen). Each of these sentences is rife with suggestiveness for structuralist and narratological interpretation. In some ways, the novel begins at the beginning, for after we have read the novel, we could say that the letting (renting) of Netherfield Park sets the story in motion. But the beginning launches an armada of questions. What is the effect of beginning the novel's telling there, as opposed, perhaps, to beginning with a history of the Bennet family, or the birth of Elizabeth Bennet, or an exposition on the condition of lesser gentry, or an exposition on the range and limits of opportunities for women of the gentry class, or the history of Mr. Darcy (which the novel ekes out one bit at a time in an irregular sequence that turns out to be crucial to the plot and its suspense), or the story of Mr. Bingley, and so on? No narratological twist has to take the turns that it ends up taking. Instead, it represents a choice from an endless menu of narratological and cultural possibilities, a choice saturated with meaning and consequence.

The famous opening sentence of *Pride and Prejudice* did not have to come first, and it did not have to get in the novel at all. We could follow the story equally well without it. Had the novel begun with Mrs. Bennet's leading question, which sets off the suspense by telling us that someone new is about to arrive in the neighborhood, nothing would look amiss. But the first sentence suggests another kind of beginning besides the beginning of the plot proper that starts a moment later with Mrs. Bennet's question. The first sentence places the novel into a set of cultural codes, on the one hand with the forthrightness of raw announcement, and on the other hand with a directness so arch that it not only announces the code but also begins to tease it, potentially even to laugh at it. It also hints at a potentially tragic distinction between how such a code might play out for women, whom the code positions as objects, compared to how it plays out for men, its vaunted subjects. In almost sarcastically parroting the code's placement of women as objects and men as subjects, the arch tone has a way of making us think about the consequences of its gendered grammar (all the more so from the perspective of reading farther into the novel and then remembering or rereading the opening sentence). Such thoughts can resubjectify women and thus put under scrutiny the whole business of dividing genders into subject positions and object positions in the first place and also put under scrutiny the idea that such a code, with its assumptions about marriage and desire, is a beginning that frames everything that follows.

This little example could be multiplied endlessly through many more interpretations and through every conceivable variation between the telling and the tale, or between multiple tellings in the same story (perhaps from the perspectives of different characters), or between any actual telling and another potential alternative telling of the same tale. The point, therefore, is that the seemingly simple rubric of the tale versus the telling offers an endless array of possibilities for interpretation, more than sufficient to carry a literature student through all the years of undergraduate and graduate study. And narratologists, ever hungry for variations and technical terminology, have charted a vast repertoire of variations in how stories play with the differences between the tale and the telling. The method carries suggestiveness not only for such obviously ripe examples as the novels of William Faulkner and the movies *Pulp Fiction* and *Memento*, which flag shifts in the sequence of the telling as part of their explicit method, but also for other novels and stories, films, reporting, conversation, and any other place where we find narrative.

Narration. Under the rubric of **narration,** we will look at four frequently discussed categories:

- embedding
- reliability
- focalization
- direct, indirect, and free indirect discourse

Let us start with the categories that are easiest to explain, recognize, and interpret: embedding and reliability.

Narrative **embedding,** or **nesting,** refers to what are also called **stories within stories,** cases where the narrative has a framing story and another story embedded, or nested, within the frame. Such nesting will also play high jinks with the relation of the tale to the telling. A reader might simply observe that a given part of a narrative is embedded, but as with any wrinkles in the relation between the tale and the telling, readers looking to interpret the text can also ask what is the effect of the embedding. The frame or outside story, for example, might make us look at the inside story more skeptically, or the inside story might make us look more skeptically at the outside story. If either wobbles, it can make the other wobble with it, sometimes setting off questions about narrative reliability.

In Percival Everett's provocative novel *Erasure*, for example, the narrator, an African American novelist, is furious that his intellectually sophisticated novels get so little attention while other African American novels that he thinks wallow in offensive stereotypes win wide acclaim. He vents his frustration by writing as offensive, stereotypical, and illiterate a ghetto novel as he can imagine, and in the middle of its narrative *Erasure* includes the entire text of the loathsome novel that the narrator writes. Together, the inside novel and the outside novel pose a binary opposition. Reading the novel and the novel within the novel together, readers might ask questions about either that we would not come up with if we read them separately. Is the inside novel so terrifically bad that it ends up as perversely good? How do the two stories and their narrators repeat or differ from each other? Does the corruption of the loathsome inside narrator hint at corruption in the seemingly sympathetic outside narrator who stoops to imagine him? Does it put the outside narrator's judgment—his reliability—in question? Or are the two narrators as fundamentally different as the outside narrator supposes? Does the inside novel make the outside narrator who scorns it look like a snob—or does it criticize the idea that popular culture might encourage us to look at middle-class blacks as snobs?

The question of narrative reliability had already received a good deal of attention before narratology came on the scene, notably in a classic of Anglo-American criticism, Wayne Booth's *The Rhetoric of Fiction* (first edition, 1961). Many high school and college students have faced questions about **reliable narrators** versus **unreliable narrators** (a binary opposition) without ever hearing of narratology. The issue of an unreliable narrator often comes up with Mark Twain's *Adventures of Huckleberry Finn*. There, the white Huck decides that he will rescue his black friend Jim from slavery, even though rescuing Jim will mean, Huck believes, that Huck will "go to hell." Having been taught that slavery is acceptable and that helping an enslaved person escape is stealing property, Huck believes that rescuing Jim from slavery is wrong, even worthy of damnation (literally going to hell). Readers, who presumably see that it is good to rescue Jim, need to understand Huck's world and his plight in different ways from how Huck understands them himself, even though Huck, who tells the story, is our only source. That makes Huck an unreliable narrator. In that sense he is typical of child narrators. When the narrator is a child, readers depend on the child's narration, yet in some ways readers usually understand the child's world better than the child understands it.

Even adult narrators can turn out to be conspicuously unreliable, as in Ford Madox Ford's *The Good Soldier*, Daphne du Maurier's *Rebecca*, Albert Camus's *The Stranger*, and Gillian Flynn's *Gone Girl*. Critics often debate whether a narrator is reliable or unreliable, such as for Ishmael in Herman Melville's *Moby-Dick*, Nick Carraway in F. Scott Fitzgerald's *The Great Gatsby*, or Jake Barnes in Ernest Hemingway's *The Sun Also Rises.* In other cases, key pleasures or insights depend on understanding characters and events differently from how the narrator understands them, as in many of Dorothy Parker's stories, Edgar Allan Poe's "The Tell-Tale Heart," or Marlowe's tale in Joseph Conrad's *Heart of Darkness.*

If we step forward from structuralism and peek ahead to deconstruction, however, we might draw on the deconstructionist sense of pervasive instability (discussed in Chapter 4) to suggest that there is no such thing as a reliable narrator. There will always be a way that some readers may choose to interpret a story differently from a narrator's way of interpreting it. Contemporary readers, for example, will often see race, gender, and class in sharply different ways from narrators of an earlier generation—or even of their own generation. And differences at so broad a level mediate different approaches to a narrative, both for melodramatic events and for mundane, barely noticeable turns of phrase and nuance, especially when we depend on a narrator to choose which events matter and how they matter.

In the same way as we question the concept of a reliable narrator, we might also question the common idea of an omniscient narrator. Many readers think of an exterior narrator (so-called third-person perspective, sometimes too casually supposed to equal the author's perspective) on the model of an all-knowing, or omniscient, god. But just as we can question the reliability of any internal narrator, we can always find something that an exterior narrator does not know, can always find ways that we do not trust an exterior narrator's knowledge or understanding. Stories would be much simpler and easier to interpret if their narrators knew everything. Sometimes narrators act as if they know everything, and they may even attract our trust, more or less, but they cannot know everything, and sometimes our trust can lead us astray. For that reason, rather than calling more or less reliable and knowing exterior or third-person narrators omniscient, I will suggest that we call them *seemingly* omniscient.

Questions about narrators and their reliability or omniscience lead to the related category of **focalization,** a narratological term for what was traditionally called *point of view* or *perspective*. Traditionally, when critics mention point of view or perspective they refer to the first-person voice of a character who narrates the story, as in the novels and stories just mentioned or in Charlotte Brontë's *Jane*

Eyre, Charles Dickens's *Great Expectations*, William Faulkner's *As I Lay Dying*, Ralph Ellison's *Invisible Man*, and so on. Narratologists renamed the concept with the awkward term *focalization* partly to signal its difference from the traditional notion of point of view. Critics typically use *perspective* or *point of view* to indicate whose voice narrates a story, but narratologists noticed that a character's perspective does not always come in the character's voice. Often, an exterior, third-person narrative voice recounts events by describing the perspective of an interior character, as in Henry James's *What Maisie Knew*, Gertrude Stein's *Three Lives*, Virginia Woolf's *Mrs. Dalloway*, Leslie Marmon Silko's *Ceremony*, and Arundhati Roy's *The God of Small Things*. Whether an **internal focalizer** comes in first-person narration (using the pronoun *I*) or third-person narration (referring to the focalizer by name or by pronouns like *she, he, or they*), the point to calling the character a focalizer is that the angle of mind comes through the character. Therefore, when we ask who is the focalizer, we cannot find the answer by checking whether the narrative comes in the first person or the third person. Instead of answering the question by checking whose words are used, we can answer it by checking whose *eyes or mind* the narration looks or thinks through.

Thus, to see how focalization works, we can ask *who is the focalizer.* The focalizer might be a character (an internal focalizer), or it might be an exterior narrator. We might also ask who (or what) is the **focalized,** the object of the focalizer's attention. Then we can ask what we can learn as an interpreter of that particular narrative by observing who is the focalizer and, perhaps, who is the focalized. What does that show about the relation between the focalizer and the focalized, and what does it say about the narrative? Is the focalizer consistent through the narrative, or does the focalizer shift? If it shifts, does it shift frequently (as in *Mrs. Dalloway, As I Lay Dying*, or Louise Erdrich's *Love Medicine*) or rarely, and how might that matter? What is the effect of the shifts? How can we tell a shift when we see it? Does anything trigger the shift? What difference does the trigger make—or the lack of a trigger? When the focalizer is a character and the focalized is another character (as opposed to, say, a focalized object or idea), does the focalized character return the attention by looking back or thinking about the focalizer?

In some ways, every internal focalizer, also called a *character-focalizer*, is also the focalized of an exterior narrator-focalizer. It works that way even if, as in a first-person narrative, the exterior narrator-focalizer is never explicit and remains merely implied. In some ways, as well, every focalizer also thinks about herself or himself and is thus partly her or his own focalized. In any narrative that catches our interest, we can consider who or what are the focalizers and the focalized and what their relation to each other can suggest, perhaps in connection to whatever issues we especially care about in that narrative.

Focalization often has a close analogue in the way that film uses a camera and editing to encourage an audience to look as if through the eyes of a character, especially in the pattern of editing known as **shot/reverse shot.** A shot/reverse shot is a film sequence that alternates between a character and an object, implying that the character is looking at the object. Often, the object is another character, perhaps during dialogue, implying that the two characters look at each other while they talk with each other. A wider shot that directly shows the two characters looking at each other often sets up or punctuates the scene. The editing and camera work then funnel the viewer's eyes into looking as if through the eyes of the character or characters. In the same way, verbal narration can set up a focalizer as a character whose view or thinking readers are invited to identify with (for better or worse, depending on the character).

Uncertain, flickering focalization often works through **free indirect discourse,** a style of narration that different critics call by different terms, including *free indirect style,* or, in French, *style indirect libre.* We can recognize free indirect discourse (FID) through its relation to its cousins **indirect discourse** (ID) and **direct discourse** (DD). Here, the term *discourse* refers to representations of speech or thought.

DD is straightforward. It represents speech or thought directly, often in quotation marks, as in *He said: "I love her."* It can come without quotation marks, though in such cases the quotation marks are implied, as in *He said: I love her,* or *He thought, I love her.* DD can use the first person (I or we), though it does not always use the first person, because people do not always use "I" or "we" when they speak or think.

ID is less straightforward but not terribly mysterious, as in *He thought that he loved her.* It shifts the tense of DD one step back, in this case from present tense (love) to past tense (loved), and in other cases from past tense (loved) to past perfect (had loved). And it uses the third person (she, he, or they) to represent speech or thought through summary rather than through direct quotation. The pivot word *that,* together with the third person, often (but not always) signal ID.

FID is trickier and more mysterious, which is why it has attracted critics' interest. Like ID, FID shifts the tense a step back and uses the third person, but it blurs the boundary between a narrator's language and a character's language, as in *He was walking down the street thinking. He loved her. He really did. This time he was sure. He crossed the street, lost in his thoughts.*

The great interest of FID comes because we cannot pinpoint the exact boundary between ID and FID, or between the character's language and the narrator's language. That interest might seem to reflect a sterile obsession with drawing lines. But in practice it can lead to provocative interpretation, because it requires readers to interpret the difference between, on one hand, the character's patterns of thought and speech and, on the other hand, the narrator's patterns. In the preceding example, the skeptical "This time" carries a different meaning according to whether we attribute it to the narrator or to the character. If we attribute it to the narrator, then the narrator can come across as knowing and the character as deluded. If we attribute it to the character, then the character can come across as wryly self-questioning, if still romantically enthusiastic. If the phrase read "This time, confound it," or "This time, damn it," then we would know it came from the character, and the words that come next would do more to fill out the character. But without expressions like *confound it* or *damn it*, we measure the words against our surrounding experience of the character and the narrator, intensifying our interpretation of both of them.

Such interpretation requires an alertness to a vast array of fluctuating and contested cultural codes and conventions, such as codes that might tell us that certain vocabularies or turns of thought— including many that some readers might object to—are characteristic of a particular gender, age, region, education, race, desire, mood, time period, prejudice, and so on. But those codes and conventions could come through either the narrator or the character, and either

DD, ID, FID, and Focalization: Connected but Not the Same

Students often confuse focalization with direct, indirect, and free indirect discourse. We can interpret direct, indirect, and free indirect discourse to describe how focalization structures narration, and we can interpret focalization to describe how free indirect discourse dips into and out of an internal focalizer's speech or thought. The representation of speech or thought through direct, indirect, and free indirect discourse overlaps with focalization, but they are not the same.

the narrator or the character (but especially the narrator) can also indulge in those codes mockingly. Readers find themselves hypothesizing interpretive patterns, supposing that a given character or narrator typically thinks in this way or that way and therefore that certain features of narration in the FID hail from the character while others come from the narrator. The slippery boundary between ID and FID provokes interpretation even from casual readers who do not know about FID, though knowing about it can redouble the provocation. Indeed, the boundary between the structuralist categories of FID and ID gets so slippery that the study of FID slides structuralism into the deconstruction that we will look at more in the next chapter.

HOW TO INTERPRET: FOCALIZATION AND FREE INDIRECT DISCOURSE

Focalization. Let us return to Walt Whitman for a more extended example of focalization, this time from section 11 of his long poem "Song of Myself" (1855):

Twenty-eight young men bathe by the shore,
Twenty-eight young men and all so friendly;
Twenty-eight years of womanly life and all so lonesome.
She owns the fine house by the rise of the bank,
She hides handsome and richly drest aft the blinds of the window.
Which of the young men does she like the best?
Ah the homeliest of them is beautiful to her.
Where are you off to, lady? for I see you,
You splash in the water there, yet stay stock still in your room.
Dancing and laughing along the beach came the twenty-ninth bather,
The rest did not see her, but she saw them and loved them.
The beards of the young men glisten'd with wet, it ran from their
     long hair,
Little streams pass'd all over their bodies.
An unseen hand also pass'd over their bodies,
It descended tremblingly from their temples and ribs.
The young men float on their backs, their white bellies bulge to the sun,
     they do not ask who seizes fast to them,
They do not know who puffs and declines with pendant and bending arch,
They do not think whom they souse with spray.

(Whitman 197–198)

Here we might ordinarily—and reliably—say that the "lady," also referred to as "she" and then as the "twenty-ninth bather," is the focalizer.

We could stop there and work with that idea interpretively, or we could elaborate. We might note that the "twenty-eight young men" are the focalized. We could also go on to note the first-person narration as it shows up in the words "I see you," and we could see the "I" as a focalizer with the "lady" as its focalized.

While readers might suppose that the "I" represents the exterior narrator, the last concentric circle of narration, every narrative also has an implicit exterior narrator, yet more exterior than the explicit first-person "I." (Of course, many narratives do not have a first-person "I.") Readers usually ignore or oversimplify the implicit exterior narrator by thinking of it as "the author," not recognizing that the exterior narrator may pursue ways of thinking that differ from what historical evidence indicates the author may have thought. Most interpretations ignore the exterior narrator. But if we choose to pay attention to it, then we could say that the exterior narrator is yet another focalizer. The focalized of the exterior narrator's focalizing would be the "I" focalizing the lady who focalizes the young men. For every character-focalizer, as already noted, is also the focalized of a yet more exterior narrator-focalizer.

We could stop there. Or we might also observe that the lady implicitly thinks about herself thinking about the young men, for, as we have also noted, every character is partly her or his own focalized, suggesting that the lady herself is another focalized of her own focalizing. Implicitly, the "I" also focalizes itself, but that remains far more distantly implicit than the lady's more visible gaze at her own thoughts as a focalized of her own focalizing.

Such a structure can be illustrated in the accompanying chart (Figure 3.3). This chart is synchronic. It does not show a chronological sequence. Potentially the "I" looks at the lady before she looks at the men, for example, but that would be a diachronic feature not expressed in the chart. While classical structuralists might stop after completing the chart, later structuralists might consider its cultural meaning. The chart appears to sustain a cultural expectation that certain people look while other people are looked at. But perhaps it also rewrites or critiques the pattern. How does it matter, for example, that a woman looks here at men? That reverses a culturally expected pattern. What if we think of queer as well as heterosexual relations mediating and mediated by this structure? Is there evidence for heterosexual or queer identifications for any of these focalizing perspectives and focalized bodies? What difference might it make if we suppose a potentially queer angle for the exterior narrator, compared to a heterosexual

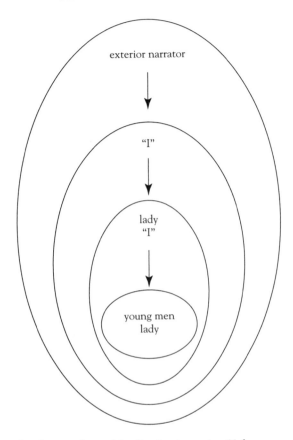

Figure 3.3 Synchronic chart of focalization in section 11 from "Song of Myself."

angle? Is there any reason to suppose that a male exterior narrator looks at the lady with heterosexual desire—or, by contrast, uses the lady to mediate and mask same-sex desire for the bathing men? What shape of desire might we see from the lady, or from the young men, who bathe with each other? For many readers, much of the interest in studying structures will magnify when we bring structuralist questions into dialogue with the methods described later in this book, such as, in this example, feminism and queer studies.

FID. At a moment of crisis in *Harry Potter and the Chamber of Secrets*, we read that Harry "could run, and no one would ever know he had been there. But he couldn't just leave them lying here. . . . He had to get help" (Rowling 202). Even if readers never realize it consciously, to understand this scene they have to sort through the FID to figure out whose mind these words represent. If we read "no one would ever know he had been there" as coming merely from the narrator, then it looks like a simple statement of fact. If we read the immediacy and directness of language as implying a third-person summary or paraphrase of Harry's first-person thoughts, so that the narration comes both through the narrator and through Harry, then we see Harry tempted to get away with something that we know he should not get away with. That, in turn, makes Harry look less than perfect and presses us to ask whether his weakness turns us against him or makes him seem sympathetically human. When we go on to read that "he couldn't just leave them" and "He had to get help," those phrases could again seem like simple statements of fact from the narrator, or, in a blur of FID, they could begin to summarize Harry's thoughts, suggesting that his sympathetic kindness wins out over his humanizing temptation to selfishness. If we miss the tone and language that signal FID and read the entire passage as direct statements of fact, then we miss out on the drama in Harry's hesitation and miss out as well on how the dance of narration—of literary form and structure—dramatizes the humanizing conflict that attracts readers to Harry and his story.

Of course, few readers of the Harry Potter books have heard of ID and FID. That does not keep them from feeling its effects, from letting it steer them into identifying with Harry's mix of mischievousness and heroism. But if we learn about ID and FID, then we can learn much about how the Harry Potter narratives steer the zigs and zags of identification with Harry and with the other characters in the Harry Potter novels.

NARRATIVE SYNTAX, AND METAPHOR AND METONYMY

Narrative syntax. The influential structuralists A. J. Greimas and Tzvetan Todorov, drawing on *Morphology of the Folktale* (1928), by the Russian formalist V. Propp, sought to describe narrative as like a sentence. Loosely summarizing this one part of their work, we can say that a sentence is a small narrative. It has a subject, predicate (verb), and object, and larger narratives also have subjects, predicates, and objects. The characters are subjects; the things the characters do are predicates; and the results (sought or achieved) are objects. Subjects can include different kinds of characters, such as protagonists, antagonists, and helpers. Predicates can include such variations as going on a journey, learning, conquering, going on a quest, and transmitting a gift. Objects can include gifts, rewards, happiness, marriage, wealth, death. In that way, at the risk of flattening out differences, narratologists can find common patterns among a variety of stories. Frodo's search for the ring in *The Lord of the Rings* can look something like Jeanette's search for independence in *Oranges Are Not the Only Fruit*. Both protagonists must find helpers and overcome antagonists as they travel the treacherous path that eventually leads to their objects or goals.

As the relation among subject, predicate, and object shapes the syntax of a sentence, so a narrative also has syntax. This insight enabled structuralists to draw on Saussure's distinction between what is variously called the **syntagmatic,** or **horizontal, axis** on the one hand and the **paradigmatic,** or **vertical, axis** on the other hand. Sometimes people in the humanities, myself included, freeze up before technical terms like this. But if you give yourself a chance to get used to them, they are not complicated. The paradigmatic or vertical axis simply means things that come in a group and can substitute for each other. For example, you can go swimming with Jane, or with John, or with a dog, so the category that includes Jane, John, and the dog is a group or paradigm. The syntagmatic or horizontal axis simply means things that follow in a sequence (Jane interprets the book) that sometimes you can rearrange (The book interprets Jane).

Thus, the numbers and letters in the "Examples of Narrative Syntax" might look forbidding, but once you see what they refer to, they are simple. Let us take three sentences: sentence 1, sentence 2, and sentence 3. Our sentences have four paradigms or groups: group A for subjects, group B for predicates, group C for objects, and group D for modifiers. We could substitute one subject for another from our pool of subjects (Jane, John, and the dog) and produce a sentence with the same structure, the same syntax, but a different meaning. Similarly, we could substitute one predicate for another, one object for another, and one modifier for another. Such movement within categories proceeds along the paradigmatic, or vertical, axis, whereas the movement from subject to predicate to object and, potentially, to modifier proceeds along the syntagmatic, or horizontal, axis (Table 3.2).

Examples of Narrative Syntax

1A Jane	1B interprets	1C the book	1D brilliantly.
2A John	2B eats	2C the sandwich	2D eagerly.
3A The dog	3B fetches	3C the stick	3D quickly.

Table 3.2 *Terms for the Vertical and Horizontal Axes*

VERTICAL AXIS	HORIZONTAL AXIS
paradigmatic	syntagmatic
vertical	horizontal, sequential
analogy, similarity	contiguity, adjacency
substitution	combination
selective, associative	combinative
metaphor	Metonymy

The vertical describes a choice among elements (individual items) in the narrative or the sentence. John, for example, can interpret or eat or fetch. The horizontal produces the narrative: what a subject does to an object and—if we use a modifier, D—how it does that. In this sense, we can keep one horizontal structure (one syntax of the sentence or narrative) while changing the vertical vocabulary, shifting, for example, from "The dog fetches the stick quickly" to "The dog eats the book quickly." Alternatively, we can retain the same vertical vocabulary while changing the horizontal structure, as in shifting from "Jane interprets the book brilliantly" to "The book brilliantly interprets Jane."

A sentence or line in a poem, a hip-hop lyric, or a novel plays vertically with the substitution of different possibilities for words and plays horizontally with the combination of different potential sequences of words. The choices in such play characterize the poem, lyric, or novel's aesthetics, style, and way of approaching and interpreting the world. In the song he calls "Hip Hop," for example, Mos Def sings:

Committed to page, I write a rhyme.
Sometimes won't finish for days.
Scrutinize my literature.
From the large to the miniature I mathematically add-minister.
Subtract the wack. Selector, wheel it back, I'm feeling that.

In ways typical of hip-hop, Mos Def combines a selectively (that is, vertically) accenting beat (I *mathematically ADD-minister*) and a series of rhymes and off-rhymes (page/days, rhyme/scrutinize, literature/miniature/add-minister/selector, subtract/wack/back/that) that play up the wittily unexpected choices in his vertical subtracting and adding (administering) with a horizontal sequencing, including the accelerations and decelerations of pace (pausing between *add* and *minister*, speeding up at *wheel*). Together the vertical and horizontal play hypes his own ability (I write, I add-minister, I'm feeling) to make such choices while modeling the ability of his listeners to make the same kinds of choices, to shape and enjoy the aesthetics of language. Together our vertical (paradigmatic) and horizontal (syntagmatic) choices craft an interpretable style, whether for Mos Def, Jane Austen, a political speech, or the next text you send or receive.

Metaphor and metonymy. Roman Jakobson drew on the relation between syntagmatic and paradigmatic structures in his influential discussion of metaphor and metonymy, based both on abstract linguistics and on studies of brain-damaged patients who retain an ability to use either metaphor or metonymy but not both. Metaphors and metonymies are rhetorical figures. A **metaphor** describes something by something else that is not connected to it. A **metonymy** describes something by something else that is connected to it or part of it.

In the classroom, I like to give examples and see if students can tell which are metaphors and which are metonymies. I might pick out a student and say that in our class discussions, she is a real *spark plug*. That is a metaphor, because the student is not connected to or part of an engine. I hold up an 800-plus-page copy of George Eliot's *Middlemarch*, one of the great achievements of British fiction, and call it a *whale* of a book. Students recognize *whale* as a metaphor, because they can see that the novel in my hand is not connected to or part of a whale. I pick out another student and say, "I want to go out tonight but my car is down, so can I borrow your *wheels*?" That is a metonymy, because the wheels are part of the car. When pundits or bloggers call for *heads to roll* at the White House, *heads* is a metonymy, because the heads are connected to, and part of, the people whom the pundits or bloggers want fired. But—to try a trickier example—we might say that *roll* is a metaphor, since heads are not connected to anything that will literally roll down the avenues of Washington like bowling balls. Even the expression *White House* could be a metonymy here, because most employees of the executive branch do not actually work in the White House, but some of them do, so that the phrase *the White House* has come, metonymically, to represent the administration overall.

Jakobson claimed that metaphor dominates in surrealist painting, and metonymy dominates in cubist painting; that metaphor dominates in romanticism and symbolism, while metonymy dominates in realism; and that metaphor dominates in poetry, while metonymy dominates in prose. For example, realism typically tends more toward prose fiction than toward poetry. If we were to write a realistic description of someone, such as the description in a novel, we might describe his or her bedroom or living space and use it as a metonymy that figures (figuratively represents) the person we are describing. A messy room suggests one thing about a personality, a sunny room another thing, and a meticulous room something else. We might also use clothing to represent the person metonymically (a tightly buttoned vest, a rakish hat), or we might characterize a particular body part to make it represent the person, such as brooding, suspicious, or cheerful eyes, a square or receding chin, or a firm or feeble handshake.

The system is far from perfect. For one thing, a person with a messy room or sloppy clothes might have an organized mind, or someone with a receding chin might be more confident and assertive than someone else who has a square chin. Such forms of metonymic representation may tell more about cultural codes and prejudices than about actual people. But that too is revealing, and it does not keep the prejudices from working figuratively in rhetoric, even in rhetoric that teases or mocks the prejudices. Having held up *Middlemarch* before my students and heard them agree that to call it a whale of a book is to use a metaphor, I then like to hold up *Moby-Dick* so that they can realize that calling *Moby-Dick* a whale of a book instead of *Middlemarch* changes the metaphor to a metonymy, because even students who have not had the pleasure of reading Herman Melville's behemoth know that it has, to say the least, a connection to a whale. Similarly, the lively student in my class may be a spark plug, and spark plug may be a metaphor, because she is not connected to or part of an engine. But what if my student is a robot with an engine? Then "spark plug" can turn into a metonymy.

Some Common Confusions

Confusion can arise because the use of the term *metaphor* as popularized by Jakobson's notion of a binary opposition between metaphor and metonymy refers to a subcategory of the more familiar use of the term *metaphor*. In that sense, a metonymy is also a kind of *metaphor*, in the usual sense of the term *metaphor*, meaning a figurative use of one thing to represent another thing. Thus, Jakobson's distinction between metaphor and metonymy distinguishes between two kinds of metaphor.

Confusion can also arise because many people already know the term *synecdoche*, referring to a figure that uses a part to represent a whole, and they often wonder about its relation to metonymy. A synecdoche is always a metonymy, but not all metonymies are synecdoches. When Christopher Marlowe, in *Doctor Faustus*, calls Helen of Troy "the face that launch'd a thousand ships," *face* is a synecdoche, and therefore it is also a metonymy. By contrast, when reporters write, "The White House announced today," the *White House* is a metonymy, because, as we have seen, it is connected to the president and the president's staff, but it is not part of them, so it is not a synecdoche.

As the context changes and metaphors become metonymies or metonymies become metaphors, the structuralist confidence in categories may seem to unravel (especially to a deconstructionist). We might then ask why we should care about the opposition between metaphor and metonymy. While structuralists may have exaggerated the value of the distinction between metaphor and metonymy, recognizing it will allow us, at the least, to follow other people's references to it. A little more ambitiously, we can follow and appreciate the uses that other critical methods bring to the distinction, especially psychoanalysis. Along the way, a familiarity with the distinction between metaphor and metonymy will help us notice previously unsuspected turns and twists of figurative language in literature and elsewhere. (And for better or worse, referring to metonymies will allow us to describe what we notice in a cool and sophisticated-sounding way.)

* * * * *

By now, as readers approach the end of this chapter on structuralism, they may feel overwhelmed with terms and categories and wonder how they can remember them all, let alone use them. While this chapter confines itself to the basic structuralist terms and concepts and those most likely to be useful, the words can seem like a blizzard when they all are new. No one would expect students to use every concept in this chapter in a course paper or a test essay, whether in a definition of structuralism or in the interpretation of a literary text or of another cultural text or genre. But readers can start to acquaint themselves with the general principles (construction, binary oppositions, systems, and so on) and then choose from among the specific tasks and strategies. The survey of structuralism here can equip readers with the key questions and approaches that structuralists have brought to literary and cultural criticism and equip readers to follow how later methods continue to draw on those questions and approaches. Students of literature sometimes find the rigor of structuralism refreshingly systematic. But sometimes they take offense at it and see the obsession with systems as a desecration or a falsifying of literary and cultural values. Out of a similar mixture of interest in structuralism and suspicion of its impulse to systematize grew the way of thinking and reading discussed in the next chapter, on deconstruction.

FURTHER READING

Barthes, Roland. "The Death of the Author." In *Image-Music-Text*. Selected and trans. Stephen Heath. New York: Hill and Wang, 1977. 142–148.

———. *Elements of Semiology*. Trans. Annette Lavers and Colin Smith. London: Cape, 1967.

———. *Image-Music-Text*. Selected and trans. Stephen Heath. New York: Hill and Wang, 1977.

———. *Mythologies*. 1957. Selected and trans. Annette Lavers. New York: Hill and Wang, 1972.

———. *S/Z*. 1970. Trans. Richard Miller. New York: Hill and Wang, 1974.

Benveniste, Émile. *Problems in General Linguistics*. 1966. Trans. Mary Elizabeth Meek. Coral Gables, FL: University of Miami Press, 1971.

Chatman, Seymour. *Story and Discourse: Narrative Structure in Fiction and Film*. Ithaca, NY: Cornell University Press, 1978.

Culler, Jonathan. *Structuralist Poetics: Structuralism, Linguistics, and the Study of Literature.* Ithaca, NY: Cornell University Press, 1975. An excellent overview.

Eco, Umberto. *A Theory of Semiotics.* Bloomington: Indiana University Press, 1976.

Erlich, Victor. *Russian Formalism: History, Doctrine.* 4th ed. The Hague: Mouton, 1980.

Garrett, Matthew, ed. *The Cambridge Companion to Narrative Theory.* Cambridge: Cambridge University Press, 2018.

Genette, Gérard. *Figures of Literary Discourse.* 1966–1972. Trans. Alan Sheridan. New York: Columbia University Press, 1982.

———. *Narrative Discourse: An Essay in Method.* 1972. Trans. Jane E. Lewin. Ithaca, NY: Cornell University Press, 1980.

———. *Narrative Discourse Revisited.* 1983. Trans. Jane E. Lewin. Ithaca, NY: Cornell University Press, 1988.

Greimas, A. J. *On Meaning: Selected Writings in Semiotic Theory.* 1970–1983. Trans. Paul J. Perron and Frank Collins. Minneapolis: University of Minnesota Press, 1987.

———. *Structural Semantics: An Attempt at a Method.* 1966. Trans. Daniele McDowell, Ronald Schleifer, and Alan Velie. Lincoln: University of Nebraska Press, 1983.

Hawkes, Terence. *Structuralism and Semiotics.* Berkeley: University of California Press, 1977. An excellent introduction.

Herman, David, Brian McHale, and James Phelan, eds. *Teaching Narrative Theory.* New York: MLA, 2010.

Jakobson, Roman. "Closing Statement: Linguistics and Poetics." *Style in Language.* Ed. Thomas A. Sebeok. Cambridge, MA: MIT Press, 1960. 350–377.

Jameson, Fredric. *The Prison-House of Language: A Critical Account of Structuralism and Russian Formalism.* Princeton, NJ: Princeton University Press, 1972.

Lemon, Lee T., and Marion J. Reis, trans. *Russian Formalist Criticism: Four Essays.* Lincoln: University of Nebraska Press, 1965.

Lévi-Strauss, Claude. *Structural Anthropology.* 1958. Trans. Claire Jacobson and Brooke Grundfest Schoepf. New York: Basic Books, 1963.

———, Claude. *Tristes Tropiques.* 1955. Trans. John and Doreen Weightman. New York: Atheneum Press, 1974.

McHale, Brian. "Free Indirect Discourse: A Survey of Recent Accounts." *PTL: A Journal for Descriptive Poetics and the Theory of Literature* 3 (1978): 249–287.

Prince, Gerald. *A Dictionary of Narratology.* Rev. ed. Lincoln: University of Nebraska Press, 2003.

Propp, V. *Morphology of the Folktale.* 1928. Trans. Laurence Scott. 2nd ed. Austin: University of Texas Press, 1968.

Rimmon-Kenan, Shlomith. *Narrative Fiction: Contemporary Poetics.* 2nd ed. London: Routledge, 2002.

Saussure, Ferdinand de. *Course in General Linguistics.* 1916. Ed. Charles Bally and Albert Reidlinger. Trans. Wade Baskin. New York: Philosophical Library, 1959.

Todorov, Tzvetan. *The Poetics of Prose.* Trans. Richard Howard. Ithaca, NY: Cornell University Press, 1977.

✻ 4 ✻

Deconstruction

Deconstruction, in and of itself, is almost dead, but it retains enormous influence on current critical thinking. While deconstruction itself peaked in the late 1970s, an evolving version of deconstruction often remains crucial to, and is even taken for granted by, contemporary cultural and literary criticism.

The founding figure and the intellectual force behind deconstruction was Jacques Derrida (Figure 4.1). His first widely influential book, *Of Grammatology*, appeared in French in 1967, and many of his later writings recast or extend the ideas of *Of Grammatology* for other contexts and issues. Advocates and popularizers saw his ideas as so revolutionary that they put him in the same light as Copernicus, Newton, Einstein, and Freud. His influence in literary studies grew so strong that many students supposed he was a literary critic or literary theorist. Still, while Derrida sometimes wrote about literature, he was primarily a philosopher, not a literary critic, even though, at least outside France, his work had little impact on philosophy until after its shock wave hit literary studies. Deconstruction has since carried its influence far beyond literary studies, not only to philosophy but also to all of the humanities and often to the social sciences, and debates still rage over its relevance for the so-called hard sciences.

KEY CONCEPTS IN DECONSTRUCTION

Multiple meanings. As I risked summarizing structuralism in one concept, relatedness, so I will risk summarizing deconstruction in one concept, multiplicity. Deconstructionists believe in multiple

Figure 4.1 Jacques Derrida (1930–2004).

meanings. They take Saussure's structuralist formula defining the sign as the signified bonded together with the signifier, and they widen the gap between the signified and the signifier, focusing on what they call *free-floating signifiers*, or the free play of signifiers. That is to say, in deconstruction, seemingly singular or stable meanings give way to a ceaseless play of language that multiplies meanings. Thus, deconstructionist thinking fit well with Roland Barthes's idea of the death of the author (reviewed in Chapter 3). No longer could our understanding of an author tie down our understanding of a text. Because, like Barthes, deconstructionists use structuralism but go beyond it, they are often called *poststructuralists*, although poststructuralism can also refer more generally to modes of criticism that came after structuralism, or to criticism that draws on deconstruction, even if it blends deconstruction with other methods, such as those discussed later in this book.

Let us clear up, early on, some common misunderstandings. People who misunderstand deconstruction often think that it says there is no meaning. Occasionally, carried away with their zeal, early deconstructionists said or implied that, but it is not representative of deconstruction. On the contrary, and most characteristically, deconstruction multiplies meaning. Instead of giving us no meaning, it gives us many meanings. Deconstructionists describe how meaning disseminates. To Derrida, *dissemination* cannot be defined, because that would limit its meaning, but it plays off the word *semen*, to suggest seed, and the word *seme*, the linguistic term for a basic unit of meaning. Dissemination thus describes how meaning scatters, spreads, and multiplies and how, in the process of accumulating, meanings can also be lost.

In a related misconception, people who know little about deconstruction often suppose that it simply means destruction. But deconstruction is not destruction. It can change the way we view things, but it does not destroy anything. It offers more, not less. In deconstruction there is always more, a surplus of meaning and rhetoric that Derrida calls a *supplement*.

With so sprawling a proliferation of meanings, deconstructionists often turn their attention to what they call *decentering*. To understand what decentering does, it can help to think about what a center does. A center holds together the things that surround it. If readers find a center, then they can see how the center organizes the things around it into a secure, stable, unified system. In a novel or a play, for example, traditional critics might pick out a particular feature—such as a pivotal scene, word, or character—and describe it as central to the overall work (whether or not they actually use the term *central* or *center*). They might argue that the scene, word, character, or other central feature shapes the rest of the play or novel, casts other scenes, words, or characters in a meaningful light that leads to a particular interpretation. Any reader will recognize that

---

Common Misunderstandings of Deconstruction

Beginners—and others who have only a casual acquaintance with deconstruction—often misconstrue it by missing that deconstruction offers more, not less. Deconstruction offers more meanings, not fewer meanings. To summarize:

- Deconstruction does not mean there is no meaning.
- Deconstruction means there are many meanings.
- Even though deconstruction means there are many meanings, it does not allow for *any* meanings. We still need convincing evidence and argument to back up a deconstructive interpretation.
- Deconstruction is not destruction. It does not destroy or take away meaning. Instead, deconstruction multiplies meaning.

Poststructuralism and Postmodernism

These related terms have caused confusion, because some people use both terms to refer to the intellectual movement spearheaded by deconstruction, while most people (myself included) use *postmodernism* to refer to contemporary developments in architecture, literature, and popular culture, saving the term *poststructuralism* for the intellectual movement. It seems to me that we can better characterize the movement in aesthetic style by its placement in a time period (after modernism) and its reaction to a previous age and style (modernism) and that we can better characterize the intellectual movement by the shape of its ideas (a response to and development from structuralism), though in many ways the shape of its ideas can also represent its time period.

way of thinking, because it is a routine way to understand any phenomenon, cultural or literary.

But deconstructionists do not believe that systems can be secure or unified or that we can capture cultural objects with single explanations. To a deconstructionist everything is multiple, unstable, and without unity. In this view, we cannot tie language down; we cannot tie the signified tightly to the signifier. Without the tight bond between the signified and the signifier that Saussure imagined, the signifiers start to float freely, even playfully, away from any particular signifieds. Deconstructionists focus intensely on those signifiers. That is, they focus on language itself, which they see as constructed out of free-floating signifiers. With their intense interest in language, they see everything as *figurative*, as dense with rhetoric and textuality. For deconstructionists, then, rhetorical, figurative meanings—the play of signifiers—proliferate so much that they displace literal meaning. For literal meaning, the signified and the signifier would have to be bound tightly together, limiting the play and the meaning of language. Without a reliable bond between the signifier and the signified, the very concept of the sign and its relation to our world and experience lack the predictable stability that we usually take for granted. Because the signifiers inevitably drift away from any one signified, the meanings of language, rhetoric, and textuality multiply beyond the possibilities of literal language, beyond the possibilities of the carefully organized systems that structuralists charted.

What Do You Call It Again—*Deconstruction?*

This is *not* important, but it can save you from putting off your readers or listeners. Few people who know much about deconstruction say "deconstruction*ism*" or "deconstruction*alism*." Perhaps people who use those terms are thinking of analogies to words like "structur*alism*." The usual terms are *deconstruction, deconstructionist,* and *deconstructive.*

How deconstructionists read. Though many deconstructionists, and occasionally even Derrida, use the verb *deconstruct* (and it has even entered the popular talk of the general public), I think that using the verb *deconstruct* and referring to deconstruction as an action misses a key point. Since deconstruction refers to a basic principle of all language, we cannot deconstruct something. As Paul de Man, one of Derrida's most famous and influential followers, put it, "The deconstruction is not something we have added to the text but it constituted the text in the first place" (de Man 17). If critics want to think deconstructively, then instead of deconstructing a text they find the way that, from a deconstructionist perspective, the text is always already deconstructed. They don't do it to a text. Instead, they expose the way that it is already done, the way that a text has always already deconstructed itself.

Deconstructionist interpretation frequently follows what has come to be called a **double reading,** a two-stage reading. In the first stage, the critic identifies a singular interpretation, free from multiplicity and deconstruction. Often it is an interpretation that a structuralist critic might propose, such as an argument about the overall system or perhaps a binary opposition or center that organizes the text into a stable, coherent system. For example, if we return to the reading of Walt Whitman's "Beat! Beat! Drums" in Chapter 2, we might say that the assumption that Whitman wanted his poem to support the United States in the Civil War provides a central idea that stabilizes the text into a coherent system, a system shaped by a firm binary opposition between pro-war (pro-Union) and anti-war. Then, in the second stage, the critic finds things that undermine the structure, things that (in deconstructionist lingo) "break down the binary," "explode the binary," or "decenter the text." Or the critic finds a moment of **undecidability** (sometimes called an aporia), showing how the free play of the text's signifiers—its language—goes beyond the capacity of the system to confine it to one meaning or set of meanings, as when our reading of Whitman's poem uncovered too many possible competing intentions for one intention to rule the poem and lock the poem's meanings to any notion of what Whitman might have intended.

Simply providing two interpretations does not add up to a deconstructive double reading. For a reading to be a deconstructive double reading, the first reading must propose a stable interpretation, and then the second reading must undo that stable interpretation by proposing an unstable reading that brings out more multiplicity in the interpreted object or text.

It is not hard to do a double reading, because we can always find something that troubles or breaks up the system. But it is harder to do a double reading well, because to do it well we have to find something that troubles or breaks up the system in interesting ways. For that reason, if you want to set up a double reading, do not make your first reading so obviously unconvincing that it is easy to knock it down. The more plausible your first reading, the more interesting your interpretation will grow when your second reading knocks the first reading over. Sometimes, instead of asking your readers to buy into your first reading and then blaming them for trusting you, you can tell them ahead of time that the first reading is provisional, a possible reading, a target that you will soon reconsider from a more critical and deconstructionist perspective.

Table 4.1 can help readers understand double readings and, more broadly, the range of concepts that lead to double readings.

Table 4.1 Deconstructive Terms

TERMS FOR NONDECONSTRUCTIVE IDEAS	TERMS FOR DECONSTRUCTIVE IDEAS
truth, substance, essence	play, free play, undecidability, aporia
center	decentering
nature	culture
stability	instability
	différance, surplus of meaning, supplement, dissemination
speech, voice, phonocentrism literalness, logocentrism	writing, textuality, rhetoric
origin, authority, authenticity	suspicion of stabilizing ideas such as origin, authority, authenticity
metaphysics of presence	Absence

Deconstructionists did not design this table, but I have put it together to illustrate deconstructionist concepts and terms, including terms that we will get to later in this chapter, making the table a reference point to return to as the chapter goes on.

The left column of the table represents standard concepts familiar outside deconstruction, grouping them roughly into three related sets. Some of the terms are familiar, while some Derrida made up or popularized (metaphysics of presence, phonocentrism, logocentrism), but they all refer to standard concepts outside deconstruction. The right column assembles a parallel set of concepts. Again, some of them are familiar terms or concepts, while some of them are Derrida's own, but they are all deconstructive concepts that Derrida sets against the more familiar concepts in the left column.

Typically, in the first stage of a double reading, deconstructionist critics will pick out a supposedly secure interpretation or structure and describe it with terms or concepts from the left column. Then in the second stage, they will say that the concepts in the left column do not really work and that the concepts in the right column work much better.

Newcomers to deconstruction often think they have discovered a fatal contradiction in Derrida's methods when they observe that Derrida and his followers use the very concepts (those in the left column) that they object to. But Derrida anticipates that objection. Indeed, he is quick to say that even though he believes we should try to get beyond the concepts that I have listed in the left column, we can never get beyond them entirely. He says that we can try to get beyond assuming secure meanings, but that sometimes we end up assuming them nevertheless. Even to criticize stable concepts and say that they are actually unstable, we still need to call on the ostensibly stable concepts. Occasionally, therefore, when Derrida uses a word that expresses a stable concept, he will write an X over the word to show that although he must use the term he does not mean to endorse it (a practice that Derrida picks up from the philosopher Martin Heidegger). In deconstructionist lingo, to cross words out that way, using them but marking the use as provisional, is called **bracketing** them or putting them **under erasure** (or in French, *sous rature*).

There are a variety of ways to pursue a deconstructionist interpretation, with or without a double reading. A double reading might give more or less equal time to the first reading and the second reading. Or it can condense the first reading into a brief gesture. Or the critic can dispense with the first reading and go directly to a deconstructionist reading, or integrate references to one or more potential first readings through the length of the deconstructionist reading.

Regardless, to produce a deconstructionist reading, critics typically pick out part of a text and study its language, rhetoric, and figuration with great intensity, searching out ways that the text unravels its own assumptions and disseminates more meaning than it can unify and more meaning than a simple structure can contain. Indeed, if you want a formula for how to read deconstructively, then reread the previous sentence, so long as you keep in mind the ironic qualification that the idea of a formula is itself antideconstructive, bracketed, under erasure. Deconstruction is thus like new criticism, in that both pursue a close attention to language. But deconstruction radically reverses new criticism through a fascination with disunity. Whereas new critics argued that the text fits together in organic balance and unity, deconstructionists might consider how a text can *seem* to fit together (the first stage of a double reading), but they end up showing (in the second stage) how it spins apart.

HOW TO INTERPRET:
A DECONSTRUCTIONIST EXAMPLE

Let us consider, for an example, Ezra Pound's celebrated two-line poem "In a Station of the Metro" (1913):

> The apparition of these faces in the crowd;
> Petals on a wet, black bough.

> (Pound 35)

A new critic might seek out symbols in the apparition, faces, crowd, petals, bough, wetness, or blackness, perhaps finding a paradoxical, ambiguous tension between the abstractness of the first line, with its hard-to-see and impossible-to-touch apparition, and the concreteness of the second line, with its touchable, visible petal and bough. The new critic would then resolve the seeming conflict into a balance that unifies the poem. A structuralist could pursue a similar reading, finding a binary opposition between the opening abstraction and the concreteness that it gives way to. The first line can work as a signifier to the second line's signified, for its abstractions give meaning to the plain facts of the petal and the bough.

A deconstructionist could ignore such interpretations and go immediately to something more multiple, or begin with those interpretations and use them as a first reading to set up a double reading. If the first line's abstractness can work as a signifier to the concreteness of the second line's signified, then a deconstructionist can just as well flip that reading and see the second line as a signifier to the first line's signified. Perhaps that could still work within a structuralist reading, because even in mirror image it retains the same binary structure. But the possibility of turning the structuralist reading on its head suggests the potential for an instability that might lead us to doubt the stability implied in reading the poem as a binary opposition or in seeing its signifiers as bound firmly to its signifieds.

To continue a deconstructionist approach, then, we could pursue any number of possibilities, so long as we choose more than one. We would likely pursue at least several angles and suggest how they also generate more possibilities, keeping the meanings circulating continuously. Often, to show how those meanings cannot settle into a stable structure, we would seek out **internal contradictions** or **internal differences** that frustrate any interpretation of the text as holding a singular, stable meaning. From a deconstructive perspective everything has internal contradictions, if we allow ourselves to see them.

In a sense, as we have noted, the first line can seem more abstract, especially in the term *apparition*, and the second line can seem more concrete because of its reliance on touchable, specific objects. On the other hand, the petals float loose, grammatically, from any article or demonstrative pronoun. That is to say, no "the" or "these" precedes them and places them in a context. The lack of such terms sets the petals' would-be concreteness in a contradictory, framing abstractness. At the same time, in the first line the definite article *the* and the demonstrative pronoun *these* make the poem refer to a contradiction: a specific ghostliness, with specific but undescribed faces in a specific but undescribed crowd. Each line thus has contradictions built within it that multiply the permutations of its opposition to the other line.

In this famously short poem the title works like a line unto itself, interrupting the potential binary opposition between lines 1 and 2. If we continue the figure of opposition, tracing the continually unraveling and reraveling opposition between the concrete and the abstract, then we might see the title as concretizing because of the way it places the poem in a specific place, the Metro, the Paris subway. Still, in the early twentieth century the Metro was abstractly a signifier of modernity at large and especially of mechanized modernity and the urban future. That future is both suggested and undermined in the lyrical petals of the second line. The petals can suggest nature, a quiet antithesis to the screeching metallic modernity of the Metro. At the same time, together with the poem's imitation of Japanese styles (such as haiku), the petals can suggest the role that Japanese understatement and Japanese ways of envisioning nature were coming to figure a new visual modernity in modern European art. After the Western powers forced Japan to trade with them, innovative painters like Edgar Degas and Mary Cassatt imitated the newly available Japanese woodcuts, just as Pound imitated Japanese haiku, so that people came to associate Japanese art with the new European modernity.

Japan also promised a new modernity militarily and economically, as it shocked the world with its defeat of Russia in the 1904–1905 Russo-Japanese War. Meanwhile, the darkness of the Metro can match the darkness of the black bough, while the lights in the Metro's underground darkness can match the sheen of wet petals set against the blackness of the bough. The poem's semicolon (which in some drafts was a colon) thus evokes a flickering hesitation between continuity (which a colon would signal, like an equal sign) and discontinuity (which a period between lines would signal). For every flicker of continuity in this poem, as these brief ruminations begin to suggest (and one could write about this reverberating little poem at much greater length), has both within it and beside it a flicker of discontinuity, not a matching flicker that settles the contradictions into equilibrium or new critical balance and unity, but rather a continuously unequal, unbalanced disequilibrium, always more and less than what it contradicts.

Such a reading suggests how deconstructive literary interpretation can work. In deconstructive interpretation, the meanings never stabilize. Deconstruction does not destroy or remove meaning but instead multiplies meanings and continues to circulate those multiplying meanings and to defy any sense of a single or stable truth or essence. But it is not as if anything goes. Deconstruction offers many meanings but, as noted earlier, it does not authorize *any* meanings. Suspicious though deconstructionists may be of systems, they still rely on evidence and argument to develop an interpretation. The logic of evidence and argument may in some sense lie under erasure, but as deconstructionists seek out internal contradictions in the objects they interpret, they also embrace deconstruction's own internal contradictions by continuing to rely on evidence and argument. That reliance makes a deconstructive reading more than an exercise in self-infatuation or anarchy. Instead, like traditional interpreters, deconstructionists seek to communicate with and convince others.

WRITING, SPEECH, AND *DIFFÉRANCE*

Writing and speech. It is time to look further at some of Derrida's specific ideas, already hinted at in Table 4.1 (deconstructive terms). (Here and over the next few paragraphs, readers may find it helpful to refer back to Table 4.1.) Whether you concern yourself closely with the details or not, a review of these ideas can help you understand the larger pattern of Derrida's thinking.

Perhaps in part to dramatize his thinking and to shock us into paying more attention, Derrida makes the counterintuitive claim that writing came before speech. Derrida thinks we put far too much emphasis on speech. He calls that emphasis *phonocentrism,* just as he coins the term *logocentrism* for the belief that signifiers, words, can contain the essence of their signifieds (*logos* is ancient Greek for "word"). That leads some deconstructionist feminists, along with Derrida, to refer to the patriarchal belief in stable meanings as *phallogocentrism,* combining the words *phallus* and *logocentrism.* Derrida thinks that Western culture is phonocentric. That is, he thinks that in Western cultures people usually take for granted that secure meanings and identities rest in the sound of the voice, as if the voice exposed a person's *essence,* revealing that person in some *essential* way. Against that notion of secure essences, against the notion of secure signifieds fastened tightly to their single signifiers, Derrida sets *writing* and the figuration or free play of language, because writing so advertises its status as the proliferation of signifiers that we cannot tie writing down to secure meanings. Thus he tries to privilege writing over speech, and so he says that writing came first.

But by *writing* he does not necessarily mean actual script. Instead of the actual script, he means the system of representation that Saussure outlines in the formula of the signified and the signifier, except that for Derrida the signifier always floats freely away from the signified. We may imagine, he argues, that speech gets outside of representation and becomes the pure signified, free from signifiers, free from *writing.* But we can never get to the pure signified, he believes, apart from the representing signifiers. We can only keep adding and multiplying the signifiers. There is no origin and no endpoint. We can never get to the *presence* itself, what he calls the "metaphysics of presence," because, in Derrida's lingo, the free-floating signifiers guarantee that there is always an *absence* between the signifier and the signified.

Différance. In the same vein, Derrida coins the term **différance,** which combines the French words for *defer* (meaning *postpone*) and *difference.* In making up this new word, he changes the second *e* to an *a* partly to make visible the difference between *différance* and *differ-ence*, even though, in French, the two words sound the same. (In Eng-lish, by contrast, we can hear the difference between *différance*, with a stress on the third syllable, and *difference*, with a stress on the first syllable.) Derrida's point and the meaning of his made-up word is that there is always difference, always a gap between signifier and signified, so that the continuous play of signifiers, instead of taking us closer to the signified, always defers the signified, thus keeping a difference be-tween the signifier and the signified. *Différance*, therefore, is Derrida's name for the inevitable gap between the signifier and the signified, the gap that keeps meanings from ever settling into something stable, the gap that keeps all meaning unstable. More colloquially, we might say that *différance* is the gunk in the gears, the imperfection—the entropy or inefficiency—that inevitably interferes with any system.

By looking at Derrida's essay on *différance* (1968), we can start to get a feel for his erudite and playful style, a style that entrances many readers and exasperates many readers as well. Here is the beginning of the essay, which, as his opening words indicate, he first delivered as a lecture read out loud to an audience:

> I will speak, therefore, of a letter.
>
> Of the first letter, if the alphabet, and most of the speculations which have ventured into it, are to be believed.
>
> I will speak, therefore, of the letter *a*, this initial letter which it appar-ently has been necessary to insinuate, here and there, into the writing of the word *difference*; and to do so in the course of a writing on writing, and also of a writing within writing whose different trajectories thereby find themselves, at certain very determined points, intersecting with a kind of gross spelling mistake, a lapse in the discipline and law which regulate writing and keep it seemly. One can always, de facto or de jure [by practice or by law], erase or reduce this lapse in spelling, and find it (according to situations to be analyzed each time, although amounting to the same), grave or unseemly, that is, to follow the most ingenuous hy-pothesis, amusing. Thus, even if one seeks to pass over such an infraction in silence, the interest that one takes in it can be recognized and situated in advance as prescribed by the mute irony, the inaudible misplacement, of this literal permutation. One can always act as if it made no difference. And I must state here and now that today's discourse will be less a justi-fication of, and even less an apology for, this silent lapse in spelling, than a kind of insistent intensification of its play. (Derrida 3)

In reading (and rereading) these words, it can help to keep in mind that Derrida's first audience, listening in French, cannot tell when, as he gives this lecture titled "Différance," he is saying *difference* and when he is saying *différance*, for in French both the familiar word and the made-up word sound the same. As readers, we can see which word Derrida is using, because one has an accent mark and has the letter *a* whereas the other has no accent and has the letter *e* near the beginning of the last syllable. By privileging the graphic over the audible, Derrida privileges writing over speech. As if that did not put up enough of an obstacle, at least for the original audience, if his listeners and readers hope to have any idea what Derrida is saying, they have to be familiar, beforehand, with the word and concept *différance*.

In short, Derrida does not begin at the beginning. Indeed, he advertises his refusal to begin at the beginning by starting off with the word *therefore*, which we might expect to find at the end. That unexpected opening can remind us that in Derrida's way of thinking, there is no beginning, no origin, and no ending, but instead a continuous circulation and deferral. In the same vein, having begun at what sounds like the end and thus undermined the idea of both beginning and ending, Derrida winks at us in the middle of the essay by saying such things as "I would say, *first* off, that *différance*, which is neither a word nor a concept," and "Let us *start*, since we are already there, from the problematic of the sign and of writing" (Derrida 7, 9; italics added to *first* and *start*). We might also notice, at the beginning, that when Derrida says that he will speak of *a* letter, the letter he speaks of is *a*. While such a pun plays perfectly into Derrida's style, the play works in English (which Derrida knew) but not in French. Regardless, each time Derrida says difference, he defers *différance* and calls attention to the difference between *différance* and difference, and each time he says *différance*, he defers difference and calls attention to the difference between the two words or concepts (or nonwords and nonconcepts) again, so that his language can never arrive at one term or the other but can only keep deferring them and signifying their endless play.

By writing in so slippery and playful a style, Derrida enacts his ideas, instead of just explaining them. He sees philosophical and critical writing as rife with multiple meanings in the same way that literary texts are rife with multiple meanings. He invites us to read his writing, and other philosophical and critical writing, in the same way that we might read the multiple, playful language of a witty, punning Shakespearean sonnet. Philosophical and critical writing, for Derrida, does not carry a truth function that sets it apart as a stable refuge from the instability of literary writing. In that sense, for Derrida, the two ostensibly different kinds of writing slide into each other and no longer seem so different. Any effort to draw a line that separates stable from unstable writing, informative writing from "creative writing," gives way to an endless *différance* that undermines what we may have supposed was a stable binary opposition.

While Derrida's detractors see such a view as a self-indulgent inflation of the literary value of philosophical and critical writing, including his own, other critics see it as an encouragement to expand our sense of the literary and to enlarge the range of what literary critics study. In that sense, deconstruction has contributed to a reluctance to draw a circle around poetry, drama, and fiction and say that only those things can be worthy of literary and critical study. Today, influenced as well by the cultural studies movement (which we discuss in Chapter 9), literary critics study much more than poetry, drama, and fiction, as presumably this book has already made clear. Today, literary critics also study film, autobiography, critical and philosophical writing, and an enormous range of cultural and popular cultural practices, from popular music to comic books and from politics to identity theory.

DECONSTRUCTION BEYOND DERRIDA

High deconstruction. By the late 1970s, deconstruction was the rage. Paul de Man, Geoffrey Hartman, and J. Hillis Miller, a group of established literary critics at Yale University, made themselves Derrida's disciples, adapting his philosophical writings to literary criticism. Famous as "the Yale School," they popularized deconstruction for Anglo-American literary studies. Deconstruction—as a word but not as a concept—entered the popular language. Usually, the people who use it have no idea what it means in critical theory and suppose, to the dismay or amusement of philosophers and literary critics, that *deconstruct* is just a sophisticated way to say *destroy*. Traditionalists were horrified by deconstruction, and sometimes they dubbed the Yale School the Yale Mafia or even the hermeneutical Mafia. Enthusiasts made it seem as if no article or book of literary criticism, outside the most old-fashioned scholarship, could be taken seriously if it did not refer to Derrida, de Man, Hartman, or Miller, and for a while they seemed to represent the future of literary criticism.

But even faster than the Yale School came to monopolize the landscape, it faded away before the force of feminism, Marxism and historicism, queer studies, and postcolonial studies, so that now deconstruction has survived not so much as a separate method but as a way of thinking that blends with and helps shape other methods. Derrida and the Yale School came to represent what we might think of as classical or high deconstruction, as opposed to the way that deconstructive thinking took new shapes as it blended with other methods, as we see later in this volume. The early leaders of deconstruction were mainly men, but soon feminists such as Hélène Cixous, Barbara Johnson, and Gayatri Chakravorty Spivak drew on deconstruction for feminist criticism. (On Cixous see Chapter 6 on feminism, and on Spivak, who translated Derrida's influential *Of Grammatology* into English, see Chapter 10 on postcolonial and race studies.) Already, in my sample deconstructionist reading of Pound's "In a Station of the Metro," I have gone beyond the limits of high deconstruction, drawing on historicism to consider how Pound's poem evokes the onset of mechanistic modernism and the new Japanese ascendancy in modern art and politics.

When deconstruction's early opponents responded to it with horror, their alarm set off a roiling scandal in English and other literature departments across the world and in the popular press. To its outraged critics, deconstruction threatened to kill off literary studies. In their minds, it replaced the rigor of new criticism and structuralism with a meaningless, anything-goes chaos that desecrated literary art in favor of abstruse, in-group philosophy and sybaritic navel-gazing. But many other critics of high deconstruction recognized that deconstruction does not mean the end of meaning, and does not mean that anything goes. They thought through its limits more patiently, and sometimes more sympathetically, even when they rejected it strongly.

As a rough consensus emerged on the limits and problems with high deconstruction, two concerns stood out. First, if everything is about the free play of language, the free play of signifiers, the dissemination of meaning, and so on, then all texts are alike. It seemed that every high deconstructionist interpretation reached the same conclusion about every text, and experienced readers could predict the ending of a high deconstructionist interpretation while they were still reading the beginning or before they started to read it at all. Second, the repetitious insistence on the free play of meaning often grew so abstract that it seemed to treat texts as isolated language games cut off from the social and material world, where particular meanings make an enormous difference in people's lives. And so to many critics, after the initial hoopla, high deconstruction—the deconstruction of Derrida, de Man, Hartman, Miller, and their followers—came to seem both predictable and irrelevant.

As it happens, Derrida intended for his writings to have social meaning, and later in his life, perhaps responding to his critics, he often made the social commitments in his writing more explicit, drawing sometimes on his African roots as an Algerian Jew who spent his adult life in France. He supported dissidents in Eastern Europe, opposed apartheid (racial segregation) in South Africa, and wrote a controversially nuanced response to 9/11. The comparative lack of social concern among the American deconstructionists, led by the Yale School, distorts Derrida's works, or at least it distorts his apparent intentions, even while many readers continue to believe that the work does not live up to those intentions. Derrida's writing and the writing of many of his followers can seem disconnected from the social world because his densely punning, mischievous, winking style of writing and thinking plays so exuberantly with the signifiers that it can seem to lose track of the signifieds.

Deconstruction and contemporary criticism. For literary or cultural interpretation, the solution to these problems is surprisingly simple. If we make the deconstructive reading our conclusion, deciding at the end of our argument that the text is about the free play of signifiers and the endless meanings of language, then our interpretations will get tiresomely predictable. But if we begin with that and then ask what consequences the play of language has in a text and in its social world or in its readers' social world, then we have exciting new leads to follow, and then deconstruction can greatly help us interpret the text and its worlds. That is why deconstruction continues to exert a strong influence on later critics, who look at what difference a particular deconstructive multiplicity might make in, for example, a feminist, queer, Marxist, historicist, racialized, or postcolonial context and in relation to specific social issues, such as those raised by environmental criticism or disability studies. In that mode, deconstruction more often goes under the label of **poststructuralism,** which helps critics continue deconstruction's sense of multiplicity without continuing the sense of social disconnection that can characterize classical, high deconstruction. While deconstruction can seem like an irrelevant language game in the hands of its early advocates, in later hands it helps poststructuralist critics understand the issues they care about most, including political and social as well as aesthetic issues, because deconstructive multiplicity shapes the crises and pleasures that run through our daily lives.

The mere fact (or claim) of multiple meanings is no longer the point. The point is how the multiple meanings work in particular historical and social settings. All this explains why almost no one does straight-out or high deconstruction anymore. It can seem cut off from the world. And yet even while classical, high, or pure deconstruction has pretty much faded away, deconstruction continues to wield enormous influence as people use it to think in ways that go beyond deconstruction itself but that still use deconstruction.

Returning briefly to our deconstructionist reading of "In a Station of the Metro," we might say that a classical deconstructionist reading would concentrate on the disequilibrium and instability of the language as ends in themselves, making and drawing on more general claims about the continuously circulating figuration of literary signification. Such a reading often ended up by concluding that the figuration of language is vertiginous, dizzying. To later critics, such a conclusion often seems formulaic and disturbingly asocial. A later reading, from critics interested in the crises of and reshapings of modernity, might dwell on the poem's disequilibrium, not simply as an abstract linguistic vertigo, but rather in relation to modernist anxieties about mechanization, warfare, colonialism, and anticolonialism, as refracted through European imitations of Japanese art and poetry and, potentially, through their political analog in Japan's rising influence. They might contrast that sense of social crisis with the poem's status as an icon of understated aesthetic experimentation, seeing the urge to pare language down to minimal images as conflicting with the recurring desire to use those images to represent cultural crisis and cultural optimism.

Simulacra and simulation. In *Simulacra and Simulation* (1981), French philosopher Jean Baudrillard, not exactly a deconstructionist, proposed an influential model that can fit with a deconstructionist sense of a mobile and nonessentialist real. Baudrillard's concept of what he calls **simulacra** can help us understand contemporary technology and media in our daily lives and aesthetic experience. The simulacrum (singular of the plural *simulacra*), or what Baudrillard calls the **hyperreal,** is the simulation or imitation of the real that grows more real than the real. During a big storm, for example, victims of the storm hunker down in their homes, cut off from the rest of the world. Without electricity, they might not know what is going on around them. Meanwhile, far away, their friends and relatives often know what is going on, because they watch the catastrophe on TV and follow it on Twitter. In that way, the hyperreal imitation of the real ends up seeming more real than the real.

In Don DeLillo's novel *White Noise*, an ordinary barn comes to seem extraordinary when it wins fame for being ordinary, and a chemical spill gets recognition as a toxic disaster not so much through anyone's direct experience of disaster as because officials and the media represent it as a disaster. In the same way, for some people, their lives on social media feel more real than their lives lived directly with people. Nothing has really happened until TV or social media say it has happened. Without the simulacrum, the hyperreal, we do not pay attention to what happens, and therefore, in some sense, without the simulacrum and the hyperreal, nothing happens. The representation of the real overwhelms the real. The exponentially multiplying media storm of contemporary signifiers overwhelms the mere signifieds. The mere real is the old real, and the old real is no longer real. Today, the simulation is the real real.

DECONSTRUCTION, ESSENTIALISM, AND IDENTITY

Both the classical deconstructionists and the later poststructuralist thinking that draws on deconstruction look skeptically at the traditional confidence in stable literary meanings, which they see as essences. The belief in essences, in turn, has come to be called essentialism, and those who object to essentialism, both in and beyond literature, are called antiessentialists. The conflict between essentialism and **antiessentialism,** propelled by deconstruction but drawing as well on many other cultural motives, has animated a great deal of critical discussion and theorizing over the last few decades and shows little sign of diminishing. We have already begun to look at the notion of essentialism in the previous chapter, on structuralism, where we used the term *essence* to describe the idea of an underlying reality independent of linguistic representation, drawing an opposition between essences and constructions. In that sense, antiessentialists are also called *constructionists*.

Actually, most people whom other people call essentialists do not call themselves essentialists. Usually, the term *essentialist* is a term of abuse, and antiessentialists use it as a way to dismiss an argument. In response, their accused opponents often say some more sophisticated form of "Whoops, sorry, I didn't realize that I'd slipped into essentialism" or, more often, "No, I'm not making an essentialist argument," and then they try to explain how their argument is not essentialist. A few critics, however, take pride in explicitly calling themselves essentialists. From my own antiessentialist perspective, though, or—to use my own more modest term—from a nonessentialist perspective, those few critics who explicitly call themselves essentialists usually

---

Wait—A Deconstructionist and a Constructionist Would Both Object to Essentialism?

Yes, it may seem confusing, but the same ideas can be both deconstructionist and constructionist, without contradiction. The two terms have different histories that converge mainly by coincidence, but the point here is that deconstructionists object to essentialism, and construction is typically seen as the opposite of essentialism. Though the terms *construction* and *deconstruction* sound like opposites, they are not. Both refer to process as opposed to essence. Language sometimes works in unexpected ways—which is exactly the deconstructionist and constructionist point.

---

have a poor grasp of the debate around essentialism and the implications of endorsing the term.

An essentialist believes that the issue at hand, whatever it may be, has an underlying essence, a basic and defining set of qualities that do not change across history and geography. To make the principle concrete through examples, we could discuss essentialism in a variety of contexts. For example, we could propose that there is an essential concept or signified for the signifier *cat*, the term we discussed in the previous chapter's review of structuralist linguistics. An essentialist would say that the signifier *cat* is unambiguous, because all cats share a set of characteristics that only cats have and that do not vary across time and place or from one cat to another. An antiessentialist might say, on the contrary, that *cat* can refer to the familiar domestic feline or to a hugely inconsistent range of felines, domestic and wild, living and extinct. It can also refer to a bulldozer, a stylish man, any of several different colleges of advanced technology, the act of masculine philandering (catting around), a backbiting woman, a catfish, a CAT scan, a catalytic converter, and so on through a long and continuously evolving list of other meanings. For antiessentialists, that list of examples may seem to prove the point that language has no essence and instead circulates continuously through chains of unstable signifiers. But in such an argument the debate can seem like an abstruse scrimmage over abstract linguistic theory. In practice, by contrast, and especially since the heyday of high deconstruction, the greatest controversies around essentialism have raged around questions of human identity.

Who are you?

And what do you think about the question *Who are you?* Most of us feel a pressure to answer that question in oversimplified ways, and many of us resent the question. Yet we repeatedly ask it—if only in our own minds—about ourselves and about others, and we repeatedly have to answer it, not only in our own minds, but also in social introductions and on official forms. Sometimes the question comes in blunter form: *What* are you? We feel that someone asking that question wants one kind of answer, but there is more than one thing that defines who and what we are. If I answer that question by saying that I am a Baptist, or an English major, or a lesbian, or a New Yorker, or a basketball fan, then my answer seems to slight the way that I am also more than one thing, and my answer can seem to reduce the many things that I am to one or merely several qualities. Moreover, it can imply that if I define myself as an English major or a lesbian, and if that characteristic defines me, then all lesbians or English majors must be alike.

And in some ways, most people believe, at least some of the time and for certain criteria, that they are alike. We attribute at least some meaning to the signifier *lesbian* or *basketball fan*, suggesting at least a degree of commonality across all the people we might describe with those signifiers. And yet at the same time, we know well that lesbians and basketball fans are not all alike, that they vary enormously, that each group is rife with internal differences. Every description of a group of people, therefore, sets off a potential tug-of-war between the impulse to describe them by things they have in common and the impulse to describe them in ways that call attention to, or at least acknowledge, differences within the group.

Essentialists believe that they can define the essence of a person's identity. That is, they believe that people have a fixed identity; that their race, ethnicity, or gender (to name only the most frequent examples) expresses that identity; and that members of a racial, ethnic, or gender group will all act and think in a shared set of patterns. Some essentialists also believe that to understand a group one must be a member of that group. For example, an essentialist might say, "Because I am a woman, I understand sexism better than men understand it." It is easy to criticize essentialism, because it can often deteriorate into plain prejudice. The person who believes that all blacks love to dance and sing is an essentialist, as well as a racist, and that kind of essentialism helps give essentialism a bad name.

But it is not always so simple. Many people believe that a woman necessarily understands sexism better than a man or that a brown

Briton or American necessarily understands racism better than a white Briton or American. Indeed, the historical pattern has much to back up such beliefs, since men as a group have a tawdry history of sexism, and American and British whites as a group have a tawdry history of racism. The difficulty comes in how we extend generalizations about a group to predicting everything about the group, for every member of the group, across all times and places. An antiessentialist might say that most women understand sexism in most ways better than most men but that to make such claims about men and women overall is unfair to both groups. When sexism is so dominant, for example, it can distort women's thinking as well as men's thinking. Such an argument can get tricky, for it can easily deteriorate into a defensive propping up of the people who, given the differences in power, may need propping up the least, and a slighting of racist and sexist history. And so the debates over essentialism take on provocative questions and may look different from different angles and for different issues.

The complications multiply and the sparks often fly when it comes to sorting out the difference between an essentialist generalization and a nonessentialist generalization. It would be an essentialist generalization to say that Chinese Americans are inherently or innately better at math than other Americans. Some might argue that it would not be an essentialist generalization to say that Chinese American families focus on math in the schools more often than most other American families. A lot is at stake in the difference between those two statements. In the same vein, while it would be essentialist and racist to say that all blacks love to sing and dance (or, speaking to more likely conditions, to *imply* that all blacks love to sing and dance), that should not remove the value of studying or admiring black musical traditions.

The problem comes—and I would say that the disrespect for African American or Chinese American intellect and culture comes—in reading the accomplishments of African American musicians or Chinese American math students as essentialist, biological, and inevitable, as in their blood rather than in their hard work and imagination. The mass media, for example, which routinely turn representations of African Americans to sports and music and neglect African American intellectual life, foster an essentialist set of expectations from the general populace, both African American and non–African American. And the model minority myth fosters an essentialist set of expectations about Chinese Americans, such as when, for example,

Chinese American English majors, who may not care any more about math than most other English majors, discover with surprise that other students in their dorm ask them for help with math. Similarly, we can see a tragically essentialist set of expectations when African American high school students tell other African American high school students not to hit the books so hard, because that is "white," or when media-saturated clichés about African Americans make students fear that other students *might think* they are "acting white."

By contrast, antiessentialists or nonessentialists typically keep at least one eye on the ways that people in any given group differ from each other and on the many different identities that one person may express. One person, for example, might identify as a man, a biology student, a math lover, a Chicano, a heterosexual, a Chicagoan, a Republican, and so on. Someone else might share some of those identifications, and so feel a common bond, but not share all of them. In one context, at a Young Republicans meeting or on a date, one identification might stand out; but in another context, perhaps a debate over global warming or a drive along Lake Michigan, another identification might stand out. People are so multiple that no one identification and no predictable group of identifications can adequately define the person for all contexts.

And yet antiessentialist arguments that focus on people's multiplicity can make many of us uncomfortable, because we often want to focus on our likeness with other people, not on our difference from them or not *only* on our difference. People who do not get the point think that deconstruction takes meaning away from identity. But that is to mistake deconstruction for a process that removes meaning, when instead it multiplies meanings. That is where generalization comes in, and the challenge is to find ways to generalize about groups of people that do not demean people by essentializing them. It is not really such a tough challenge, but the cultural habit of relying on thought and language that takes essentialism for granted, that reduces people to only one or two of their many identities, can make it seem tough.

It can help to keep in mind that people have reasons for essentializing. People take pride, for example, in women's identity or Puerto Rican identity or many other identities. But these identities are historical and cultural processes and constructions, not essentialist absolutes, as we can see when we think how the connotations would shift if we talked about pride in white identity. Deconstruction and poststructuralism can help us find ways to generalize about identities that see them as historical and cultural processes rather than as stable essences.

We can find a helpful model in the cultural studies scholar Stuart Hall's discussion of cultural identity. (On Hall, see also Chapters 9, 10, and 11.) Born and raised in Jamaica, Hall has lived his adult life in Britain and written about both Jamaican and black British identities. He notes that some people have described Jamaican identity as African, others as European, and others as American. Rather than allowing any one of these influences to characterize Jamaican identity by itself, Hall chooses all three, so that he reads each history in multiple ways. He triangulates the three histories to describe Jamaican identity, not as an essence, but as a process. "Perhaps," writes Hall, "instead of thinking of identity as an already accomplished historical fact, . . . we should think, instead, of identity as a 'production,' which is never complete, always in process, and always constituted within, not outside, representation" (Hall, "Cultural Identity" 68). In this view, identity is not a stable signified that a single signifier passively represents. It is a continuous process of multiple signifiers and signifieds circulating through each other, *producing* identities through representation, that is, through language, not merely labeling identities that are already statically there. In addition to applying Hall's model to Jamaican identity, we could choose a similar structure, with different particulars, for any other identity we might want to describe. What, you might ask, are the multiple components of your identity or one of your identities or the identity of someone else you know?

Frequently Asked Question

Students often wonder how they can offer a deconstructive reading of a film or work of literature that obviously proclaims its own deconstruction. They worry, for example, that to point out that Gertrude Stein's poem "Tender Buttons," James Joyce's novel *Finnegans Wake*, Borges's stories, or films like *Being John Malkovich*, *Memento*, and *Primer* can be read deconstructively is only to point out what any reader or viewer already knows. But even when a work is not self-evidently deconstructive, it takes no great insight to point out that it is deconstructive after all. Because if deconstruction is a principle inherent to all representation, then it is a routine rather than a distinguishing

Continued

quality of any particular representation. Therefore, whether the work is obviously self-deconstructive or not, the goal is not to point out that it is deconstructive. Instead, the goal is to point out what difference its deconstruction makes for something that you care about in the work—its approach to gender, art, religion, or whatever most stirs your interest and imagination.

For example, the hypergenius baby that narrates Percival Everett's *Glyph*, a comical novel that takes its title from a word that deconstructionists often use to signal writing, reads Derrida and Barthes and is steeped in narratology. As he writes his narrative, he writes about the narratology of his own narrative. But—writing obsessed though he is—he never speaks. For as we might recall, Derrida argues that writing came before speech. Besides, babies can't talk. And so readers cannot always tell how much the novel makes fun of structuralism and deconstruction and how much it comically devotes itself to them. Perhaps that is a perfectly deconstructionist dilemma. But the deconstructionist dilemma does not remove meaning. It multiplies meaning. As readers realize that the genius baby is an African American baby in a sophisticatedly theoretical novel by an African American who resents being pigeonholed by the clichés about African Americans, *Glyph* makes a deconstructionist point. It offers an antiessentialist reading of African Americans, and by spoofing the wildly inaccurate cliché that African Americans, and nonwhites in general, don't do critical theory, it also offers a deconstructionist reading of critical theory.

HOW TO INTERPRET: FURTHER DECONSTRUCTIONIST EXAMPLES

Let us take two more examples. In the United States most people, over the years, have thought of the American populace through the lens of a black/white binary, as if all Americans were white or black (and certainly not white and black). Americans often essentialize black and white so thoroughly that they do not realize that the American schema of black and white, or black versus white, does not hold for much of the rest of the world, which often sees itself in other terms. In Great Britain, to take one example, the term *black* includes people of African and South Asian ancestry, while in the United States it includes only people of sub-Saharan African ancestry. Americans tend to think of race as an essence, rather than as a construction, but as we will see in Chapter 10 (on postcolonial and race studies), the study of race, partly influenced by deconstruction, has increasingly led to seeing race as a changing idea constructed by culture rather than as a biological essence. Americans—with and without the influence of deconstruction—are gradually recognizing that the black/white binary vastly oversimplifies American and global culture and demography.

But the cultural pressure driving (and constructing) the black/white binary remains forceful, such as in opinion polls that purport to tell us that whites think this and blacks think that, which can pressure members who identify with either group to think the way that they are told their group thinks, producing a self-fulfilling prophecy. From a deconstructive perspective concentrating on the figurative force of language, the terms *black* and *white* thus carry a figurative force in the American setting in excess of their truth value. That figurative force generates a truth effect, characterizing white and black as essences and as opposites, misrepresenting both whites and blacks and, in the process, misrepresenting the millions of Americans who do not identify as white or black. The black/white binary is thus a falsely totalizing polarity, magnetizing a wide range of variables into two opposite poles. Along the way, as it cuts out of the calculus the millions who are neither black nor white, it also oversimplifies both whites and blacks by characterizing each group as if all its members were all alike, as if there were no internal differences within the group, making each race look like an essence and denying its multiplicity.

For a final example, imagine a magazine advertisement with a picture of a gorgeous car. Think of the car as a signifier. Can we tie it to a secure signified? Can we pick out its essential meaning? If we chase after the signifier and catch it, will we arrive at the signified? Presumably not. Presumably we will never reach satisfaction (as the Rolling Stones complained), because there is always a gap between the signifier and the signified. Once we get the car (if we get it), the signifiers will keep multiplying, because there is always *différance*. We may seek the object of our desire, but we can never reach it (we can never reach the signified), because something always defers it, producing another desire, so that we want something to go with or substitute for the car, which is itself already a substitute for a previous desire, which in turn is a substitute for a still-earlier desire. There is no origin and no endpoint. A classic deconstructionist might stop there, content to show that the system is unstable and has no essence, but we can begin there and then go on to ask what that instability says about the vast social systems of representation in the car and in the desires and practices (of work, play, sex, travel, industry, mineral exploitation, landscape, ecology, and so on) that the car produces, frustrates, and continuously defers satisfying.

People who do not get deconstruction sometimes suppose that it is all about what we cannot say. We cannot believe any longer that things are natural, because in deconstruction they are cultural, the result of construction and process. Instead of truth, deconstruction offers play or undecidability. Instead of asking what is the authentic voice of, say, African Americans or African American women or any other group, deconstruction offers a swirl of internal differences and contradictions within the group. Instead of understanding history by pointing out an origin, deconstruction replaces the idea of a single origin with continuous process and disequilibrium. To people who do not get deconstruction, all this seems like loss. But that is to miss the point. For the point is that in turning our attention to process, discontinuity, disequilibrium, internal differences, culture, and undecidability, we find more, not less. The point is not to say, "No, we cannot believe in such things," but, rather, to say, "Yes, let us see what happens to culture and interpretation when we look at them, not as a settled and complete thing, but instead as something ongoing and rife with questions."

FURTHER READING

Barthes, Roland. *The Pleasure of the Text*. 1973. Trans. Richard Miller. New York: Hill and Wang, 1975.

Baudrillard, Jean. *Simulacra and Simulation*. 1981. Trans. Sheila Faria Glaser. Ann Arbor: University of Michigan Press, 1994.

Culler, Jonathan. *On Deconstruction: Theory and Criticism after Structuralism*. Ithaca, NY: Cornell University Press, 1982.

De Man, Paul. *Allegories of Reading: Figural Language in Rousseau, Nietzsche, Rilke, and Proust*. New Haven, CT: Yale University Press, 1979.

———. *Blindness and Insight: Essays in the Rhetoric of Contemporary Criticism*. New York: Oxford University Press, 1971.

Derrida, Jacques. *A Derrida Reader: Between the Blinds*. Ed. Peggy Kamuf. New York: Columbia University Press, 1991.

———. *Of Grammatology*. 1967. Trans. Gayatri Chakravorty Spivak. 2nd ed. Baltimore: Johns Hopkins University Press, 1998.

———. *Writing and Difference*. 1967. Trans. Alan Bass. Chicago: University of Chicago Press, 1978.

Hartman, Geoffrey H. *Criticism in the Wilderness: The Study of Literature Today.* New Haven, CT: Yale University Press, 1980.

———. *Saving the Text: Literature, Derrida, Philosophy.* Baltimore: Johns Hopkins University Press, 1981.

Johnson, Barbara. *The Critical Difference: Essays in the Contemporary Rhetoric of Reading.* Baltimore: Johns Hopkins University Press, 1980.

———. *A World of Difference.* Baltimore: Johns Hopkins University Press, 1988.

Leitch, Vincent B. *Deconstructive Criticism: An Advanced Introduction.* New York: Columbia University Press, 1983.

Miller, J. Hillis. *Ariadne's Thread: Story Lines.* New Haven, CT: Yale University Press, 1992.

———. *Fiction and Repetition: Seven English Novels.* Cambridge, MA: Harvard University Press, 1982.

———. *The Linguistic Moment: From Wordsworth to Stevens.* Princeton, NJ: Princeton University Press, 1985.

———. *Theory Now and Then.* Durham, NC: Duke University Press, 1991.

Norris, Christopher. *Deconstruction: Theory and Practice.* 3rd ed. London: Routledge, 2002. An excellent introduction.

Ryan, Michael. *Marxism and Deconstruction: A Critical Articulation.* Baltimore: Johns Hopkins University Press, 1982.

❊ 5 ❊

Psychoanalysis

The profile of psychoanalysis in literary and cultural criticism has zigged and zagged over the years since psychoanalysis first attracted wide interest early in the twentieth century. The early popularizers of psychoanalytic criticism attracted as much derision as interest for their confidence that readers could reduce art to biography and make writers' early childhoods and a few phallic symbols explain everything about their writing. Beginners may still think that is what psychoanalytic criticism is, but as you read this chapter, I hope you will discover something far more mysterious and challenging.

Later, as structuralism and poststructuralism emerged in literary, film, and cultural criticism, critics found a model in the psychoanalytic narrative of gender. They built on the structuralist and poststructuralist rereading of Freud (Figure 5.1) by the French psychoanalyst Jacques Lacan (Figure 5.2), and they also built on feminist critics' rethinking of gender. In these ways, during the 1970s and 1980s, psychoanalytic criticism reinvented itself in poststructuralist and often in feminist clothing. While many feminists looked at psychoanalysis with all the enthusiasm of a cat for a dog, other feminists saw it as offering a potentially feminist description of entrenched patriarchy.

Meanwhile, the growth of socially focused criticism, under the flags of Marxism, historicism, cultural studies, and environmental studies, brought yet another challenge. Some socially focused critics saw a chance to build on the new excitement about psychoanalytic criticism, while others saw a conflict between the psychoanalytic interest in individual minds and the Marxist, historicist, or cultural and environmental studies interest in broader social structures. For a while, the sparks cast by these conflicts kept psychoanalytic inquiry at the trendier cutting edges of literary, film, and cultural criticism. But in recent years the ascendancy of socially focused criticism (as discussed in the remaining chapters of this book), combined with a sense from some (but not all) critics that psychoanalysis describes white European and Euro-American thinking better than it describes the rest of the world, moderated the influence of psychoanalysis in contemporary criticism.

That has not deterred psychoanalytic critics, however. Their ways of thinking have less widespread influence than they had a generation ago, but their influence remains strong, and psychoanalytic critics continue to develop and intensify their ideas.

CLINICAL PSYCHOANALYSIS

Since psychoanalytic criticism developed in response to psychoanalysis, and psychoanalysis is a clinical practice, psychoanalytic criticism has origins of a different kind from the other critical methods discussed in this book. That is to say that Sigmund Freud, the founder of psychoanalysis, developed his ideas through the observation and treatment of patients, which plays no role in the history of the other critical methods that this book discusses. While some contemporary critics overlook the continuing influence of psychoanalysis' history of clinical practice, a brief (and necessarily selective) review of clinical psychoanalysis can help introduce psychoanalytic thinking, clarify popular misconceptions, and ground psychoanalytic criticism in its history.

Psychoanalytic critics (with rare exceptions) are not psychoanalysts, in part because it takes a long apprenticeship to become a psychoanalyst. Ten years of preparation and study are not unusual—and that is ten years *after* a doctorate (an MD or a PhD). To become a psychoanalyst, you also have to be psychoanalyzed.

Contrary to common misconceptions, psychoanalysis is not ordinarily for psychotics. That is, it is not for those who suffer from radically impaired functioning and an extreme disconnection from a socially recognized sense of reality. Freud believed that psychotics might be beyond the help of psychoanalysis. Instead, he saw psychoanalysis as something for ordinary neurotics—which is to say, for most of us.

Psychology, psychiatry, and psychoanalysis are not the same thing. Psychology is the umbrella term, but there are many forms of psychology, and psychiatry and psychoanalysis represent two of those forms. Psychiatry is medical psychology. To be a psychiatrist, you need an MD. Psychiatrists can prescribe drugs, which for many years have played an increasing role in psychological treatment. Psychologists who do not have an MD cannot prescribe drugs, though they sometimes work with psychiatrists to integrate drugs into treatment.

Psychoanalysis is the branch of psychology that works in the tradition founded by Sigmund Freud. If measured by the number of clinical practitioners, it is a small branch. If students of the humanities cross the campus green to walk, for example, from the English, French, comparative literature, or history department to the psychology department, they will find little or no teaching or research in psychoanalysis. The psychology professors might even laugh or sneer at the very idea of psychoanalysis. They might tell students that if you want that, you had better go to the English department. But even in the humanities, where there may be psychoanalytic critics, there almost never are actual psychoanalysts. The academic home of psychoanalysis lies not in colleges and universities but rather in psychoanalytic institutes (which sometimes are affiliated with universities). Psychoanalytic institutes themselves vary widely, depending on how closely they hold to Freud or identify with any of the various post-Freudian directions that have emerged since late in Freud's career.

Clinical psychologists can provide therapy. The therapy they provide comes in many varieties and usually has little to do with psychoanalysis. Only psychoanalysts can provide psychoanalysis, a relatively rare practice that differs from the many other varieties of therapy. For psychoanalysis, the therapy must work in accord with the psychoanalytic understanding of the human mind, which we will soon describe. The analyst and the analysand (the patient) must also meet frequently. Five or six days a week used to be the norm, but practicalities gradually eroded that dogma. Now three days a week is acceptable. Regardless, the frequent meetings indicate the intensity of the process, and so does the duration. Psychoanalysis often takes years. One year would be relatively quick. The analysand lies on a couch (we will soon see why), comical as that may seem to the unfamiliar eye. Some psychologists and psychoanalysts also offer therapy that works in accord with psychoanalytic thinking but is less intense, might not take as long or require as frequent meetings, and might not use a couch. That is psychoanalytically oriented psychotherapy but not psychoanalysis.

KEY CONCEPTS IN PSYCHOANALYSIS: THE PSYCHOANALYTIC UNDERSTANDING OF THE MIND

What, then, is the psychoanalytic understanding of the human mind? Three key principles can provide a context and overview that will help us go on to develop the picture in more detail, and then we can see what happens when psychoanalysis leads to psychoanalytic criticism. While Freud's model changed over the years, for our purposes we will focus less on the trees and more on the forest—less, that is, on the changing story of his developing ideas and more on the general pattern, especially as it has gone on to influence recent cultural and literary criticism.

1. The **unconscious.** Do not confuse Freud's term *the unconscious* with its pop offshoot, the *subconscious*. No one who is knowledgeable about psychoanalysis talks about the *subconscious*. *Sub-* suggests something underneath but still fairly accessible if we just dig a layer or two down. *Un-*suggests something more radical, something not just underneath awareness but utterly without awareness. (*Unconscious* means not conscious, not aware, but it does not refer to *conscience*, which is another term altogether.)

2. **Repression, drives** (instincts), and **defenses.** When we feel threatened by our drives, we often defend against them by repressing them. That generates the unconscious, which consists of repressed drives. Freud argued that excess repression of psychological drives leads to neurosis. But contrary to many common misunderstandings, Freud did not see repression as inevitably a bad thing. If not for repression, we would all be having sex with each other and killing each other. Therefore, we need repression. While some repressions can hurt us psychically, in many ways we also thrive on repression. We **sublimate** repressed drives, meaning that we redirect them to other activities, which is how we build culture and civilization.

3. The **clinical method of psychoanalysis,** which we have already begun to review, calls for the analysand to talk to the analyst, so that psychoanalysis is sometimes called "the talking cure." The analyst asks the analysand to **free associate**— to say anything and everything that comes to mind, no matter how random or irrelevant it may seem. The analyst

listens. Contrary to popular misconceptions, the analyst says little and, ordinarily, does not give advice. The analyst might give advice and go well beyond listening if that could deter a suicide or crime, or might give advice far along into the analysis (perhaps after years). Also contrary to popular misconceptions, the analyst says little or nothing to interpret the analysand, at least not until far into the analysis. Mainly, the analyst listens, sometimes responding with the simplest of remarks or questions. For example, an analyst might say something like "How does that feel?" or "What do you think about that?" or might respond with a slow, contemplative "hmmmm." Such minimal but mysteriously suggestive responses from the analyst return the process to the analysand's thinking and emotions. And such responses, especially if they come at the right time and in the right way, can encourage an analysand to think more deeply (in the sense of thinking through feelings), more questioningly, and—gradually—more honestly.

Meanwhile, the analysis is shaped by what psychoanalysts call **transference.** During psychoanalysis, analysands, preoccupied with their own concerns, can transfer onto the analyst emotions that apply to someone else, typically another authority figure, such as the analysand's mother or father. We might think that transference would interfere with an analysis, cluttering it with an obstacle course of troubled emotions. But since those emotions likely have much to do with the analysis, analysts who understand transference can take advantage of it to help analysands work through their neuroses. Even so, analysts run the risk of not understanding transference, because they themselves can mask their perception of analysands by what psychoanalysts call *countertransference.* That is, just as analysands transfer their emotional life onto the exchange with analysts, so analysts transfer their emotions onto the exchange with analysands. Analysts, for example, might see their analysands as versions of the analysts' children or siblings. Again, that threatens to undermine the analysis but will not undermine it if the analyst understands the process. And to understand their own entanglements in countertransference, psychoanalysts believe that they need to have been analyzed themselves, which is why someone has to complete psychoanalysis before becoming a psychoanalyst. Transference also explains the couch. By lying down in a relaxed position without facing the analyst, the analysand can associate freely without the transference overwhelming the free association.

While literary and cultural critics typically pay far less attention to transference then practicing psychoanalysts do, transference has attracted the interest of critics, who propose that it can describe the way that readers or audiences respond to a literary text or any other cultural text—a film, a song, a pop star, or a cultural crisis such as war, terrorism, disaster, or political controversy. We read and interpret cultural issues and objects much as analysts and analysands read and interpret each other, transferring our own concerns onto cultural events in ways that shape our response to those events. That is partly why different individuals and to some extent different groups (different classes, age groups, races, religions, genders, regions, and so on) interpret the same events in different ways.

Transference and other features of our emotional architecture also influence our understanding of and response to psychoanalysis itself and to psychoanalytic criticism. Psychoanalytic thinking takes it for granted that our encounter with psychoanalysis will provoke resistance, because psychoanalysis studies the unconscious, and we have a psychic stake in keeping the unconscious unconscious. That makes the study of psychoanalysis differ from the other ways of thinking discussed in this book. While we can learn to itemize the features of psychoanalytic thinking more or less as easily as we can itemize the other ways of thinking in this book, psychoanalysis takes longer to absorb. Typically it takes years, because it is an emotional as well as an intellectual perspective. Indeed, psychoanalysts see "intellectualization" as a **defense,** a means of repressing threatening emotions. While psychoanalysis is harder to absorb than more specifically intellectual patterns of thought, we can still begin to absorb it here. And whether readers are interested in absorbing it into their own thinking or not, we can introduce psychoanalytic thinking and, at the least, equip readers to follow other people's use of it.

Freud's goal was far more limited than the popular understanding of Freud recognizes. He did not usually set out to cure people. Instead, he sought, much more modestly, to transform neurotic suffering into ordinary unhappiness.

As you read this chapter and think about the questions it raises, I recommend that you do not try to disprove psychoanalysis. Psychoanalysis has an irritating, frustrating response to efforts to disprove it: It sees them as a defense against psychoanalysis and thus as evidence for what they seek to refute. In that sense, psychoanalysis is a closed system that, at least from the perspective of that closed system, we cannot disprove. We can disagree with it, or with parts of it (and psychoanalysts and psychoanalytically influenced thinkers disagree among themselves about many things), and we can decline to accept it, but we cannot disprove it. I recommend that rather than trying to prove or disprove psychoanalysis, to see it as true or untrue, right or wrong, you simply try to get used to it and look at it as a way of thinking, in the broadest sense of thinking, which includes emotion.

SIGMUND FREUD

Let us approach an introductory overview of Freud's ideas, especially as they have influenced contemporary literary and cultural criticism, by describing Freud's account of gender as literary and cultural critics have come to understand it. Practicing psychoanalysts sometimes focus on the patterns that gender hardens into, using language that can seem essentialist to cultural and literary critics. Cultural and literary critics, by contrast, draw on the deconstructive critique of essentialism and the sense of culture as a process, an ongoing construction. In that way, they call attention to the antiessentialist implications in Freud's narrative of gender. From their perspective, Freud's account undermines the routinely taken-for-granted stereotypes that see gender as an essence, that suppose one stable and correct way to be feminine and one stable and correct way to be masculine. The focus on the psychoanalytic narrative of gender as a construction also draws on and feeds back into the dialogue between psychoanalytic criticism and criticism that comes out of feminism and queer studies.

Freud's interpretation of the construction of gender tells a story. People are born, according to Freud's story, in **polymorphous perversity.** *Polymorphous* means "many forms," and *perverse* means "turning upside down or overturning." Thus, Freud means that people are born without any particular sexual or gender identity. Instead, infants begin with sexual drives that toss and turn randomly in any and all directions. Typically, then, the process of growing up narrows human identity and desire. In Freud's model, the child typically moves through a series of stages, from polymorphous perversity to desires that focus on the oral (as infants approach the world through their mouths), then on the anal (as they take pride in learning to control their bowels), and then on the phallic, finally leading, for most people, to the adult, heterosexual, genitally focused sexuality that Freud saw as the goal of

Figure 5.1 Sigmund Freud (1856–1939), 1907.

healthy sexuality. Within this model, all humans have homosexual and heterosexual desires as part of their polymorphous perversity, but some of those drives remain unconscious, while other, more conscious drives go on to define a person's adult sexuality. (For a critique of the term *homosexuality*, see Chapter 7.)

Many contemporary cultural critics reject Freud's story. They see it as naturalizing masculinity and heterosexuality, as if those were a norm and everything else, including femininity and queerness, were a deviation from the norm. Yet many contemporary cultural critics, including many feminist and queer studies critics, find Freud's narrative an illuminating description of how gender often works, even though it does not always end up at the heterosexual masculinity that Freud took as a goal and a norm. Such critics may object to how gender often works, but, in part because they object to it, they find Freud's description revealing.

Freud's story takes one path for infant boys and another for infant girls. Writing from the sexist presumptions shared by most men in his time and place, Freud took his story of boys as the foundation of his thinking. He turned to the ancient Greek story of Oedipus, familiar to many readers through Sophocles's play *Oedipus Rex*, to describe the path of gendering for boys. Through a fateful series of events, Oedipus—without realizing what he is doing—kills his father and marries his mother. In Freud's model, the infant boy feels an attraction to his mother. That much might be no surprise.

But Freud extended the story from there. He saw the boy as beginning to look at the father as a rival for the mother and thus as feeling an unconscious desire to kill the father, so as to have the mother to himself. Moreover, the boy observes that the mother has no penis, and he supposes (still unconsciously) that the mother has been castrated. He fears, therefore, that he too might be castrated, and more specifically he fears that the father might castrate him for desiring the mother. That is what Freud called **castration anxiety.**

Meanwhile, the erotic desire for the mother, the desire to kill the father, and castration anxiety all represent forbidden emotions that must be repressed. In repressed form, these forbidden emotions stay alive, but only in the unconscious. The father's threat of castration, Freud believed, produces what Freud called the *superego*, which we can describe as conscience, authority, and law. (Again, you will not want to make the beginner's mistake of confusing the words *conscious* and *conscience*.)

Typically, the boy seeks to win his mother's love by identifying with his father. Identifying with his father helps the boy defend against the desire to kill his father, because it denies and represses such desire. Through identifying with his father, then, a typical boy grows into adulthood as a heterosexual. As an adult, he displaces his desire for his mother onto a gender-similar "object," a woman who is not his mother, and he lives his adulthood heterosexually. But if the boy fails to defend against his desire for the mother by identifying with the father, then he can identify with the mother and grow into adulthood as a homosexual.

Working from this model, Freud sees adult neuroses as deriving from early childhood traumas that interfere with the child's psychic development. The child's development can stall at the oral, anal, or Oedipal stage, or it can move on partly but still have trouble growing completely out of those stages. And in what Freud called the **return of the repressed,** repressed drives can pop back up in the form of neurotic symptoms, disguised representations of unconscious desires. Indeed, he observed, neurotics repeat the same symptoms over and over, a pattern that Freud called the **repetition compulsion.** Through analysis, he believed, people could "work through" their neuroses, coming to a more comfortable sense, or at least a less uncomfortable sense, of how to live with emotions that may have taken a troubling form but that at their root are ordinary and do not need to offer an obstacle to well-adjusted adulthood.

Freud admitted, notoriously, that he was perplexed about the gendering of infant girls, and his story about girls has more twists and turns than his already intricate story about boys. It begins like the boys' story: The infant girl feels an attraction to her mother. Again, the desires that Freud describes for the infant girl are unconscious. Like the boy, the girl observes the mother's supposed castration, and she feels disillusioned by the mother's castration and by her own supposed castration. She thus renounces her love for her mother and turns her attraction to her father, but she senses that her attraction to the father is not allowed, and so she turns back to identifying with her mother. Identifying with the castrated mother, she suffers from what Freud calls *penis envy*, so that she desires a baby from her father as a substitute for her supposedly castrated penis. As an adult, she displaces her desire for her father onto a gender-similar object, a man who is not her father, and she lives her adulthood heterosexually. But if the girl remains fixated on her love for her mother, then she can grow into adulthood as a homosexual.

Frequently Asked Questions

- When first exposed to Freud's ideas, many people wonder how his model can work for infants who never know their parents, since such infants do not necessarily turn out differently from infants who do know their parents. Psychoanalysts do not worry about that, however, because they see nonparental caregivers as filling more or less the same psychic role as parents in the construction of gender. They also see the general role of authority in the culture at large as filling the psychic role of parents, even when actual parents are not there.

- Sometimes, people who do not know much about psychoanalysis say that Freud must be wrong because they know a son who adores and wants to be like his father or a son who despises his mother. Therefore, they suppose, sons do not necessarily hate their fathers and love their mothers, so

Freud must be wrong. But such thinking shows little under-standing of Freud's ideas. To Freud, a son who unconsciously hates his father will often defend against the hate by iden-tifying with his father, and a son who unconsciously desires his mother will often defend against his dangerous desire by turning away from his mother. In that sense, Freud wins either way. If the son despises his father, that proves Freud's point, and if the son loves his father, that also proves Freud's point. As we noted earlier, Freud's ideas offer a closed system. We can reject them, disagree with them, or object to some of their details, but we might find the overall system hard to disprove.

- Beginners sometimes react with outrage to Freud's notion of childhood sexuality, believing that children do not have sexual desires. Such outrage usually underestimates how thoroughly Freud sees childhood sexual desires as uncon-scious and as part of the fundamental life drive that ani-mates all human beings. For Freud, childhood sexuality is not so much about lust as about the infant's dependence on its mother. If the infant does not center its desire and psychic energy on its mother, it will die. From within the closed system of psychoanalysis, the outrage at Freud's ideas looks like evidence of a wish to keep those desires uncon-scious. Outrage—as opposed to neutral disagreement—suggests an emotionally intense need to repress what Freud invites us to acknowledge.

Critics and psychologists unsympathetic to psychoanalysis often reject Freud's account in its entirety, as we have noted. But many continue to believe in it or take the general outline with great seri-ousness, even if they reject some of the details (and there are more details than a short summary can include). Still others, as we will see, work within classical psychoanalysis (and here the term *classical* means Freudian) while continuing to develop it in new directions. Notably, Freud's description of women as, in effect, failed men de-fined by their "lack" of a penis and suffering from penis envy has not appealed to all feminists, as you might imagine. And yet feminism is divided about Freudian psychoanalysis, for some feminists (encour-aged by Juliet Mitchell's influential *Psychoanalysis and Feminism*, 1974) insist on its value as a description of how patriarchal culture works for women and men, a description of what feminists want to change. As you also might imagine, Freud's account of the construction of gender as ideally culminating in healthy heterosexuality has not appealed to critics who respect queer desire. Even so, many queer studies cultural critics find that psychoanalysis offers a valuable description of how heterosexist culture works, just as feminists sometimes value its description of patriarchal culture. In these ways queer studies and feminism also draw on each other.

Freud's story of gender also holds value for queer studies critics who more or less accept the outline of the story without accepting Freud's sense that the story has a predetermined and preferred goal. While Freud took what he saw as healthy, adult, genitally focused heterosexuality as a goal, others look at the story he tells and note that, as Freud himself observed, it often turns in directions other than the direction that Freud preferred. Repression does not always narrow the polymorphous variety of possibilities for sexuality and gender into genitally focused heterosexuality. Freud's idea that everyone begins in polymorphous multiplicity and retains polymorphous desires, at least unconsciously, can also help us understand how many people, and in some ways all people, reach adulthood driven by a wide range of desires outside the usual definitions of mainstream heterosexuality. In that sense, beyond what Freud had in mind, his model not only offers a logic for heterosexuality. It also offers a logic for queerness.

HOW TO INTERPRET: MODELS OF PSYCHOANALYTIC INTERPRETATION

Film, literary, and cultural critics write about cultural practices. They are not psychoanalysts. Movies, magazines, poems, and pop songs, for example, do not lie on a couch, free associate, and hope to find a healthier way to live daily life. Critics thus try to draw on psychoanalysis as a way of thinking without actually doing psychoanalysis. And over the years a variety of strategies has emerged, beginning with strategies closer to actually doing psychoanalysis and then expanding from there. There are many ways to divide up the possible goals of psychoanalytic critical interpretation, but I will divide them into the following general categories. Psychoanalytic criticism can interpret authors. It can interpret characters. It can interpret the literary form itself. Or it can interpret audiences, that is, readers and their surrounding culture.

The Tripartite Model of the Psyche

Late in his career, Freud proposed his famous tripartite model (also called the *structural model*) of the psyche, consisting of the ego, the id, and the superego. The id is the seething cauldron of basic drives in their primitive, selfish, unorganized state. At the opposite end of the spectrum, the superego is the moralizing conscience, with its rules and sense of right and wrong. Meanwhile, the ego is the realist organizer and planner that mediates between the id and the superego. (If we put Freud's German into English instead of the Latin chosen by Freud's translator, the id is the *it*, the ego the *I*, and the superego the *over-I*.) Though the tripartite model was central to 1950s and 1960s "ego psychology" and is often talked about in popular culture, it no longer plays a major role in literary and cultural criticism. Most contemporary psychoanalytic thinkers, especially cultural and literary critics, see the tripartite model (if they pay attention to it at all) as inviting oversimplified interpretations. For example, critics trying to work with the tripartite model to interpret a film or novel might assign a wild, impulsive character to the id, a follow-the-rules, proper character to the superego, and a central character—who must learn to choose a path between extremes—to the ego. That might sound sensible at first, but it tends to oversimplify the intricacies and internal contradictions of the id, ego, and superego as well as of the characters and the ups and downs of a storyline.

Authors. Critics can interpret an author psychoanalytically, almost as if they were psychoanalyzing the author. Interpreting the author often catches readers' interest. It has the fun of gossip and storytelling, but it has more to do with biography than with literary or cultural criticism. It can also risk treating authors as if they were the sole producers of the works they write, versus the structuralist sense that the overall system of writing produces a given piece of writing (as in the discussion of "the death of the author" in Chapter 3), and versus the Marxist sense that social practices, not just romantically isolated individuals, produce writing. The psychoanalytic description of authors will continue, but in these ways most critics usually find it limited as literary and cultural criticism.

Characters. Critics can also interpret characters psychoanalytically, such as characters in a play, movie, novel, or story. While that continues to hold appeal for many critics, its appeal has limits, because it treats characters as if they were people. The distinction between characters and people often proves challenging when readers first hear of it. Some readers respond by asking, why not treat characters as people? Isn't that what we read literature for, enticingly realistic characters? That is one reason we read, though one among many reasons, including the pleasure or interest we find in language, art, social interpretation, plot, structure, humor, philosophy, and so on. But characters are not people, and to pretend that they are can falsify their status as literary characters, as verbal and filmic artifacts. When I sit next to a stranger on the bus or joke with friends, I assume that they have lives outside our bus ride or friendship, and that assumption influences how I think about them. But characters in a novel or film exist only in that film or on the pages of that novel. They do not have a life before, after, or outside the events of the novel or film.

Some characters are more like people, such as characters in so-called realistic novels or movies, and some are less like people. But because we often take realism for granted, it is hard for many readers and viewers to recognize the frequency of characters who are less like people, unless we mention a wide range of examples, such as characters in cartoons, romances, horror stories, adventure tales, or satires, whether in novels, poems, plays, and stories or in movies and TV shows. In such cases, ranging from *The Spanish Tragedy, Pilgrim's Progress, Alice's Adventures in Wonderland, Peter Pan, Six Characters in Search of an Author, The Lord of the Rings,* and the *Harry Potter* series to *Mission Impossible, Pirates of the Caribbean, As the World Turns, Kill Bill, True Blood,* and *Marvel's The Avengers,* to interpret the characters psychoanalytically as if they were nonfictional people would often misconstrue them grotesquely.

Psychoanalytic interpretation beyond the interpretation of authors and characters varies greatly and remains less standardized, less agreed on, and less familiar to most readers and even to many professional critics. Still, we can summarize a wide range of uncoalesced practices by saying that psychoanalytic critics can also interpret the form of a literary work or they can interpret the audience and culture that reads or views the work.

Form, audience, and culture. For example, Catherine Belsey has proposed a psychoanalytic interpretation of the form of realist fiction. She focuses on Arthur Conan Doyle's Sherlock Holmes stories, especially a story called "The Adventure of Charles Augustus Milverton" (easily available on the Web, because the copyright has expired). As we have noted, most readers take realism for granted. They do not even recognize it as a form, as a distinct set of conventions (as structuralists would say) that shape realist writing. In that sense, realist writing is not a reproduction of reality so much as a repetition of a form so familiar that we often suppose it reproduces the reality outside the fiction, even though it does not. We hold a realist novel, for example, in our hands. It fits on a screen or on pages glued together between covers, unlike the world outside the book that we often suppose that a realist novel reproduces.

Supposedly, realist writing tries to tell a true and complete story. But to tell some parts of a story, it must always conceal other parts, for it can never tell everything. The telling can never tell the entire tale. In that sense, even a realist text that presents itself as telling the whole tale has an unconscious tale that it represses. While a new critic might set out to describe a literary work as unified, a psychoanalytic critic might find conflicts between what a literary work proclaims or a film makes most visible and what at the same time these works try to repress. Where a new critic looks to find how everything fits coherently together, a psychoanalytic critic, especially if influenced by deconstruction, might seek out internal contradictions, impulses that jar against each other and compete for control.

Belsey observes how the Sherlock Holmes stories circle obsessively around women's sexuality and desire while at the same time keeping women's sexuality and desire invisible. In "The Adventure of Charles Augustus Milverton" Holmes and his sidekick Dr. Watson come to the aid of "the Lady Eva Brackwell, the most beautiful *débutante* of last season," who "is to be married in a fortnight to the Earl of Dovercourt." But as Holmes explains to Watson, the evil blackmailer Milverton "has several imprudent letters—imprudent, Watson, nothing worse—which were written to an impecunious young squire in the country. They would suffice to break off the match" if Milverton shows the letters to the earl. Holmes, therefore, crafts a plan. Disguised as a "rakish" plumber, the inveterately single Holmes cozies up to and even proposes to Milverton's housemaid to get the information he needs to burgle Milverton's house. "But the girl, Holmes?" asks Watson, concerned about trifling with the maid's emotions and casting her aside to save the Lady Eva. Holmes shrugs his shoulders and responds that he has little choice, but that "I have a hated rival who will certainly cut me out the instant that my back is turned"—and then in the same breath he changes the subject by proclaiming "What a splendid night it is!" (Doyle 159–163).

While Holmes calls the Lady Eva's letters merely imprudent, describing them in the passive voice as letters "which were written," as if she did not write them but they wrote themselves, Milverton, by contrast, calls them "sprightly—very sprightly." But the story never quotes the letters or reveals what they say. By not telling us what the letters say, Belsey implies, the story dances around and evades the Lady Eva's sexual desire, just as it dismisses the housemaid's desire. If readers knew what the letters said and found it salacious, they might lose sympathy with the Lady Eva, which would take the point out of Holmes's scheme to rescue her from Milverton's evil machinations. On the other hand, if readers knew that the letters were innocuous, then readers could lose sympathy with the Lady Eva's desire to marry a man who would reject her for something so trivial. Either way, the story represses feminine sexuality while at the same time teasing us with the continuing consequences of the feminine sexuality that it represses. In deconstructive contradiction, the story depends on what it also conceals.

And that, Belsey argues, is how realist literary form works. Even the extreme realism of the Sherlock Holmes stories, which define themselves by a compulsion to uncover and explain, depends at the same time on a corresponding compulsion to hide and repress, the unconscious other side of the realist coin. In that sense, we can read the realist and detective compulsion to uncover and explain partly as a symptom, as the return of the repressed, as a repetition compulsion that flamboyantly keeps pointing at the feminine sexuality that it also represses. And so the Sherlock Holmes stories, in so many ways stories about masculine friendship—the intense friendship between Holmes and Watson, as well as, in this story, the "sporting" rivalry between Holmes and Milverton (Doyle 164)—reveal as well an intricate dependence between public masculine friendship and the urge to keep feminine sexuality private.

Already, in this reading, we can see how a psychoanalytic interpretation of form can lead to an interpretation of the audience and the culture that help produce the story. In writing the stories of Sherlock Holmes or the many other stories, including other detective stories, that circle around women's sexuality, writers do not produce these stories by themselves. The stories are partly a product of a culture that writes the stories through its writers. (Here I am drawing again on the idea of the death of the author, from Chapter 3.) In that sense, the culture helps produce the stories and helps produce audiences, readers, who want to read the stories and who therefore make stories like these and other realist detective stories into a cult phenomenon. An interpretation of stories like these can therefore offer a broader interpretation of a culture and its readers. It invites us to question the ways that the world we live in privileges men's sexuality and friendship over women's sexuality. The culture yearns to acknowledge women's sexuality. Yet at the same time, the culture respects women's sexuality so little that it props up an array of habits and teases, even in realist fiction, that reveal a compulsion to belittle and repress the same sexuality of women that it also wants to acknowledge.

FROM THE INTERPRETATION OF DREAMS TO THE INTERPRETATION OF LITERATURE

Freud gave special attention to dreams, especially in his book *The Interpretation of Dreams* (1900), because he believed that dreams offer a window to the unconscious. And Freud's ideas about the interpretation of dreams have interested literary critics because the interpretation of literature is like the interpretation of dreams.

Many people think Freud believed that dreams represent wish fulfillments, but that is not exactly what Freud argued. In *The Interpretation of Dreams*, he proposed that "a dream is a (disguised) fulfillment of a (suppressed or repressed) wish" (Freud 160), a far more interesting and intricate idea than saying that dreams themselves directly represent wish fulfillments. In other words, a lot happens on the road between the unconscious and its representation in dreams. Sleep relaxes the defenses, allowing the impulses in the unconscious to try making their way out of the unconscious and into the dream. But a range of processes gets in the way, and Freud called those processes the **dream work.** The dream work gets in between the unconscious and the dream and then between the dream and our memory of the dream. In that way, the dream work mediates between the **latent content** of the unconscious and the **manifest content** of the dream.

The Dream Work Comes between the Unconscious and the Dream

latent content →   dream work   → manifest content

While the manifest content of a dream, the dream itself, may be more open than the consciousness of waking life to impulses from the unconscious, the dream does not represent a wish fulfillment directly, because the unconscious repressed wishes still seem so threatening, even in a dream, that they can only appear after the dream work changes them. In that sense, the dream work comes between the unconscious and the dream. It mediates and thus changes the unconscious repressed wishes as they travel from the unconscious to the dream. The dream work operates through the overlapping mechanisms of **censorship,** which rejects threatening unconscious wishes, and **compromise,** which allows them to enter the dream only after they have changed into something less threatening. The dream itself, therefore, is a compromise between impulse and repression. Censorship and compromise come in four forms, which Freud called **displacement, condensation,** secondary revision, and considerations of representation.

Displacement. Displacement refers to the psychic process of representing one desire by another, less threatening and more acceptable desire. The wish to take revenge on the father, for example, might appear in a dream in the less threatening form of a joke about the father or a punch on a punching bag or a fantasy of outperforming the father at a particular task. More defensively, it could appear as a wish to identify with and be like the father, thus taking shape indirectly, in the form of denying the desire for revenge. The same censorships and compromises can shape the mind in waking life, but the censorships and compromises in dreams often take more unexpected and perplexing forms when we are asleep.

Condensation. Condensation refers to the psychic process of merging multiple wishes into fewer, less threatening, and more acceptable wishes. A memory of being punished for masturbation, for example, might combine with a memory of being teased for an interest in

---

How Dream Work Operates

dream work

↑

censorship and compromise

↑

displacement, condensation, secondary revision,
considerations of representation

the arts and end up in a dream as a desire to destroy a sculpture or—depending on the dream and the degree of compromise and denial—to produce a sculpture. (**Denial** is a defense, an unconscious repression and refusal to recognize something.) Worries about an overly protective mother might condense with less threatening worries about an overly protective teacher, leading to a dream about the teacher that also expresses, in disguised form, the anxieties about the mother. Such a dream displaces the mother onto the teacher and condenses the two together.

Secondary revision. We all know how hard it sometimes is to describe a dream or even to remember it. Our memories of the few dreams that we remember do not usually last long. When we try to recount a dream, the difficulty of recounting it makes us change the dream, sometimes knowingly, yet unable to help ourselves, and sometimes, Freud suggested, not knowingly, unconsciously. The same process of displacement and condensation that makes the dream work, mediating the unconscious impulses on their route to the dream, comes in again and mediates the retelling of a dream, which Freud called *secondary revision.* In that sense, the dream work takes place twice, making it still harder to identify the remembered, narrated dream with the wishes and unconscious desires from the beginning of its history.

Considerations of representation. Meanwhile, the dreaming mind might not find acceptable words or objects that represent its impulses accurately, a problem that Freud called *considerations of representation.* And so the dreaming mind chooses from what it finds available. It draws on recent, innocuous memories, what Freud called "the day's residue," such as memories from the previous day about ordinary people, objects, and events, the bric-a-brac and busyness of daily life—perhaps a lost hat, a bug in the bathtub, or an engrossing TV show. A fascination with incest, for example, might get displaced in a dream or in the secondary revision of a dream onto a more acceptable fascination with a familiar thing from daily life that is not related but has a similar sound, such as insects. Or a fear of seeing a parent's forbidden genitalia, evocative of seemingly threatening sexual drives, might get displaced onto and condensed, in a dream, with a fear of some more familiar thing that is also hairy, such as a furry pet, or—circling back to condense with the previous example—a hairy-looking insect or a family member's hair in the bathtub. In these ways, displacement, condensation, secondary revision, and considerations of representation overlap and merge with each other. In that light, we might see secondary revision and considerations of representation as variants of displacement and condensation, thus simplifying the four categories into two categories. We might even see condensation itself as displacement, condensing the four categories into one.

Moreover, Jacques Lacan—expanding on a suggestion from Roman Jakobson—proposed that we can see displacement as metonymy and condensation as metaphor. (For Jakobson's account of metaphor and metonymy, see Chapter 3.) Indeed, the overall process of the dream work as a mediation between the latent content and the manifest content, that is, between impulse and dream, calls to mind the use of literary language and film technology as mediations between psychic impulses and art, between psychic impulses and a poem, film, novel, play, painting, or song. When writers and filmmakers transform impulses into literary writing or film art, those impulses must adapt to the shape and the limits of literary language and film technology. When we interpret film and literature, therefore, we look at their art as something like psychic dream work, as a mediation of impulses meaningful both for what it disguises and for what it does in the place of what it disguises.

HOW TO INTERPRET: FURTHER PSYCHOANALYTIC EXAMPLES

When Vardaman Bundren, the traumatized five-year-old boy of William Faulkner's novel *As I Lay Dying*, proclaims, in a famous passage, "My mother is a fish" (Faulkner, *As I Lay Dying* 84), he displaces his anxieties over the loss of his mother onto the loss of a recently caught fish. Like his mother, the fish has just died. But he finds it less traumatizing to process the death of a fish than the death of his mother. Displacing his fears over the death of his mother onto the death of a fish can help him process the death of his mother. Still more, it can help process the blow he has received all his life from the emotional loss of his mother, since she cares far more about some of her other children. For the young Vardaman, her death threatens to expose and intensify that earlier loss, because once she has died he can no longer deny the neglect he has suffered all his life. In response, Vardaman defensively grasps at the straw of the dead fish, condensing and displacing all these anxieties onto one less threatening object.

We might even say that he poses the fish as a metonymy disguised as a metaphor. That is to say, in the fish Vardaman chooses an object that appears to have no connection to his mother, allowing him to pretend, psychically, that the displaced emotions he anguishes over through the fish have no (metonymic) connection to his mother but, instead, have only a more safely distanced (metaphoric) capacity to figure his emotions over his mother.

In the same way, the little girl of Elizabeth Bishop's poem "First Death in Nova Scotia" pauses in perplexity, trying to understand the unexpected death of her little cousin Arthur. Unable to process his death, as she approaches his body at his wake, she displaces and condenses her emotions onto a stuffed loon in the same room. Like little Arthur, the loon is dead. But she finds it less traumatizing to ponder the mysterious death of a stuffed loon than the more threatening death of her cousin. By displacing her sense of her own vulnerability, exposed by the death of Arthur, onto the death of a bird, and onto the lifeless photographs of the royal family that loom over the stuffed bird, she can process Arthur's death and its foreboding of her own death or the death of others around her.

And yet Vardaman and the little unnamed girl of Bishop's poem are characters, words on paper, not people. As words, the character Vardaman and the character in Bishop's poem offer analogies to psychologizable people, but those analogies stop short of the three-dimensional range that might apply to a person. Structuralists and deconstructionists might say that a person, like a character, is still a text, still a set of representations. But even so, a person offers seemingly infinitely more text than a character offers.

To turn a psychoanalytic reading in more literary directions, then, directions that consider the literary form itself, we could say that Vardaman's desperate displacement and condensation dramatize an ongoing process of displacement and condensation across the novel and its literary modernist architecture. As Vardaman displaces his psychic energy from his mother to a fish, so *As I Lay Dying* keeps shifting from one focalizer to another with each of its many shifts between narrators (one narrator per chapter, with 15 narrators across 59 chapters). Flamboyantly, those shifts epitomize the modernist literary fascination with multiple perspectives. They expose the inadequacy of any one perspective, much as psychoanalysis recasts essentialist ideas of gender and personality into narratives that could have gone and could yet go in multiple directions. Any given telling of a story becomes one version, slanted to evoke a way of seeing that offers only one among many competing ways of seeing.

The kaleidoscope of shifting displacements invites us to ask what other displacements they can represent, leading psychoanalytic interpretation into the interpretation of culture. For example, we might think of the displacement of racial conflict in *As I Lay Dying*. Vardaman's name comes from James K. Vardaman, a notoriously racist white Mississippi politician. Racial conflict was pervasive across the world that Faulkner writes about, and yet though Faulkner signifies it through Vardaman's name, racial conflict otherwise remains almost unmentioned in the novel. In effect, *As I Lay Dying* displaces racial conflict into the class conflict that overlaps with it. At the same time, it also displaces class conflict by condensing widespread and tragic poverty into one trivial family of buffoons, making poverty appear minor and dismissible. Such displacements risk allowing the social criticism in the novel to degenerate into comic oddity. Evasive displacement is a form of denial, then, socially as well as psychically.

In Ernest Hemingway's short story "Cat in the Rain," we see another revealing series of psychic displacements. The story focuses on an American woman traveling in Italy and aching with a vague sense of dissatisfaction. Looking out a window, she sees a cat in the rain and hurries out to rescue the cat from the downpour, as if rescuing the cat can somehow reverse her dissatisfaction. But when she reaches the place where she saw the cat, it is gone, and she finds herself returned more forcefully to an aching emptiness. Maybe, she thinks, she should let her hair grow long again. "I want to pull my hair back tight and smooth and make a big knot at the back that I can feel. . . . I want to have a kitty to sit on my lap and purr when I stroke her." "Yeah?" her husband asks, unimpressed. "And I want to eat at a table with my own silver and I want candles. And I want it to be spring and I want to brush my hair out in front of a mirror and I want a kitty and I want some new clothes" (Hemingway 169–170). While a new critic might ask what the cat "symbolizes," we would oversimplify the emotional resonance of the cat's free-floating vagueness if we tried to reduce it to representing one desire, like the desire for a baby that some critics have imagined might explain the story. Part of the mystery lies in the inability of the cat or any other object to contain, to condense, the restless displacement of dissatisfaction.

The many objects of desire in the woman's serially expanding list each evoke dissatisfaction with her condition as a woman. She complains that her hair is short, like a boy's. Staying in a hotel, far from home, she imagines that the accoutrements of conventional white middle-class American feminine domesticity—long hair, a kitty, a table, silver, candles, new clothes—might fill the emptiness that haunts her. But each time she names an object of desire, it cannot fill the needs that she asks it to fill, and so she must name another object and then another and another, in a chain of metonymic displacements that gradually unravels any expectation of satisfactory completion. Her choice of objects depends on clichés of femininity. She grasps after the clichés with so little hope that she ends up exposing the hollowness both of the clichés and of her restless desire, including its inability to speak to the range of feminine possibility and fulfillment. Yet she continues to hunger for fulfillment, as if she does not know how to see or believe in other, less clichéd models of feminine possibility. And so she finds herself stuck between desire and an inability to pin down any satisfactory objects for her desire.

In this way, the psychic impasse of a character dramatizes a broader social impasse about women's desire and about the restless incapacity of literary language to express desire beyond a culture's entrenched patterns and clichés. Structuralists call those patterns and clichés *cultural codes and conventions*, and Marxists, as we will see in Chapter 8, call them *ideologies*, unconscious patterns of social assumptions. Deconstructionists might call the restless incapacity of literary language to express desire an instance of *différance*, of the incapacity of free-floating signifiers to produce stable expressions of signifieds. Thus a panoply of ways of thinking, from feminism, structuralism, and deconstruction to Marxism and psychoanalysis, can help critics converge on a set of closely related and overlapping questions.

Let us look to Shakespeare and turn once more to Faulkner for more traditionally psychoanalytic examples. As we will see, even a more traditionally psychoanalytic example can draw on a diversity of critical methods. Believing that the central problem in Shakespeare's *Hamlet* is Hamlet's delay in killing his uncle Claudius in revenge for Claudius's murder of Hamlet's father, Freud argued that the Oedipus complex can explain Hamlet's delay. When Claudius kills Hamlet's father and marries Hamlet's mother Gertrude, Claudius lives out the Oedipal fantasy that Freud supposed would shape Hamlet psychologically. For Hamlet to kill Claudius, therefore, would feel to Hamlet unconsciously like suicide, like killing a version of himself. But as soon as Hamlet's mother dies, Hamlet finally kills Claudius. Freud argued that Hamlet can kill Claudius once Gertrude dies because her death releases her son from the burden of seeing Claudius as living out Hamlet's unconscious fantasies.

Freud's argument, expanded on by his follower Ernest Jones, has attracted skeptics as well as adherents. Skeptics reject the idea of unconscious Oedipal anxieties altogether or find Freud's explanation too convoluted, or else they find that such an interpretation treats a dramatic character too much like a person. But we should be clear about one issue that often confuses beginners. It does not matter, for Freud's argument, that Shakespeare lived three hundred years before Freud and could not have read or heard about Freud's ideas. Psychoanalytic interpretations of literary texts do not require that the author read or knew about Freud, because psychoanalysis describes patterns of thought and emotion that began long before Freud described them.

In Faulkner's novel *Light in August*, the Oedipal anxieties stand out more explicitly than in Shakespeare's *Hamlet*. Joe Christmas never knows his biological parents, but he responds Oedipally to his adoptive parents, Simon McEachern and "Mrs. McEachern" (we never learn her first name). Joe fears affection from Mrs. McEachern and prefers punishment from Simon (who is usually called just "McEachern"). Affection from his adoptive mother would threaten to make conscious his unconscious and dangerous love for her, or at least for the possibility of feminine, motherly affection that she represents. In the same way, to defend against his unconscious desire to kill the brutal McEachern, Joe identifies with him. Even when McEachern beats Joe, Joe postures his body just like McEachern's, their "two backs in their rigid abnegation of all compromise more alike than actual blood could have made them" (Faulkner, *Light in August* 148). Joe continues that identification with McEachern later in life, beating his roommate, Lucas Burch, with the same rhythmic strokes of the hand that McEachern used to beat Joe. Finally, though, Joe gives in to his desire to kill the father. He smashes a chair onto McEachern's head and then runs off, for all he knows having killed his adopted father.

His immediate response, however, is not guilt but instead a burst of delight and desire, "exulting of having put behind now at once and for all the Shalt Not, of being free at last of honor and law," qualities that, from a psychoanalytic perspective, boys learn Oedipally through identifying with the father and his threat of castration, the threat that originates concepts like honor and law. "He cried aloud, 'I have done it! I have done it!'" (207). Then he instantly decides that his crime against his stepfather means that he should get married, as if killing his rival makes him a mature adult. As an adult, he no longer needs to block his affection for the feminine, apart from the need to displace it from his mother or stepmother onto another woman. (Joe chooses an older, more experienced woman, who therefore ironically echoes the stepmother she displaces.)

In this sense, psychoanalysis has it both ways. Whether the son hates his father or loves his father, hates his mother or loves her, a psychoanalytic interpretation can read the intense psychic investment through an Oedipal lens that makes either hate or love a version of the same desire. It may come directly, or it may come indirectly, in the form of a defense that denies desire or denies hate. But either way, as the opposite of indifference it shows the deep psychic investment that Freud describes in Oedipal terms.

Light in August also invites us to carry this interpretation beyond treating characters as if they were people. In pitiable imitation of his adoptive father's violence, Joe gets stuck in a repetition compulsion, adopting his father's violence as a way of cutting off affection from women. He beats and brutalizes women (arguably including rape and murder), trying to protect himself from the vulnerability he feels in the face of feminine affection and assertion. In a world where women had recently won the right to vote and, more largely, in a world of changing gender assumptions that the expanding right to vote can represent, self-pitying American masculinity often saw itself as threatened by women's increasing public and domestic power. Defending against that sense of shifting gender relations, men often seek to establish their own toughness. They code toughness as masculinity, but since such toughness is a reaction (what psychoanalysts call a *reaction formation*) rather than a stable truth of gender that has to be that way, it always lies under threat, both from women's toughness, which challenges the exclusiveness of a supposedly masculine domain, and from women's affection, which threatens to expose men as vulnerable to emotions outside the defensively contrived rhetorics of toughness.

Just as Joe beats and brutalizes women, therefore, he also beats and brutalizes men, especially men who threaten his stereotypically brutal masculinity by coming too close to him in masculine affection. When Joe and some neighboring white boys show off to each other by paying a black girl for sex, he reacts by furiously fighting with the other boys, without even knowing why. In one sense, he could identify with the black girl and want to stop the white boys from taking advantage of her, for though at that point in the novel he lives as a white person, he believes he may have black ancestry. But he also seems to sense that by taking turns with the abused girl,

Incest and Incest Anxiety in Literature and Literary Criticism

Freud's notion of the Oedipus complex supposes that men and women repress a desire to commit incest with their parents, and that healthy adult sexuality comes from displacing incestuous desire onto culturally more acceptable objects, that is, onto lovers who are not our parents. Drawing on Freud's ideas, literary critics routinely discuss incest anxiety in literature as if it were like any other literary motif, like a color pattern or an image pattern. I think it is important, however, for critics, teachers, and students to take a step back from that ordinary sense of literary motif and think about the risk of approaching incest anxiety or incest itself as a routine literary motif in a world where, as we have come to realize since Freud, actual and terribly abusive incest—as opposed to mere incest anxiety—is not as rare as Freud supposed.

Within psychoanalytic circles, there is heated debate about the frequency of actual incest as compared to the frequency of incest fantasies. Freud eventually came to see his patients'—especially women patients'—memories of incest as fantasies, but some later scholars, led by Jeffrey Moussaieff Masson, have argued that many of Freud's patients were actual incest victims.

Whether Freud or Masson is right about Freud's patients, in the classroom when we discuss incest anxiety in a work of literature I remind myself that there are likely to be incest victims in the classroom, just as there are likely to be incest victims reading this book. Treating incest as merely a literary motif can rebrutalize incest survivors by making light of their trouble. But silence about incest, even literary incest, can also make light of their trouble by sweeping it under a rug of denial. Thus I take a moment in the classroom to reflect explicitly, as I am doing here, on the seriousness of the incest which, regardless of where we stand on the Freud–Masson debate, lies at the root of psychoanalysis. I ask us to take seriously the sad routine of abusive relations in many families. Perhaps then as we read and contemplate the abuses and anxieties portrayed in film and literature, we can go beyond passively reflecting the crisis and can help ourselves speak back to the trauma of child abuse.

with each boy putting his penis where the other boys put theirs, the boys express a relation with each other more than with the poor girl whom they otherwise do not know and whom they do not associate with as peers. At that point, by the frightened standards of a homophobic world, their male-to-male bond of friendship veers threateningly close, for a queer-fearing world, to a sexual bond, and so Joe's explosion into violence against his male friends seems unconsciously to defend against the threat to his self-conception as heterosexual. Similarly, when he takes on a male roommate, he ends up beating his roommate, trying to protect himself from imagining the possibility or even the appearance of gay desire.

Joe's compulsively repeated rhetoric of stereotypically heterosexual masculine toughness in posture, gesture, language, and violence does more than just passively reflect these defensive cultural dynamics of gender that psychoanalysis can help us understand. As we will see in the discussion of new historicism in Chapter 9, literature is not simply a passive reflection of culture. It also actively participates in, even helps generate, the culture it reflects. In that sense, Faulkner's novel engages in the implied cultural debates about gender that it also depicts. Like Joe, it evokes a fear of changing masculinity. Changing femininity takes on its power, in this masculine-centric story, not as much on its own terms as through its implications for changing masculinity. In the process the repetitive shape of the narrative, dramatizing its own helplessly compulsive repetition of patterns of gender, also challenges the patterns that it portrays. For in one sense, these compulsions lock the novel in a cultural neurosis. But in another sense, they also portray the psychic prison of that neurosis and invite, even plead with, readers to look critically at troubled patterns of gender and begin to change them.

JACQUES LACAN

As Freud's long career went on, his ideas evolved and changed, and his followers divided between those who held to classical, Freudian psychoanalysis and others who veered off in many different directions. Of the various offshoots of classical psychoanalysis, those that have most influenced literary and cultural studies include Jungian psychoanalysis, developed by Carl Jung and—by far the most influential—the ideas of the French psychoanalyst Jacques Lacan.

Jung's notion of archetypes shared by different peoples in a "collective unconscious" attracted interest in literary criticism, especially in the 1950s and 1960s. Critics brought Jung's ideas together with those of anthropologist James G. Frazer, whose famous *The Golden Bough: A Study in Magic and Religion* (first edition, 1890) tracked myths that different cultures share, such as myths of death and rebirth. But just as anthropologists no longer take Frazer's work seriously, so Freud and most other psychoanalysts and psychologists have rejected Jung's ideas. Jung has had more influence in popular culture, impelled by the writings of Joseph Campbell, than in scholarship or psychology. Nevertheless, the study of myths and archetypes gradually won a modest profile in literary studies, leading to "myth criticism" or "archetypal criticism" and culminating in the sophisticated writings of the Canadian critic Northrop Frye. Frye's ideas, especially influential in the 1960s, still attract respect, especially in Canada, though their influence on contemporary literary criticism has faded.

Lacan's writing is notoriously difficult to read, let alone summarize, the more so because, like Freud's, his ideas evolved and changed over many years. I will focus, therefore, less on a comprehensive description of Lacan's ideas for their own sake than on describing them as they have exerted the most influence on literary and cultural criticism. In that light, I will introduce Lacan's notion of the mirror stage and then summarize his ideas according to his triad of three related *orders*, the imaginary, the symbolic, and the real.

The mirror stage. According to Lacan, at six to eighteen months infants go through what he called **the mirror stage.** In the mirror stage, the infant, before developing a sense of its own subjectivity, sees its reflected image and identifies with the reflection. The mirror image, Lacan says, "symbolizes the mental permanence of the *I*, at the same time as it prefigures its alienating destination" (Lacan, *Ecrits* 2). It makes the seemingly fragmented bits and pieces of the infant's body seem to cohere for the first time, impelling a coherent image of *I* (that is, of ego, subjectivity, or self), a coherence that, as we will soon see, Lacan argues will eventually give way to alienation.

The imaginary. For Lacan, infants—responding to the seemingly coherent image of wholeness in the mirror stage—come to live their psychic lives in **the imaginary.** In the imaginary, there is no difference and no absence. Instead, there is fullness and immediacy. In the imaginary, therefore, there is no alienating sense of self versus other, no sense of distance or incompleteness. While Lacan and Jacques Derrida (on Derrida, see Chapter 4), rivals for the acclaim of French poststructuralism, usually remained silent about each other and, when they acknowledged each other, liked to make much of their differences, we might say that the imaginary is like what Derrida called the *metaphysics of presence*, full presence with no absence.

But the imaginary cannot last in unquestioned fullness. After all, it is imaginary. The Oedipus complex disrupts the imaginary through the threat of castration. Lacan redescribes the Oedipus complex. He calls the father's opposition to the son's desire for the mother **the Father's No,** or **the Law of the Father,** or **the Name of the Father.** The Father's No does not need to be explicit and does not depend on the presence of an actual, literal father. It is so woven into the culture that the infant will respond to it, regardless of whether the father is there or explicitly sets out to interrupt the infant's desire. The Law of the Father, the father's prohibition of incestuous desire, is the origin of ideas about propriety or right and wrong, the origin of rules and law. For Lacan, it is a patriarchal origin, sustained by passing the Name of the Father on to the next generation, as in the patriarchal privilege and control evoked by the custom of passing the father's— but not the mother's—family name onto the next generation. As you can see, Lacan was far from feminist. Yet many feminists value his ideas, as they value Freud's, for their description of the patriarchal cultural assumptions and patterns that feminists abhor.

The symbolic. When the Father's No interrupts the imaginary, it casts the infant out of the imaginary and into **the symbolic,** into language. While in the imaginary there is no difference and no absence, in the symbolic, difference and absence reign. Instead of the fullness and immediacy of the imaginary, in the symbolic there is alienating incompleteness and distance, characteristics inherent to language and representation. Instead of sounding like the metaphysics of presence, the symbolic is like Derrida's description of writing and all language, fraught with an irreconcilable gap between signifiers and signifieds. In that way the symbolic is like the difference, deferral, and absence that Derrida called *différance.* Any idea of the self or the subject, for example, depends on an idea of the loss of the self, because we cannot recognize selfhood unless we compare it to its absence. Presence, therefore, depends on absence, and absence depends on fullness.

The real. Through most of Lacan's career, he paid little heed to **the real,** the underlying intransigent that resists definition. For that reason, as Lacan's influence gathered force in cultural and literary criticism, the imaginary and the symbolic received most of the attention. Later in his career Lacan wrote more about the real, and some recent Lacanian critics, including the provocative Slovenian philosopher Slavoj Žižek, give it special attention. The real is a mysterious concept that is not the same as reality. We can represent reality with signifiers, but we cannot represent the real. The language we would use to represent the real evokes our distance from the real. The real is the raw kernel over which the imaginary and the symbolic operate and compete. It cannot be explained or described, but only inferred, as when Žižek likens the real to the alien in the movie *Alien*. The real is the origin of hunger and the trauma of the indescribable that can never reach meaning. It is the in-between of competing explanations, shaping reality without being part of reality. While dedicated Lacanians like Žižek now often focus on the real, on what cannot be explained, most other critics continue to address the imaginary and the symbolic, with little concern about the real.

The relation between the imaginary and the symbolic. So goes a highly summarized outline of Lacan's version of Freudian psychoanalysis. We can understand this outline better if we think of the symbolic as adding to, rather than utterly replacing, the imaginary. To make sense of that, it can help to expand our sense of what the imaginary can refer to. Drawing on the ideas of the Marxist philosopher Louis Althusser, which influentially expand from Lacan's idea of the imaginary, we can think of the imaginary as referring to social spaces where we focus more on identity than on difference. For example,

Figure 5.2 Jacques Lacan (1901–1981).

it can refer to ethnic or national spaces where people identify with each other because they see themselves as sharing the same ethnicity or nationality. In this sense, the imaginary is ideological. Althusser defined ideology as an imaginary relation to real conditions. (For a fuller discussion of Althusser's view of ideology, see Chapter 8.) In that sense, when we recognize ourselves in the imaginary, when we see ourselves in its mirror reflection, Lacanians see the recognition as a misrecognition. We see something different from ourselves and imagine that it is the same as ourselves. That is to say, the imaginary captures an emotional commitment and investment that may differ from the true picture of things. After all, it is imaginary.

In this sense, when we focus more on our likeness with others, we focus more on the imaginary, and when we focus more on our difference from others, we focus more on the symbolic. We never live in the imaginary alone or in the symbolic alone. The imaginary is like a comfort zone. When we feel a sense of oneness or merging with parents, family, friends, with people we might never even see who share a religion, a homeland, a race, nationality, or set of political beliefs, with fellow sports or music fans (think of crowds cheering at a political rally, a sports event, or a concert), when we feel a sense of oneness or merging in love, in all such emotions of union and likeness, we dwell in the imaginary. That sense of oneness is similar to what the historian Benedict Anderson (not drawing on Lacan) calls an **imagined community.** By contrast, when we feel a sense of difference or even conflict, sometimes in the same settings where at other times we might dwell in the imaginary, then we dwell instead, or at least dwell more, in the symbolic. We live in the symbolic when we confront ideas and beliefs that we see as hostile or strange or when we confront competitors, enemies, or strangers. But we can also feel that sense of difference among parents, family, or friends. People who share a religion or homeland, a race or nationality, a set of political beliefs, or even a love for the same music or team can still argue with each other, and lovers, of course, do not always see things the same way.

Mostly, then, we live in the symbolic. Life can hurt. It is not all or even mostly comfort. But while we live in the symbolic, we also spend much of our lives chasing after the imaginary. The symbolic and the endless deferral and difference that Derrida calls *différance* mostly keep us from reaching the imaginary. Desire has trouble getting to its object. Difference, deferral, and *différance* keep interfering. Instead of the signifier and the signified merging, the gap between them remains stubborn. When we wake up in the morning and look in the mirror, most of us, on most mornings, are at least partly questioning or critical. We do not relax into pure comfort. Instead, we see difference and absence. We think we should wash or comb. We wish we could cover over this or change that.

And yet we do achieve the imaginary, relatively, more at some times and in some places. We even make choices between the imaginary and the symbolic. When we work for a political party or join with a religious, racial, national, or ethnic group, we choose to focus more on our likeness with the members of that group and less on our difference from them. Sometimes we even delude ourselves into forgetting the difference. If we essentialize a group of people, supposing that they are all alike (that all Jews or Chinese, all blacks or Muslims, all Christians or women or men are alike), we give way to the imaginary so much that we risk denying the symbolic. Still, we can focus on the imaginary without denying the symbolic, as when we form alliances with others that enable us to focus on what we have in common without denying the differences. Imagined communities can do good things or not-so-good things. They can abuse those who do not fit in or help those who do and those who do not fit in. It depends on what people make of the imagined communities.

The phallus, the gaze, the look. Lacan and Lacanians often discuss what they refer to as the **phallus,** and they also discuss what they call **the gaze** or **the look.** Much as the distinction may make unfamiliar readers laugh, it helps to understand that the phallus is not the penis. For Lacanians, who—like Freudians—see women as psychically castrated versions of men, the phallus refers to patriarchal authority in general, not necessarily to the physical male organ.

The gaze or the look refers to what Freud called "the scopic drive," the way that looking itself is steeped in the erotic. Looking plays a crucial role in literature, popular culture, art, and—not least—film. We might think of the gaze or the scopic drive as the symbolic visually pursuing the imaginary, trying to collapse the distance and difference between desire and the object of desire. We stare at a film with desires that it appeals to, desires that it invites us to satisfy by looking, but that no film can ever satisfy. The look itself can be so hypnotizing that, as film theorist Christian Metz argued, film uses the look to erase what Marxists call its means of production. It can mesmerize us into seeing a film as if we were in the imaginary, as if the film were simply natural and not the product of elaborate editing, intricate technology, and the cooperation and struggles of a huge crew of filmmakers, financiers, marketers, and of traditions and conflicts among filmmakers and audiences.

Within a film, on a stage, or in the text of a play, novel, or poem, characters, actresses, and actors gaze at each other or at something else, while audiences and readers gaze at the characters, actresses, and actors gazing. When we gaze at the other, however, we do not see the other itself. Instead, we construct the other by projecting onto it what we wish to see, fear seeing, or know how to see. In Lacan's cryptic words, "When, in love, I solicit a look, what is profoundly unsatisfying and always missing is that—*you never look at me from the place from which I see you*" (Lacan, *Four* 103). We cannot see the other. In between the subject and the object comes the symbolic that interrupts the imaginary, the *différance* that interrupts the link between the signifier and the signified. When we look at each other, then, we see not the other itself but instead what our own desires project onto the space of the other. When we suppose that we see the other itself, we misread, or Lacanians might say *misrecognize*, the symbolic as the imaginary, but sooner or later the symbolic will rear up and remind us that the other is not what we desire or imagine it to be. It is not the same. It is different.

Lacan's writing. Here it can help to look briefly at an example of Lacan's cryptic, knotted, and mischievous writing. Lacan's essay "The Agency of the Letter in the Unconscious or Reason since Freud" (1957) has held particular interest for literary critics, perhaps in part because it draws directly on Saussurean linguistics and discusses figurative language, sometimes in a style that itself draws on the figurative play of literary writing, including Lacan's interest in surrealist poetry. This is the essay where Lacan connects Jakobson's description of metaphor and metonymy to Freud's description of dream work, aligning metaphor with condensation and metonymy with displacement. In the process, he reconsiders Saussure's model of the sign as a construct of the signified attached to a signifier. Lacan imagines the signified as two doors that look alike and the signifier as a word on each door. On one door, the signifier is "Ladies," and on the other door the signifier is "Gentlemen." Lacan insists that his example of "twin doors . . . symbolizing . . . the laws of urinary segregation" is not merely a "low blow," for it shows "how in fact the signifier enters the signified, namely, in a form which, not being immaterial, raises the question of its place in reality" (Lacan, *Ecrits* 151).

Thus signifiers segregate us, in this case by gender. In that way, signifiers produce differentiation and structure. For Lacan, then, drawing on Saussure, differentiation and structure model and define language. As we observed in Chapter 3, Saussure saw language as a structure of differences, of signifiers differentiated from signifieds and of signifiers differentiated from each other. For Lacan, then, signifiers and language are not "immaterial," not mere labels written onto reality after the fact, but instead are themselves reality, are themselves truth.

The differentiating truthfulness of language matters because, as Lacan proclaims in a phrase he often repeats, a phrase that brings Saussure and structuralist linguistics to Freudian psychoanalysis, "the unconscious is structured like a language." That means, in part, that the unconscious is not a random hodgepodge of chaos. It has structure, for it speaks through recognizable patterns of figurative language, leaving us, as a poem leaves us, "at the mercy of a thread woven with allusions, quotations, puns, and equivocations" (Lacan, *Ecrits* 169–170).

> Who, then, is this other to whom I am more attached than to myself, since, at the heart of my assent to my own identity it is still he who agitates me?
>
> His presence can be understood only at a second degree of otherness, which already places him in the position of mediating between me and the double of myself, as it were with my counterpart.
>
> If I have said that the unconscious is the discourse of the Other (with a capital O), it is in order to indicate the beyond in which the recognition of desire is bound up with the desire for recognition.
>
> In other words this is the Other that even my lie invokes as a guarantor of the truth in which it subsists.
>
> By which we can also see that it is with the appearance of language the dimension of truth emerges. (Lacan, *Ecrits* 172)

Like a poem, then, the Other that is the unconscious can be interpreted, but it cannot be erased into paraphrase. An interpretation of a poem can mediate a poem, can understand it at the distance of "a second degree," but even while it signifies the signified that is the poem, an interpretation cannot replace the poem. It cannot merge the signified and the signifier into one thing, for one still mediates the other. "In other words," as Lacan puts it to describe "the Other" of the unconscious, there is always mediation, always difference, always structure. For Lacan, as for Saussure, mediation, difference, and structure are language, which is the "truth" that Lacan uses to describe the ceaseless figuration of signifiers that express the unconscious through metaphor and metonymy.

HOW TO INTERPRET: A LACANIAN EXAMPLE

Returning, then, to Hemingway's "Cat in the Rain," we might think of a moment when the American woman tries to appease her dissatisfaction by looking at her reflection. She is long past the mirror stage. "She went over and sat in front of the mirror of the dressing table looking at herself with the hand glass. She studied her profile, first one side and then the other. Then she studied the back of her head and her neck." She asks her husband, "Don't you think it would be a good idea if I let my hair grow out?" He answers that he likes "it the way it is," but she responds: "I get so tired of it. . . . I get so tired of looking like a boy" (169). When she looks in the mirror, she does not see anything comforting. She does not see an identity between herself and her desire. She sees only difference and deferral. She even looks at one mirror through another mirror, trying to see past difference, trying to escape the limits of her reflection, but seeing only more reflection, seeing the reflection of reflection, difference multiplying its own difference. She turns to her husband, hoping to find an identification with him, but he declines to identify with or reflect her dissatisfaction. Ironically, he identifies with the way she looks, but he cannot identify with her dissatisfied looking at the way she looks. She is so wrought up in difference that she feels difference in, and even feels thwarted by, his identification with her.

She supposes that she looks like a boy, and she would rather look and feel like what she supposes that a woman should look and feel like. But as we have seen before, the expectations for women, the codes of femininity, while culturally powerful, are yet so culturally unstable that despite her hopes she can muster no confidence that one or another signifier of femininity will close the gap between how she looks and her hunger for a way of looking and feeling that can transform her emotions into an imaginary stability of fullness and presence, free at last from the pangs of difference and dissatisfaction. When she looks in the mirror, therefore, she sees her femininity cut off. She sees her bobbed hair, what Lacanians might see as her psychic castration, the Father's No or the Law of the Father. Mired in the symbolic, she sees herself as a lack, not a presence. She gazes at her absence as if it were her only form of presence, and in that way she defines what she is by what she is not, by what she lacks and has cut off.

Such a reading can go beyond simply interpreting character. The conflicts it describes dramatize and join in a broader cultural debate, in the age of the bob-haired flapper and the newly acquired vote, about women's cultural and psychic future. The conflicts that such a reading describes ponder, in effect, whether women's kernel of desire must remain elusively in the real, escaping over the horizon like the cat, never describable but always almost there, half-threatening and half-inviting, or whether women can escape beyond the vision of femininity as a lack and find a way to assert an alternative future.

We could see such defining of women by what they supposedly lack as misogynist, and many feminist critics read Lacan and psychoanalysis that way. At the same time, as we have noted, many feminists see Freudian and Lacanian psychoanalysis as rooted in misogyny but still providing a revealing description of misogynist cultural assumptions, practices, and burdens, a description that offers a potentially feminist diagnosis of what feminists seek to change. Indeed, feminism and psychoanalysis came to the fore of criticism at roughly the same time, and so we move from psychoanalysis in this chapter to feminism in the next chapter.

FURTHER READING

Brenner, Charles. *An Elementary Textbook of Psychoanalysis*. Rev. ed. New York: International Universities Press, 1973. A short summary of classical psychoanalysis.

Chodorow, Nancy. *The Reproduction of Mothering: Psychoanalysis and the Sociology of Gender*. Berkeley: University of California Press, 1978.

Fenichel, Otto. *The Psychoanalytic Theory of Neurosis*. New York: Norton, 1945. A comprehensive reference for classical psychoanalytic ideas.

Fink, Bruce. *Lacan to the Letter: Reading Écrits Closely*. Minneapolis: University of Minnesota Press, 2004.

Freud, Sigmund. *The Freud Reader*. Ed. Peter Gay. New York: Norton, 1989.

Gallop, Jane. *Reading Lacan*. Ithaca, NY: Cornell University Press, 1985.

Grosz, Elizabeth. *Jacques Lacan: A Feminist Introduction*. London: Routledge, 1990.

Horney, Karen. *Feminine Psychology*. New York: Norton, 1967.

Jones, Ernest. *Hamlet and Oedipus*. New York: Norton, 1949.

Lacan, Jacques. *Ecrits: The First Complete Edition in English*. Trans. Bruce Fink. New York: Norton, 2007.

Malcolm, Janet. *Psychoanalysis: The Impossible Profession*. London: Gollancz, 1981. An excellent introduction to clinical psychoanalysis.

McCannell, Juliet Flower. *Figuring Lacan: Criticism and the Cultural Unconscious*. Lincoln: University of Nebraska Press, 1986.

Mellard, James M. *Using Lacan, Reading Fiction*. Urbana: University of Illinois Press, 1991.

Mitchell, Juliet. *Psychoanalysis and Feminism: A Radical Reassessment of Freudian Psychoanalysis*. 2nd ed. New York: Basic Books, 2000.

Muller, John P., and William J. Richardson, eds. *The Purloined Poe: Lacan, Derrida, and Psychoanalytic Reading.* Baltimore: Johns Hopkins University Press, 1988.

Ragland-Sullivan, Ellie. *Jacques Lacan and the Philosophy of Psychoanalysis.* Urbana: University of Illinois Press, 1986.

Rose, Jacqueline. *Sexuality in the Field of Vision.* London: Verso, 1986.

Wollheim, Richard. *Sigmund Freud.* New York: Viking, 1971.

Wright, Elizabeth. *Psychoanalytic Criticism: Theory in Practice.* 2nd ed. London: Routledge, 2003. A comprehensive survey.

Žižek, Slavoj. *Looking Awry: An Introduction to Jacques Lacan through Popular Culture.* Cambridge, MA: MIT Press, 1991.

———. *The Žižek Reader.* Ed. Elizabeth Wright and Edmond Wright. Oxford: Blackwell, 1999.

❋ 6 ❋

Feminism

To this critic's thinking, at least, no movement in intellectual and cultural history has done more to change literary criticism than feminism. Though the word *feminism*, as a term for supporting women's rights, did not enter the English language until the 1890s, feminism can trace its history back to Mary Wollstonecraft's *A Vindication of the Rights of Women* (1792) and earlier. But feminist literary criticism, in some ways like feminism in general, gathered its force gradually, moving through such landmarks as Virginia Woolf's *A Room of One's Own* (1929), Mary Ellmann's less well-known *Thinking about Women* (1968), and Kate Millett's galvanizing *Sexual Politics* (1970) and then finally coalescing in the late 1970s and the 1980s.

For literary criticism, feminism is not a method in the sense that new criticism, structuralism, deconstruction, and psychoanalysis are methods. It does not zero in on codifying a set of operations that one might turn like a crank to produce a new epistemology or a new literary criticism, though it produces those things nevertheless. While feminist criticism certainly has method and has changed literary critical method in general, it is not so much a method in itself as an area of interest and even a commitment. In that sense, the shift to feminism marks a change in this book that will continue through queer studies, in some respects through Marxism (which may define itself more by its methods but which also defines itself by its commitment), and through postcolonial studies, race studies, ecocriticism, and disability studies.

WHAT IS FEMINISM?

At its most fundamental level, feminism is a simple concept. It is about taking women seriously and respectfully. It sets out to reverse a pattern and history of not taking women seriously, a pattern so deeply ingrained that it can seem natural, like mere truth. Feminists sometimes use the word **misogyny** for that habit of not taking women seriously, not respecting women, and misogyny is part of the broader cultural history and practice of centering on men while underestimating women, which feminists dub **patriarchy.**

Like queer studies and in some ways postcolonial, race, and disability studies, feminism derives also from an identity category. Thus, the principles that feminists have thought through often overlap with, feed into, and feed off similar issues in other identity-related studies, including African American studies, Latina/o studies, Asian American studies, and American Indian studies, to name only those that have the most visible space in contemporary academia (where their position nevertheless often remains precarious). As feminists think through identity, they draw on and contribute to the debates about essentialism and identity that we have seen in the previous chapters on deconstruction and psychoanalysis. In a spirit that runs partly parallel with deconstruction and that partly intertwines with deconstruction (including feminist deconstruction), we can say that feminism sees women not as one thing but as many different things.

Indeed, there are many ways to be a feminist, not one way, as Roxane Gay reminds us by calling herself, with irony, a "bad feminist." Gay makes fun of the idea that feminists have to sign up to follow a prepackaged idea of the good feminist. Feminists can disagree with each other, like people in any large group. There are close-minded feminists, as there are close-minded people in any group, but many feminists value perspectives that they disagree with and make a point of discussing, debating, and learning from many different feminists and many different feminist ideas.

First-, second-, and third-wave feminism. The variety of feminist debates leads us to a rough historical outline that loosely tracks feminism through a series of three waves. **First-wave feminism,** propelled by Wollstonecraft's arguments for women's education, focused on establishing women's rights, such as the right to own property and the right to vote, officially recognized in the United Kingdom partly in 1918 and fully in 1928, and in the United States in 1920. **Second-wave feminism** defined itself along a broader cultural agenda, beginning in the 1960s. While in practical politics second-wave feminism often concentrated on achieving equal rights, like first-wave feminism, the theoretical movements most associated with second-wave feminism concentrated more on describing or even celebrating the distinctiveness and specialness of women, sometimes under such rubrics as *cultural feminism*, which claimed a women's culture that was kinder, gentler, and more peaceful than the dominant culture, or *difference feminism*, which was less interested in equal rights than in establishing women's difference and superiority. Second-wave feminism often focused on a sense of sisterhood and shared identity among all women.

But to some feminists, that sense that all women shared the same identity came to ring false. For that reason, many feminists reacted against second-wave feminism so that a **third-wave feminism** developed. Third-wave feminism objected to second-wave feminism as essentialist and sought instead to build a feminism that focused more on the variety of women, making a point of including women of all races and building coalitions across racial and national boundaries. In these ways, third-wave feminism often engaged with the antiessentialist impulses of deconstruction.

In practice, most feminist critics and theorists today do not define themselves entirely through this or that wave. They may favor third-wave feminism, but they draw on all three waves to pursue nonessentialist, political, and cultural agendas.

Postfeminism?

To my mind, we live, loosely speaking, in an extended age of third-wave feminism, but some people say that we have reached an age of *postfeminism*. What is postfeminism? It is different things to different people. To antifeminists, the term offers a chance to make people believe that feminism has come and gone. To others, however, the *post-* suggests a dialogue between feminism and poststructuralism, including a reaction against second-wave feminism. But I would suggest that third-wave feminism already expresses that dialogue, while the prefix *post-* threatens to undermine the feminist side of the conversation, relegating feminism to the past. To yet others, including some poststructuralist feminists, the term *postfeminism* suggests an ongoing readiness to reimagine feminism for changing times. To my thinking, the idea that we live in an age of postfeminism is a lamentable form of cultural consumerism. It treats feminism like a consumer product, something to be used up and gotten rid of so that we can go on to use up another product that we will soon get rid of in the same way. It reduces feminism to a fashion of the moment. In that context, it is no surprise to hear people referring not only to postfeminism but also to post-postfeminism. I would rather that we get used to it and accept it: Feminism is here to stay.

While the division of feminism into a series of waves oversimplifies overlapping histories and dialogues, the movement from second- to third-wave feminism roughly parallels the history of feminist literary criticism. Early feminist literary criticism had much to do with second-wave feminism. It revolutionized critical thinking and laid the ground for a dialogue with the poststructuralist, Marxist, queer, and historicist thinking that characterizes more recent movements in feminist criticism. The popular feminism that most people encounter in journalism, in the mass media, and in the caricatures from fearful antifeminists continues to rely on second-wave feminism to represent all feminism. Similarly, the ideas that drove early feminist literary criticism continue to dominate what most readers understand about what feminist literary criticism might be.

For that reason, this chapter sets out to acquaint readers with the specific strategies of early feminist criticism so that readers can recognize them as distinct strategies, much as the chapter on new criticism sets out to help readers who took new criticism for granted come to recognize it as a specific set of strategies. In each case the goal is also to pose alternatives, whether to new criticism or to the approaches of early feminist criticism, thus allowing readers, and perhaps even encouraging them, to critique those approaches. Then readers can decide either to continue the practices of early feminist criticism more knowingly or to engage with more recent and less publicized feminist alternatives.

The later chapters of this book, then, follow contemporary feminist criticism and theory as it helps shape and is shaped by queer studies, Marxism, historicism, cultural studies, postcolonial studies, race studies, and ecocriticism, all central to the dialogues of third-wave feminism. As second-wave feminism sometimes proclaimed the sameness of women, so third-wave feminism, as we have begun to see, takes an interest in the variety of women—and, we might add, the variety of men. Contemporary, third-wave feminism enlarges the dialogue between feminism and the study of gender, seeing women less as a separate group and more as integral to the world across local and global gender formations, geographies, and cultures.

EARLY FEMINIST CRITICISM AND CONTEMPORARY FEMINIST CRITICISM

Images-of-women criticism. Early feminist literary criticism, as Toril Moi notes, focused on what came to be called **images of women** (after the title of a 1972 anthology of feminist criticism), at first primarily in male-authored works but eventually also in female-authored works. Images-of-women criticism judges a work (novel, film, music video, song) according to whether it provides "positive images" of women. If it portrays good women, then according to images of women criticism it is a good film, song, or novel. If it does not portray good women, then it is not so good a work. By now, many feminist critics see the focus on "images of women" as limiting and old-fashioned, because it tends to imply that women characters must be good "role models," which seems to confine literature to a narrow, predictable range of possibilities. For example, it excludes parody and much comedy, such as in feminist writing that makes fun of particular kinds of women or feminist writing that may set out to portray unrealistic characters. In feminist writing, as in most writing, characters can come in all kinds—good, bad, or too unrealistic to be either good or bad.

We can all remember classes or conversations where people say that they do not like this or that movie or book or play because a character is unrealistic, including times when they object to a work because it portrays an unrealistic stereotype, perhaps even a demeaning stereotype. In that sense, we need "images-of-women" criticism, and it has close parallels in criticism that focuses on images of African Americans or images of American Indians or Catholics, immigrants, Muslims, or old people, and so on. In all these areas images criticism plays a huge role, but to later feminist critics it came to seem that images criticism played far too large a role.

Perhaps it comes down to this: When do the characters work as role models, inviting people to imitate or differ from them? And when do the characters end up, far more, doing any of the many other things that literary characters can do, such as make us laugh or feel sad, dramatize a story, make us think about language or a social issue, probe our psychologies, or astound us with their unpsychological but entertaining difference from actual people? Readers and viewers like such movies, TV shows, novels, and plays as *Crash*, *The Hours*, *Pride and Prejudice*, *Gravity*, *Broadchurch*, and *The Bodyguard* partly for their more or less realistic portrayals, but like *Angels in America*, *Atanarjuat: The Fast Runner*, *The Incredibles*, *Inglourious Basterds*, the Harry Potter series, *Crouching Tiger, Hidden Dragon*, or *Game of Thrones* partly for their thought-provoking, entertaining, or some-times scary sliding away from and distorting of realistic portrayals. The movement away from realistic characters that offer role models for the audience does not make these works aesthetically or ethically bad film or bad writing.

Many contemporary movies—far more than older movies—feature skillfully active, adventurous female leads, as in, for example, *The Descent*, *Salt*, *The Hunger Games* series, and *Wonder Woman*. Such characters might seem to reinforce a feminist desire for women to break past traditional barriers and control their own lives. The energetic, skillful action of such characters reacts against the earlier pattern of weak or passive female characters. The reaction against a continuing expectation that women do not typically act boldly and skillfully can make such characters look like welcome feminist cri-tiques of misogynist assumptions. But it can also make them look like antifeminist, defensive overcompensations that mock the supposed weakness of real women outside of movies.

When we watch secret agent extraordinaire Evelyn Salt outsmart and outfight one man after another in rapid succession, we might see her talents on their own terms, as we probably see the talents of secret agent extraordinaire Jason Bourne in the Bourne movies and novels. But viewers might also see Salt's talents as somehow even less cred-ible than Bourne's, as playing against the cultural gendering of our expectations. Deconstructively we can take both views, for neither tells the whole story. Similarly, in *The Descent* and its sequel we might admire the Amazon spelunkers' skill and boldness, but when adven-ture turns to horror and the films send the women to their gruesome fates, we might wonder if the films punish their heroines for crossing boundaries that women supposedly should never cross (Figure 6.1).

Figure 6.1 "What was that?" Natalie Mendoza and Shauna Macdonald in *The Descent.*

In such ways, a feminist interpretation depends not so much on the characters themselves as on the broader social contexts that shape how we process the characters. In both examples, there is no objective and true images-of-women litmus test that tells us that the characters are good or bad role models. Even if we wanted to model ourselves after them, they are too unrealistic (entertainingly so) for us to suppose we could do what they do. Instead, the maelstrom of interpretive possibilities sets characters spinning in a broader cultural dialogue about the history of how we think about gender, what audiences expect, and what we think audiences should expect.

But there is a test from the heyday of images-of-women criticism that combines an acid sense of feminist humor with a searching feminist critique. Known as the Bechdel test, it gauges the individual characters less than the film itself, or the novel, play, TV show, or any other work with a plot. In her comic strip *Dykes to Watch Out For,* Alison Bechdel proposed the following three criteria for judging a film as worth watching: It must have two women. The women must talk to each other. And they must talk to each other about something other than a man (Bechdel 22–23). We could apply a similar test for other identity groups. Do they get at least two characters? Do the characters talk to each other? Do they talk to each other about themselves and their own interests? Such questions offer a basic gauge of respect, agency, and dignity.

It is remarkable how many works flunk the Bechdel test. And certainly the test has its limits, like other images-of-women criticism. As we have seen, for example, *The Descent* passes the test with flying colors and yet may bait us into expecting a more female-friendly outcome than many viewers might think that we end up getting. Works that seem feminist may flunk the test while others that seem misogynist may pass it. Sometimes, going outside the boundaries of respect, agency, and dignity makes for the interest of a plot. But often, energizing the plot by breaking those boundaries seems like an excuse for wallowing in patriarchal disrespect. Whatever its limits, the Bechdel test offers both readers and writers a bracing reminder of how few options they will find in the patriarchal cul-de-sac of much traditional film and literature, and how many other options await us if we give them a chance. With the danger and the advantage of prescribing specific but refreshingly simple standards, the Bechdel test shows that even while we may want to question images-of-women feminist criticism, we may do well to keep it as one possible consideration among whatever other critical questions we go on to ask.

Prescriptive realism and the authority of experience. Feminist critics study many topics and issues besides character. A focus on expecting realistic character, as in the Bechdel test, can lead to **prescriptive criticism** or even **prescriptive realism,** which tells writers how to write, prescribing how they should write rather than describing how they do write. Prescriptive realists tell writers that they should present realistic characters or characters that offer "positive role models." We can see why early feminist criticism would err in the direction of prescriptive criticism, because there was so urgent a need to point out the powerfully misogynist traditions of cultural history, literary history, and literary criticism. There is no sign that that task will end soon, but given the success that feminist critics have had in that domain, they have grown more and more interested in doing other things as well.

Prescriptive realism is also sometimes referred to by the title of another early (1977) anthology of feminist criticism, *the authority of experience.* The problem there lies in the assumption that one kind of experience is authoritative, as in the statement "As a woman, I know what sexism means," whereas to many feminists, including poststructuralist, third-wave feminists, experience varies, and so does the interpretation of any given experience. After all, another person could say, "As a woman, I appreciate it when men protect me from having to work, manage money, or vote and save me from bothering my little head with going to college and reading all those difficult books." For poststructuralists, including Lacanians (as we saw in Chapters 4 and 5) and many poststructuralist feminists, experience is never stable. It is always mediated by culture, which leads different people to understand experience in different ways.

As we will see in Chapter 11, on reader response, critics have debated whether, when different people read the same text or interpret the same experience, their different projections onto it mean that they end up seeing different texts and experiences rather than the same texts and experiences. Poststructuralist feminists might argue, therefore, that if we believe in the authority of experience, then we think that we can lock the signified onto one signifier and isolate that signified from other signifiers. But in poststructuralist criticism, both *authority* and *experience* have often become suspect words, especially *authority*. What looks like authority to one person may look like opinion to another. What one person says is an authoritative perspective on women's experience may look to another person like a misogynist perspective ("I'm so glad that men protect me"). To many feminists, authority seems like the enemy of feminist criticism, not the justification for it.

The word *experience*, however, continues to provoke debate. To many critics it seemed for a while that poststructuralists, including poststructuralist feminists, had put an end to appeals to experience, at least among critics who kept up with the debates in cultural criticism. But in recent years a number of critics have come to the defense of experience, especially critics of color, notably bell hooks, who fear that if we banish experience from critical thinking, then in many people's minds white experience will blot out the experience of people of color. Such critics realize that the concept of experience is open to abuse, because different people have different experiences, so that no one experience is authoritative. But they also point out that all criticism depends on experience, even if different people have different experiences and interpret them in different ways. We may find value in the variety of experience, rather than merely finding bias. The point then becomes not to do away with reasoning from experience, but on the contrary to reason in ways that take into account, and even learn from, the multiplicity of experience.

Expanding the canon. Feminist criticism began by studying the often-disturbing images of women in literature written by men and opposing those images to the authority of women's experience, but the concentration on writing by men quickly came to seem as limiting as the idea that women all had the same experience. Feminist critics turned increasingly to women's literary writing, contributing to a massive movement to read beyond the traditional set of literature that critics and teachers typically studied and taught. The traditional set of literature came to be called **the canon.** Feminist critics of all colors and heritages worked to "expand the canon," joining with critics of African American literature and then increasingly of Latina and Latino literature, Asian American literature, American Indian literature, Black British literature (such as works by British writers of Caribbean, South Asian, and African heritage), and literature from around the world, including English-language literature in English departments, and—beyond English departments—literatures in other languages. As part of this project, literary critics have dug into the archives to uncover forgotten works of literature, ranging from works once famous and then forgotten or not taken seriously (frequent problems for women's writing) to works never published. These recovery efforts have dramatically enlarged the range of literature that critics, teachers, and students read and study, bringing into the classroom—to name only a few examples— such widely taught and revered writers as Aphra Benn, Mary Shelley, Harriet Jacobs, Charlotte Perkins Gilman, and Nella Larsen.

Beyond celebration. In this context, feminist critics not only study "images of women" in works by men or even in works by women but also bring all the wide-ranging resources of literary criticism to study women's literary writing of all kinds. Feminist literary criticism and history, therefore, are not about "celebrating" women's writing. Such celebration had its place in early feminist criticism, which had the uphill task of making it known that there was a great deal more women's writing, and a great deal more deeply admirable and appealing women's writing, than most readers realized. But after a time such celebration starts to seem demeaning, starts to suggest that we doubt women's writing and need to compensate for our doubt by celebrating women's writing. Feminist literary criticism and women's writing overall have now come so far that we can accept the value of women's writing without needing to worry about such doubts. Now, instead of making feminist literary criticism about proving that women's writing is worth reading and studying, we can take that as a given and bring to it the full resources of our critical methods and energies.

Indeed, the now-dated focus on the "celebration" of women's history and writing—and of the overlapping categories of history and writing from the variety of racial, ethnic, and national peoples who have left a literary legacy—has long since reached the point where it can turn counterproductive. It can play into the hands of reactionaries who protest that African American studies or feminist studies, for example, are not serious intellectual pursuits but are just about celebration.

Celebrating had its time and place and still has value on special occasions, but women's studies, African American studies, and the many other studies programs that now play a role in college, university, and international intellectual life, including—to speak to the immediate point—feminist literary criticism, are not about throwing a party. They may often be fun, and they may be proud, but as this chapter can show, they are now also as serious intellectual pursuits as any others.

Women as victims versus women as agents. By setting out to expose the abuses of patriarchy, early feminism and early feminist criticism sometimes seemed to see women mainly as objects and as victims. Partly in reaction to that exaggeration, more recent feminism increasingly draws attention to women's "subjectivity," their "agency"— that is, their ability to imagine and shape their own lives. The term *subjectivity* has a variety of histories (see Chapter 8), but for our purposes here the relevant history is the structuralist notion of a subject versus an object in a sentence as a model for subjects versus objects in cultural practices. Subjects do, and objects are done to. Feminist criticism continues to pay attention to what is done to women, to pay attention to women's role as objects, but it also pays serious heed to women as doers, as subjects and agents, seeing a dialogue between women as objects of patriarchy and women as agents of their own future. Popular critics of feminism sometimes complain about what they call "victim feminism," which shows how little they have kept up with contemporary feminist thinking. Contemporary feminism, while it continues to value the study of what patriarchy has done to women (and to men), has also gone far beyond that early focus to concentrate on what women do and, in the case of literature and literary criticism, on what women write.

Some Antifeminist Myths About Feminism

1. It's all about victimization.
2. It's all about affirmation and celebration.
3. It's anti-lesbian.
4. It's anti-heterosexual.
5. It's anti-pleasure; it's humorless.
6. It's anti-male; it's about hating men.
7. It's for "radical kooks," bra burners, and "feminazis."

Myths 1 and 2, 3 and 4, 2 and 6, and perhaps 2 and 5 are each opposites: That is how prejudice works. Many such myths come from people who feel their privilege or comfort threatened by feminism. Sometimes they find something in feminism—or in what they wrongly suppose is feminism—that they do not like, and then they try to use that to define all feminism.

All these myths have to do with what has come to be called *straw feminism*. Straw feminism puts ridiculous ideas in the minds of people or of TV, film, or literary characters whom antifeminists inaccurately describe as typical feminists. By misrepresenting feminism and feminists as ridiculous, and perhaps by pasting a ridiculous label on them like "feminazi," antifeminists try to make feminism and feminists look silly, like something just for kooks, and definitely not like something for people with any sense.

But any movement as wide-ranging and changing as feminism is too multidimensional to be defined by its frightened opponents or its least convincing advocates. Those who believe in the expressions listed under myth 7, or in similar expressions, resort to derogatory name-calling as a substitute for argument about the issues. Burning bras might have been amusing, but there is no record of feminists burning bras anywhere except in the fantasies of antifeminists. As this chapter shows, feminism is not any one thing. Instead, like other methods of criticism, it keeps changing and growing as feminists debate among themselves.

SEX AND GENDER

In her influential *The Second Sex* (1949), the French philosopher Simone de Beauvoir famously proclaimed: "One is not born, but rather becomes, woman" (Beauvoir 283). Later, in 1975, Gayle Rubin described what she called the "sex/gender system" (Rubin 159), using the word *sex* for what Beauvoir says one is born with and the word *gender* for what Beauvoir describes as what one becomes. In the 1980s and usually continuing through current feminism, feminists—often influenced by Beauvoir or Rubin—use the terms *female* and *male* to refer to **sex,** and the terms *feminine* and *masculine* to refer to **gender.**

In this way of thinking, sex comes from biology and anatomy, while contemporary feminist theory usually sees gender as the constructed product of culture rather than the natural, inevitable product of biology and anatomy. In the word *constructed* we can hear the influence of structuralism and deconstruction. *Female* and *male* refer to essences, whereas poststructuralist feminists think in terms of constructed gender rather than of essences. Since the onset of third-wave feminism, then, the distinction between sex and gender has become a cornerstone of contemporary, nonessentialist feminist theory, because it suggests that gender proliferates into many different forms, like what Derrida calls the free play of signifiers or the free play of language.

All this means that there are many different ways to enact gender, many different ways to live as a female or a male, not one essentialist way. Feminists see this sense of multiplicity as liberating. It means that it is best for women to choose how to live as women, whether that means going to college or not, and working outside the home or working in the home to raise children, whether it means heterosexual desire or lesbian desire, driving a truck or baking cookies, wearing a pink dress or wearing jeans, studying physics or French, or any combination of these. And along the way, the hope is that feminism can also help men feel at liberty, like women, to choose how to enact their gender.

With its interest in the multiplicity of gender, as opposed to an essentialist notion of what women are and can be, contemporary feminism draws from Derrida and deconstruction, although some feminists suggest that feminist thinking anticipated Derrida. In its opening to many different ways to be female and male, this strain of feminist theory has overlapped with, helped with, and been helped by the growth of lesbian, gay, and queer studies. As we saw in the

---

Feminist (and other words)

This will seem too obvious to many readers, but experience and the pleading of many teachers suggest that a little clarification can save beginners from comical goofs. Do not confuse *feminine* with *feminist*. *Feminine* refers to a style of gender, whereas *feminist* refers to a commitment to respecting women. And *feministic* is not an accepted word, so it sounds clueless and might even make your readers laugh or groan.

previous chapter, it has also helped bring out the way that Freudian psychoanalysis tells a story about the construction of gender, instead of supposing that sex and gender form a single essence.

Meanwhile, to some feminists—in a strain of argument often associated with the philosopher Judith Butler, though it did not begin with her—even the liberating distinction between sex and gender seems constraining. They argue that even sex is constructed, rather than inherent, because we cannot understand sexual anatomy apart from cultural ideas about gender, which structure how we construct, understand, and interpret anatomy. As it happens, anatomy books differ over the centuries in the ways that they present sexual anatomy (as Thomas Laqueur has shown), because how we see is shaped by how we think, and how we think varies across time and geography and even from person to person. In this way of thinking, sex is always already gender, that is to say, always already constructed. Each culture sees what it supposes is essentially female or male in different ways from other cultures, and even within a given culture we can find variations and differences. These ongoing discussions put two different but related binary oppositions under accelerating scrutiny:

1. the binary opposition between female and male, and
2. the binary opposition between sex (female and male) and gender (feminine and masculine).

Today, for example, we increasingly take note of what we now call intersex, namely, biological categories that do not fit wholly into the conventional biological definition of female or male. Our increasing awareness of intersex people challenges the traditional division of people into females or males, seeing it as an essentialist binary opposition between two supposedly internally consistent and entirely opposite categories. Meanwhile, the movement to challenge discrimination against transgender people as illegal sexual discrimination, while contested, seeks to establish a legal norm that no longer necessarily reads sex as a stable, unchangeable biological given established at birth, so that sex and gender emerge as two names for what at least sometimes is the same category.

FEMINISMS

French and Anglo-American feminisms. For a time beginning in the 1980s, many writings in feminist theory and criticism made a distinction between French feminism and Anglo-American feminism, a distinction that now seems exaggerated but still carries a legacy.

Whatever its limits, the opposition between French feminism and Anglo-American feminism helped call Anglo-American readers' attention to provocative challenges from French feminists. Three influential writers, Hélène Cixous, Luce Irigaray, and Julia Kristeva, came to dominate Anglo-American readers' awareness of French feminism, even though none of them is originally French. Cixous was born and grew up in Algeria, Irigaray in Belgium, and Kristeva in Bulgaria, though they each moved to France as adults. And as we might imagine, there are many other French feminist writers. Cixous, Irigaray, and Kristeva have differences among themselves, and their ideas have developed and varied across many writings, but they each see the predominant language as masculine, or *phallogocentric*, and they each try to imagine feminine alternatives to phallogocentric language.

Cixous [pronounced *seek-soo*] argues that feminine writing, or *l'écriture féminine* (*écriture* is French for "writing"), has its source in the infant's prelinguistic relation to the mother, supposedly before the infant establishes boundaries and differentiations between the self and the rest of the world around it, that is, before the onset of what Lacan calls the symbolic. For her, the free play of language (we can hear Derrida's influence on Cixous) and linguistic celebration of the body evoke the prelinguistic relation to the mother. A woman's voice, for Cixous, "physically materializes what she's thinking; she signifies it with her body. . . . There is always within her at least a little of that good mother's milk. She writes in white ink" (Cixous 251). At other times, however, Cixous makes a point of saying that gender does not come directly from bodies, that men can be feminine and women can be masculine (Figure 6.2).

Figure 6.2 Hélène Cixous (1937–).

Irigaray advocates a specifically woman's language that she sees in the language of women's pleasures and in the bodily shape of women's sexuality. For Irigaray, who sometimes writes in poetic rhythms that enact the language she advocates, woman "touches herself in and of herself without any need for mediation, and before there is any way to distinguish activity from passivity. Woman 'touches herself' all the time, and moreover no one can forbid her to do so, for her genitals are formed of two lips in continuous contact. Thus, within herself, she is already two—but not divisible into one(s)—that caress each other" (Irigaray 24). As women, she writes, "We are luminous. Neither one nor two. I've never known how to count. Up to you. In their calculations, we make two. Really, two? Doesn't that make you laugh? An odd sort of two. And yet not one. Especially not one. Let's leave *one* to them: their oneness, with its prerogatives, its domination, its solipsism: like the sun's" (Irigaray 207).

Kristeva describes what she calls the *chora* or *semiotic*, based on the fetus's prelinguistic relation to the mother in the womb. (Her use of the term *semiotic* differs from other people's use.) By connecting women's writing to the prelinguistic relation to the mother, Kristeva and Cixous suggest, much as Irigaray suggests, that women's writing flows in rhythms outside the stultifying logic and systemizing of language and linguistic structures. They see women's writing as evoking a freedom and unpredictability that they believe acculturated, rule-bound language tries to exile from our imaginations.

In effect, Cixous, Irigaray, and Kristeva ask whether women and men think and write in contrasting ways, and, if they do, then why? They suggest that women as a rule, or perhaps as a tendency and not as a rule, do more than men to retain their prelinguistic, imaginary relation to the mother. Or perhaps differences between women's bodies and men's bodies, as Irigaray argues, lead to differing ways of thinking and writing. Some feminists react against the idea that women and men write differently. They fear that to believe so is to resurrect the very stereotypes that feminists set out to oppose. In that vein, they criticize French feminism, as associated with Cixous, Irigaray, and Kristeva, as essentialist, as believing in an inherent, bodily femaleness rather than a culturally constructed feminine, that is to say, as seeing sex where other feminists say that we should see gender. Some more admiring readers see the French feminists, by contrast, as teasingly, exaggeratedly, even ironically essentialist for the sake of provocation.

Monique Wittig, another prominent if not as well-known French feminist, far more explicitly challenged essentialist notions of gender, astonishing her audience, in a 1978 lecture, by announcing that "lesbians are not women." For Wittig, who wrote novels, theory, and hybrids of fiction and theory, the very idea of gender, including the very idea of women and men, depends on taking heterosexual norms for granted. Wittig rejects second-wave feminist claims for a specifically women's culture, seeing such claims as depending on the sexist divisions between genders that they set out to oppose. She argues that lesbians have no place in the heterosexual way of thinking that naturalizes heterosexuality and centers on the experience of men. Therefore, she believes, the very presence of lesbians exposes a fraud in those heterosexual assumptions.

Many feminists see the linguistic, playful, theoretical, poststructuralist, and sometimes psychoanalytic interests of Cixous, Irigaray, and Kristeva, and the provocations of Wittig, as different from the more empirical and historical approaches taken by influential English-writing innovators from the same era of feminist literary criticism. Rather than trying to find a specially feminine language, English-writing critics such as Nina Baym, Sandra Gilbert, Susan Gubar, and Elaine Showalter try to recover a history of women's writing and its interests and dialogues. For example, Gilbert and Gubar's *The Madwoman in the Attic: The Woman Writer and the Nineteenth-Century Literary Imagination* (1979) sees Charlotte Brontë's novel *Jane Eyre* as a metaphor for the state of nineteenth-century women's writing. In Brontë's novel, Rochester proposes marriage to Jane while he secretly remains married to Bertha Mason, the "madwoman" he keeps locked in the attic. Seeing Bertha, Rochester's secret wife, as a double for Jane, his proposed public wife, Gilbert and Gubar read Bertha's caged expressiveness, her madness, as a metaphor for how patriarchal culture viewed women's writing.

Beyond French and Anglo-American feminisms. Feminist critics from outside the French/Anglo-American divide, such as the Norwegian Toril Moi and the Indian Gayatri Chakravorty Spivak (on Spivak, see Chapter 10), have launched major critiques of Anglo-American feminist critical theory and literary critical practice, prodding Anglo-American critics to think more internationally and theoretically and to look critically at their own practices. Spivak, for example, notes that Bertha Mason is a Jamaican Creole, and Spivak therefore sees the British Rochester's caging of Bertha as figuring not only a cultural idea about women but also a colonialist idea about the colonized

world and about the battered-down lives of colonized women. As critics who write in English and teach in English-speaking countries,
such feminists as Moi and Spivak have reached English-speaking audiences more than many other international feminists.

Meanwhile, many feminists of color, including the African American novelist Alice Walker, Chandra Talpade Mohanty, Kimberlé
Crenshaw (Figure 6.6), and the contributors to *This Bridge Called My
Back: Writings by Radical Women of Color*, edited by Cherríe Moraga
and Gloria Anzaldúa, called needed attention to the way that many
early Anglo-American feminists sometimes wrote about women as
if all women were white. Concerned that such narrowness came to
define feminism, Walker proposed **womanism** as an alternative term
to rename a feminism that no longer centers on white women. While
some feminists—or womanists—still use the term *womanism*, it has
a lower profile than the rethinking of feminist ethnocentrism that
Walker, Spivak, Anzaldúa (on Anzaldúa, see Chapter 10), bell hooks,
Mohanty, Crenshaw, Sara Ahmed, and other critics of color have encouraged. Crenshaw's concept of *intersectionality* underlines the need
for feminists to move beyond thinking of women as if they were ordinarily white and underlines the need to include gender with other
categories of identity. She studies the obstacles that black women
face when the law and the courts respond to prejudice against women
by seeing all women as if they were white, and respond to racism by
seeing all blacks as if they were men. Crenshaw argues that such approaches overlook the specific, compound position of black women.
(For more on intersectionality, see later in this chapter.)

In this light, feminist critics note, for example, that in Bharati
Mukherjee's short story "Jasmine" (not to be confused with Mukherjee's novel of the same title), the privileged white American feminist, Lara, can enjoy her new feminist liberties in part because she
has the power to hire Jasmine, an undocumented immigrant from
India, to take care of Lara's child and help with the cooking and
housework. Jasmine leaps at the scraps of opportunity she finds in the
United States, including her job as a "mother's helper," because, without the privileges and cultural contexts that Lara has, she is ill prepared to understand when Lara and Lara's husband take advantage
of her, both economically and sexually. The two women's different
positions put them in competition with each other, but their dangerously cliché sense that a working-class woman like Jasmine has
as much chance to control her future as Lara has keeps them from
seeing how women can work against each other's interests. In short,

not all women are alike, and not all women have the advantages that some women have. Feminism best serves its purpose of respecting women when it takes into account the differences among women and advocates for less privileged as well as for more privileged women, no easy task when women's interests compete across variations in class, nationality, education, and race.

It is now almost as routine for women of every race and region where women have access to public intellectual life to call themselves feminists as it is for Anglo-American women to call themselves feminists. Indeed, French feminism, Anglo-American feminism, and the rest of the world's feminism have long since moved beyond the unfortunate binary opposition that for some years seemed to oversimplify feminism into French feminism versus Anglo-American feminism. Now, feminists from across the globe reject the idea that feminism is a western export imposed on the rest of the world. Nigerian writer Chimamanda Ngozi Adichie, for example, dismisses the idea "that feminism was not our culture, that feminism was un-African" (Adichie 10–11). More and more, feminists of all stripes learn from each other, and feminist thinkers come from every race and class and from all over the world.

HOW TO INTERPRET: FEMINIST EXAMPLES

We might imagine a variety of feminist approaches, for example, to Ernest Hemingway's novel *The Sun Also Rises* or Dorothy Parker's story "A Telephone Call" (not as widely taught as Hemingway's novel, but still a widely read, easily available classic). We could argue that Brett Ashley, the femme fatale flapper of *The Sun Also Rises*, shows Hemingway's sexism, or his novel's sexism, because she is reduced to a mere sex object or because she makes a mess of her life. Or we could argue that in Parker's story the frantic monologue of a pitiful woman desperate for her lover to call shows Parker's sexism, or her story's sexism. After all, the desperate narrator has made herself depend entirely on a man's affection (and implicitly not just on any man but on a cad), and like Brett, she makes a mess of her life. Such arguments work in the typical manner of early feminist criticism, including images-of-women criticism. The point lies in interpreting characters (not so much form, ideologies, or language), and the goal is to ask whether they are good characters or bad characters. According to whether the characters are good or bad role models for readers, such arguments issue a verdict for or against the novel or story.

While such readings were routine in early feminist criticism and remain on the table today, especially in classroom discussions, they now seem too simple. Even within images-of-women criticism, we can start to play with such readings in more challenging ways. We might see these works' portrayals of unfortunate women not as representing a belief that that is how women are, in their essence, but rather as critiquing that way of imagining women's possibilities and so suggesting that women can differ from Brett or from the anguished monologuist of "A Telephone Call" waiting for the telephone to ring. Suddenly, by that gambit, without changing our observation of details, we turn the interpretation upside down, and what at first looked like antifeminist writings can now, from this other perspective, look like feminist writings.

The possibility, then, of turning an interpretation upside down offers great promise and yet also great danger for images-of-women feminist criticism and for all critical judgments based on characterizing models of identity, including gender, race, religion, disability, sexuality, nationality, and many other categories. If we find a portrayal offensive in a movie or a novel, for example, then we—or someone else—could also flip that judgment upside down by reading the same portrayal as a critique of the offensive image, rather than an endorsement of it. Such flexibility offers powerful resources for interpretation and judgment, but it also carries risks. We probably want to retain the ability to say that certain representations disturb us. We might even want to advise writers and moviemakers to keep away from those disturbing representations. If we can turn any critical judgment upside down, then we risk making it seem as if anything goes, as if we have to endorse any representation. And we might find that outcome ethically and culturally dangerous. Writers and moviemakers could use the logic of reversible judgment to rationalize the most disturbing images and stories. In that light, as much as we may find images-of-women criticism too simple and constricting, we may sometimes still want to hold on to it.

We probably cannot find a one-size-fits-all-texts and all-readers solution to this provocative contradiction between opposite interpretive possibilities. We have to keep both possibilities in mind and go through the sometimes difficult—but not always so difficult—process of sorting them out case by case. The possibility of flipping an admiring or a rejecting interpretation upside down might give us pause and encourage caution and modesty before we indulge in broad-brush rejections or endorsements along the lines of binary absolutes like antifeminist versus feminist.

Instead of leaping to condemn or praise the characters, we might ask what happens to gender in these works, not only in the characters but also in the form that renders them. "A Telephone Call" poses questions, for example, about the gendering of dialogue, of telephone calls (or today of texting or social networking as well as telephone calls), of asking questions ("What are you doing Saturday night?"). There is nothing inherent in the form of dialogue to require that some people get to call while others can only be called or that we blame some people for calling while we blame others for not calling. Cultural convention draws those lines between categories of gender: men call (women), and women are called (by men). But we could have drawn the lines in other ways, such as for same-sex couples, or not drawn the lines at all. The rules are cultural constructions, not inevitable consequences of sexual difference.

We might wonder at the *defamiliarization* (to use the Russian formalist term from Chapter 3) that allows readers to recognize and laugh at, and perhaps look critically at, patterns of gender that get so taken for granted that readers might not have thought much about them before—including patterns of rationalization or self-serving resort to religion, as when the woman in the story pleads with God to make her boyfriend call her on the telephone. Yet the character herself seems to see through her own self-deceptions. Even so, she cannot make her ability to see through them keep her from getting stuck in them. In these ways, gender comes freighted with cultural compulsion. Sometimes, we see how it confines us, yet we keep running headlong into those confinements, even when we know better.

While the telephone—excitingly almost new at the time of this story (1928), at least for individual middle-class residences and single women—might seem to promise a bridge to more flexible structures of gender, its liberating potential ends up bowing down in subservience to the same old demeaning hierarchies. We might wonder how that compares to the new technologies of our own time. Here we have a woman who cannot converse, at least not with the person she wants to converse with, yet right before her is a technology that promises to open the gates of dialogue.

At the same time, though the character cannot converse, Parker can, for her story reaches an audience. It comically shows a woman—Parker—defying the limits on women that trap the character in the story. Feminine agency and feminine reduction to mere object status thus sit together on a fence of alternating critiques and possibilities, like the narrator's flitting back and forth between the urge to call her lover and the conviction that it would court disaster to call him. The continuously shifting options spoof the reduction of gender relations to a tortuous power imbalance that paints women as mere victims—and set off a painful laugh at the same imbalance, leaving us to debate whether the laughter helps crack the barriers it spoofs, or not.

Brett Ashley in *The Sun Also Rises* may seem like an opposite figure, for she would certainly telephone her lover or any other man, straight or gay—or just walk up to him. But even in their opposition to each other, both Parker's and Hemingway's characters are provocative clichés of the feminine. Lady Brett parades through Hemingway's novel as a femme fatale and an iconic figure of Woman, whether endorsing such clichés, parodying them, or—deconstructively—both at once. But she is also portrayed as masculine, from her name to her short hair to her quenchless erotic initiative. Under this light, sex starts to reappear as gender, and gender no longer seems like so certain a category, for Brett blends and bends masculinity with femininity in ways that might make us question the conventional identifications between female and feminine and male and masculine, and question the idea of feminine as passive and masculine as active.

At the same time, everything we learn about Brett comes mediated through the narration and focalizing of the narrator, Jake Barnes, and so in a sense characterizes his gender as well as hers and perhaps characterizes his more reliably than hers. Yet that obsessive mediation also makes his gender needily dependent on hers or on his perception of the relation between his and hers. His interest in her masculine femininity and her feminine masculinity invites interpretations of him, but it also invites interpretations that, as the reference to formal features such as his narration and focalization may suggest, go beyond the old-fashioned criticism that only addresses character.

A variety of cultural issues arise in the preoccupation with watching Brett, or with Jake's watching of Brett, or Jake's watching of himself and others watching Brett, or Hemingway's watching Jake watch. And they arise with our watching as well, or with the history of many critics and readers watching so much watching and feeling compelled to use it to pit one character's model of gender against another's, as if to weigh and judge them. Gender starts to appear as a topic and means for a culture to debate its future, and before long, in *The Sun Also Rises*, it connects to conflicting ways of thinking about war, economics, sports, nationality, ethnicity, commodification, and on and on. No interpretation can take on all the possibilities, but any interpretation that gets beyond the basics will pursue its choices far beyond the opening gestures I have pointed to here—and that is where the interest lies. Feminist criticism is not about labeling books as good or bad, sexist or nonsexist. It is about interpreting them in light of the feminist rethinking of women and women's positions. By respecting women and by thinking through the implications of that respect, feminist criticism leads us to think through anything in culture that has to do with women and gender, which potentially is everything.

FEMINISM AND VISUAL PLEASURE

Laura Mulvey's "Visual Pleasure and Narrative Cinema" (1975), one of the most influential articles in feminist criticism, can help us consider feminist film criticism as well as feminist literary and cultural criticism. I will also use it as a point of departure to a variety of issues in more recent feminist criticism that go well beyond what Mulvey's article addresses.

Bringing psychoanalysis and structuralist narratology together with feminism, Mulvey (Figure 6.3) describes classic Hollywood cinema as organized around a binary opposition between a masculine spectator, the subject, and what we might call a feminine spectated, the object. The spectator enacts what, drawing on psychoanalysis, has come to be called the *gaze*. The masculine subject gazes, and the feminine object is gazed at. To Mulvey, this process goes beyond what we see on the screen. It reaches out and draws in the audience. Conventional film editing, the norm in classic Hollywood cinema and still so pervasive a norm in contemporary film and video that most spectators are not even aware of it, aligns spectators in the audience with the masculine spectator in the film through subjective camera and shot/reverse shot editing. The expression *subjective camera* refers to camera work that looks as if through the eyes of a character, thus constructing a visual focalizer, like the focalizer in verbal narrative. As we saw in Chapter 3, *shot/reverse shot* refers to editing that invites us to look through the eyes of a character. Mulvey describes how the combination of subjective camera and shot/reverse shot editing leads audiences to look through the eyes of an actor gazing at an actress, and to identify with the actor's gaze at the actress. The process that she describes is sometimes called the **masculinization of spectators,** because through gendering the camera and the editing, the conventions of film can sway spectators—women and men both—into identifying with a masculine subject position (stance or point of view).

The Feminist Critique of Objectification

Mulvey's argument is a version of the standard, and to most readers probably familiar, feminist critique of objectification. Many people misunderstand that critique, because the term *objectification* can have two different but related meanings. It can mean turning someone into a mere thing. Or it can mean treating someone as an other, that is, seeing someone, grammatically, in the position of an object (the one who is acted upon) in relation to someone else in the position of a subject (the one who acts). The first meaning, treating someone as a mere thing, describes a disturbing objectification, but the second meaning describes an inevitable objectification.

In the second sense, then, objectification itself is not the problem. There is nothing necessarily wrong with objectifying something or someone as an other. It is even inevitable. We all look at others and are looked at by others, and not only in the narrow sense of looking. For whether we are sighted or blind, we look at others in the broader sense of perceiving others. And when we look or are looked at, we often respond with indifference or with pleasure.

Looking in itself, therefore, is not a problem. And seeing someone as an object, in the sense of seeing someone as an other, is not a problem. The problem comes with reducing women (or anyone else) to little or nothing except their status as an object, when by object we mean a mere thing, or a merely sexual thing. The sexuality, then, is also not a problem. The problem is the abusive reduction of the object to her or his sexuality and to nothing else. Mulvey associates abusive objectification with classic Hollywood cinema and stereotypical masculine patterns of the gaze.

Mulvey also argues that classic Hollywood cinema tends to film men (those who look) in three-dimensional space, granting them movement to either side or backward and forward within the filmed space. By contrast, it tends to film women (the looked-at objects) in two-dimensional space. They often hold relatively still, suggesting stasis, especially while male characters look at them and while the audience is drawn into looking at them through a male character's gaze. The women often appear in a framed space, perhaps standing in a door frame or before a window frame, underlining their position as two-dimensional static objects, like pictures in a picture frame. With the male gaze focused on women, this style of filmmaking, so standard and conventional that viewers do not usually even recognize it as a style, associates men with voyeurism, control, and authority, expressed as a will to investigate and fetishize women. Mulvey sees that will as sadistic for men and as confining for women.

For Mulvey, writing before DVDs, YouTube, streaming, or mobile phones that can show or make movies, the pattern she describes is specific to traditional film, shown to a large audience on a big screen in a dark theater:

> The mass of mainstream film, and the conventions within which it has consciously evolved, portray a hermetically sealed world which unwinds magically, indifferent to the presence of the audience, producing for them a sense of separation and playing on their voyeuristic fantasy. Moreover the extreme contrast between darkness in the auditorium (which also isolates the spectators from one another) and the brilliance of the shifting patterns of light and shade on the screen helps to promote the illusion of voyeuristic separation. Although the film is really being shown, is there to be seen, conditions of screening and narrative conventions give the spectator an illusion of looking in on a private world. (Mulvey 17)

Though Mulvey points her argument specifically to classic film, we can see related patterns in contemporary film, in music videos, and in written literature. Written literature often lingers over a narrator's or a focalizer's erotic gaze at a focalized character and often at a focalized woman.

Mulvey declares boldly: "It is said that analysing pleasure, or beauty, destroys it. That is the intention of this article" (16). She sees traditional cinema as a corrupt pleasure, and she believes that filmmakers can invent a new cinema beyond the sexism that defines the old cinema, if they reconceive film in a way that destroys its corrupt pleasure. She therefore calls for filmmakers "to free the look of the camera into its materiality in time and space and the look of the audience into dialectics and passionate detachment" while believing that "this destroys the satisfaction." "Women," she concludes, "cannot view the decline of the traditional film form with anything much more than sentimental regret" (26). Mulvey thus calls for a radically new style of film that is not based on the "look," the "gaze," or subjective camera and focalizing narrative. The alternative style that she calls for would be fragmented rather than dreamily continuous and hypnotic. Characters—if there were characters at all—might step out of their roles to address the camera or the audience and break the audience's identification with the characters, splintering the subjective camera and editing typical of mainstream film.

After Mulvey: expanding visual pleasure and critical spectatorship. Mulvey's argument—which she herself has gone on to rethink through later perspectives—has carried great force in feminist film criticism and beyond, in literary studies and in gender studies in general, but critics have also raised objections to her model. Even among critics who disagree with her, though, many of the ideas that Mulvey offered continue to propel critical discussion, even while the arguments take a shape opposite to what Mulvey suggested. In that sense, by reviewing the critiques of Mulvey's argument we can sample a good variety of additional and more contemporary feminist theory and criticism, using Mulvey's work as a bridge to more recent questions in feminist theory and in the many other strains of theory that contemporary feminism engages with.

Although Mulvey often gets credited or blamed for describing the so-called *male gaze*, and at one point she does use that expression, her argument actually goes against the idea that the gaze is male or necessarily male. Instead, she discusses the gaze as masculine (gender), rather than as male (sex). More specifically, she describes the gaze as heterosexual and masculine, and still more specifically, as an abusive version of masculine heterosexuality.

Still, some critics see Mulvey as essentialist. They believe she paints gender as an absolute category rather than as a category that varies across different times and cultures. They read her as saying that this is what men do: they look, and they look in abusive ways; and this is what women do: they are looked at, and they remain passive. Mulvey can invite that objection, can seem to see women and men as frozen in a binary opposition. But such an objection can miss that she does not accept the sexist patterns that she describes. She opposes them. She does not see those patterns as frozen in time and space, for she believes that describing them can help us change them.

Others object that Mulvey writes prescriptive criticism, because she argues that filmmakers should make certain kinds of films. That is, they object because she tells filmmakers what to do. She assumes that a given form—fragmented film without the gaze and without subjective camera and editing—will necessarily produce a given

Figure 6.3 Laura Mulvey (1941–).

politics. More specifically, she assumes that traditional form necessarily produces a sexist politics and experimental form necessarily produces a feminist politics.

That assumption requires a belief in what communications theorists call **technological determinism,** the idea that a given technology produces a predictable result. For example, when people say (as once people did say) that telephones will lead to equality by letting anyone call anyone else, that word processing will destroy writing, that fax machines, cell phones, or social networking will bring electoral democracy to China, or that the Internet will free people to challenge mainstream culture through an open exchange of ideas, they suppose that a given technology necessarily produces a predictable cultural change. They usually say as well that the technology is valuable, or dangerous, depending on what they think of the change. Skeptics see technological determinism as a fallacy (along the lines of the intentional and affective fallacies described by new critics), because the same technology often produces dramatically different results. In the Facebook-launched Arab Spring of 2011, an eruption of protest against repressive governments, the same technology led to different results in different countries and even in different parts of the same countries. For that reason, skeptics see the technology itself as unable to determine the outcome. They see culture as determining the consequences of technology at least as much as technology determines the culture.

From this skeptical perspective, Mulvey gets caught in the fallacy of technological determinism. As it turns out, the experimental film forms that Mulvey advocated soon grew commonplace in, for example, music videos, but I doubt that any serious critic would propose that the fragmented, disruptive cinematic form of many music videos has usually led to feminist filmmaking. The same form can work in a sexist or a feminist way, depending on how we use it, just as two poems can use the same meter and stanza form and yet produce dramatically different effects. The form in itself will not predict the outcome. But by buying into technological determinism, Mulvey essentializes form.

Mulvey has also taken criticism for supposing that the text (the film) shapes or determines the spectator (the audience, the reader). The film, she believes, constructs all spectators as masculine spectators, in effect converting women to a masculine subject position. More specifically, although she does not say so, in her model the film constructs all spectators as masculine heterosexual spectators. By taking the heterosexuality for granted and not making it explicit, Mulvey naturalizes heterosexuality. She ignores queerness. More generously, we might say that she reads classic cinema as ignoring or masking queerness. She does not consider queer spectators of any kind—trans, bi, lesbian, or gay—or any spectators who take into account a variety of potential sexualities in themselves or in others. In Mulvey's model, spectators may or may not walk into the theater with any variety of desires in their minds or histories, but the film turns them all into masculine heterosexual spectators.

Of course, that is part of the power and provocativeness of Mulvey's argument. But as many of her readers have insisted, it just isn't so. Some spectators, for example, will look at the feminine sex object on the screen and feel little or no sexual attraction. Some spectators will feel attracted to the masculine spectator on the screen. In this sense, when Mulvey supposes that the text determines its spectator, she leaves out the possibility that the spectator also determines the text, as in reader-response criticism. (For more on reader-response criticism, see Chapter 11.) Even masculine heterosexual spectators might see a film inviting them into an abusively objectifying model of masculine heterosexuality and respond by saying "No," or respond with less enthusiasm than some other masculine heterosexual spectators. Queer spectators might simply not participate in the heterosexual invitation, or they might participate satirically.

Indeed, Mulvey's approach, with its prescriptive sense that film-makers need to provide good examples for their audience, leaves no room for irony or humor. On the screen a heterosexual invitation can come across, in some spectators' eyes, as a parody of heterosexual presumptions, even as camp. Similarly, Mulvey does not anticipate the possibility of what has come to be called **critical spectators,** that is, active spectators who resist the system, as opposed to spectators who passively allow the system to seduce them into naturalizing its assumptions.

Different critics hold different beliefs about how easy or difficult it is to resist dominant cultural assumptions that film or any other media set out to draw us into. To some critics, resistance seems easy and routine. To others, the dominant assumptions shape us so subtly and deeply that they make resistance almost impossible. In that view, much of what passes for resistance never adds up to much more than allowing us to think that we are resisting, so that we keep ourselves from realizing how little we really resist and how much more we remain compliant. As we will see in Chapter 8, Marxist theorists have developed models for how to think through this debate over how people do or do not resist prevailing cultural assumptions.

Viewers' various social positions may prepare them to respond more critically than Mulvey anticipates. bell hooks, for example, responding to Mulvey in an essay called "The Oppositional Gaze: Black Female Spectators," has argued that race relations can en-ergize the capacity to gaze as a critical spectator. hooks notes how blacks, in the first two-thirds of the twentieth century, especially in the American South, were still not allowed to look directly at whites in public. Black spectators responded, hooks says, by enjoying the freedom to stare at representations of whites in the movies and on TV, and they resisted racist assumptions by laughing at the ridicu-lous white representations of blacks on early TV. hooks recognizes that black spectators sometimes went along with cinematic social assumptions, just as Mulvey says, but she also sees black spectators as more likely to critique what they looked at. By not differentiating spectators racially, hooks argues, Mulvey describes all spectators as if they fit her model of implicitly white, compliant, uncritical spec-tators. hooks's argument shows the oversimplification in Mulvey's powerful generalization about spectators, as if all spectators always fit the same dominant social pattern racially and sexually (white, straight, patriarchally objectifying). By contrast, if we differentiate

Figure 6.4 Classic Hollywood cinema: What do spectators do—with their eyes and with their thoughts and desires—when the camera gazes at the star? Lauren Bacall in *To Have and Have Not*.

spectators by the social groups they belong to—racially, sexually, politically, and so on—then we might find more of the variety that Mulvey encourages.

As part of Mulvey's underestimation of critical spectators, and in much the same way that she naturalizes heterosexuality, she idealizes the theatrical setting and naturalizes one version of cultural patterns that vary greatly. Let us return, for example, to Mulvey's description of a traditional film shown to a large audience on a big screen in a dark theater, where the film seems to unwind magically and seduce the audience into a dreamy world of spectators isolated from each other, reduced to their individual relation to the film on the screen. Surely spectators are not always isolated. Many people go to the theater partly to enjoy their erotic relation to another spectator sitting next to them. Others spend an entire movie craning to peer around a taller person in front of them or lamenting a nearby loudmouth or, now, a distracting cell phone addict. We all recognize the difference between watching a movie with a large, talking, laughing audience and watching a movie in an empty theater or in the darkened theater that Mulvey describes as isolating spectators from each other, reducing them to their gaze at the actresses and actors on the screen.

Figure 6.5 Music Videos: What do spectators do—with their eyes and with their thoughts and desires—when the camera gazes at the star? Do contemporary music videos overlay spectatorship with a difference-making irony? Or does the irony end up preserving an updated version of the same old same old? Lady Gaga in *Paparazzi*.

When I was an undergraduate, before we had the technology to watch movies at home, and in the heyday of new excitement about campus feminism and the heyday of film as a campus social outing, it was routine for spectators—men as well as women—to hiss at moments of a film that we found misogynist. That was part of the fun of going to movies, and it helped politicize spectatorship and make it a communal rather than an isolating pleasure. White, middle-class audiences typically speak back to a movie less than black audiences, especially in comedies that play with black social expectations. All of us have seen films that speak from cultural assumptions that we do not share, whether in terms of politics, class, sexuality, religion, race, or our personal histories. And contrary to Mulvey's notion of the passive spectator, we sometimes—though Mulvey might say not often enough—explicitly reject a film's presumptions, even while, as Mulvey says, the film unwinds before us as if magically. Sometimes, with today's technology in the privacy of our homes, we yell at the screen. And sometimes, even at the cineplex, spectators yell out and make an entire theater angry or make it burst into laughter or both.

It may be that as a rule, spectators remain too passive, too accepting of a film's cultural assumptions and, as Mulvey says, of the cultural assumptions embedded in the very technology of camera work and editing, including sexist assumptions. But spectators are not the passive victims that Mulvey supposes. Mulvey deserves credit for helping women get out from under the passivity they may have suffered from under sexist film practices, but her rejection of filmic pleasure comes out of an earlier, victim-focused stage of feminist criticism. We can see why feminist criticism went through that stage in its early years, even succumbing, sometimes, to what may now seem like antipleasure feminism, but women and men both have come a long way since then, even if not a long-enough way. Both on screen and in the audience, women, queer or straight, are not always passive victims of an abusive masculine heterosexual gaze. Women on the screen now more often move through three-dimensional space, even if sometimes in the explicit gender reversals of films like *Thelma and Louise*, *Million Dollar Baby*, *The Hunger Games*, and *Wonder Woman*, which necessarily depend on the patriarchal expectations that they reverse or spoof. Even in classic Hollywood films, women are not only gazed at. They have their own gaze, whether looking back at those who look at them or just looking—on their own initiative. And women in movies or watching movies look at both women and men.

Mulvey herself looks. She describes how the erotic gaze at a woman, often a "performing woman,"

> takes the film into a no man's land outside its own time and space. Thus Marilyn Monroe's first appearance in *The River of No Return* and Lauren Bacall's songs in *To Have and Have Not*. Similarly, conventional close-ups of legs (Dietrich, for instance) or a face (Garbo) integrate into the narrative a different mode of eroticism. One part of a fragmented body destroys the . . . illusion of depth demanded by the narrative; it gives flatness, the quality of a cut-out or icon, rather than verisimilitude, to the screen. (19–20)

We can see the same process in verbal narrative when a focalizer's or narrator's eye slows the pace of narrative to gaze lingeringly at a focalized character. At such moments the mobile focalizer halts, interrupting his mobility (I say *his*, since Mulvey writes about masculine gazers). The static position of the immobile, flat feminine space gains ascendancy, with a mix of recovered power and constrained stasis. We can hear that sense of feminine power in Mulvey's excited description of such iconic figures as Monroe, Bacall, Dietrich, and

Garbo, actresses whose characters often look at men as the men look at them (Figure 6.4). And sometimes they look at other women, as women spectators surely both gaze at the actresses and identify with their position of being gazed at and, sometimes, of gazing back.

As women look, perhaps some are "masculinized," as in the model that Mulvey proposes for classic Hollywood films. But surely many women do not limit or sway their gender to match a film's expectations. Either way, women do not become any less women through their looking.

Moreover, after Mulvey's article appeared, now that movies and video have reached the home and seemingly everywhere else, viewing habits have changed (Figure 6.5), as Mulvey herself has discussed in her later writing. The lights are on. The conversation often continues while the film shows. People walk in and out. We stop the film, replay it, slow it down, leave it on while we walk away, or leave it on as background for other activities, and often we watch it again (or at least play it again) over and over. Mulvey's technological-determinist formula might lead us to expect that such changes would loft us away from sexist film, but while popular film may not be as pervasively demeaning to women as it used to be, it is hardly a paragon of feminist equality. The broader culture, still saturated with sexism, continues to help shape how people produce and interpret film and other cultural processes, more than the technology itself determines the culture.

INTERSECTIONALITY AND THE INTERDISCIPLINARY ETHOS OF CONTEMPORARY FEMINISM

Contemporary feminism is energetically interdisciplinary. Feminists build alliances with other areas of study. As we will see in later chapters, especially as we review queer studies, postcolonial studies, and ecocriticism, contemporary feminist theory often engages with and reshapes other areas of critical theory. The interdisciplinary energy of contemporary feminism comes across especially through the growing discussion of intersectionality.

In 1989 and 1991 legal scholar Kimberlé Crenshaw published articles about what she calls **intersectionality**, and those articles have gradually grown in influence. Writing from an intersection of feminist antiracist, black antisexist, and critical race studies perspectives (on critical race studies, see Chapter 10), Crenshaw argues that people working against antiblack racism tend to think of blacks as men and overlook black women. Meanwhile, people working against sexism

Figure 6.6 Kimberlé
Crenshaw (1959–).

tend to think of women as white and, again, overlook black women.
Without realizing it, antiracist and antisexist theorists and activists
often suppose that we can describe the plight of black women by
adding together the plight of blacks and the plight of women. But
Crenshaw argues that merely adding the categories erases the specific
obstacles that work against black women.

Crenshaw gathers a devastating series of examples. She begins with
a legal case. Before 1964, General Motors hired no black women. Then,
when the economy sunk into recession in 1970, GM fired all its black
women employees, following the pattern of "last hired, first fired." Five
fired black women sued for discrimination against black women. The
court ruled that the fired black women could not sue as black women.
As blacks, they could sue for discrimination against blacks. And as
women, they could sue for discrimination against women. But they
could not sue for discrimination against black women. It did not
matter to the court that the fired black women were last hired as a
consequence of GM's previous unwillingness to hire black women at
all. The black women were caught in a feedback loop, hired only in

a time frame that also got them fired. The court's indifference to the feedback loop made the specific vulnerability of black women legally invisible.

Similarly, Crenshaw looks at the position of black women in the prosecution of rape. She shows, as other scholars had shown before her, that black men accused of rape are much more likely to be convicted than white men accused of rape. And when convicted, black men tend to receive much longer prison terms than white men. Black men especially receive longer terms when convicted of raping white women. But Crenshaw extends those earlier observations by noticing that studies of such patterns pay attention to the convicted rapists without paying much attention to the victims, especially when the victims are black women. She shows evidence that black women's testimony against accused rapists is far less likely to be believed than white women's testimony. Prejudices against black women's behavior tend to trivialize or discredit their testimony because of a belief that black female victims probably "asked for it" or were already too "ruined" to be hurt by rape. Crenshaw notes a study (of Dallas County in Texas) that showed that men convicted of raping black women received average prison terms of two years. Men convicted of raping Latina women received average prison terms of five years. And men convicted of raping Anglo women received average prison terms of ten years (Crenshaw, "Mapping" 1269). Women of color, she concludes, do not get the same recognition and respect as white women.

Crenshaw also enters the vexed debate about racism and misogyny in certain hip-hop lyrics and in the critique of those lyrics. She notes three much-discussed responses to controversial lyrics. One response defends allegedly misogynist lyrics as artful satire in a black tradition of satire. Another response attacks the criticism of the lyrics, calling such criticism racist (for the way it paints black male rappers as animals). A third, feminist response attacks the lyrics as sexist. Crenshaw argues that all three of these responses typically leave out the intersectional position of black women. Defenders of the lyrics who would not otherwise tolerate racist jokes as satire accept the same kinds of jokes when they degrade black women. The racist attacks on the lyrics trouble Crenshaw not only for their racism but also for the same critics' indifference to similar lyrics from white performers and their indifference, again, to the position of black women. And feminist critiques of misogynist hip-hop lyrics tend to sensationalize white women victims of black men's language of violence and misogyny while, once more, Crenshaw argues, they erase the black women who often bear the biggest burden of offensive lyrics.

Through these and many other examples, Crenshaw argues that we can only understand the position of black women by thinking of black women as both blacks and women, not as blacks plus women or as women plus blacks. Everyone has more than one identity, and we cannot understand the perception of identity by thinking about identities one at a time. A "contradiction arises," she argues, "from our assumptions that" black women's

> claims of exclusion must be unidirectional. Consider an analogy to traffic in an intersection, coming and going in all four directions. Discrimination, like traffic through an intersection, may flow in one direction, and it may flow in another. If an accident happens in an intersection, it can be caused by cars traveling from any number of directions and, sometimes, from all of them. Similarly, if a Black woman is harmed because she is in the intersection, her injury could result from sex discrimination or race discrimination.
>
> Judicial decisions which premise intersectional relief on a showing that Black women are specifically recognized as a class are analogous to a doctor's decision at the scene of an accident to treat an accident victim only if the injury is recognized by medical insurance. Similarly, providing legal relief only when Black women show that their claims are based on race or on sex is analogous to calling an ambulance for the victim only after the driver responsible for the injuries is identified. (Crenshaw, "Demarginalizing" 149)

Especially in her more recent work, Crenshaw notes that her argument is not so much about identity as about the legal and institutional structures that respond to identity through cultural assumptions and through laws and court rulings about discrimination and rape, and even in specific institutional practices such as decisions about who can—and who cannot—get admitted to shelters for battered women. In these ways, the concept of intersectionality gains special force for feminist inquiry in black studies, where Crenshaw partly begins, and also for feminist inquiry in race studies at large, including all races, and in queer and postcolonial studies. That is to say, the concept of intersectionality gains special force wherever institutions and cultural practices take singular identities so much for granted that they overlook the distinctive positions of multiple, less powerful identities.

The concept of intersectionality has everything to do with the interdisciplinary ethos of contemporary feminist theory. A review of intersectionality could fit in other chapters of this book as well as in this chapter on feminism. As we will see in the chapters to come, contemporary feminists pay particular attention to parallel, reinforcing, and crisscrossing routes of intersectionality across gender, sexual orientation, disability, ability, class, race, postcolonialism, and environmentalism.

* * * * *

In that spirit of interdisciplinary alliance, readers can probably see, by now, that it would be hard to think seriously about women and the feminine without also thinking seriously about men and the masculine, and so feminism has led to gender studies. And some feminists and women's studies scholars believe that feminism has reached a point where the women's studies programs that feminists built in colleges and universities, often against great odds, should now evolve into gender studies programs. Other feminists think that changing women's studies programs into gender studies programs will sacrifice or betray many of feminist scholars' hard-won advances. Especially in a world that continues to undervalue the role of women, they believe, we need to sustain women's studies as an enclave for intellectual work that otherwise might not get done. Some programs try to have it both ways, changing from women's studies programs to programs in women and gender studies or gender and women's studies. Among other things, the rubric of "gender" can seem to offer a safe place for queer studies, especially in public universities that may fear a taxpayers' backlash against queer studies.

Fourth-Wave Feminism?

Contemporary technologies have also launched what some feminists have dubbed fourth-wave feminism, often centered in social media. Even as social media has provided an avenue for virulent misogynist attacks on women, it has also made a space for feminist activism, most famously in the #MeToo movement. Through a variety of tech venues, ranging from the Everyday Sexism Project (where women document everyday sexism) to the viral video *10 Hours of Walking in NYC as a Woman* to such outbursts of hashtag feminism as #BeenRapedNeverReported,

#YesAllWomen, and #MeToo, contemporary feminists have sought justice for women and opposed the culture of harassment, rape, and sexism in schools, workplaces, and popular culture from politics to video games. In some people's eyes, this surge of electronic feminist activism and social-media-boosted women's marches adds up to a new set of ideas, a fourth-wave feminism. In other people's eyes, it provides a powerful contemporary medium for recasting and expanding earlier waves. Either way, or both ways together, against a continuing culture of misogyny the new online feminism has energized activism, debate, and education, both group self-education and education of the culture at large.

Intellectually, however, feminist studies and women's studies have generated so much momentum toward rethinking gender that it would be impossible to practice them thoughtfully without rethinking heterosexuality and queerness, as we have seen through the discussions provoked by thinking about feminism and film. Feminism and queer studies are not the same, but queer studies, the topic of the next chapter, has found some of its intellectual momentum in feminism, and feminism in turn has drawn on the intellectual challenges of queer studies.

FURTHER READING

Adichie, Chimamanda Ngozi. *We Should All Be Feminists*. New York: Anchor, 2014.

Ahmed, Sara. *Living a Feminist Life*. Durham, NC: Duke University Press, 2017.

Baym, Nina. *Feminism and American Literary History: Essays*. New Brunswick, NJ: Rutgers University Press, 1992.

Beauvoir, Simone de. *The Second Sex*. 1949. Trans. Constance Borde and Sheila Malovany-Chevallier. New York: Random House, 2010.

Carby, Hazel V. *Reconstructing Womanhood: The Emergence of the Afro-American Woman Novelist*. Oxford: Oxford University Press, 1987.

Célestin, Roger, Eliane DalMolin, and Isabelle de Courtivron, eds. *Beyond French Feminisms: Debates on Women, Politics, and Culture in France, 1981–2001*. New York: Palgrave Macmillan, 2003.

Cixous, Hélène. *The Hélène Cixous Reader*. Ed. Susan Sellers. New York: Routledge, 1994.

Collins, Patricia Hill. *Black Feminist Thought: Knowledge, Consciousness, and the Politics of Empowerment*. New York: Routledge, 1990.

Crenshaw, Kimberlé. "Demarginalizing the Intersection of Race and Sex: A Black Feminist Critique of Antidiscrimination Doctrine, Feminist Theory and Antiracist Politics." *University of Chicago Legal Forum* (1989): 139–167.

Crenshaw, Kimberlé. "Mapping the Margins: Intersectionality, Identity Politics, and Violence against Women of Color." *Stanford Law Review* 43.6 (July 1991): 1241–1299.

de Lauretis, Teresa. *Technologies of Gender: Essays on Theory, Film, and Fiction.* Bloomington: Indiana University Press, 1987.

Ellmann, Mary. *Thinking about Women.* New York: Harcourt, Brace & World, 1968.

Felski, Rita. *Literature after Feminism.* Chicago: University of Chicago Press, 2003.

Friedan, Betty. *The Feminine Mystique.* New York: Norton, 1963.

Fuss, Diana. *Essentially Speaking: Feminism, Nature, and Difference.* New York: Routledge, 1989.

Garland-Thomson, Rosemarie. "Integrating Disability, Transforming Feminist Theory." In *Feminist Disability Studies.* Ed. Kim Q. Hall. Bloomington: Indiana University Press, 2011: 13–44.

Gilbert, Sandra M., and Susan Gubar. *The Madwoman in the Attic: The Woman Writer and the Nineteenth-Century Literary Imagination.* New Haven, CT: Yale University Press, 1979.

Haraway, Donna Jeanne. *Simians, Cyborgs, and Nature: The Reinvention of Nature.* New York: Routledge, 1991.

Hirsch, Marianne, and Evelyn Fox Keller, eds. *Conflicts in Feminism.* New York: Routledge, 1990.

hooks, bell. *Feminist Theory from Margin to Center.* Boston: South End Press, 1984.

Irigaray, Luce. *The Irigaray Reader.* Ed. Margaret Whitford. Cambridge, MA: Basil Blackwell, 1991.

Irigaray, Luce. *This Sex Which Is Not One.* 1977. Trans. Catherine Porter with Carolyn Burke. Ithaca, NY: Cornell University Press, 1985.

Kaplan, E. Ann, ed. *Feminism and Film.* Oxford: Oxford University Press, 2000.

Kristeva, Julia. *The Kristeva Reader.* Ed. Toril Moi. Oxford: Basil Blackwell, 1986.

Marks, Elaine, and Isabelle de Courtivron, eds. *New French Feminisms: An Anthology.* Amherst: University of Massachusetts Press, 1980.

McCann, Carole R., and Seung-kyung Kim, eds. *Feminist Theory Reader: Local and Global Perspectives.* New York: Routledge, 2010.

Millett, Kate. *Sexual Politics.* Garden City, NY: Doubleday, 1970.

Mohanty, Chandra Talpade. *Feminism without Borders: Decolonizing Theory, Practicing Solidarity.* Durham, NC: Duke University Press, 2003.

Mohanty, Chandra Talpade, Ann Russo, and Lourdes Torres, eds. *Third World Women and the Politics of Feminism.* Bloomington: Indiana University Press, 1991.

Moi, Toril. *Sexual/Textual Politics: Feminist Literary Theory.* 2nd ed. London: Routledge, 2002.

Mulvey, Laura. *Visual and Other Pleasures.* Bloomington: Indiana University Press, 1989.

Oliver, Kelly, and Lisa Walsh, eds. *Contemporary French Feminism.* Oxford: Oxford University Press, 2004.

Plain, Gill, and Susan Sellers, eds. *A History of Feminist Literary Criticism.* Cambridge: Cambridge University Press, 2007.

Russ, Joanna. *How to Suppress Women's Writing.* Austin: University of Texas Press, 1983.

Showalter, Elaine. *A Literature of Their Own: British Women Novelists from Brontë to Lessing.* 2nd ed. Princeton, NJ: Princeton University Press, 1999.

Silverman, Kaja. *Male Subjectivity at the Margins.* New York: Routledge, 1992.

Thornham, Sue, ed. *Feminist Film Theory: A Reader.* New York: New York University Press, 1999.

Walker, Alice. *In Search of Our Mothers' Gardens: Womanist Prose.* San Diego: Harcourt Brace Jovanovich, 1983.

Warhol-Down, Robyn, and Diane Price Herndl, eds. *Feminisms Redux: An Anthology of Literary Theory and Criticism.* New Brunswick, NJ: Rutgers University Press, 2009.

Wittig, Monique. *The Straight Mind and Other Essays.* Boston: Beacon, 1992.

Woolf, Virginia. *A Room of One's Own.* London: Hogarth Press, 1929.

✳ 7 ✳

Queer Studies

Just as deconstructionists see everything as multiple and feminists see many ways to be a woman and many ways to enact gender, so queer studies suggests that there are many ways to enact gender and sexual desire. The growth of feminism helped prepare the ground for the growth of queer studies, which in turn led to rethinkings of feminism. We can see that multidirectional cross talk in the discussion of post-Mulvey ideas about feminist film theory in the previous chapter, where we saw how the feminist issues that Mulvey posed gave critics new ways to pursue queer interpretations, which in turn helped critics rethink the feminist issues.

Again, as in feminism, the motive for queer studies comes not so much from a method per se, though it may lead to new methods, as from thinking about an identity category (or an unstable, shifting constellation of identity categories). It comes also from thinking about the way that across history, cultures have understood or repressed queer acts, enacted queer identities, or abused or denied the existence of queer people. In this context, I will echo the introduction to feminism in the previous chapter and say that queer studies is a simple concept. It is about taking queer acts, life, and thought seriously and treating them respectfully.

Queer studies has grown out of and can include lesbian studies and gay studies, but queer studies does gay and lesbian studies with a difference. Lesbian and gay studies address sexual orientation and people who identify as lesbian or gay and compare them to people who identify as straight. In the process, lesbian or gay studies sometimes takes on a sound of essentializing lesbians, gays, or straight people and pitting lesbians or gays or "homosexuals" against straights as binary opposites. Just as deconstruction tries to go beyond the binary oppositions that structuralists believe organize our thinking, so queer studies—drawing on and contributing to deconstruction—tries to go beyond the binary oppositions and essentialism that it sometimes sees as characterizing gay or lesbian studies. The concern is that some people use terms such as *lesbian* and *gay* or use lesbian or gay studies to suggest a belief in stable characteristics that can describe all gays or all lesbians across geography and time and that definitively separate gays and lesbians from each other and from straight people. By contrast, the term *queer* suggests instability and continuous process. We might say that queer studies is a deconstructive version of gay and lesbian studies, a version that contemplates a wider variety of sexualities and orientations than can fit under the labels of gay and lesbian.

KEY CONCEPTS IN QUEER STUDIES

The desire for a deconstructive version of lesbian and gay studies speaks to the larger project of reconstructing ideas of identity and sexuality, moving away from **the naturalization of heterosexuality** and away from **compulsory heterosexuality.** The naturalization of heterosexuality is the assumption, typically made without thinking, that everyone is heterosexual unless labeled otherwise. When people naturalize heterosexuality, they suppose that heterosexuality can be taken for granted and that anything else is a special case.

Once, for example, a student in a theory class I was teaching cheerfully referred to the scene in the movie *Top Gun* where a group of hunky, bare-chested men play volleyball, calling it an episode that women get excited about watching. Without realizing it, she slid into naturalizing heterosexuality by speaking as if all women were heterosexual. That could have provided a good teaching opportunity, easily managed with a laugh. Besides noting that not all women might respond that way, I could have mentioned that the scene has also attracted interest for a playfully gay suggestiveness, and that the film is often read as rife with same-sex desire. But— fearful of embarrassing or offending the student by putting her on the spot—I didn't say anything. My caution naturalized heterosexuality yet again.

Clarifying the Naturalization of Heterosexuality

When students first learn about the concept of the naturalization of heterosexuality, they sometimes think that the mere presence of heterosexual acts, characters, or desires in a film or work of literature shows the naturalization of heterosexuality. But it doesn't. You can have heterosexuality without supposing that everyone is naturally and definitively heterosexual, just as you can have queerness without supposing that everyone is naturally and definitively queer.

Such moments have the effect of enforcing *compulsory heterosexuality*, a term popularized in a 1980 essay by the poet and essayist Adrienne Rich (Figure 7.1). Compulsory heterosexuality refers to the impression, explicit or implicit, that people should be heterosexual or else something is wrong with them. Compulsory heterosexuality can also take a direct form, especially for women; each year men and patriarchal economics pressure or force millions of women around the globe into marriage, rape, or concubinage. Even in its implicit form, compulsory heterosexuality costs many people—especially people who favor same-sex desire—great and needless suffering, and it has much to do with the tragically high suicide rate among queer youth. Insisting on compulsory heterosexuality is a way of protecting illusions that the increasing visibility of queerness puts in doubt. The naturalization of heterosexuality drops a curtain over a great deal of human desire, and in many ways queer studies begins simply by lifting that curtain and acknowledging the range of human desire and the utter routine of the world beyond compulsory heterosexuality.

For queer studies, once the heterosexual/gay or heterosexual/lesbian binary breaks, then the line between heterosexual and queer no longer looks so firm as the conventional insistence on compulsory heterosexuality can imply. Within the binary model, some people have same-sex desire and others do not. Alternatively, same-sex desire and opposite-sex desire are potential in everyone. As you may recall from Chapter 5, Freud believed that infants are polymorphously perverse, meaning that they can find erotic pleasure in any body part. The term *perversity* in this sense carries no moral judgment. It simply describes desire that persistently turns in unpredictable directions, and *polymorphous* means that the unpredictable desire takes many forms.

Figure 7.1 Adrienne Rich
(1929–2012)..

In this model, everyone has the potential for any sexual orientation. But as most infants grow older, the surrounding world structures and streamlines their polymorphous perversity into standardized patterns, such as gay, lesbian, or straight. Whether Freud had that exactly right or not (and people disagree on that issue), the larger queer claim is that people's desire is more multiform than the rigid binary opposition between straight and queer can account for.

Though compulsory heterosexuality and the naturalization of heterosexuality would deny it, in our daily lives we routinely see multiform sexuality around us and perhaps within us. Some men who identify as heterosexual find some "masculine" women attractive, perhaps an athletic woman or a take-charge woman. Some women who identify as heterosexual find attraction in a "feminine" man, perhaps seeing something refreshing in a freedom from machismo. Heterosexuals often find pleasure in staring at sports stars, celebrities, or fashion models of their own sex, such as at websites or magazines about sports, music, movies, fashion, or bodybuilding. We can multiply these simple examples many times over. The point is not to out anyone (see later in this chapter for more on outing) but instead to reconceptualize heterosexuality and queerness in less binarizing, less mutually exclusive ways.

In tune with deconstructive feminism and gender studies, then, the point is also to challenge essentialized notions of what feminine and masculine might mean. Hence my earlier quotation marks around *feminine* and *masculine* mark stereotypes worth reconsidering. And the point is also to challenge the automatic assumption that feminine means a desire for masculine/male and that masculine means a desire for feminine/female. For in the culture around us, each desire has a way of teasing itself to an interest, at least, in its opposite desire. The places that supposedly harbor the most intense gender conservatism—a beauty parlor, perhaps, or a football team, or the military (where the military is still male-dominated, a pattern now changing)—are also entrenched bastions of erotically charged same-sex admiration. Meanwhile, other places that may seem the most skeptical of gender conservatism—a drag queen revue or some butch, femme, or transgender choices in clothing, hairstyle, makeup, or facial hair—might also seem, ironically, to reinforce conservative notions of the gender binary by enacting stereotyped models of femininity and masculinity. Or perhaps they reinforce those models so ironically or so differently that they deconstructively undermine what to some people they might seem to uphold. In this queering of daily life, every style of desire is only a turn of the corner away from becoming, at the same time, or instead, the opposite of what it might seem.

Just as such a way of thinking can threaten conservative models of gender and sexuality, so it can also threaten essentialist models of lesbian and gay or straight identity, models that claim a stable sense of what lesbian is, what gay is, what heterosexual is, and how each supposedly remains firmly separated from the others. From within such models, the term *queer*, with its insistent, deconstructive instability, can seem to obscure differences between gay and lesbian or between same-sex desire and heterosexual desire or between the differing cultures and histories associated with each group.

For that reason, some people interested in what I am here calling *queer studies* resist the term *queer* in favor of saying *gay* or *lesbian*. In practice, however, lesbian, gay, and LGBT (lesbian, gay, bisexual, and transgender) studies often mean more or less the same thing as queer studies. While *queer theory* implies a more deconstructive, theoretical approach and *queer studies* implies a more practical approach, people sometimes put aside these differences, as I mostly do here, and use the terms interchangeably. Individual critics may or may not keep up these distinctions, depending on the context and their preference.

The differences can matter, but when other issues come to the fore, some critics blur the boundaries.

In the early euphoria of new dialogue between deconstruction and queer studies in the 1980s, it sometimes came to seem that queer theorists turned their deconstructive energies on the categories of gay and lesbian, making it seem as if deconstruction were a special quality of gay and lesbian identities and not of straight identities. In response, the novelist Dorothy Allison and queer studies scholar Esther Newton comically but trenchantly produced a call to "Deconstruct Heterosexuality First" (Duggan 7). By now, queer studies has gone much further to meet that call, and all identities are up for discussion. In that context, the question still common in the general populace, *What makes people gay or lesbian—or trans or bi?*, is partly a way of avoiding the question, *What makes people straight?* Many straights want to avoid that question, because to recognize their heterosexuality as a construction is a way of recognizing that they did not and perhaps do not have to be heterosexual. It could have turned out differently.

In a similar way, in the early euphoria of dialogue between deconstruction and race studies, it came to seem as if critics eagerly produced deconstructive readings of black identity while leaving white identity as if it were a stable quality, unchanging across time and place. Just as we can hardly understand queer identities without thinking of straight identities, and vice versa, so—in an American context—the same mutual dependence holds for black and white identities. And black and white identities are only a limited part of the American and the global range of possibilities. Eventually, however, there arose a provocative and by-now-massive scholarly enterprise of whiteness studies (see Chapter 10), often led by African American writers and taking its cue from historical observation at least as much as from deconstructive philosophy. In these ways, the growth of queer studies and its dialogue with deconstruction is part of a panoply of other dialogues across many different, sometimes overlapping identities, each thinking through many of the same issues.

As the everyday culture of queer life and the academic culture of queer studies expand and grow, the vocabulary also grows. Terms change, evolve, attract support and opposition, and new or newly popular terms help us think through what they describe, misdescribe, or fail to describe. The terms *genderqueer, nonbinary, gender nonconforming*, and *agender* can help routinize the deconstructive instability of gender and queerness. The terms *cisgender* or *cis* describe people whose gender identity matches the sex they were assigned at birth, as when someone assigned female identifies as female and someone assigned male identifies as male. By contrast, the terms *transgender* or *trans* describe people whose gender identity differs from the sex they were assigned at birth, as when someone assigned female identifies as male and someone assigned male identifies as female. The feeling of a mismatch between gender expression and assigned sex is sometimes called *gender dysphoria*.

Each of these terms has its advocates and critics. For example, some critics question how well such terms accommodate intersex people. Some people object that the term *gender dysphoria* sounds too much like a clinical diagnosis or relies too much on a binary concept of gender. Traditionalists fear that new terms authorize concepts and identities they object to. Others value the way that new terms, even when imperfect, or simply by the way they highlight the possibility of changing and evolving language and identities, help make space for queerness. Even pronouns change, as English-language speakers increasingly favor gender-neutral, gender-inclusive pronouns or invent new pronouns (*ze, em, hir*, and so on) to take into account genderqueer identities. In that spirit, the pronouns *they* and *their* have gained wide and increasing acceptance as a way to refer to individual people without assuming or making a point about how they perform gender.

Gender and performance. Following an argument especially iden.i-fied with the philosopher Judith Butler (Figure 7.2), especially her book *Gender Trouble: Feminism and the Subversion of Identity* (1990), many cultural critics express the constructedness of sexual and other identities by describing identity as performed rather than as a static essence. Because no two performances come out the same way, performance suggests variation and continuous process rather than an interior core of essential selfhood. At its most celebratory, the idea of identity as performance can suggest that anything goes, that people can choose whatever performance they want. But even performances work from a script. We do not make up from scratch the range of possible performances. Instead, we inherit models of gender, sexuality, and identity, and the surrounding culture often forces or pressures those models on its members, even as its members sometimes try to mix ways of repeating the inherited models with ways of inventing new variations.

Figure 7.2 Judith Butler (1956–).

We build models of gender through repetition, Butler argues. Performing gender, and watching it performed in more or less the same way over and over, produces a taken-for-granted idea that certain ways are natural and right. Yet repetitions are never perfect. We never do the same thing exactly the same way twice. And some repetitions vary from the model more than others. Thus, even as repetition irons in the model of an essentialized notion of gender, it also undermines that model, proliferating what it repeats into a series of variations. While we can see patterns in the ways that people perform gender, then, we can also see repetitions that change the patterns and even, with a sense of humor, repetitions that spoof the patterns.

Butler proposed drag as one way to spoof seemingly rigid patterns of gender. A drag queen, for example, can seem to spoof masculinity by offering a campy, comical, fabulous variation on masculine gender. At the same time, a drag queen can spoof femininity by exposing the repeated patterns of femininity as a performance that bears no necessary relation to the sexuality of the performer that the patterns supposedly represent.

Butler's claim about drag, though only a small part of her overall discussion, set off arguments about whether drag inevitably challenges conservative models of gender. Instead, drag might reinforce the models that it seems to spoof. For as people watch a drag queen, they might respond by thinking that after all, she, or he, is not really a woman. And so they might intensify their belief that after all, he is really a man and that against Butler's argument, there is an essential difference between men and women, corresponding to an essential difference between masculinity and femininity. When a drag queen performs, he mimics a structuralist poetics of femininity. That is, he mimics repeated patterns of dress, gesture, and speech that a traditional model of gender associates with femininity. While the mimicry can mock those patterns, as Butler supposes, it can also intensify people's belief that those patterns, in a woman, *are* femininity. In that sense, drag can work in opposite directions at once, perhaps more in one direction for some people and more in another direction for other people.

Moreover, the performer cannot control the outcome. To Butler's chagrin, some readers took her as arguing that people can choose their own performances of gender, an argument sometimes described as *voluntarism*. But if, as Butler argues, there is no core identity of gender, then there is no one home to do the volunteering, for, in Butler's deconstructive argument, people do not have a preexisting self that then performs identity. Instead, the performance of identity constructs the self. Or, in more poststructuralist lingo, the performance of identity constructs the subject. The subject or self is not the cause of what people do. It is the effect of what people do and, still more, of what people keep doing. Gender, like subjectivity, is not an essential core but a constant production. People produce gender and subjectivity not *by* the ways they express them, as if the signifiers and signifieds were separate causes and effects, so much as *in* the ways they express them.

While people can perform gender in ways that spoof and undermine the preexisting menu or structuralist poetics of possibilities for gender, there are limits on our freedom to perform gender, for observers do not necessarily read gender in the way that its performers desire. A comfortably straight woman or man can be read by some people as masking her lesbianness or his gayness. A dyke comfortable with her own performance can be read by some people as a man or as a failed woman. A comfortably gay man can be read by some people as an inept performer of his true gender, as another failure. In a world that naturalizes heterosexuality, a lipstick lesbian and a gay man in a business suit can be naturalized as straight and rendered invisible as queer or can be misread as not accepting their own queerness. In contemporary culture, the options and the visibility of options are both expanding. Even so, as much as we influence how we perform gender and how others read our performance of gender, we do not control how people read our performances. We do not even control how we ourselves read them, for, like any audience, within our individual selves we can multiply the models of interpretation, mixing the conventional and the unconventional and even making competing interpretations give urgency and meaning to each other.

HOW TO INTERPRET:
A QUEER STUDIES EXAMPLE

In the movie *The Crying Game* (1992), Dil explains herself to Fergus by saying such things as "A girl has to have a bit of glamour" and "A girl has to draw the line somewhere." In effect, she proposes a structuralist poetics of femininity. Each time she calls on that poetics by explaining her actions and preferences as matching what a girl has to do, she performs a feminine role. But because repetition, as Butler reminds us, produces difference as well as likeness, when Dil calls attention to her performance as a role (see Figure 7.3), she also suggests an ironic possibility that not all girls have to have a bit of glamour or have to draw the line in the same place. Once Dil is revealed as a he, or for viewers who suspect all along that she is a he, or who know from watching the movie before or hearing about it before that she is a he, then Dil's remarks about what a girl has to do multiply in their already multiple meanings. A girl might have to do certain things, by one model, but a guy might not have to do those things. Or a guy who is also a girl or is performing girlness or who, we might say today, is a trans girl or woman might feel even more pressure to do them or might find pleasure or relief in doing them. Or he, or she, or they might find pleasure in vexing Fergus's more conservative notions of what gender requires from Fergus or from men or from couples. When Fergus desires Dil, supposing she is a woman, or a woman performing a woman, and then discovers that she is a man—at least in his thinking—or a man performing a woman, then Fergus can find himself desiring another man. In that way, he can also find himself rethinking his understanding and performance of his own desire.

Audience members might go through the same rethinking, if they have specularized Dil in the way that (as we saw in Chapter 6) Laura Mulvey proposes that audiences specularize movie showgirls as feminine heterosexual objects and icons. Fergus discovers that he has

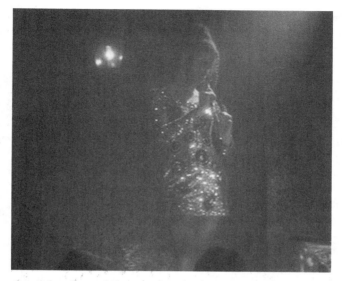

Figure 7.3 Dil as showgirl chanteuse. Jaye Davidson in *The Crying Game*.

been performing heterosexuality, and his newfound sense of his heterosexuality as performance can compromise its stability as heterosexuality. Suddenly, things he did not understand earlier in the film cascade into a series of newfound recognitions, such as his memory of Jody's (Dil's previous boyfriend) words about Dil, his own bonding with Jody, and his conflicted feelings about his attraction to Dil and his unlikely commitment to pursue her.

As Jody, Dil, and Fergus perform their gendered identity and sexuality, they also perform and show the mobility of their colonialist identities. As a black Briton, Jody can fit among the colonized, but the new, would-be postcolonial Britain invites him to join the colonizers by enlisting in the army. By joining the colonizers, Jody sacrifices his chance to join his potential peers and allies among the colonized Irish. The power of the colonializing metropole offers an attraction too strong for Jody to resist. Meanwhile, his potential allies among the colonized Irish are not so welcoming. Except for Fergus, when the Irish Republican Army fighters look at Jody they see only his collaboration with the colonizers. From their perspective, he is just like the other colonizers or, in a sense, worse. For by joining the colonizers' army he has consented to their rule. He has, in effect, colonized himself.

Or so it might seem. For when Jody points Fergus to Dil, another black Briton, he upsets the equation. Just as he breaks a racialized taboo in following the Irish white woman, allowing a heterosexual interlude to deflect Fergus from recognizing that Jody might also desire a man, so Jody breaks several taboos in directing the white, Irish, and ostensibly heterosexual Fergus to Dil: taboos of nationality, of race, and of gender. Each forbidden connection intensifies its parallel forbidden connections.

In these ways, *The Crying Game* trades on Fergus's heterosexual desire and queers it, or reveals it as always already queered. It asks whether a queer desire drives Fergus's heterosexual pursuit of Jody's girlfriend Dil, who too conveniently performs the ostensibly heterosexual stereotype of the showgirl chanteuse. Queer studies often proceeds by taking ostensibly heterosexual practices and unveiling a queerness within them, making *queer* into a verb. When Fergus pursues the girlfriend of another man, in a sense he also pursues the other man. He tries out the position of erotic relations, mediated or once-removed, with the other man, and all the more so when Dil turns out to be more like Jody than Fergus anticipated. As Fergus found himself unexpectedly facing and touching Jody's penis when Jody was a tied-up hostage and Fergus agreed to help him urinate, so he again unexpectedly faces (and almost touches) Dil's. Similarly, even among heterosexuals the familiar pattern of competition between people or literary characters for the same man or woman can end up expressing desire not only for the person they compete for but also, potentially, for their rival, as they bond with their comrade in the chase.

More generally, once we think of gender as performance, then queer and straight practices do not run along independently of each other. Instead, like the opposite but not really so opposite poles of any binary opposition, they define and depend on each other, and in a sense they actually inhabit each other. Just as Marilyn Monroe or John Wayne, Mae West or Ernest Hemingway, perform heterosexuality so extravagantly that they overperform it, so—like the stereotypical gunslingers and tough-guy detectives of film and fiction—they end up performing a role so conspicuously scripted and iconic that it carries the possibility of flipping into its opposite and spoofing the heterosexual confidence that it supposedly exemplifies. In that sense, overperformance of straightness protests so much that it ends up exposing doubt. Queerness ends up queering straightness.

QUEER STUDIES AND HISTORY

The Oscar Wilde trials. In the spirit of deconstructive queer studies that sees practices and beliefs as changing across time, scholars study queer history. From one approach, the notorious trials of Oscar Wilde in London in 1895 look like a landmark in the public recognition of queerness, particularly for gay men. Wilde, the brilliant playwright, poet, wit, and aesthete (champion of art for art's sake), was convicted of "gross indecency," a euphemism for gay sex. Through the Wilde trials, a gay male subculture came into the wider public eye and consciousness, which many historians see as transforming an awareness of gay acts to an awareness of gay identity and culture.

Foucault. In that vein, in *The History of Sexuality, Volume I* (1976), Michel Foucault (Figure 7.4; pronounced so that it rhymes with *to know*) proposed that the very idea of homosexuality as an identity is a relatively recent invention. While there have always been people who engage in practices that we now associate with queerness, Foucault argued that those practices did not generate or represent an identity until a medicalizing discourse obsessed

Figure 7.4 Michel Foucault (1926–1984).

with repressing sexuality arose in the nineteenth century. Ironically, the zeal to repress sexuality produced a massive discourse of sexuality, including psychoanalysis, that centered identity on sex. In Foucault's thinking, then, acts do not represent or emerge from preexisting homosexual identities. Instead, a pattern of thinking emerged that imposed identity on acts. For Foucault, "the psychological, psychiatric, medical category of homosexuality was constituted . . . less by a type of sexual relations than by a certain quality of sexual sensibility, a certain way of inverting the masculine and the feminine in oneself. Homosexuality appeared as one of the forms of sexuality when it was transposed from the practice of sodomy onto a kind of interior androgyny, a hermaphrodism of the soul. The sodomite had been a temporary aberration; the homosexual was now a species" (Foucault 43). Eventually, then, Foucault argued, the identity came to be taken for granted, as if it came from the acts themselves rather than from ways of thinking about the acts. Before the invention of homosexuality, according to Foucault's controversial thesis, people might engage in same-sex erotic acts, but they would not be homosexual. Beginning with the invention of homosexuality in the nineteenth century, what you did became what you are, whether straight or queer. (For more on Foucault, see Chapter 9.)

Not all historians agree with Foucault. They continue to debate how we should interpret the relation between the long history of queer practices and the history of queer identities. It remains clear, nevertheless, that the interpretation of queer practices has changed across time and space. In ancient Greece, erotic love between men

---

Stonewall

One evening in 1969 in New York's Greenwich Village, the police raided a gay bar, as they had countless times before. But this time, the customers and a gathering crowd at the bar, called the Stonewall Inn (Figure 7.5), fought back. And they fought back successfully, first by hundreds and then by thousands. "Stonewall," as the event came to be known, or sometimes the Stonewall riots or the Stonewall rebellion, inspired queer political organizing and marked a turning point in the development of "gay pride" and the organized, public assertion of queer rights.

Figure 7.5 The Stonewall Inn.

and boys was honored among the aristocracy, including the military and the leaders of culture and government. While scholars continue to sift the evidence and debate the details of ancient Greek pederasty, the Greek example shows how ideas about sexuality vary. It can help remind us that acts considered gay or lesbian in the twenty-first century West do not necessarily look that way in other cultures and times. In many countries, for example, public hand-holding among same-sex heterosexuals is routine. Passionate expression of love between heterosexuals of the same sex was routine in the nineteenth-century United States. In some countries, a man may penetrate another man anally without being thought of as gay or bi. The sexual categories and assumptions of any time and place, including our own, have a history. They are not essences. They have changed over time, and they continue to change.

Homosexual and heterosexual. The very term *homosexual* did not appear until 1869. In the late nineteenth century, it came into prominence as a diagnosis for what many doctors then considered a sickness. Because of its history as a medical term connoting illness, many people now reject the term, and I do not ordinarily use it in this book. (In an influential series of statements beginning in 1973, the American Psychological Association declared its judgment that "homosexuality" is not a disorder or illness.) The relative newness of the term, historically, corroborates the idea that queerness as a distinct identity, or an identity in something like its current or recent form, did not emerge until well into the nineteenth century. At least it corroborates the idea that during that time gay and lesbian identities went through dramatic changes, whether in themselves or in the public awareness of them or both. The word *heterosexuality* did not appear until 1880, suggesting that our concept of heterosexuality is not an essence, but instead, as structuralists might say, part of a binary opposition that makes the concept of heterosexuality depend on the concept of "homosexuality," and perhaps vice versa. From a poststructuralist perspective, however, or in the eyes of many historians and cultural critics, from a historicist perspective, that binary opposition—though often supposed stable—varies so widely across times, places, and groups of people and individuals that it looks dramatically unstable.

The lesbian continuum. In 1980, Adrienne Rich proposed a way to describe that instability for women. She suggested that there is a *lesbian continuum*, "a range—through each woman's life and throughout history—of woman-identified experience," that fits somewhere on a lesbian continuum, regardless of whether "a woman has had or consciously desired genital sexual experience with another woman" (648). Rich's proposal attracted considerable interest, partly because, by naturalizing lesbianism and seeing it as routine, ordinary, and pervasive, it turns the tables on the naturalization of heterosexuality, and partly because some feminist and lesbian critics find it oversimplifying. They fear that it desexualizes lesbianism or mutes its specificity. The concept of a continuum can reestablish its opposite poles, leaving a subtler form of the old binary opposition between straight women and lesbian women. It might also invite others to propose a heterosexual continuum, the same continuum as it appears from the other side of the binary. Regardless, in the 1970s and 1980s especially, Rich's notion and the ideas of other lesbian feminists helped turn feminism and gender studies away from naturalizing heterosexuality, so that lesbian studies influenced feminism even as feminism and gender studies influenced lesbian and queer studies.

Universalizing views and minoritizing views. Rich's concept of a lesbian continuum has what the literary critic and queer studies scholar

Eve Kosofsky Sedgwick called a universalizing implication. That is, it can apply to all women. Queer studies scholars often ponder how queer studies and queerness itself might apply to all people as well as, more specifically, to queer people. For example, Foucault's discussion of a homosexual identity can represent what Sedgwick calls a minoritizing view. It identifies queer or homosexual people as a minority. By contrast, Freud's view that everyone begins in polymorphous perversity, with a capacity for sexual desire that points in any direction, presents another universalizing view. It sees all people as potentially desiring women and men. At various points, according to the needs of the moment, the same people might adopt either a minoritizing or a universalizing view.

Either view can be and often is used to defend or attack queer desire. From the minoritizing view, queer people might look like a minority that deserves respect—or, to some people, like one that deserves rejection. From the universalizing view, queer people might be anyone, and so deserve respect—or, to some people, they might be anyone, and so all people need to look at others, and at themselves, with suspicion. Under policies that discriminate against queer people in housing or employment, for example, queer people are a minority with a distinct identity. Whether they participate in same-sex erotic acts or not, they can be denied an apartment or a job in the military (sometimes) or in the classroom because of their orientation.

By contrast, under laws that make certain sexual acts, such as so-called sodomy, illegal, the act is the crime, not the identity. Such laws have a universalizing dimension, because any people who commit the act might be criminalized, regardless of how they understand their identity. To notice that distinction, however, is to observe, deconstructively, a Foucauldian distance between acts and identity. It means that acts are not a reliable signifier of a signified identity. That is, some people who identify as heterosexual are not sexually active or engage in (or have engaged in) same-sex erotic acts, while some people who identify as queer, gay, or lesbian are not sexually active or engage in (or have engaged in) opposite-sex erotic acts. To queer the distance between acts and identity is to throw into question the rigid binary oppositions often set up to divide straight from queer or straight from lesbian, gay, trans, or bi.

Meanwhile, within queer studies—or some would say outside it—there has often been tension between lesbian and gay studies. Many scholars see it as the productive tension of an alliance, while others resent the potential for gay studies or lesbian studies to overshadow the other or to overshadow or be overshadowed by queer studies. In a still patriarchal culture, some critics see gay studies as especially at risk of overshadowing lesbian studies. At their best, an alertness to each of these possibilities helps keep scholars—and gay, lesbian, and queer people more generally—more attentive to the consequences and nuances of their practices and assumptions. Meanwhile, more recently, these potentially productive tensions have also sometimes found themselves mirrored in similar suspicions and provocation between, on the one hand, lesbian, gay, or queer studies and, on the other hand, transgender studies, an emerging area of interest and scholarship that overlaps with each of these other categories while still laying claim to its distinctiveness.

OUTING: WRITERS, CHARACTERS, AND THE LITERARY CLOSET

In the classroom, the hardest idea for me to get across about queer studies is that queer studies, and especially queer literary criticism, is—as I like to put it—not about **outing.** Outing is the controversial process of publicly exposing people for living in the **closet,** that is, for keeping their queer desires private rather than public. To many people's thinking, outing is a terrible violation of privacy.

Amid continuing controversy, a modicum of consensus has developed that suggests that outing is abusive—except when it comes to outing people who abuse their position in the closet by advocating homophobic public policy. For example, queer activists threatened to out closeted politicians who voted against the interests of queer people.

The controversy is vexed because the very concepts of the closet and of outing presuppose a homophobic cultural setting. If the cultural environment were not homophobic, then no one would want to hide in the closet, and it would make no difference whether someone were outed or not. But in a homophobic setting, those who look on outing with suspicion fear that it may hurt people, or that people at least fear that they could be hurt by being outed, by coming out of the closet, and they believe (as I do) that it is no one's right to make that decision for someone else. Nevertheless, staying in the closet can help perpetuate a homophobic cultural environment by helping to sustain a public perception that there is something wrong with being queer. By coming out of the closet—or never going into the closet in the first place—people can help make queerness visible as something ordinary.

When journalists say—as they often do—that someone in the public eye is "openly" or, even worse, "admittedly" lesbian, transgender, gay, or queer, they slam the closet door in the guise of sliding it open. They spotlight queerness as if it were something to be ashamed of. Similarly, the US military tried to paint queerness as shameful through the recently repealed policy of "Don't ask, don't tell." Such practices help make the environment that leads, for example, to the epidemic of queer teen suicides. Policies like "Don't ask, don't tell" are a form of queer-bashing, however unwitting. In the process, such language also fetishizes the status of in versus out of the closet, making the process of fingering someone's sexual "preference" (as if it were a consumer choice) the binary be-all and end-all of much of the broader public's dialogue about queerness. In that binary obsession, people can get reduced to "they are" or "they are not" queer, as if it were always that simple and as if the on-off switch on that overly simple binary opposition defined everything that matters about someone. You never see a journalist describing someone as openly— let alone admittedly—heterosexual. For example, when an American president—George W. Bush—called for a ban on same-sex marriage, news reports did not describe him as openly heterosexual, implying that he bore some undue bias because of his own history. But when queer politicians and activists speak out on the same issue (and on many other issues), news reports routinely introduce them with the "openly" or "admittedly" tag.

Besides making for shoddy journalism, such a practice encourages a crudely oversimplified notion of queer literary and cultural criticism. It leads students—and many critics—to suppose that queer criticism is about pointing out that particular writers are or were lesbian or gay or that certain characters are lesbian or gay. I call that a form of outing. But the goal of queer criticism is not to out writers or characters. A focus on outing—even without using the term *outing*—can sometimes go against the ideas and goals of queer studies. For one thing, to out writers or characters or to allow outing to seem like the organizing motive of queer criticism reinforces, rather than undermines, the binary opposition between queer and straight, because it suggests that we can divide everyone into two categories: They are queer or they are not queer. Usually (depending how we do it), to out writers or characters by announcing that certain writers or characters are lesbian or gay can invite the assumption that all the rest are straight, as if everyone were straight unless otherwise noted. It also risks reducing queer writers or characters to their sexuality, in a way that we do not typically do for straight writers or characters. And it suggests a transhistorical essence for such categories as *lesbian* and *gay*, as if those terms applied in the same way to all times and all people and as if all queer people fit perfectly within those terms and understood exactly how they fit in them. To call Shakespeare gay— or to say that he was not gay—supposes that three hundred years before the Wilde trials or almost four hundred years before Stonewall, Shakespeare's way of understanding his identity and sexuality would fit snugly into the assumptions and practices of a later age.

To be sure, in many ways they might fit the assumptions of a later age, and historians debate what has stayed the same in queer and straight life and what has changed. Increasingly, for example, critics argue over whether we can determine Shakespeare's sexual orientation or at least the sexual orientation of the speaker in his sonnets, who passionately addresses most of his love sonnets to a man, while sometimes writing of his love for a woman and sometimes of his love for both the man and the woman. For some critics, it seems presumptuous to apply our own categories of "sexual orientation" to so different an age. To others, the gay or bisexual stance of the sonnets seems explicit. We can also recognize many characteristics associated with later gay stereotypes in some of Shakespeare's characters, such as Richard II, and in characters of other playwrights from his time, such as Christopher Marlowe's Edward II, a partial model for Shakespeare's Richard II. In that sense, to argue against outing writers and characters risks encouraging a practice that could slide into denying the queerness of writers or characters, which would undermine the goals and practices of queer criticism. But there is a difference between focusing on outing, which can reduce queerness to something that critics point at and finger like an essence logoed on the forehead, and recognizing queerness as an integral, sometimes shaping part of a picture but not necessarily in itself the goal and end-all of literary interpretation. Now and then, these opposed concerns may clash, but that can make for a productive dialogue that helps keep queer criticism queer by keeping it unstable and self-questioning.

HOW TO INTERPRET: OUTING THE CLOSET

Even in the same plot, different attitudes to outing carry different implications about the daily routine of queer life and the role of literature and film in representing and influencing the way people think about queer life. In the movie *Brokeback Mountain*, for example, the plot begins with Ennis and Jack discovering their gay desire and their passion for each other. Part of the fun and part of the implicit humor in the film, and in the story by Annie Proulx that inspired the film, come from the way they flout the cowboy stereotype, that bastion of supposedly confident, heterosexual masculinity. In Jack's first appearance on screen, he tries so hard to show off his masculinity that he ends up parodying it (Figure 7.6). He kicks the fender of his pickup truck, squirms his shoulders, and rocks his hips—as if he had just climbed off a horse—in an intense effort to perform like a stereotypically manly cowboy. But all that gyration makes him look almost as if he is dancing with his truck. His performance is so over-the-top that it suggests a craving to prove something about his masculinity, at least to himself if not also to Ennis, even though Ennis mostly pretends not to look at him. It also suggests a pleasure in masculinity as performance rather than essence, which opens the path to more varieties of performance than Jack is yet ready to act on.

But after Ennis and Jack fall in love, the rest of the movie, like the story, concentrates on their battle with the closet. *Brokeback Mountain* shows why the closet is so powerful, for Ennis knows that coming out of the closet, in the fiercely queer-fearing world where he and Jack live, puts them at risk of getting beaten and murdered, as Ennis's father brutally taught him. Thus, when Jack dies and Ennis plausibly imagines he was beaten to death, the terrible ending seems to corroborate the sorrowful logic of Ennis's caution. (On the motives behind queer-bashing, see the next section of this chapter.) Audiences could walk away from *Brokeback Mountain* supposing that the closet, much

Figure 7.6 Jack straining to show off his pickup-truck masculinity for Ennis and for himself. Jake Gyllenhaal in *Brokeback Mountain.*

as the movie paints it as heartrendingly tragic, looms almost irresistibly as the dominant fact of queer daily life.

By contrast, in Christopher Isherwood's novel *A Single Man* and the film based on it, we see George simply living and loving as a gay man. *A Single Man* is set at the same time that *Brokeback Mountain* begins, and both take place in the American West. But there is a difference between the West of George's Los Angeles and the rural Wyoming and Texas of *Brokeback Mountain*, and there is a difference between the social position of Ennis and Jack, "high school dropout country boys with no prospects, brought up to hard work and privation" (Proulx 254), and George's position as an English professor with a good income and a fashionable house. We do not see George having to discover that he is gay or see him struggle with or feel guilty about his sexuality. We never see him even think about closeting himself. Instead of saving his gay sexuality for supposed "fishing trips," as in *Brokeback Mountain*, he lives happily with his lover. *A Single Man* makes part of its charm come through its depiction of George and Jim's domestic life together, the pleasure they take (in the movie version) simply in sitting together in their house and reading novels. In *Brokeback Mountain*, by contrast, to be queer is by definition to live in crisis.

We might even say that in *Brokeback Mountain* to be queer is to be tragic. In the other film, while being queer still means facing prejudice—George, for example, is not invited to Jim's funeral—such crisis as George faces comes not from being queer but from losing his lover to the random tragedy of a car accident, a tragedy that has nothing to do with George or Jim's sexuality. In these ways, critics can move beyond favoring or opposing outing, however urgent and necessary such choices may be, to think historically, interpreting the ways that different films and works of literature and different regions and social worlds think about living in or out of the closet and the role such choices play in queer lives and in the representation of queer lives.

HOMOSOCIALITY AND HOMOSEXUAL PANIC

The homosocial. The category of the **homosocial** speaks to historical questions about changing notions of sexual practices and identities over time and how those changes influence our understanding of literature, including character and literary plot. The term *homosocial* refers to intense relations between people of the same sex that might not be sexual but that through their intensity can suggest an erotic charge. In an influential 1975 article, "The Female World of Love and Ritual: Relations between Women in Nineteenth-Century America," feminist historian Caroll Smith-Rosenberg describes the intense friendships typical of many ostensibly heterosexual nineteenth-century American women, often expressed in passionate letters and diaries that seem, to later ears, erotic but that bear no direct evidence of sexual relations. Such friendships were routine for many ostensibly heterosexual men as well as women. Some of them must have included sexual contact, but apart from homosocial kissing and hugging, most of them probably did not.

Historians are left to ask what changed to make such once-commonplace friendships unusual or even taboo and what changed to make the passionate language of such friendships, once routine among ostensible heterosexuals, now sound erotic, sound "homosexual," whether lesbian or gay, rather than homosocial. By themselves, the Wilde trials cannot explain the change, but they can signify a shift in people's sense of possibility, a shift that the Wilde trials grew out of, catalyzed, and made visible. In some ways, visibility and public awareness make things better by showing both the queer and straight public the ordinariness of queer life. But in the face of continuing homophobia and even queer-bashing, visibility and public awareness also pose a threat to lesbians and gays and to anyone else whom a homophobic culture might suppose is lesbian or gay. That threat, in turn, appears to have changed the profile of homosociality, because the same acts and expressions of passionate affection that once could happily coincide with a heterosexual self-identity soon came to look lesbian or gay in a culture that often saw lesbian and gay life as abhorrent.

As a result, homosocial friendships changed, at least in the Anglo-American and western European world. They lost much of their passionate language and openness of touch, but they did not disappear. Indeed, **homophobia** and the continuation of homosociality have much to do with each other. Homophobia refers to a prejudice against and fear of so-called homosexuals. The term takes the heterosexist idea that "homosexuality" is a psychological problem and turns it upside down, lifting the burden of psychological disorder ("phobia") from queer people and putting it instead on those heterosexuals who fear and object to queer people. Where homosociality remains powerful, in such places as sports teams, monasteries, convents, and the military, homophobia is often especially strong (which is not to say that it succeeds in stamping out queer acts or emotions—far from it).

As Eve Kosofsky Sedgwick (Figure 7.7) has argued in *Between Men: English Literature and Male Homosocial Desire* (1985), homosociality also plays a key role in heterosexual relations and heterosexual marriage.

Sedgwick argues that in crucial ways marriage has, historically, been a homosocial institution, much as that might at first seem counterintuitive. Marriage and heterosexual relations, according to Sedgwick, have traditionally been a homosocial exchange **between men.** She draws on the structuralist argument by Claude Lévi-Strauss that cultures structure themselves through the **traffic in women,** also called the **exchange of women.** Working from assumptions that now leap out at us as sexist, Lévi-Strauss proposed that men structure their relations to each other—which he saw as the relations that define culture—by using women. The women cement or figure alliances among men, and they figure masculine status. The feminist anthropologist Gayle Rubin, in a landmark article called "The Traffic in Women: Notes on the 'Political Economy' of Sex" (1975), offered a feminist rereading of Lévi-Strauss's model, arguing that the traffic in women reduces women to objects of exchange between men.

When I first describe the exchange of women to students, they usually look at the idea with skepticism. They think of that as something that other cultures do, not their own culture. They see their

Figure 7.7 Eve Kosofsky Sedgwick (1950–2009).

own culture as envisioning marriage through romance, and traditionally through heterosexuality, not through dowries or arranged
marriages. But students start to get more of a feel for the exchange
of women if we mention the familiar notion of the "trophy wife,"
including Thorstein Veblen's idea that men use women for conspicu-
ous consumption, to show off their success to other men. Still more,
students see the point if we refer to the tradition of the father of the
bride "giving" the bride to the groom, as if a wedding were a deal
between men, as it often is and as, in many parts of the world and at
many points in history, it is explicitly.

Traditionally, classic British novels and dramatic comedies end in
heterosexual marriage, as if heterosexual marriage were the goal and
end of all that matters, especially for women. Sedgwick proposes that
male characters negotiate and use those marriages and the brides to
shape their homosocial relation to other male characters, not simply
to shape a heterosexual relation between husband and wife. In many
a Shakespearean comedy, for example, and not only when the characters finally marry at the end, men use marriage between women
and men to resolve their conflicts with other men.

Men use women to shape men's relations with other men in a
variety of ways across a variety of cultural activities and literature,
from explicit instances, as in Robert Browning's "My Last Duchess"
and Shakespeare's *The Taming of the Shrew, Much Ado about Nothing,*
and *The Tempest,* to surreptitious instances, as in Henry James's *The
Portrait of a Lady,* to many variations in between. In Jane Austen's
Pride and Prejudice, for example, former friends Darcy and Wickham,
now rivals and enemies, use Elizabeth and Lydia Bennet in part to
negotiate their relation to each other. In Nathaniel Hawthorne's *The
Scarlet Letter,* for another example, Roger Chillingworth and Arthur
Dimmesdale use Hester Prynne to negotiate their relation to each
other, without their fully understanding or saying so, so that generations of readers unattuned to the exchange of women or unattuned
to erotic emotions between men often missed that reading. Yet contemporary readers, increasingly attuned to queer possibilities, see it
far more often and more provocatively.

Often, the interest lies in the ways that the traffic in women is not
a done deal but instead gets negotiated, successfully or not, by women
as well as by men. Drawing, therefore, on the discussion of feminist
interest in women's agency in Chapter 6, we might read Shakespeare's
The Merchant of Venice as showing women's reaction against men's
using women to shape relations between men. We could see Portia as

controlled by her father's directions for her marriage, or we could see her as using the song to turn her father's directions to her own purposes and then taking charge through the trial and the rings. Similarly, Desdemona in Shakespeare's *Othello* resists her father's plans for her and thus shows feminist agency, or we could see her resistance as a disaster that ends up reinforcing the value of patriarchal wisdom.

The teasingly half-erotic or almost erotic side of homosociality has made a comeback in the *bromance*, as in such films as *Superbad* and *I Love You, Man*. Bromances have an earlier history in the form of male buddy films, which grew especially popular around the 1970s (*Butch Cassidy and the Sundance Kid, Lethal Weapon*) in reaction, some critics have supposed, to the growth of feminism and women's rights. While the female friendships in *Fried Green Tomatoes, Thelma and Louise, Waiting to Exhale,* and *Wanted* seem partly analogues or responses to the male buddy films, films and novels about women's friendship have yet to achieve the high profile of films and novels about men's friendship. In the contemporary bromance, the hint of gay desire sparks the thrill of risk and the self-protective mockery of satire. At the same time, most buddy movies and bromances, from *Butch Cassidy* and *Lethal Weapon* to *Good Will Hunting, Superbad,* and *I Love You, Man*, protect themselves from the supposed contamination—and the box-office risk—of gay desire by carefully establishing the heterosexuality of their bromancers. In that way, the men's heterosexuality is not so much about their relation to women, as we might have supposed, as about their relation to men.

Homosexual panic. In *Between Men* and later works, Sedgwick also discusses the concept of **homosexual panic,** which develops from her discussions of homosociality. Homosexual panic refers to the fear by straight people or by people of uncertain sexuality that others might think they are lesbian or gay in a homophobic culture. Homosexual panic is a powerful cultural force. It leads, for example, to queer-bashing, whether through harassing acts and language or through physical violence. As heterosexuals in a homophobic culture fear that they are, or might be, or could be thought to be queer they sometimes worry over the queerness or potential queerness they fear in themselves and project it onto others. Then they try to reassure themselves by abusing that queerness as if it were not part of themselves. They want to see it as utterly separate from themselves in a binary opposition. But the binary opposition is so shaky that they must keep propping it up to prevent it from toppling over.

We might see anti-queer legislation as a form of homosexual panic, including laws against equal rights in housing, employment, benefits, hospital visitation, and so on. Those who oppose such rights seek to reassure themselves about their own threatened heterosexual status. From this perspective, the idea that heterosexual marriage must be protected by legislation exposes a fear that it is vulnerable, that heterosexuality cannot stand up by itself but instead needs to hold itself up by putting limits on nonheterosexuality. That can remind us that heterosexuality needs and depends on nonheterosexuality. Without queerness to compare it to, heterosexuality cannot be recognized as heterosexuality.

Homosexual panic is an especially helpful concept to introduce to college students, who will make up many of the readers of this book, because it does a great deal to shape the lives of many adolescents and young adults. In a world where many people conflate femininity and masculinity with the cisgender, binary oppositions of stereotypically heterosexual femininity and masculinity, adolescents, younger adults, and people of other ages as well frequently feel pressed to prove their masculinity, femininity, and heterosexuality, perhaps by acting or dressing a certain way on Friday or Saturday night, by drinking as much as or more than the next person, by putting on the right swagger in the locker room, or maybe by a queer-bashing wisecrack that tries to say: *They* are like that, but *I* am not. Or maybe by staying silent when someone else makes a wisecrack. We see it academically when straight students fear that if they talk about or ask a question about queer studies in the classroom or in a paper, or if they check out queer studies books from the library, or if someone sees them looking at queer books in a bookstore or looking at queer websites or even reading this chapter, then someone might think they are queer.

The term *homosexual panic* is misleading. We might better call it heterosexual panic, since it refers to a panic by (more or less) heterosexuals. Already-out gays and lesbians are immune to homosexual panic, because other people already know they are queer. The new visibility figured in the Wilde trials made homosocial acts look like queer acts in a queer-bashing world, thus intensifying homosexual panic and reshaping the pleasures and anxieties of same-sex friendship. If we think critically about homosexual panic and recognize the ordinariness of queer life and queer desire, then we can help the panicky heterosexual stop worrying about what someone else might think and just decide that *it's ok*.

Daily life, movies, popular culture, and literature are fraught with homosexual panic, with people and characters desperate to prove a stereotypically heterosexual, cis masculinity or femininity or, more

---

"That's So Gay!"

In recent years, the expression "That's so *gay!*," meaning "That's so *stupid!*," spread widely, especially among younger straight people. If asked, they sometimes hurry to say that the expression has nothing to do with gays or queers, that it's just an expression. But what does it express?

Some people also say "That's so *Jewish!*" or "That's so *retarded!*," intending the same meaning: "That's so stupid." People who never imagine that they themselves might join in queer-bashing routinely use these expressions or stay silent when they hear others use them. In much the same way, the expression "No homo," by supposing an exaggerated need to deny queerness, insists that there is something wrong with queerness.

The widespread use of expressions like "That's so *gay!*" and "No homo" can direct us, whatever our sexual orientation and behavior, to think about what role such phrases or the sentiments they express might play in encouraging queer depression and even the tragically high rate of suicide among young queer people. They also encourage homosexual panic. They say that *you* or someone else might be gay, but *I* am not, so don't worry about me—worry about yourself. In those ways, ironically, expressions like "That's so *gay!*" and "No homo" worry very much.

---

subtly, so self-conscious about the desperation to prove it that their desperation also provokes curiosity about what they fear. The desire to prove people's heterosexuality seems especially intense after the shift represented by the Wilde trials. It is intensely visible, for example, in Ernest Hemingway's fiction, where characters (both female and male) often live in fear of and fascination with queerness and their own femininity and masculinity.

HETERONORMATIVITY, THE ANTI-SOCIAL TURN, AND QUEER TIME

Mainstream queer culture invests in a liberal, progressive commitment to increasing and establishing queer rights, such as the right to marry, to adopt, to work, to serve in political office, and even to buy a cake (as in the famous court case about a baker who refused to design a cake for a same-sex wedding). Michael Warner has critiqued the preoccupation with mainstream rights as an embrace of what he calls *heteronormativity*, as an effort to lull lesbians and gays into the culture of naturalized heterosexuality—so long as lesbians and gays act in the ways that conventional heterosexual culture has celebrated as "normal." From a heteronormative perspective, lesbians and gays are welcome, but only on the condition that they live up to a heteronormative model of married, monogamous couples who keep their sex in their private homes, go to sleep early, raise children, and don't behave too queerly or disruptively, too visibly, fabulously, or flamboyantly. Heterosexuals themselves do not always conform to that model of heteronormative respectability, but many of them still use it to exile queerness. To Warner and many other queer-focused critics and theorists, however, gaining recognition for the right to marry or adopt and gliding smoothly into a model of heteronormative respectability seems less like an achievement and more like an assimilationist threat to queer difference.

One controversial strain of contemporary queer theory, sometimes called the anti-social turn, expands on the rejection of heteronormative respectability. Identified especially with Leo Bersani and Lee Edelman, the anti-social turn critiques the focus on rights as undermining a norm-busting shock and disruption that it sees as definitional of queerness. It even goes so far as to embrace what angry homophobes say about the socially destructive potential of queerness—except to value the destruction instead of rejecting it. Edelman observes how cultural norms gather around investments in futurity, valuing our lives for the ways they serve the future by shaping the present around the children that many queer people choose not to have. In his eyes, we too often fear the unsolvable mysteries of the present. Trying to compensate for a present we cannot understand, we deceive ourselves by chasing after an unreachable future sentimentalized in the figure of the child. Edelman does not oppose rights, but he sees the preoccupation with rights and raising children as threatening an anti-reproductive queer logic that defies reproductive futurity and mainstream respectability.

As you might imagine, responses to the anti-social critique of reproductive futurity range from finding it inspirational, to finding it dangerously apolitical and self-defeating, to arguing that it underestimates the range of possible futures. Regardless, Edelman and other critics, such as Jack Halberstam—including critics who do not necessarily agree on all points—have turned our attention to the relation between queerness and time. In a world where masses of people live or fear living lives radically cut short by AIDS, and by caring for people with AIDS, time took on heightened intensity and urgency. Queer ways of living time can even merge familiar models of queerness with other rejections of convention, queering alternative ways of living outside the reproductive and familial time organized around birth, marriage, reproduction, child-rearing, and the expectation of a long life. A variety of subcultures, whether self-identified as queer or not, live in short, sometimes queering bursts of intensity, organizing their lives around youth, drugs, risk, or experiment, living in the now more than in preparation for the future. In that light, a novel, film, play, story, or poem can consign its plotting and its characters, queer or not, to expectations of long lives or short lives, to socially uplifting or to antisocial and disruptive relations to time and futurity, as when the young, homosocially proud, school-skipping pool players of Gwendolyn Brooks's "We Real Cool" slam the door on time, ending the poem suddenly with the words "We / Die soon," or when Tony Kushner's AIDS-saturated *Angels in America* ends with unexpected reconciliation, healing, and hope for a long future.

QUEER OF COLOR CRITIQUE

A good number of queer studies scholars focus on queer life and culture in specific racialized populations or communities. (On *racialization*, see Chapter 10.) Richard T. Rodríguez, for example, has written about the connections that gay Chicanos make to Chicano/Chicana traditions of *la familia*. Robert Reid-Pharr, for another example, has written about intersections between black queer identities and debates around black politics, queer politics, and academic efforts to ground interpretation in identity or release it from identity. Sharon Holland has written about the daily life of antiblack racism in relation to erotic desire. She questions the way that many critics think about queer sexuality without thinking about race.

José Esteban Muñoz, to take another example, proposed a model he called *disidentification*. He argued that queer-of-color performance art recycles white heterosexual styles and images but changes them, often with a critical, satirical edge. In that way queer-of-color performance makes alternative spaces by disidentifying both with dominant white heterosexual patterns and with clichés of queer and racialized life, disidentifying with stereotypes that might suggest a queer-of-color world utterly separate and different from white hetero norms. In Muñoz's eyes, the imaginative disidentification of queer-of-color art helps build a space of alternative queer agency outside the conventional binary oppositions of assimilation versus separatism and sexuality versus race.

Despite the wide range of patterns across many different Native American peoples, a variety of queer Native traditions and contemporary identities cohere, partly, under what has come to be called two-spirit people. The diversity of Asian, transnational Asian, and—for example—Asian American, British Asian, and Pacific Islands histories challenges generalization across sexualities, classes, languages, political boundaries, and time frames of travel and return across those boundaries. But that diversity also offers the opportunity to study particular traditions, such as the effects of immigration law (which sometimes favored Asian male immigration and suppressed Asian female immigration) on Asian sexuality and on perceptions of Asian sexuality. In their landmark anthology *Q & A: Queer in Asian America,* David L. Eng and Alice Y. Hom can be taken to argue that the multiplicity and ongoing fluidity of Asian formations and Asian American coalitions make the study of Asian American queerness central to an underlying ethos of Asian American studies, even when it challenges a history that has sometimes naturalized Asian heterosexuality. The range of scholarship about queerness and race is growing rapidly, and these examples only hint at emerging avenues of study, including the ways that queer cultural variations and traditions continue to reshape themselves as they engage with each other and with many other dimensions of contemporary culture.

Some queer studies scholars have developed what they call *queer of color critique.* Drawing on the concept of intersectionality that we reviewed in Chapter 6, queer of color critique produces a reading of queerness and race like Kimberlé Crenshaw's reading of the cultural invisibility of women of color. Institutions and dominant cultural habits, whether straight or queer, whether among whites or people of color, often take for granted—or try to take for granted—that queer people are white and that people of color are (or should be) straight. We cannot correct that energetic denial simply by adding the categories of color and queerness, just as Crenshaw argues that we cannot see the distinctive position of black women simply by adding black and female. The intersection of multiple categories shapes the categories in different ways compared to the shapes they are imagined to take on individually. I say *imagined* because no one category defines anyone. But we are trained, culturally, to believe in the definitional power of individual categories of identity. As Crenshaw argues that the belief in the definitional power of individual categories erases black women and women of color more generally, so critics working with queer of color critique argue that the belief in the definitional power of individual categories erases much of queer life in general and especially erases the specific conditions faced by queers of color.

As simple addition cannot make the distinctiveness of queers of color coherent, neither can analogy. The understandable impulse to argue for queer rights through analogy to the more widely (if often superficially) recognized rights of people of color can mask differences and, again, mask the distinctive positions of people who live their daily lives as both queer people and people of color.

Siobhan B. Somerville, Chandan Reddy, and others propose that such arguments by analogy can also serve the liberal state at the cost of potentially more radical queer alternatives. To take one provocative example, when Europeans and Americans advocate for the rights of queer people by analogy with the rights of racial minorities, they center on rights within the Western state as the criterion of value. In that way, according to Reddy, the liberal state recruits queer people to go along with its policies by saying that queers too can join the military or get married. Those liberal reforms leave queers and their allies less likely to complain when the state acts abusively in other areas. From such a perspective of queer critique, as many queer studies critics argue in a variety of contexts, a focus on same-sex marriage as the wedge of advocacy for queer rights risks focusing value on state regulation and approval, reforming the mainstream rather than offering a genuine alternative. Reddy argues that by using its expanding respect for queer rights and the rights of racial minorities, the state brushes up its image as an icon and defender of human rights, and then uses that image to legitimize violence against immigrants and against non-whites internationally. In his reading, the state seeks a monopoly on legitimate violence (meaning legal, supposedly acceptable violence) and uses liberalism toward its queer citizens and citizens of color to help get away with racist violence beyond the state's borders.

Not everyone will accept Reddy's argument. Some critics may want to dissociate the politics of citizens' rights from the politics of immigration and international war. Liberal and conservative critics may see American wars overseas partly as defending rather than merely attacking people of color. In their eyes, Reddy's view of policymaking may seem too conspiratorial. Reading the state as a unified whole, in the same way that a new critic finds unity in a poem, Reddy may underestimate the role of separate responses to different conditions. After all, it is not as if Reddy objects to recognizing the rights of queers and people of color. From his perspective, however, the suppressed connection between supposedly separate patterns of thought is exactly the point. Such arguments go beyond merely adding or analogizing categories of race and sexuality. Instead, they suggest a network of interrelatedness and intersectionality, of conscious and unconscious patterns of thought that propel otherwise hard-to-fathom, unspoken assumptions influencing how people understand individual categories and larger aggregations of race and sexuality.

HOW TO INTERPRET: ANOTHER QUEER STUDIES EXAMPLE

Those new to queer studies sometimes slide into thinking about queer criticism only for texts they think of as explicitly queer. But part of the concept of queer studies, including the idea that heterosexuality and queerness define each other, is the conviction that queerness relates to all texts. Having already looked at explicitly queer-focused works like *The Crying Game* and *Brokeback Mountain*, let us look now at Shakespeare's *A Midsummer Night's Dream*, which might seem exclusively heterosexual. The point is not to out the characters, play, or playwright so much as to ask what insights we can gain by drawing on some of the questions that queer studies asks.

In *A Midsummer Night's Dream*, the opening scene shows men trying to control the fate of women, and that control may seem to draw on men's supposed right to exchange women. But we do not see any actual exchange negotiated, and the patriarchal system remains far from perfect or complete. Egeus wants his daughter, Hermia, to marry Demetrius, but we never learn what Egeus might get in return, so that Egeus's wish never emerges certainly as an attempted exchange. Meanwhile, Hermia and Lysander, her choice for a husband, protest Egeus's arrangement. That puts Egeus and Demetrius on one side, with Lysander on the other side, so that men do not all fit into a general conspiracy of men exchanging women. Nor do they exclude Hermia from the discussion. She gets her say, just as they do. Thus, men's exchange of women lies implicitly on the table, but it is also up for debate. Then Lysander goads Demetrius, and goads the reigning assumptions about sexuality, by saying: "You have her father's love, Demetrius, / Let me have Hermia's; do you marry him" (Shakespeare, *Midsummer Night's Dream* 1.1.93–94).

Lysander's verbal jab protests men's efforts to control women's desire. It also suggests that something might be going on, erotic or otherwise, between Egeus and Demetrius and that they want to use Hermia as the proverbial feminine pawn as they negotiate their relations between themselves, of whatever kind.

Lysander's jab has two additional, contradictory effects. On the one hand, it throws before us an aggressive, homophobic syllogism with something like the following bitter logic: (1) Marriage, love, and sex between men (three different things here implicitly blended together) are obviously ludicrous. (2) You—Demetrius and Egeus— want Hermia to marry Demetrius because of your love for each other, rather than because of any love for Hermia. (3) Therefore, your plan for Hermia to marry Demetrius is obviously ludicrous. The upshot of such logic, apart from its immediate meaning for the fates of these particular characters, is to skip past the initiating assumption that same-sex desire is ludicrous and allow it to linger unchallenged in the background. Caught in the momentum of plot and drama, an audience can get swayed by the logic for the characters, the conclusion in number 3, and allow the broader cultural logic and assumptions in number 1 to hover in place as unnoticed yet active cultural dictates. (That is what Marxists call ideology, as we will see in the next chapter.) Cultural assumptions like that can rumble through an audience's emotions, setting off homosexual panic and punishing people for actual or potential same-sex desires. After the play concludes, an audience's concern for the characters' fate may end or diminish, but the cultural logic underlying the dialogue and plot continues to help regulate the unthinking logic and momentum of daily life, and in this case that logic is homophobic.

On the other hand, when Lysander suggests that Demetrious marry Egeus, and implies that such a marriage is obviously ludicrous, it might not in every respect and to every member of the audience seem as ludicrous as the homophobic logic demands. In that sense, the point is not so much what Lysander's bitter wit may suggest for the other characters as it is the deconstructively unstable multiplicity of Lysander's comment, more for the audience than for the characters. The point is not to out the characters. Demetrius and Egeus, or, if not them, then two other men, could love each other or could feel drawn to each other sexually, and sometimes they negotiate their feelings for each other through the exchange of women. Or they could put aside the exchange of women and negotiate their feelings for each other more directly. Some men, of course, express their feelings for each other more directly, and so do some women. That is to say, even homophobic hints that queerness is ludicrous can turn themselves upside down and expose their own ludicrousness when juxtaposed against the nonludicrous routine of queer life.

Indeed, such questions might lead to more questions, particularly for A *Midsummer Night's Dream*, which soon goes on to experiment with a host of sexual shenanigans: rapidly shifting erotic allegiances, an ostensibly heterosexual couple (Oberon and Titania) fighting over their passion for a lovely changeling boy, and Titania falling head over heels for someone who, by class and species, lies outside her culturally assigned range of appropriate lovers. One kind of sexual transgression can begin to suggest another kind. Once someone opens the door to the instability of sexual alignments, no one can shut it. A work of art, literature, or popular culture, such as A *Midsummer Night's Dream*, can expose, reflect, and help provoke an instability of cultural logics and assumptions about all sorts of things, by all means including queerness.

None of this has much to do with saying that Shakespeare or Egeus or Demetrius is—or is not—gay. Queer criticism is about the cultural logics of queerness and heterocentrism, not about outing or pinpointing the supposed sexual orientation of writers or characters.

QUESTIONS THAT QUEER STUDIES CRITICS ASK

If you wish to think about possibilities for queer criticism, then you can ask yourself what underlying cultural assumptions about queerness seem to be at work in a literary text or in another cultural text, such as a political speech, a law, a court ruling, a movie, a song, a website, a TV show, a tweet or text message, or a painting. You can find those underlying assumptions in references to queerness. Sometimes, you can also find them in references to heterosexuality. Who desires whom, and what suggestions, if any, seem to be at work about who should or should not desire whom, and what are the consequences of those desires? Do characters or plots seem to take anything for granted about the possibilities for who feels attracted to whom? How do they enact their taking-for-granted, and does their taking some things for granted have the effect of silencing, calling attention to, or resisting other possibilities? Is heterosexuality naturalized? Is cisgender identity naturalized? If so, are they comfortably naturalized, or do you see cracks in the effort to naturalize them?

How do characters with queer desires respond to the cultural resistance to queer desire? Can they ignore it? Do they oppose it? Do they internalize and accept it, or find themselves caught between ignoring, opposing, and adopting such attitudes? Do you see any homosexual panic or any encouragement of homosexual panic? Do men conduct their relations with each other by manipulating women? Do women go along?

How do assumptions about lesbian, gay, bisexual, and heterosexual desires compare to each other? Do illicit heterosexual desires receive a different treatment from illicit same-sex desires? Can illicit heterosexual desires in any way serve as a stand-in for illicit same-sex desires? Do characters or the texts themselves take pleasure in or find fear in identity as a performance that may in some ways float free from a sense of identity as an essence? How does the text understand masculinity and femininity, and does it assume connections between patterns of masculinity or femininity and patterns of sexual desire? Do those patterns work, or does something resist them? Are there multiple or competing conventions of masculinity or femininity or competing patterns of feminine or masculine desire? How do the thinking and assumptions about gender and sexual orientation match up, or not, with thinking and assumptions about race or about particular racial groups?

With Marxist, race studies, and feminist critics, queer studies critics can ask how the space of a film, play, novel, poem, or other cultural object gets divided or not divided according to gender and sexual orientation—who is where, and who goes where, and with or without whom? And when do they do it? That is to say, how does time (which sometimes connects to space) get divided or not divided according to sexual orientation (and race, or class, or age)? For example, who chooses or is sent to the night, the office (and what kind of office), the desk, the street, the family, the couple, the sunlight, the stage, the beach, to this web or gaming environment or to that web or gaming environment? Who chooses or is sent to the pub or bar (and what kind), the opera house, the boardroom, the closet, the kitchen, the children's room, the school, the church, mosque, or temple (and which one), the alley, the park, the urban, the rural, the suburban, the sports field or locker room, the negotiation, the legislature, the funeral, the hospital, the sickroom, and so on? Who is allowed and not allowed, who is made to seek, and who chooses to seek or not seek this or that time or place?

When the text ponders questions like these, does it worry over them? Does it tease them or laugh over them? How does a focus on seriousness or laughter or a mix of seriousness with laughter speak to cultural debates and assumptions about queer possibilities and the resistance to them? What variations do you see within these debates and within the work's assumptions or the characters' assumptions about sexual identities and about same-sex and opposite-sex desires?

FURTHER READING

Bersani, Leo. *Homos*. Cambridge, MA: Harvard University Press, 1995.

Butler, Judith. *Bodies That Matter: On the Discursive Limits of "Sex."* New York: Routledge, 1993.

———. *Gender Trouble: Feminism and the Subversion of Identity*. New York: Routledge, 1990.

Castle, Terry. *The Apparitional Lesbian: Female Homosexuality and Modern Culture*. New York: Columbia University Press, 1987.

Dollimore, Jonathan. *Sex, Literature, and Censorship*. Cambridge: Polity Press, 2001.

———. *Sexual Dissidence: Augustine to Wilde, Freud to Foucault*. Oxford: Oxford University Press, 1991.

Duggan, Lisa, and Nan D. Hunter. *Sex Wars: Sexual Dissent and Political Culture*. 2nd ed. New York: Routledge, 2006.

Edelman, Lee. *Homographesis: Essays in Gay Literary and Cultural Theory*. New York: Routledge, 1994.

———. *No Future: Queer Theory and the Death Drive*. Durham, NC: Duke University Press, 2004.

Eng, David, and Alice Y. Hom, eds. *Q & A: Queer in Asian America*. Philadelphia: Temple University Press, 1998.

Faderman, Lillian. *Surpassing the Love of Men: Romantic Friendship and Love between Women from the Renaissance to the Present*. New York: William Morrow, 1981.

Ferguson, Roderick A. *Aberrations in Black: Toward a Queer of Color Critique*. Minneapolis: University of Minnesota Press, 2004.

Foucault, Michel. *The History of Sexuality, Volume One: The Will to Knowledge*. 1976. Trans. Robert Hurley. New York: Pantheon Books, 1978.

Freeman, Elizabeth. *Time Binds: Queer Temporalities, Queer Histories*. Durham, NC: Duke University Press, 2010.

Halberstam, Judith [Jack]. *Female Masculinity*. Durham, NC: Duke University Press, 1998.

———. *In a Queer Time and Place: Transgender Bodies, Subcultural Lives*. New York: New York University Press, 2005.

———. *The Queer Art of Failure*. Durham, NC: Duke University Press, 2011.

Halberstam, J. Jack. *Gaga Feminism: Sex, Gender, and the End of Normal*. Boston: Beacon Press, 2012.

Johnson, E. Patrick, and Mae G. Henderson, eds. *Black Queer Studies: A Critical Anthology*. Durham, NC: Duke University Press, 2005.

Martin, Robert K. *The Homosexual Tradition in American Poetry*. 2nd ed. Iowa City: University of Iowa Press, 1998.

McRuer, Robert. *Crip Theory: Cultural Signs of Queerness and Disability*. New York: New York University Press, 2004.

Muñoz, José Esteban. *Disidentifications: Queers of Color and the Performance of Politics*. Minneapolis: University of Minnesota Press, 1999.

Reddy, Chandan. *Freedom with Violence: Race, Sexuality, and the US State*. Durham, NC: Duke University Press, 2011.

Reid-Pharr, Robert. *Black Gay Man*. New York: New York University Press, 2001.

Rich, Adrienne. *Blood, Bread, and Poetry: Selected Prose, 1979–1985*. New York: Norton, 1986.

———. *On Lies, Secrets, and Silence: Selected Prose, 1956–1978*. New York: Norton, 1979.

Rodríguez, Richard T. *Next of Kin: The Family in Chicano/a Cultural Politics*. Durham, NC: Duke University Press, 2009.

Rubin, Gayle. "The Traffic in Women: Notes on the 'Political Economy' of Sex." In *Toward an Anthropology of Women*. Ed. Rayna R. Reiter. New York: Monthly Review Press, 1975: 157–210.

Sedgwick, Eve Kosofsky. *Between Men: English Literature and Male Homosocial Desire*. New York: Columbia University Press, 1985.

———. *Epistemology of the Closet*. Berkeley: University of California Press, 1990.

———. *Tendencies*. Durham, NC: Duke University Press, 1993.

Sinfield, Alan. *Cultural Politics—Queer Reading*. 2nd ed. London: Routledge, 2005.

———. *Gay and After*. London: Serpent's Tail, 1998.

———. *On Sexuality and Power*. New York: Columbia University Press, 2005.

Sinfield, Alan. *The Wilde Century: Effeminacy, Oscar Wilde, and the Queer Moment*. London: Cassell, 1994.

Smith-Rosenberg, Carroll. "The Female World of Love and Ritual: Relations between Women in Nineteenth-Century America." In *Disorderly Conduct: Visions of Gender in Victorian America*. New York: Knopf, 1985: 53–76.

Stockton, Kathryn Bond. *The Queer Child, or, Growing Sideways in the Twentieth Century*. Durham, NC: Duke University Press, 2009.

Stryker, Susan, ed. *The Transgender Studies Reader*. New York: Routledge, 2006.

Warner, Michael. *The Trouble with Normal: Sex, Politics, and the Ethics of Queer Life*. New York: Free Press, 1993.

❊ 8 ❊

Marxism

You might wonder why we would care about Marxism today. Didn't it die when the Berlin Wall fell in 1989? That is what many Americans believe. Actually, well over one out of five people still live in Communist countries, most of them in the People's Republic of China but many of them in Vietnam, North Korea, Laos, and Cuba, and Communist parties or their descendants are active in many other countries. But while contemporary Communism varies widely, contemporary Marxist criticism has little to do with Communism. Many Marxist critics believe that the Soviet, Maoist, and other Communist ruling parties since the Russian Revolution of 1917 hijacked the socialist ideals of Marxism and merged them with totalitarianism, often leading to *state capitalism*, which concentrates power in the hands of party and national leaders, as it was once concentrated in the hands of capitalists. Marxist critics often see contemporary Communists as blending state capitalism with corruption and, especially in China, with plain old capitalism. For these reasons, this chapter on Marxism has little to do with Communism.

In the mid-nineteenth century, Karl Marx (Figure 8.1) and his colleague Friedrich Engels developed the ideas that came to be called Marxism. Without attempting to give a full account of Marxism, this chapter introduces the elements of Marxism—and especially contemporary Marxism—that matter most to current literary and cultural criticism.

KEY CONCEPTS IN MARXISM

For Marx, human history begins with the desire for food and shelter. Marx took a **materialist** perspective, as opposed to the idealist perspective of traditional European philosophy from Plato to Hegel. That is to say, he understood the world as made up of natural, physical things, including food and shelter, rather than idealistic or spiritual abstractions like beauty, truth, and the supernatural. He believed that life shapes consciousness, as opposed to consciousness shaping life. "It is not the consciousness of men that determines their existence," he wrote, "but, on the contrary, their social existence determines their consciousness" (Marx, *Contribution* 11–12). Thus, he saw the material, economic world as a **base** and the rest of the world as a **superstructure** produced by that base. Marx's notion that economics is the cause of everything else is called **economic determinism** or **economism.**

As people joined together to produce food, shelter, and clothing, they assigned different work to different people, which began what Marx called the *division of labor*, which in turn led to different classes with competing interests. When agriculture grew enough to make surplus crops, that led to trade, until gradually capitalism replaced feudalism. The new class of capitalist merchants, the **bourgeoisie,** exploited the class of workers, the **proletariat.** For Marx, this process culminated in his own time, at the height of the industrial revolution and the growth of factories, with a small number of owners and a large number of workers. He saw the world as divided between a class of people who labor to produce goods and who sell their labor, and a class

Figure 8.1 Karl Marx (1818–1883).

of people who have capital, use their capital to purchase labor through wages, and exploit the labor to accumulate wealth for themselves.

For Marx, **capital** is more than simply money that people exchange for goods or labor. It is money that capitalists use to purchase goods or labor for the purpose of making a profit. Typically, the profit comes from purchasing goods and then selling them again. One hundred dollars, therefore, is not capital unless someone uses it to buy something with the goal of selling it again for more than $100. Hence, *capital* refers to money that is used to make more money, which is used again to make more money and again more, in continuous circulation.

Capitalists see their practices as natural, because capitalists privilege capital over labor, whereas Marx privileged labor over capital. Rather than seeing history as a series of wars and changing ideas, he saw it as an ongoing class struggle between those who labor and those who own. Marxists often use the term **dialectic** to evoke that ongoing struggle. The concept of dialectic has a long history in philosophy, but for Marxists it usually refers to the way that contradictory arguments and economic forces engage with each other (as in dialogue) to produce something else. In particular, Marx supposed, the back and

The Bourgeoisie and the Proletariat

The terms *bourgeoisie* and *proletariat* often confuse readers not familiar with them. I have seen beginners come up with such variations as *bugoisie* (which sounds like an insect) and *proliterate* (which of course would mean something else), so you may want to note the spelling. *Bourgeoisie* is a noun, with *bourgeois* as the adjective, and *proletariat* is a noun, with *proletarian* as the adjective, so we might say that the bourgeoisie usually thinks in bourgeois ways, and the proletariat usually thinks in proletarian ways. The first syllable of *bourgeois* and *bourgeoisie* rhymes with *store*, though some people pronounce it *boo*. Regardless, the term *proletariat* applies only after the massive growth of wage labor that began with the industrial revolution. While the term *bourgeoisie* might sometimes fit the merchant class before the industrial revolution, neither of these terms typically applies to preindustrial conditions, such as Elizabethan England or the world before the Renaissance.

forth of class conflict and contradictory ideologies, which Marxists call *dialectical materialism* or *historical materialism*, would eventually resolve into a socialist future. The proletariat would spontaneously rise up in revolution, overthrow capitalism, and establish a socialist state without class divisions or private property.

Marx did not anticipate the ways that capitalism would adapt to the clamor for socialist change. Through a variety of reforms—increased voting rights (by class, gender, and race), unions, laws against child labor, a limited work week, income taxes, unemployment compensation, welfare, pensions and social security, publicly funded or supported healthcare, and so on—capitalism adapted. In the eyes of people more or less like today's Democrats in the United States or social democrats in Europe, such reforms make almost as much progress as we can reasonably hope for, though they require continuous effort to preserve them and to adapt them to changing conditions. To conservatives, such reforms often go overboard and threaten to convert capitalism into socialism, while to democratic socialists (who have a higher profile in Europe than in the United States), the reforms seem like mere reforms that do not go far enough. Regardless, no one any longer expects the proletariat to lead a spontaneous revolution and create a classless, propertyless state. Instead, contemporary socialism favors democratic change.

And contemporary Marxist criticism is often less about provoking social change than about using Marxist ideas to interpret culture. Some critics lament that contemporary Marxist criticism is not enough about social change. Indeed, most of the ideas we will review from Marxist criticism could also work for a right-wing or a liberal critic as well as for a Marxist critic. The difference between a Marxist critic and another critic who draws on Marxist ideas is simply that the Marxist critic keeps in mind the ultimate purpose of revolution or at least of dramatic, socialist-directed change.

Alienation and commodification. Under the division of labor in industrial capitalism, Marx argued, much as his contemporary Henry David Thoreau argued in *Walden*, workers are subjected to the **alienation of labor.** In earlier times, people made their own clothes. Even people producing goods for the market, such as farmers, blacksmiths, and shoemakers, saw the process through from beginning to end and could see and take pride in the completed product without feeling alienated from their own labor. Factory workers, by contrast, work on only one small part of a product and may never see the finished product, let alone use it themselves. Today, we do not make our own Nikes or Levis, build our houses or apartments, plant and harvest our pizzas or cheeseburgers or sodas, or design and assemble our tablets, apps, and smart phones. Instead, hundreds of thousands of people from around the globe play a role in making those products, and therefore, like us, they feel alienated from their labor.

In precapitalist times, workers used the objects they produced, and so those objects had what Marx called **use value.** In the age of alienated labor, workers produce objects for sale on the market, and so those objects, which Marx called **commodities,** have what he called **exchange value.** Exchange value in the widely dispersed and often-distant market seems more abstract than use value, and so laboring for exchange value redoubles the alienation of labor. Meanwhile, Marx argued, exchange value takes on a power of its own, for commodities provoke a desire for yet more commodities, leading to what Marx called a **commodity fetish.**

If Marx in the middle of the nineteenth century saw a world mesmerized by commodity fetishism, surely that concern has magnified many times by the twenty-first century. Many critics, from the conservative new critics to contemporary Marxists, have wondered about the role of art and literature as commodities as well as about the role of art and literature in competition with other commodities. Some commodities achieve exchange value not so much because of their use for those who purchase them as because of the status they

---

Buying, Selling, and Commodities

Newcomers to Marxist theory often suppose that any valued object is a commodity. But for an object to be a commodity, it has to be bought and sold. The seashell or rock that you find on the beach or in the woods and treasure for its shape and colors is not a commodity—unless you market it and sell it. A mountain is not a commodity—unless someone sells it, perhaps to a rancher or a mining company, or charges admission for others to look at it or hike on it. The water in a lake is not a commodity when we stare at the waves—but we turn it into a commodity when we pay to pipe it to businesses and homes. An object with use value is not a commodity, therefore, unless it also has exchange value.

represent. Your cool shoes, for example, may have no more immediately practical value than my uncool shoes and may even have less; but if they are the latest thing, then they signify status and bring you what Marx called **sign exchange value.** For most practical purposes, your Rolex may not work any better than my Timex (especially after someone steals the Rolex). But because you have the sign exchange value of a Rolex and I do not, people will think that you are special and that I am . . . an English professor.

The growth of a commodity economy and a commodity culture takes us steadily further from practical, unalienated labor and use value, leading people to value each other mainly as producers and purchasers of commodities. Eventually, in a process that Marx called **commodification,** people themselves are commodified, valued not as people but instead as numbers, statistics, and cogs in an abstract economic machine.

LUKÁCS, GRAMSCI, AND MARXIST INTERPRETATIONS OF CULTURE

Early Marxism and literature. For many years, Marxist criticism made little difference for most literary critics. It tended to paint with a broad brush, identifying a writer with the writer's class and seeing the literature as reflecting the writer's class interests. To most critics, especially those not so sympathetic to Marxism in the first place, that felt clunky and oversimplified. In the 1930s, with the growth of Communism, the Great Depression, and the rise of the left internationally, Soviet leaders and many of their followers in other countries called for *socialist realism*, literature that explicitly endorsed a romantic, idealized vision of the common people and a Communist vision of their future. To many artists, writers, and critics, that kind of prescriptive criticism, criticism that tells writers (prescribes for them) how to write, seemed unreflective intellectually and oblivious to the aesthetics of literature.

In the English-speaking world, in the years before World War II, many left-wing writers called for a proletarian literature and debated what that might mean. At its crudest, it echoed socialist realism, and proletarian literature often continues to be remembered in socialist realist terms. In its subtler modes, it could call instead for art that encouraged people to think critically about capitalist assumptions or to imagine socialist possibilities without necessarily speaking to readers didactically or idealizing the proletariat. Indeed, the proletariat, far from offering a socialist vanguard, often believes in capitalism as fervently as the bourgeoisie. After World War II, as western Europe and the United States turned against the left to pursue the Cold War, and with the rise of new criticism and its attention to the details of literary form, it often seemed to Americans and western Europeans that Marxist criticism cared little for the nuances and particulars of a literary text or for literary art and aesthetics.

Meanwhile, mostly away from Anglo-American eyes, two major Marxist theoreticians, Georg Lukács and Antonio Gramsci (Figure 8.2), pursued work that would later figure largely in the thinking of Marxist literary criticism. Lukács, a Hungarian philosopher, literary critic, and politician entangled in sometimes-brutal Communist party politics, served as People's Commissar for Education and Culture in the Hungarian Soviet Republic of 1919, the world's second Communist government, which lasted only four months, and as Minister of Culture in the anti-Soviet government of 1956, which lasted less than two weeks before the Soviet tanks rolled in.

Unlike the new critics, who during the same years celebrated innovative literary form without taking much interest in social meaning, Lukács, as a Marxist, gave special attention to the social meaning of literary form. Lukács expanded on Marx's notion of **reification** (from *res*, Latin for "thing"). Sometimes called *thingification*, reification refers to the way that commodification reduces social relations, ideas, and even people to things, thus intensifying alienation. Things take on their own momentum, independent of human life, evoking the bewildering fragmentation of alienated, capitalist modernity. Amidst commodity fetishism, things take over human life as consumers lose touch with the actual labor of the proletariat that global corporations "outsource" to a distant, unseen elsewhere. In contemporary terms, we might see reification when people merge with their phones to the point that they shut out the world around them.

Controversially, Lukács decried modernist fiction, such as the novels of James Joyce, Franz Kafka, Robert Musil, William Faulkner, and Samuel Beckett, because he believed that in such novels as *Ulysses* and *The Sound and the Fury* the fragmentation of modernist form decadently and uncritically reproduced the alienated reification of modern life. He saw the modernists as writing for form and technique rather than for social representation, and he saw their form, as in modernist stream of consciousness, as swept up in merely individualist virtuosity. By contrast, he championed what he saw as realist novels, including the fiction of Sir Walter Scott, Stendahl, Honoré de Balzac, Leo Tolstoy, and Thomas Mann. He believed that realism, though produced by bourgeois writers, represented not modernist fragmentation, but rather the totality of society, including history and dialectical class conflict, which can lead readers beyond reification to revolutionary class consciousness. The dialectics of realist fiction, readers might infer, seem more convincing than the triumphant proletarianism of socialist realism, which replaced boy-meets-girl with boy-and-girl-meet-tractor to make the working class live happily ever after. But especially in the 1930s, when Lukács was beholden to the sometimes-brutal Communist advocates of socialist realism, he could not put the case so bluntly.

Gramsci. Gramsci was a leader of the Italian Communist Party. Imprisoned by the Italian Fascist dictator Benito Mussolini, Gramsci wrote most of his influential works in prison, sometimes in secret, and under censorship that forced him to couch many of his ideas in an indirect, fragmented way that readers must struggle to decipher. Gramsci's prison notebooks, smuggled off to Moscow and published long after his death, have held great interest for contemporary Marxists, especially because he criticized the classical Marxist notion of economic determinism. He distinguished between what he called the *state* (government and politics) and *civil society* (culture), and he concentrated his writings on civil society, which makes his writings appeal to cultural critics who want to explain things in cultural terms rather than explaining everything by economics.

Writing in Fascist Italy in a Fascist prison, Gramsci wanted to understand how the right had risen to such dominance. He wanted to understand why the proletariat had not revolted, as Marx predicted it would. Yet more, he wanted to understand why the masses, for the most part, not only held back from revolution but actually supported the far right, against what Gramsci saw as their own interests. This question has remained central for Marxist thought, because Marxists need to understand why the masses do not overthrow capitalism to set up the socialist system that, according to Marxists, would make the world a far better place for the masses.

Gramsci reasoned that the right maintained its **hegemony,** its dominating cultural influence and power, not so much by violence or **coercion,** as we might expect, as by leadership that won the seemingly spontaneous **consent** of the masses. The government can step in with coercion if necessary, through the police and the army. But according to Gramsci, the more effective way to sustain hegemony comes through cultural leadership. The bourgeois capitalists' cultural prestige makes their way of thinking seem like common sense to the

Figure 8.2 Antonio Gramsci (1891–1937).

masses, and so the masses come to identify with bourgeois ways of thinking, leading them to consent to bourgeois dominance.

For example, we might think of the seemingly irresistible drive to consumerism. We could argue that instead of choosing to buy and consume, people have the drive to buy and consume imposed on them, culturally. The menu of "consumer choices" is chosen for us. But the feeling of a menu deceives people into thinking that they consent, that they have choice and are only doing what they individually want, even when they buy a mass-produced product that they have been made to want via marketing and peer pressure. The marketing and peer pressure create a demand that was not there before, even when the products pollute the environment and come from factories that help prop up antidemocratic, misogynist, repressive, corrupt governments. When I buy a pair of shoes (let alone the many pairs that so many of us buy, because the menu of consumer choices makes us feel a need to buy again and again), I do not usually think I am choosing to support a system that starves women and keeps them from voting while corrupt oligarchs live in luxury. I think I am choosing some cool shoes. But perhaps I have been swayed into letting the delusion of consumer choice keep me from realizing that I am acting against the interests of working-class people around the world, people who under a different system could be my allies.

We might change bourgeois cultural dominance, Gramsci argued, not by a spontaneous proletarian revolution, which no longer seemed

likely, but instead by changing people's cultural assumptions, a grad-
ual process of making alliances with other groups to form a "historic
bloc" that can eventually achieve its own hegemony. At the helm of
that process of cultural change Gramsci saw what he called **organic
intellectuals,** not the traditional intellectuals who think they are different from and better than other people, but instead leaders who
arise from within the people and can use civil society—education and
the media—to express the people's ideas that the people might not be
ready to express for themselves. With his focus on process and cultural
change, therefore, Gramsci moved away from the classical Marxist
sense of inevitable revolution and to a sense of *praxis* (practice), a
sense that the future will come through the doing of it, through alliances and contingencies, rather than through absolute and abstract
theoretical laws. In this way, his thinking has appealed to Marxists
influenced by structuralism, who see everything through its relation
to something else, as well as to Marxists influenced by deconstruction, who see culture as a continuous shifting of multiple forces.

The Frankfurt School. In the middle decades of the twentieth century, a group of Marxist philosophers pursued what they called *critical
theory* (in a narrower sense of that term, versus the broader sense of
critical theory that is the overall topic of this book). Associated with
the University of Frankfurt am Main, in Germany, they came to be
known as the Frankfurt School. Led by Max Horkheimer, Theodor
W. Adorno, Herbert Marcuse, and, in the next generation, Jürgen
Habermas, they sought to reinterpret the relation among reason, art,
modernism, and public debate. Without the proletariat leading a revolution, as Marx predicted it would, the Frankfurt School sought to understand how capitalist ideology deters revolutionary consciousness.
They concentrated their attention, like Gramsci, on the superstructure, on culture rather than on economic determinism. Fleeing to the
United States to escape the Nazis, they later reestablished themselves
in Germany after World War II. While in the United States, they
saw technology and the commodifying, commercial "culture industry" (the entertainment industry—movies, music, the media, sports,
and so on) reproducing capitalist ideology from one generation to the
next, drawing the consuming masses to take capitalist assumptions
for granted. The world of corporate entertainment, they lamented,
turns art into another commodity, encouraging political complacency instead of revolutionary or critical thinking.

Adorno saw the discontinuities of modernist art as a reprieve
from the false promises of Enlightenment rationalism. In the shock

of Nazism and World War II, he reacted against traditional art and beauty as ways of painting over the horror of modernity. Adorno called instead for a modern, avant-garde art that would disrupt traditional complacency, an argument not accepted by those who see art and beauty as relatively independent of the corrupt cultures that sometimes produce them.

Habermas, more appreciative of Enlightenment rationality, sees Enlightenment models of public debate, which he dubbed the **public sphere,** as offering a space between the state and civil society and offering the best alternative to the threatening fragmentation of modernist art and life. He values the role of "communicative reason," as opposed to poststructuralist and postmodernist skepticism. While Habermas sees the corporate mass marketing of politics as displacing the public sphere's rational debate, others have argued that he idealizes the historical public sphere, neglecting the many groups that it excluded, such as (to name only the largest group) women.

Walter Benjamin, who was more loosely associated with the Frankfurt School, seems to have committed suicide while fleeing the Nazis. He took a more sympathetic approach to the relation between modernism and culture. He acknowledged that new technologies pushed away the traditional "aura" of the work of art. For example, he described how oral storytelling gave way to the printing press, and then to movies and radio. But he also saw new technologies as potentially encouraging critical thinking, depending on how we use them. While the Frankfurt School philosophers, especially after arriving in the United States, saw corporate, mass, consumer culture as producing consenting, conforming consumers, Benjamin thought that it could also produce critical consumers. The Frankfurt School thinkers were themselves critical consumers, though we could argue that critical consumers are the exception rather than the rule.

CONTEMPORARY MARXISM, IDEOLOGY, AND AGENCY

Contemporary Marxism. Gradually, many forces converged to form what we might almost call, ironically, a revolution in Marxist criticism, including the disappointment with Communist governments; the growing theoretical challenges from structuralism and deconstruction; a radicalizing professoriate in the wake of the civil rights movement, the war in Vietnam, and the growth of feminism; and the persistence of the British left, which—compared to the American left—has a stronger tradition of leftist critique. Amidst continuing debate and controversy, there gradually arose what came to be called *new Marxism*, *post-Marxism* (the *post* suggests a later Marxism and a dialogue with poststructuralism), or *contemporary Marxism*, which sets itself against the earlier Marxism that it sometimes calls *classical* or, more dismissively, *old* or *vulgar Marxism*.

Contemporary Marxism in this mode looks critically at the base/superstructure model of classical Marxism, sometimes observing that though Marx proposed that model, in some of their writings Marx and Engels also sought more flexible ways of understanding the relation between economics and culture. As we have indicated, in classical Marxism (at least as new Marxists describe it and certainly in the classrooms and officially sanctioned thinking of Communist countries), the base is economics, and everything else—including art, literature, music, politics, and popular culture—is the superstructure. The base is the cause and the superstructure is the effect, the direct reflection of the base. That model can seem clunky, because many people think that attributing so much to one cause, economics, oversimplifies the variety and unpredictability of human behavior, especially for the arts. We typically think of music, literature, and the visual arts as enclaves of imaginative unpredictability too quirky to be explained in any one way. For that reason, as Marxists—often in the tradition of Gramsci—looked more skeptically at economic determinism, their rethinking of Marxism appealed to many literary and cultural critics.

Ideology, and interpellation. In that context, literary and cultural critics turned with special interest to the writings of the French Marxist Louis Althusser (Figure 8.3), especially his contributions to an ongoing discussion about what Marxists call *ideology*. In "Ideology and Ideological State Apparatuses" (1970), Althusser famously defined ideology as "the imaginary relationship of individuals to their real conditions of existence" (162). Althusser used the term *imaginary* in Jacques Lacan's sense of the term, as we introduced it in Chapter 5 on psychoanalysis. According to Althusser, we misrecognize the world around us, like the infant that Lacan describes, who misrecognizes itself as identical to its mirror image. By misrecognizing imaginary conditions as real, we do not see the real conditions. Althusser's phrasing can make sense even to readers unfamiliar with Lacan's special use of the term *imaginary*, if they understand that Althusser saw ideology as an unconscious process.

Confusion arises because, like other Marxists, Althusser did not use the term *ideology* in the usual way we do in English, outside the lingo of Marxist and critical theory. In ordinary English usage, ideology refers to a conscious, deliberately chosen set of political beliefs. In that sense, we ask political candidates to explain their ideology. But for Althusser, **ideology** refers to an *unconscious* set of beliefs and assumptions, our imaginary relation to real conditions, especially to real conditions that may not match what we imagine. In Althusser's sense, therefore, we cannot explain our own ideologies, because they are unconscious. In Althusser's sense of the term *ideology*, we mostly misrecognize the world around us and so we misunderstand what makes us act the ways we act.

For example, if asked why they went to college, many college students, especially the humanities-oriented, culturally and intellectually ambitious students who will often read this book, might say

Figure 8.3 Louis Althusser (1918–1990).

that they go to college to learn, to grow culturally, intellectually, and imaginatively, perhaps even—as the well-worn phrase puts it only half ironically—to discover themselves. From an Althusserian perspective, however, those students are deluding themselves, because the real reason they went to college is, as I will put it in deliberately less inspiring terms, to reproduce the managerial economy.

No one will get excited to hear that. But the truth is, most of the students reading this book will become middle managers. They will be the easily replaceable cogs in the vast machine of the managerial economy that reproduces itself from generation to generation. They will not change things much, at least not on a big scale. They will make small adjustments to help reproduce the system better rather than to change it.

But the kind of people who take the classes where they might read this book are not likely to feel a thrill surging through their veins at the thought that their future is to reproduce the managerial economy. If universities advertised, "Come to our great university and major in English so that you can reproduce the managerial system," potential students—if they survived their dumbfounded perplexity—would immediately turn about-face and go somewhere else. It sounds dull and uninspired. Nevertheless, from the notion of ideology that I am describing here, the dull and uninspired life of small adjustments and middle management is exactly the fate that awaits those students.

That is also why the culture at large, let alone the individual universities, dares not admit that fate to itself or to would-be students. By encouraging students to believe that their fate is to grow and learn and to discover themselves culturally and intellectually, the system baits them into a much duller fate that they would refuse to go along with if they knew its real conditions. Thus students' imaginary, unconscious relation to real conditions tells them that their motives are discovery. But the real conditions that actually drive what they decide to do are the far more impersonal managerial economy's built-in structures of self-replication, which allow it to reproduce itself from generation to generation.

That system needs to remain unconscious and imaginary, because if it were conscious, no one would go along. It recruits its next generation of managers by encouraging them to believe that they act out of individual selfhood, whereas the real conditions are that individual selfhood is a delusion that makes it possible for them to act out of socially (not individually) determined motives that they remain unconscious of, oblivious to. They must remain unconscious of or oblivious to those motives, or they would not go along. English and other humanities majors would become revolutionaries instead of managers, and then the whole system would fall apart. (Or else the former English majors, as failed revolutionaries, would languish in prison.)

Althusser used the term **interpellation,** not the most elegant choice of terms, to describe the engine that keeps the system reproducing itself. Literally, *interpellation* means "calling." Althusser said that the system calls to us, or **hails** us (in the sense of saying "hello!") and we answer. When we answer, we become **subjects** of interpellation, like subjects to a queen or king or subjects to the law. And so we get drawn into ideology more by what Althusser called *ideological state apparatuses* (ISAs), echoing Gramsci's term *civil society*, which include the schools, media, churches, families, unions, and entertainment culture, than by the repressive state apparatuses (RSAs), echoing Gramsci's term the *state*, which include the police, courts, prisons, and military. The ISAs can recruit us into ideology more subtly than the RSAs, making us imagine that we have chosen the actions that real conditions have chosen for us.

Thus when the buzz around a new product makes us wonder which new phone, game, shoes, deodorant, or flavor of ice cream we want, we think it through and then choose this one or that one. We may even think—and the system encourages us to think—that we have a genuine choice and that our choice expresses our individuality. In the process, we have been interpellated or hailed into unconsciously accepting the assumptions underneath the question, accepting our imaginary relation to real conditions. We do not respond by saying, "Wait, I don't need a phone" (or new game, shoes, deodorant, or ice cream). And we do not say that the system that baits us into thinking we need them leads to an economic structure that distributes income and political power unequally and abusively. Instead of expressing our individuality, we let a screen of bogus individuality (a prepackaged set of options) block us from realizing that we are acting more or less like everyone else around us.

In this sense, *interpellation is the process of being passively, unconsciously drawn into dominant social assumptions.* (Note the spelling of *interpellation* so that you do not make the common mistake of confusing it with *interpolation*, a completely different term.) At those rare times when we can step outside interpellation enough to see it, we might say that at the point where the interpellation takes place, such as the point when a flashing neon sign or an ad on Facebook or TV makes us think we need that ice cream or new video game, the ideology *congeals* (one of Althusser's less important but more evocative terms). That is to say, it becomes palpable, like oil (or, as I think of it, like peanut butter or even like slime). A question such as "What would her husband think?" for example, when asked about someone whose sexuality and marital status we do not know, can interpellate us into supposing that she and everyone else is hetero-sexual and wants marriage or should want marriage. In that way, the naturalization of heterosexuality is a form of interpellation, like the naturalization of whiteness, the assumption that people are of course white unless indicated otherwise. Interpellation is the engine that re-produces taken-for-granted (unconscious) cultural assumptions from generation to generation, preventing radical change.

Such is the Marxist and Althusserian theory of ideology, at its grim-mest and most inflexible. But it is not always so completely grim. After all, the students reading this book no doubt vary a great deal. Some of them go to college because, in the world where they grew up, college is just expected. Others come from a world where hardly anyone expects them to go to college, and they have overcome enormous obstacles to graduate from high school, let alone move on to college. Some of them think they can avoid middle management by becoming teachers, but that just makes them part of the machinery that manufactures the raw material of other students into middle management or into more middle management makers (that is, into more teachers). Others, however, will do almost anything they can to avoid working in middle management. Perhaps most of those avoiders will eventually change their minds, as practicalities mount later in their lives, but some of them will hold out. Yet others, meanwhile, consciously go to school specifically in the hope that school will lead to a job in middle management.

In these ways, the picture is intricately diverse. The grim view ex-plains a lot, but it might not explain everything. Few English majors will become revolutionaries, but many of them—including some of the middle managers—will work in politics or social services, whether within their jobs or beyond their jobs, and many of them will vote. None of that seems likely to lead to revolution, but it might sometimes contribute to incremental changes for the better, and, over the years, changes might build on changes. Maybe the system will revise itself only as much as it needs for it to keep reproducing itself, or maybe some of the changes will add up to more than a mere reproducing of the system.

Agency and relative autonomy. You may think that people sus-tain enough individuality, perhaps a little here and a little there, to change the system, but Marxists would probably not put it that way. Instead of looking to individuality as the potential route to **intervention** (the technical word for changing the system or at least for trying to change it) or **agency** (the ability to make things happen), Marxists would probably look to what Althusser called **relative autonomy,** a related but decidedly different term that refers to the superstructure's partial independence from the base. *Relative autonomy* suggests at least a little independence from the clutches of the system, from interpellation, but such independence does not have to come in the form of individualism.

Subjects and Subjectivity

When Althusser uses the term *subject,* readers can get confused because, depending on the context, the terms *subject* and *subjectivity* have different meanings. Let us begin with what we do *not* mean in critical theory by these terms. When we say *subject,* we do not mean it in the sense of topic (as when people ask what topics or subjects interest you). And when we say *subjectivity,* we do not mean it in the sense of bias (as when people say that someone's view is biased or subjective). Those are perfectly acceptable meanings, and sometimes people use them in critical theory. But using the terms that way can cause confusion with the usual and more technical meanings of the terms in critical theory.

In the usual and more technical sense, the term *subject* has two different but related meanings. One meaning we have already seen in our discussion of structuralism. Based on the grammatical model of a sentence, the subject is the agent, the one who does, as opposed to the object, which someone does something to. In that sense of the term, the subject holds a position of relative or potential power, similar to a self or an individual but not the same as a self or an individual. Those who equate subjectivity with selfhood miss the point. The terms *self* and *individual* suggest a romantic individualism, whereas the term *subject* refers to a position, and to a position that can be held by a group as well as an individual, such as when we speak of feminist or Asian American subjectivity. In this sense, we might think of subjectivity as a structuralist, impersonal answer to what, from the perspective of structuralism, can seem like an overly personal and romantic notion of individuality and selfhood.

Althusser, by contrast, uses the term *subject* to refer to having less power, as in being subject to the law or subject to a queen or king, or, for Althusser, subject to a dominant ideology. Althusser's use of the term focuses on how the subject is interpellated and made into a subject by being interpellated. The subject's delusion of selfhood and individuality keeps it from recognizing that it is a subject, not a self or individual.

Thus, in the structuralist sense of the agent or the subject of a sentence, the term *subject* suggests having a degree of control and power, but in the Althusserian sense it suggests thinking you have control and power without realizing that you are mostly being controlled. In both senses it offers an alternative to the romantic and consumerist exaltation of selfhood and individuality.

Given the Marxist interest in thinking socially, not just individually, relative autonomy, agency, and intervention can come from groups, not just from individuals. For example, if you somehow find a way, at least now and then, to think critically and resist interpellation, your ability to resist may remain modest, may be only relative, which makes the term *relative autonomy* far less romantic and less misleading than the term *individuality*. And you may gain that relative autonomy not just because you are, romantically, a unique person (pat yourself on the back), but because you are part of a group of people whose history and partially collective thinking help you learn to think critically. And perhaps that history and collective thinking even interpellate you into what we might think of as a subideology, a way of thinking different from and potentially counter to the dominant ideology. Maybe the group you belong to is an economic group, such as the working class, or a racial group, such as African Americans, or a religious or regional identity, a campus organization, an immigrant, ethnic, or national identity, or a political organization. Whatever the group, and possibly with whatever dash of individuality some people may add to the mix, your relative autonomy, though only relative and not complete, and your exposure to a sub- or counterideology help you to think critically about the dominant ideology, or, as José Estaban Muñoz puts it (see Chapter 7), to disidentify from the dominant ideology. The critical thinking and disidentification can lead to agency and intervention.

Those who do not understand relative autonomy rush to convert it into bourgeois individualism. They end up using the term *relative autonomy* in romanticizing ways that turn it back into the capitalist individuality that the very notion of relative autonomy seeks to undermine, much as those who do not understand the term *subject* use it as if it meant the same thing as *individual* or *self*, which misses the point of the term.

It is easy to say where ideology comes from. It comes from a culture's dominant assumptions, its hegemony. It is harder to say where relative autonomy comes from, but it seems to come from imperfections in the overall system of any ideology. Especially in light of deconstruction, any system seems incomplete, imperfect. Gaps in the dominant system, wrinkles or loose threads in the hegemony, make its imperfections visible, which leaves openings for relative autonomy. It works both ways, however, because relative autonomy also produces gaps, wrinkles, and loose threads in the system. When we pull on a loose thread we sometimes hit a knot, so that not much more comes loose, but sometimes we find ourselves pulling out more and more thread until the system begins to unravel.

We might see the Marxist term **false consciousness** as the opposite of relative autonomy. *False consciousness* refers to a way of thinking that is so interpellated into oppressive ideologies that it leads people to act against their own interest. For example, when you ride a motorcycle, you put yourself at so high a risk of injury or death, especially when you ride without a helmet, that though you think you are acting cool, you might reach that thought out of a false consciousness that keeps you from seeing that riding a motorcycle, and, even more, riding without a helmet, is against your own interest. More provocatively, we might say that when voters support amending the United States Constitution to ban flag burning, their false consciousness makes them think they are acting in a wonderfully patriotic way, but the real conditions are that they undermine their own national polity by trivializing the Constitution and jeopardizing free speech. Or we might say that by advocating lower taxes, my false consciousness leads me to believe that I help myself by reducing my tax burden, whereas the real conditions are that I damage the larger cultural and social world, including my own life in that world, by sabotaging schools, police and fire departments, public transportation, healthcare, libraries, and a host of other public services.

Among Marxists, however, the notion of false consciousness has a bad reputation, because it can seem presumptuous to suppose that we can put ourselves in a superior position that allows us to understand other people's interests better than they understand their interests themselves. In that light, each of the examples listed in the preceding paragraph is loaded and arguable (though I myself stand by them). Other people might respond that by riding a motorcycle instead of driving a car, they use less gasoline and therefore help the broader good by acting more environmentally. Or they could say that banning flag burning keeps Americans from trivializing the Constitution's protection of free speech and so helps uphold genuine debate. Or, from a right-wing perspective, reducing taxes makes governments healthier by encouraging them to cut waste and privatize public services, and it boosts the economy by rerouting private money from taxes into investment. Recognizing, therefore, that people have genuine reasons for disagreement, Marxists often criticize the notion of false consciousness, though they have to assume at least some degree of false consciousness, or else they have no way to explain why people have not made the radical changes that Marxists call for, even though those radical changes, according to Marxists, would work in people's own interest.

This leaves us with relative autonomy, agency, and intervention on one side of a continuum and ideology, interpellation, and false consciousness on the other side (as illustrated on p. 250). We can see critics or cultural commentators who focus more on the relative autonomy, agency, and intervention side of the continuum as more optimistic Marxists and see those who focus more on the ideology, interpellation, and false consciousness side as more pessimistic Marxists. (In the case of Althusser, different readers put him at different positions on the spectrum, sometimes varying according to which of his essays or which parts of the essays they weight the most.)

HOW TO INTERPRET: AN EXAMPLE
FROM POPULAR CULTURE

For an example, let us consider the debates around misogynist hip-hop. The very concept of "misogynist hip-hop" has the potential to rile readers of this book, who include many hip-hop fans. Indeed, several professor readers have expressed fear that this example is too controversial for their students. But the controversy is the point. After all, the debates within the hip-hop world take us to complicated issues with more than two sides to them, for not all hip-hop is alike—far from it—and not all fans of hip-hop agree. Hip-hop listeners have a long history of debates about hip-hop lyrics, and hip-hop scholars such as Tricia Rose sometimes fit those debates into issues like those about Marxist criticism that we are considering here. Thus, instead of lecturing to hip-hop fans, a discussion of the controversy over lyrics can come from within the debates that many hip-hop fans have among themselves.

In *The Hip Hop Wars*, for example, Rose argues that the most popular hip-hop has degraded over the years, centering more and more on what she calls the tragic trinity of gangstas, pimps, and hoes, degrading the people, particularly the African American people, that it supposedly celebrates. She tries to understand who makes the decisions, who is the agent, when someone decides to listen to gangsta, pimp, and ho hip-hop. In the process of asking about agency, Rose considers the cultural setting of hip-hop, including the economic setting, not just the setting of its listeners but also the setting of its producers and, not least, its distributors (the music industry, the radio stations). She sees the site of agency as dispersed across more agents than the individual listeners who think and to some extent are made to think that they make their own decisions when instead they choose from a menu that in many ways others provide for them. Thus, Rose argues that hip-hop does not emerge merely from individual, personal choices by musicians or listeners. Instead, many cultural agents mediate the supposedly direct expression of the music and the lyrics.

We can make Rose's questions concrete by supposing, for example, an imaginary thirteen-year-old girl—let's call her Danielle—who listens to hip-hop and especially likes to listen to misogynist hip-hop. From the more pessimistic way of thinking, Danielle is a victim of false consciousness, interpellated into the commercial ideology of consumerism that leads her to buy and listen to misogynist music and maybe even share it with her girlfriends, helping to interpellate both herself and her friends into ideologically, unconsciously accepted and abusive assumptions about women, blacks, and commercial culture.

From the more optimistic way of thinking, all that might still make sense, but it is not the whole story. Danielle might download misogynist music, and she might listen to that music with her girlfriends, but she might not pay much attention to the lyrics. She might even interpret the lyrics as ironic, as making fun of misogynist ideas (a defense of misogynist hip-hop that I rarely find convincing). Regardless, whether or not she pays much attention to the lyrics, those lyrics might play little role in her imagination compared to other uses she finds for her music. She might listen to the music partly as a signifier of resistance to authority, perhaps in the form of parents, teachers, or her general sense of what people in authority think is right for a thirteen-year-old girl. While such resistance can seem immature, we might be harsh to dismiss it as self-destructive. Instead, we can see it as beginning to include, and as carving a path to, genuine cultural criticism—including agency, intervention, and relative autonomy—as Danielle matures. By sharing her music with friends—listening together, talking about the music in person and through social media, reading rap websites, and swapping fanzines—Danielle may also bond with other girls in ways that allow her to set up a community of girls that helps give her the means to resist or criticize some of the misogyny of daily life, despite the misogyny of the lyrics. Maybe the music even inspires her to experiment with making her own music or writing lyrics, perhaps nonmisogynist lyrics or lyrics that play with misogyny in convincingly ironic or satirical ways.

The interest for a critic lies not so much in pasting on a label of ideology, interpellation, and false consciousness or a label of relative autonomy, agency, and intervention and then calling that the end of the story. Instead, the interest comes in the intricate negotiations across the interlocking possibilities in any particular cultural activity, including poems, movies, video games, novels, plays, clothing styles, music, political campaigns, sports, websites, magazines, and so on. As critics, any of us may tend to lean more toward the optimistic side or more toward the pessimistic side. (I lean more toward the pessimistic side.) Or we may prefer both equally or vary widely from case to case, but the interest usually comes in how we interpret the particulars rather than in imposing a predetermined tendency to pessimistic or optimistic interpretations.

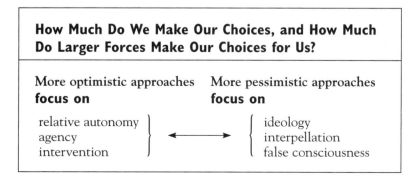

How Much Do We Make Our Choices, and How Much Do Larger Forces Make Our Choices for Us?

More optimistic approaches **focus on**

More pessimistic approaches **focus on**

relative autonomy
agency
intervention

ideology
interpellation
false consciousness

In light of this overview of Marxist and Althusserian notions of ideology and the resistance to ideology, we can return, for another example, to the discussion of Laura Mulvey's "Visual Pleasure and Narrative Cinema" from Chapter 6. When Mulvey interprets classical Hollywood cinema as masculinizing its audience, as unconsciously coaxing its viewers, whether women or men, queer or straight, into an abusive version of masculine heterosexuality, we can now see her as arguing that classical Hollywood film interpellates or hails its audience into a particular sexist ideology. Mulvey then tries to make an intervention, tries to crack the shell of that ideology so that, by exposing it to our conscious scrutiny, we can generate enough relative autonomy to resist its enticements and begin to imagine alternatives. Once we notice the workings of powerful, dominant ideologies and bring them to consciousness, then we have begun to look, at least partly, from outside the ideologies, and looking from outside the ideologies makes it possible to resist them.

VARIATIONS IN MARXIST CRITICISM

Brecht and the alienation effect. Similarly, the German Marxist playwright Bertolt Brecht called for a new style of acting, which he dubbed the **alienation effect,** which would encourage readers *not* to identify with the actresses and actors on the stage or the roles they play. Contrary to the usual Stanislavskian, or "method," acting that asks performers to absorb themselves into their roles and invites audiences to lose themselves in a trance of realism, Brecht asked for staging and acting that calls attention to itself as performance. Let the lights go on, he said (versus the classical Hollywood assumptions of a darkened theater, as described by Mulvey), and let the lights be visible, and let the performers act in ways that expose their role as actresses and actors, so that audiences can have a critical distance that allows them to question ideological assumptions instead of letting interpellation smother their skepticism. We might transfer Brecht's argument about staging into parallel arguments about poetry or fiction that calls attention to itself as performed, constructed writing instead of encouraging audiences to see the literary text as a passive window to or transcript of unquestionable truth and realism.

Relative autonomy, race, and gender. Political change sometimes reinforces contemporary Marxism's rethinking of classical Marxism. In classical Marxism, because the base of economics determines everything else, class, an economic category, was thought to determine race, a cultural category. In the eventual classless state that Marxists predicted, race would disappear. But as antiracist, anticolonial, and postcolonial thinking increasingly led to reflection about the cultural role of race, it grew harder to see race simply as a product of class. While in many countries whites tend to have more economic power than people who are not white, so that race and class may seem parallel, nevertheless people of all races belong to every class. Race is therefore a relatively autonomous determinant of cultural variation, of who we are and what we do. Racism may feed off economic exploitation, but economic exploitation also feeds off racism.

Similarly, so long as Marxists tried to explain everything by economics, they had a difficult time accounting for gender, since people in the same family, and hence in more or less the same economic class, do not all share the same gender. For that reason, classical Marxists often ignored feminism and ignored women's concerns. But as feminism revolutionized cultural criticism, feminists convinced Marxists (and sometimes the Marxists and the feminists are the same people) to see gender, like race, as a relatively autonomous determinant of culture. Much as in the relation between racism and economic determinism, misogyny feeds off economic exploitation, but economic exploitation also feeds off misogyny. In the new Marxism, cultural categories such as gender and race shape our lives in a dialectical relation with economics.

Bourdieu and cultural capital. In tune with the rethinking of economic determinism, the French sociologist Pierre Bourdieu, who was critical of Marxism, expanded the traditional Marxist notion of economic capital to include **cultural capital.** Most people think of their aesthetic taste as something they choose for themselves. But in Bourdieu's model, developed especially in *Distinction: A Social Critique of the Judgment of Taste* (1979), we do not freely choose our aesthetic style, our taste in music, clothing, movies, or home décor, or even our style of speaking. Instead, class position, defined not so much by economic capital as by the related qualities of family and formal education, goes a long way to influence aesthetic taste.

Drawing on extensive sociological study in France, Bourdieu argued that working-class taste tends to favor realism and escapism in literature and favor realistic or functional painting and photography. Elite taste, by contrast, favors—and has the luxury to favor—an appreciation for form and style in themselves in literature, music, abstract painting, and artistic photography. Those with less formal education tend to favor matter, while those with more formal education tend to favor manner. It often requires more education and aesthetic experience to appreciate an art that imitates or plays off other art than to appreciate an art that imitates nature. Just as cultural capital produces an elite taste in art and elite patterns of speech and behavior, so those tastes and patterns of speech and behavior produce cultural capital, so that social stratification reproduces itself from generation to generation. Thus cultural capital, and not simply economic capital, makes working-class people stay in the working class and makes upper-class people—defined now by their aesthetic taste and not merely by economic wealth—stay in the upper class. For Bourdieu, then, art serves a social function: It reproduces and legitimates social hierarchies.

Terry Eagleton and Fredric Jameson. The most widely read contemporary Marxist literary theorist and critic is Terry Eagleton, whose broad learning, steady eye on the political consequences of aesthetic and critical practices, and spirited style of writing, together with a massive output of criticism and theory, nearly defy summary. For more than a generation of critics, Eagleton's books have sorted through the ideas of his predecessors in critical and literary theory, especially Marxist theory. He played a leading role, for example, in bringing Althusser to an Anglo-American audience. Meanwhile, his literary criticism has ranged across a host of mostly well-known British writers, from Shakespeare to the present, with particular attention to the historical and political embeddedness of literary writing. As a theorist, he is probably more influential in the model he sets for attending to theory and its political consequences, as seen from the left, than for any one theoretical argument, and deliberately so, for he prefers to direct theoretical debate to the purposes of Marxist political change, as opposed to studying theory for its own sake.

The most influential American Marxist literary theorist is Fredric Jameson. After early books that introduced central European Marxist theory and offered a Marxist critical introduction to structuralism and Russian formalism, Jameson continued on to a massively dialectical weaving of Marxist theory, structuralism, and formalism with poststructuralism, psychoanalysis, and the study of popular culture and capitalist globalization. His governing Marxist slogan is "Always historicize!" (Jameson 9). Jameson sees literature and other cultural productions and movements as shaped by unacknowledged social meanings that he calls the *political unconscious,* evoking a social dimension to psychoanalysis and to bourgeois culture's investment in repressing its recognition of its own desperate motives. In *The Political*

Unconscious: Narrative as a Socially Symbolic Act (1981), Jameson criticizes the bourgeois belief that art is pure and separate from history and politics. He sees that way of thinking as impoverishing bourgeois life, in the same way that the bourgeois interest in individuality desperately tries to separate bourgeois subjects from the social world. Jameson thus follows how literary form evokes the growth of bourgeois culture and aesthetics from realism to its disintegration into modernist and postmodernist fragmentation.

In postmodernism, as he argues in his influential essay "Postmodernism, or, the Cultural Logic of Late Capitalism" (1984, 1991), modernist fragmentation multiplies itself until parody, with its biting cultural criticism, gives way to postmodernist pastiche, imitation without the political bite of parody. The fragmentation of modernist style implied a critique of capitalist commodification, Jameson argues, but the cultural logic of late capitalism and postmodernism is the ascendancy of commodification as an end in itself. Modernist styles degrade into postmodernist codes, into conglomeration without direction, randomly cannibalizing the history of style in a purposeless hodgepodge of kitsch, schlock, and clutter, an effort to escape history that is itself a sign of history.

Jacques Rancière. The French philosopher Jacques Rancière, who began his career as a student of Althusser, has crafted an idiosyncratic offshoot of Marxist theory that focuses on the relation between politics and aesthetics. To Rancière, what we can and cannot see and say shape our art and politics and tie art and politics together as versions and causes of each other.

Rancière's roots in Marxism center his thinking on a pervasive sense of equality across all people. He insists on seeing people of all classes as equally intelligent, from the humble worker to the intellectual and the political leader. Early in his career, Rancière's fundamental belief in equality led him to break from Althusser. Rancière objects to a harsh binary opposition in Althusser's theory of ideology, an opposition sometimes not highlighted in Anglo-American ways of drawing on Althusser's ideas. When Althusser sees most people most of the time as passive dupes of ideology, he puts himself and other Marxist intellectuals and leaders in a superior position, because he suggests that they can see the truth that ordinary people cannot see. By drawing on a supposedly scientific Marxist truth, Althusser and other Marxist leaders believe that they can interpret and lead culture from a space outside and above ideology. To them, ideology is about other people, not about them. For Rancière, such a view condescends to the rest of us, including workers, students, undocumented immigrants, the unemployed, and pretty much everyone not part of the Marxist intellectual vanguard.

Rancière developed his ideas about equality partly by observing and joining workers and students as they rebelled against the French government in 1968. Even though the students' and workers' strikes eventually fizzled away, Rancière saw ordinary people rise to rebellion without Marxist intellectuals like Althusser to lead them. Rancière also developed his ideas as part of a philosophy of education that argues against the idea that teachers teach best by assuming a position of superiority to their students. He believes, on the contrary, that students learn best when encouraged to see themselves as their teachers' equals and take their own initiative to lead their own education.

In political philosophy, Rancière's concept of equality translates into an opposition between what he calls *consensus* and *dissensus*. He sees contemporary politics as caught up in the sway of a liberal, managerial consensus that relies on experts and professional politicians to establish the boundaries of what we can think and do politically. They have their disagreements with each other, but they stay within the range of a consensus about what it is permissible to think. Outside the consensus live undocumented immigrants, the unemployed, the indifferent, those who do not fit into the dominating managerial agreements about what counts and about what we can and should sense. The concept of what we can and should sense, what we can see, think, understand, hear, do, make, and say, leads Rancière to theorize what he calls the aesthetics of politics. It also leads, in turn, to what he calls the politics of aesthetics.

Specifically, it leads to what Rancière calls *the distribution of the sensible*. (Here *sensible* does not refer to having common sense. It means perceptible through the senses.) Rancière describes three dominating patterns in the history of the distribution of the sensible. First came *the ethical regime of images*, then *the representative regime of art*, and then *the aesthetic regime of art*. When a new regime arises, the earlier regimes do not disappear, though they sometimes grow less prominent. The same work of art can even include more than one regime, for art is rife with inconsistency and internal contradictions.

The key philosopher of the ethical regime is Plato. Plato judged the arts by an ethical standard of truth and accuracy. He banished poets and artists from his ideal republic, because he saw their work as untruthful lies, and therefore as dangerous ethically.

By contrast Plato's student, Aristotle, the key philosopher of the representative regime of art, saw value in the arts. Aristotle saw artistic representations not as failed distortions, lying images that signal an ethical failure, but instead as valuable fictions that follow their own logic and rules, their own consensus. For example, he saw tragedy as the genre for noble characters, and comedy and satire as genres for common folk. In this sense, according to Rancière, the representative regime of art follows a sense of what is proper. It follows rules of taste, realism, and plausibility. Different characters differ from each other, responding to the same circumstances in different ways, but the social class of the characters matches their style of speech in a consistent pattern, implying a political consensus. Plot follows a logic of cause and effect, as the hierarchies of social class imply that it is only natural and right that the nobility rule over the rest of us. The representative regime even sees art as superior to history, because the rules of art require a logic of propriety and of cause and effect that the mere reporting of history lacks.

Then, according to Rancière, in the nineteenth century, with the emergence of the aesthetic regime of art, the rules of genre began to drop away. Now, any work can use any style or language. Therefore, the aesthetic is the regime of the modern and of democracy and equality. Art is no longer about representing something else. It is about its own language and expression rather than about representation. It is singular, autonomous, pure suspension. In the aesthetic regime, aesthetic form is about form itself, but it is not separate from the social world. Instead, the form, language, and visual images of art and of politics shape the way that the social world sees and understands itself. Released from the rules of genre in art and in politics, we can summon the freedom to see and say beyond the ideologies that Althusser supposed we have shrunken to, and in that way the aesthetic regime of art makes for a democracy and an equality unimaginable to Althusser or to Althusser's brand of Marxism.

Rancière's Story of the Changing Distribution of the Sensible

1. The ethical regime of images
2. The representative regime of art
3. The aesthetic regime of art

To Rancière, then, politics and aesthetics shape each other. The intentions of the filmmakers, poets, novelists, and painters cannot control the limits of what they make. Some artists have politically appealing intentions, while others do not. But once their art moves out into the world it takes on a momentum of its own, because different audiences will read the same art in different ways. Indeed, all art includes contradictions. The intentions behind a work of art may contradict its effects. The fragmented aesthetic of Modernist art may seem to throw aside politics in favor of nihilism, but it may also show us the alienated disaffection and chaos of capitalism. As in our earlier discussion of how changes in film form do not guarantee predictable feminist or antifeminist effects (see Chapter 6), Rancière argues that a given form, whether Modernist fragmentation or any other form, does not necessarily produce a given, predictable politics. When neither the artist nor the form can constrain the aesthetic regime's distribution of the sensible, then art can reshape our sense of democratic and egalitarian possibility. Art can no longer be shut into the locked room of Aristotle's rules. Now, in the aesthetic regime, and even more with the accelerations of contemporary technology, all classes and all parts of the population have access to the arts. Art's capacity to go in any direction undermines the oppressive hierarchies that constrain freedom and that constrain politics and the aesthetic imagination. In the aesthetic regime of art, therefore, Rancière sees a door opening onto irrepressible democracy and equality.

HOW TO INTERPRET: FURTHER MARXIST EXAMPLES

To bring Marxist insights into a film or a literary text that has characters and a plot, we might ask whose labor makes it possible for the characters to do the things they do and makes it possible for them not to do the things they do not do. We can also ask how much the text makes that labor visible. Often, for example, in the novels of Jane Austen, Henry James, and Edith Wharton as well as many other novels and films, some of the characters lead privileged lives, never dirtying their hands with the work that makes their privilege possible. If labor is invisible or rarely visible, its invisibility can interpellate readers into assuming that labor somehow matters less than other activities, and that people who labor in the working class somehow matter less than people whose class position separates them from the working class. Their dependence on the working class may even grow invisible, or nearly invisible. Or perhaps the novels or films themselves critique their own characters' obliviousness to the work that upholds their privilege.

When a character in a novel or a historical movie rides in a carriage and the carriage appears magically, as if by itself, or attracts little or no additional mention, then at that point the ideology congeals. It hails readers into the assumption that the privileged life of carriage-takers is somehow better and more valuable than the laboring life of those who care for and harness the horses, maintain and fetch the carriage, drive it, keep their mouths shut, and clean up afterward. Some novels and stories, by contrast, such as Elizabeth Gaskell's *Mary Barton*, Harriet Beecher Stowe's *Uncle Tom's Cabin*, Rebecca Harding Davis's "Life in the Iron Mills," and Richard Llewellyn's *How Green Was My Valley*, call attention to those workers, writing from the workers' point of view or showing them mistreated. This is not to say that *Uncle Tom's Cabin* is (or isn't) better than Henry James's *The Portrait of a Lady*. Rather, it is about understanding some of the cultural and ideological assumptions that works of art and other cultural acts reflect and contribute to.

In Austen's *Sense and Sensibility*, one chapter begins this way: "Before the house-maid had lit their fire the next day, or the sun gained any power over a cold, gloomy morning in January, Marianne, only half-dressed, was kneeling against one of the window-seats for the sake of all the little light she could command from it, and writing as fast as a continual flow of tears would permit her." Similarly, at another point, while two characters talk they are "interrupted by the servant's coming in to announce the carriage being at the door" (Austen, *Sense* 133–134, 215). While this passage refers to *the* servant, not *a* servant, suggesting a familiarity with her presence, she never again speaks or acts in the scene. As far as the narration cares, the interruption is about the other characters, not about the servant, for her announcement pressures the others to finish their conversation. In both instances, servants pop into the narration for atmosphere, like the sun or a doorbell. Then they disappear. Nevertheless, their nearly invisible work produces many of the conditions that make the rest of the novel possible, including its social assumptions—and its characters' assumptions—about class and privilege. The same might be said for a more recent novel, or for the world where you sit as you read this book now, where much of the work that makes your reading possible gets done not by nearby servants so much as by forgettably distant and alienated factory workers. Most of us see the factory workers even less than the upper-class characters of novels see their servants who drive and care for a carriage and horses, but we still depend on their labor.

In Austen's *Persuasion*, when Sir Walter Elliot and his daughter Elizabeth—minus his daughter Anne—leave their home at Kellynch Hall, Austen describes the scene in these words: "The last office of the four carriage-horses was to draw Sir Walter, Miss Elliot, and Mrs. Clay to Bath. The party drove off in very good spirits; Sir Walter prepared with condescending bows for all the afflicted tenantry and cottagers who might have had a hint to shew themselves" (Austen, *Persuasion* 34). The servants get no mention.

By contrast, the 1995 film of the novel draws out the same moment at length (Figures 8.4 and 8.5). As the camera shows Anne standing in front of the house to say goodbye, a servant, larger than Anne, stands beside her at awkward attention. A line of servants stretches from the house to the carriage, standing with a similar awkward formality. The camera pans slowly across their faces, allowing their eyes to shift and suggest uneasiness about the incongruity between Sir Walter's spendthrift habits, which force him to leave his home, and his taking for granted that he deserves all those servants standing there, lavishly liveried, for no reason but to pay homage to his flimsy grandeur. Yet more servants stand by the carriage, interrupting the camera's view. One of them, with needless but therefore meaningful

Figure 8.4 and 8.5 Anne and her servant in *Persuasion*, awaiting Sir Walter's departure. A moment later, Sir Walter departs before a line of servants.

courtesy, assists Elizabeth and Sir Walter into the carriage. When they then drive off in good spirits, neither Sir Walter, Elizabeth, nor Mrs. Clay, of course, does the driving. Instead, three servants hover on the carriage above them, two in back and one in front to drive. As the carriage rolls away, it reveals a long line of tenants and cottagers standing to watch it depart. While Sir Walter offers a feeble, condescending wave with the fingers of his white-gloved hand, nothing in the film exactly matches the comic sarcasm in Austen's description of tenants and cottagers showing up merely out of obligation, "afflicted" to see him leave.

The film replaces the sarcasm by extending its gaze. We see individualizing close-ups of the tenants and cottagers' grim faces, and then we see close-ups of the oxen that carry off the Elliot belongings, as if to suggest, metonymically, that to Sir Walter and Elizabeth the tenants and cottagers are beasts of burden, too. Next, the camera lingers over the backs of two servants left behind as they watch the carriage leave. As if that were not enough, the next scene—not in the novel—returns to Anne, but the camera gives at least as much attention to the servants as they cover or cart off the furniture, remove a painting, and dust off and pack books. One servant speaks a modestly inaudible word to Anne, but otherwise they remain silent. Only the Elliots speak. In all these ways, the film finds visual analogues for the novel's satire of Sir Walter's vanity, but the film expands the novel's attention to class differences. It sneers at the hypocrisy in Sir Walter's pride by contrasting his pride with his dependence on his servants. It shows Anne, by contrast, as more responsible. Almost like a servant herself, she stays behind to do the work, supervising the servants and packing her own belongings.

Let us conclude with two more examples, beginning with a reading of Edwin Arlington Robinson's "Richard Cory" (1896).

Whenever Richard Cory went down town,
We people on the pavement looked at him:
He was a gentleman from sole to crown,
Clean favored, and imperially slim.
And he was always quietly arrayed,
And he was always human when he talked;
But still he fluttered pulses when he said,
"Good-morning," and he glittered when he walked.
And he was rich—yes, richer than a king—
And admirably schooled in every grace:
In fine, we thought that he was everything

To make us wish that we were in his place.
So on we worked, and waited for the light,
And went without the meat, and cursed the bread;
And Richard Cory, one calm summer night,
Went home and put a bullet through his head.
(Robinson 9–10)

Richard Cory attracts the gaze of the working-class poor, the "people on the pavement" who "looked at him." They seem to know little about his internal life, but they project onto him the antithesis to themselves, for he is a "gentleman," meaning a man wealthy enough that he does not work. Short of money, they must crimp on meals, cursing their monotonous diet of bread without meat. Yet though he can eat better than they can, he is still "imperially slim," as if to suggest that the wealthy have some mysteriously inherent superiority, much like the mystique of royalty. His class position shows all the way up to his "crown," and he is "richer than a king," richer than those who achieve their wealth naturally, by divine right. In other words, the imperially crowned kings and Corys of the world do not labor to earn their wealth; they simply are wealthy. Nothing in the poem acknowledges that Cory's wealth comes from the labor of others. In that way, the poem mystifies the privilege of capital, taking it as natural, rather than explaining or thinking critically about the economic system that produces inequality.

Still, the poem criticizes the owners of capital, even satirizes them for their inability to appreciate their privilege. From the focalized stance of the poem, "we" work hard, and "we" suffer. Our suffering is real, but Cory's woes are the effete suffering of the privileged, whose internal angst comes across as one of wealth's privileges. The "we" of the poem want to be in Richard Cory's "place." Perhaps, having lived their hard lives, they would know how to appreciate his privilege better than he can. Or if wealth corrupts them, then at least their history of hard times would help them better appreciate the opportunity to make their suffering as refined as his.

Yet even as the poem criticizes the Corys of the world who own the capital and who profit from the labor of others, the "we" of the poem cannot criticize the structure that produces the unequal distribution of wealth that Cory represents. They can criticize the person but not the system. Ideologically, they have been interpellated into taking unequal distribution as natural and inevitable. That allows them to think they are resisting the way of the world when they look skeptically at Cory, but looking skeptically at Cory keeps them from realizing that they still accept the system he represents. After all, when Cory bids them "Good-morning," their pulses flutter. Instead of looking doubtfully on his condescension, they let his greeting hail them, interpellate them, into his mystique and the social exploitation that it masks. In that way they consent to their own degraded position, so alienated from their own labor that they refer to it merely as work without caring to mention what kind of work, and certainly they give no hint of any pleasure in their work. Instead of doing something to change the system, they passively wait for the light, hoping that Cory's mystique will someday be theirs. They have been interpellated into a craving to get theirs, and that craving shuts off the impulse to think critically about the overall system that keeps them and others like them from getting it. With so little to challenge it, the system can reproduce itself from generation to generation, occasionally changing who fills the position of the rich Richard Corys but not changing the overall structure.

If it is all that bleak, then the "we" of the poem are utterly victims of false consciousness, deluded into believing that if they work hard enough and crimp on their meals, then someday, maybe, they too can grow wealthy like Cory, when of course they never will. With the hard finality of its devastating last rhyme, this poem offers little hope. If we insist on finding relative autonomy regardless, then perhaps we might see a hint of possibility for breaking outside the suffocating grip of ideology and false consciousness in the poem's crafted meter and pointed rhyme, offering a glimpse of aesthetic values not entirely run down by the hard lives of the poem's half-starved workers.

Critics sometimes ask how to bring Marxism together with questions about gender, and so we can look at one more example that brings those two ways of thinking together. Kate Chopin's "The Story of an Hour" (1894) begins with the following sentence: "Knowing that Mrs. Mallard was afflicted with a heart trouble, great care was taken to break to her as gently as possible the news of her husband's death" (Chopin 352). These opening words seem likely to interpellate readers into a variety of ideologies, sets of cultural assumptions that readers participate in unconsciously, that is to say, without stopping to think about it or to recognize the ideologies. The character is defined by her marriage (the first word to describe her is "Mrs."), labeled by her husband's name rather than by any name that she brings to the marriage. She comes across as delicate and vulnerable, at least in the eyes of those who see her as Mrs. Mallard. We get a sense of women as vulnerable and as dependent on men and marriage. But the story drops us so firmly into the middle of an ongoing narrative that, at least on a first reading, we probably get swept up in the suspense and allow such ideologies of gender to absorb us without our recognizing them. That is how ideology works (how it interpellates and hails us), and in retrospect we might say that when we return to the story and recognize how it begins in those assumptions about femininity, we can perhaps see that, right at the beginning of the story, the ideology has already congealed.

But Mrs. Mallard, it soon seems, might not be so utterly vulnerable and dependent as the opening sentence can suggest. She has her own room, and she can go away to it and even close and lock the door. In her own space, she exudes a bodily solidity and self-sufficiency: She sinks down into a "comfortable, roomy armchair," throws her head back on a cushion, and gives way to "physical exhaustion," with "her bosom" rising and falling "tumultuously" (352–353). The woman in this story languishes indoors, finding refuge in domestic privacy and physical repose, while the men move about outdoors, following another silent but suggestive ideology of gender binaries. Working first through Mrs. Mallard's languishing corporeality and then through the emotional shift that gradually overwhelms her, the story eventually cracks the shell of its interpellations into the dominant ideologies of gender by leading Mrs. Mallard to a new and suddenly critical view of her dependence, along with a newfound delight in her imagined future of independence, marked abruptly by the shift from the interpellating "Mrs. Mallard" to the more personal "Louise" (354).

And then, in the shock at the end—just when Louise exults in her new freedom—her supposedly dead husband returns home very much alive, and her feeble heart catches up to her and kills her. Thus, the story follows the interpellation, then exposes it, and then kills the character off for exposing it—and it runs readers through the same emotional slalom. When the story submits, then rebels, and then punishes its rebellion, where does that leave its relation to the patterns of ideology that it exposes? In some ways it ends up suppressing resistance, critical thinking, and feminine independence. Louise's independence might even degrade into mere petulant self-ishness as she thinks (in free indirect discourse) that "she would live for herself " (353). Or perhaps the story rethinks such options as feminine independence, critical thinking, and resistance to patriarchal ideology, not so much by suppressing them as by bringing them to light in ways that refrain from romanticizing them as easy, complete, or free from internal contradictions. After all, dependence has its pleasures as well as its burdens. When Louise enjoys her independent life in her own room, she yearns for freedom and implicitly yearns for a mobility that this story associates with men, not with women. The men's movement in the world outside—Richards in the newspaper office and from the newspaper office to the Mallard house, Brently Mallard out on what could be a business trip, the "peddler . . . crying his wares" (352) in the street below—all suggest the labor that pays for Mrs. Mallard's room in a house big enough to have an upstairs and a downstairs. By hinting at the labor behind her luxury, the story enjoys her luxury but does not idealize it. We do not know whether she envies the men's labor, but she profits from it, and she envies their mobility.

When the story exerts so much effort at unearthing Louise's desires, then, it is hard not to see the story as making a feminist intervention. But after the devastating conclusion, it is also hard to tell whether the story finally lands more on the side of endorsing an ideology of feminine dependence or more on the side of yearning for relative feminine autonomy. Perhaps it is too simple to characterize the story as all on one side or all on the other. Even so, the dialogue between opposed possibilities can end up legitimizing a skepticism about dominant gender roles, a skepticism that the story also punishes. Meanwhile, to think of the story as punishing Louise's relative autonomy might underestimate the story's humor, a sense of comic irony that lightens the closing tragedy and keeps alive, for readers, the hopes that finally die for Louise.

Given that "The Story of an Hour" was first published in *Vogue* magazine in 1894 (Figure 8.6), a fashion magazine aimed at economically prosperous women in New York City, the emotions in this story are commodified. Chopin sold the story to the magazine, which sold it to readers, who read it for their own pleasure in its emotions and because the editors used the story as bait to sell the magazine. The editors sold the magazine to readers and to advertisers who paid the magazine to help sell fashion to women like Louise Mallard, who typically depended on their husbands or fathers to fund the fashions that the story helped market to them. Thus the story, as a commodity within a commodity that marketed yet more commodities, helped reproduce the same dependent position of women that it also struggles to think about, partly resisting and partly embracing.

For those who see popular culture as leading us away from questioning dominant ideologies, the commodification of "The Story of an Hour" would seem to deflect readers from thinking critically

Figure 8.6 A fashion page from the December 6, 1894 issue of *Vogue*, where "The Story of an Hour" first appeared.

about their own immersion in commodity-obsessed consumer culture. But for those who see popular culture as encouraging relative autonomy, "The Story of an Hour" might work against some of the consumerist principles that must have led *Vogue*'s editors to put it in their magazine. Women's fashion, after all, need not be entirely about commodification. It can also be about women's aesthetic expression. In that sense, the story as a commodity can also help set up a forum for women's artistic expression, commodified or not. And the story's questioning of women's dependence on marriage might make female readers critique their economic reliance on men, including their reliance on men for access to the fashionable world of feminine expression and communal feminine pleasure.

In these ways, it is hard to sort out the story's cultural consequences for its readers, who after all may vary a good deal, both from reader to reader and even within individual readers. Those individual readers—as anyone versed in deconstruction can tell us—are rife with their own internal contradictions. And so, even if we could poll a cross section of readers, what those readers say that they think, in a world of ideology, might not accurately reflect the emotional resonance that the story carries for them. But "The Story of an Hour" can help us see how relative autonomy and hidebound ideology can tangle into each other. How we interpret that tangle will vary with our purposes and predilections, anywhere from seeing rebellious thinking as terribly defeated to seeing the door to its temptations opened just enough so that however abruptly the end of the story tries to slam shut the door, it cannot keep skeptical thoughts from slipping in and inviting us to recognize and rethink ideological assumptions.

* * * * *

As we will see in the next chapter, historicism and cultural studies pick up on the questions and debates within Marxism that we have reviewed here and continue to work with them, turning them especially to questions about literature and popular culture.

FURTHER READING

Adorno, Theodor W. *Aesthetic Theory*. 1970. Trans. Robert Hullot-Kentor. Ed. Gretel Adorno and Rolf Tiedemann. London: Athlone Press, 1997.

———. *Negative Dialectics*. 1966. Trans. E. B. Ashton. New York: Seabury Press, 1973.

Althusser, Louis. "Ideology and Ideological State Apparatuses." 1970. In *Lenin and Philosophy and Other Essays*. Trans. Ben Brewster. New York: Monthly Review Press, 1971: 127–186.

Arato, Andrew, and Eike Gebhardt. *The Essential Frankfurt School Reader*. New York: Urizen Books, 1978.

Belsey, Catherine. *Critical Practice*. 2nd ed. London: Routledge, 2002.

Benjamin, Walter. *Illuminations*. Ed. Hannah Arendt. Trans. Harry Zohn. New York: Harcourt, Brace & World, 1968.

———. *Reflections: Essays, Aphorisms, Autobiographical Writings*. Ed. Peter Demetz. Trans. Edmund Jephcott. New York: Harcourt Brace Jovanovich, 1978.

Bourdieu, Pierre. *Distinction: A Social Critique of the Judgment of Taste*. 1979. Trans. Richard Nice. Cambridge, MA: Harvard University Press, 1984.

Brecht, Bertolt. *Brecht on Theatre*. Ed. and trans. John Willett. London: Methuen, 1964.

Eagleton, Terry. *Criticism and Ideology: A Study in Marxist Literary Theory*. London: NLB, 1976.

———. *Ideology: An Introduction*. London: Verso, 1991.

Gramsci, Antonio. *Prison Notebooks*. Trans. Joseph A. Buttigieg. 2 vols. New York: Columbia University Press, 1991.

Habermas, Jürgen. *The Structural Transformation of the Public Sphere: An Inquiry into a Category of Bourgeois Society*. 1968. Trans. Thomas Burger with Frederick Lawrence. Cambridge, MA: MIT Press, 1989.

———. *The Theory of Communicative Action*. 1981. Trans. Thomas McCarthy. 2 vols. Boston: Beacon Press, 1984, 1987.

Hardt, Michael, and Antonio Negri. *Empire*. Cambridge, MA: Harvard University Press, 2000.

Horkheimer, Max, and Theodor Adorno. *Dialectic of Enlightenment*. 1944. Trans. John Cumming. New York: Continuum, 1982.

Jameson, Fredric. *Marxism and Form: Twentieth-Century Dialectical Theories of Literature*. Princeton, NJ: Princeton University Press, 1971.

———. *The Political Unconscious: Narrative as a Socially Symbolic Act*. Ithaca, NY: Cornell University Press, 1981.

———. *Postmodernism, or, the Cultural Logic of Late Capitalism*. Durham, NC: Duke University Press, 1991.

Lukács, Georg. *The Meaning of Contemporary Realism*. 1958. Trans. John and Necke Mander. London: Merlin, 1963.

———. *Studies in European Realism: A Sociological Survey of the Writings of Balzac, Stendhal, Zola, Tolstoy, Gorki, and Others*. 1948. Trans. Edith Bone. London: Hillway, 1950.

Marx, Karl, and Friedrich Engels. *The Marx-Engels Reader*. 2nd ed. Robert C. Tucker, ed. New York: Norton, 1978.

Mojab, Shaharzad, ed. *Marxism and Feminism*. London: Zed, 2015.

Nelson, Cary, and Lawrence Grossberg, eds. *Marxism and the Interpretation of Culture*. Urbana: University of Illinois Press, 1988.

Rancière, Jacques. *The Politics of Aesthetics*. 2000. Ed. and trans. Gabriel Rockhill. London: Bloomsbury, 2004.

Williams, Raymond. *Marxism and Literature*. Oxford: Oxford University Press, 1977.

❊ 9 ❊

Historicism and Cultural Studies

While deconstruction grabbed headlines in the popular press, igniting controversy and shaping the debates of literary criticism, a restlessness was stirring through literary studies. The new critics, the early structuralist literary critics, and the deconstructionist literary critics, different though they were, shared a formalist approach to interpreting literature. They gave little attention to history and culture, preferring to concentrate on literary form. Sometimes new critics and deconstructionists even suggested a sneering condescension to historical and cultural interpretations of literature, looking down on such ways of reading as naively old-fashioned. But many critics felt that formalism betrayed the social and historical interests that help make many readers and critics care about literature. Other critics shared the formalism of the new critics, structuralists, and deconstructionists, seeing literary form as integral to the very idea of literary study, and yet felt that an interest in history and culture could fit together with, rather than oppose, an interest in form.

Critics hungered for a way to draw on what they learned from deconstruction and bring it together with cultural and historical inquiry, and out of that hunger emerged what came to be called *new historicism*.

NEW HISTORICISM

New historicists see literary studies, from the new criticism through deconstruction, as tending to evade history or to use history only for what new historicists call *old historicism*. To new historicists, old historicism relegates history to mere *background* and *context*, with the literature merely *reflecting* the history. We have all been students in classrooms—and some of us have been teachers in classrooms— where the teacher begins by providing historical background and then leaves the history as mere background without going on to pay much attention to it as we talk about the literature. To new historicists, old historicists also see history as certain and stable, as a set of secure facts, which allows us to make such claims as "the Elizabethans believed" such and such, claims that, after deconstruction, seem too general and confident to new historicists. After all, as deconstruction helps us understand, people have internal contradictions. Some Elizabethans believed this but other Elizabethans believed that, and all Elizabethans believed more than one thing, including contradictory things.

By contrast with old historicists, new historicists try to read history and literature together, with each influencing the other, and without a sense of stable facts. For new historicists, history is just as uncertain and complex as literature. Apart from the basic facts (though maybe for basic facts too, as we will soon see), it simply will not work to make claims about history by saying that this or that happened or the Elizabethans believed such and such and then leave it at that. Just as it would be too simple to make broad-brush, absolute claims about a literary text ("*Romeo and Juliet* idealizes adolescence"), so it would be too simple to make broad-brush, absolute claims about history ("the Elizabethans believed in deference to authority, represented by the great chain of being").

When we study literature, after deconstruction, we take multiple perspectives into account and consider how different perspectives lead to different interpretations. It is not a matter of throwing up our hands and saying that anything goes. But it is a matter of saying that multiple things go, and that we will distinguish among those multiple things on the basis of what interests us (perhaps feminism or figurative language or class or focalization and so on) and on the basis of whether we can put together an interesting argument that connects to our political, artistic, or cultural commitments.

For new historicists, those same principles that we bring to literary interpretation should also direct how we read history. It is not just about saying here is the historical background and then applying that historical background, as if it were a mere lump of inflexible facts, to the supposedly more nuanced challenge of interpreting literature. For new historicists, the history already has as much multiplicity and

---

Old Historicism vs. New Historicism

Old historicism: history ⟶ literary text
New historicism: histories ⇄ literary text

---

nuance as any work of literature (and maybe more, to say the least). Moreover, literary texts influence the sociohistorical world that influences the literary texts, so that the textuality of history and the historicity of texts shape and reshape each other in a continuous cycle of mutual influence.

New historicists thus see themselves as recovering history for literary studies, after the move away from history in new criticism and sometimes in structuralism and deconstruction. By studying history with the close attention to its multiplicity that we associate with deconstruction, new historicists see themselves as merging historical study with deconstruction, rescuing literary study from a tendency to ignore history and rescuing historical study from a tendency to oversimplify, to see things as absolute and definite (a mistake that the best historians would not make, but still a problem in much historical study and especially in old historicist literary study).

From a new historicist perspective, the facts that old historicists rely on may not be so reliable after all. New historicists argue that what makes a fact depends on the perspective we look from; it is a construction, not an essence. To illustrate the point, let us consider some routine "facts." The sun rises in the morning and sets in the evening. Summer comes in June, July, and August. Columbus discovered America in 1492. Gold is heavier than paper.

From another perspective, the sun does not rise or set, but the earth rotates on its axis, making the sun appear to rise or set—at least on a sunny day. Summer comes in June, July, and August north of the equator, but south of the equator it comes in December, January, and February. In 1492, the name *America* did not even exist, and what Columbus did was no discovery if discovery means being the first person to find something. Untold millions of people knew about "America" before Columbus, and they did not think of it as the "New World" either. By tagging Columbus as the discoverer of America and the New World, we keep ourselves from looking through the perspective that would characterize him as an invader and conqueror, and as a brutally genocidal invader and conqueror. But surely, you may respond, there is no question about some facts. Surely it remains a fact that an ingot of gold is heavier than a sheet of paper. Still, a sheet of paper in one gravitational field (such as the Earth's) may weigh more than an ingot of gold in another gravitational field, or in weightless space. And some paper—such as your birth certificate when you apply for a passport—is heavier, metaphorically, than an ingot of gold.

Or, more ideologically, we might question why we resort to scientific facticity as the last bastion of facts and truth. From another perspective, we might choose God instead of science as our ideal realm of truth and fact. And from another perspective, we might choose love or beauty or the need for food and shelter. What we choose to represent facts, and what perspective we look from, determine what we choose to call facts, which allows new historicists, drawing on poststructuralism, to see history itself as contingent (meaning that it depends on variables) and constructed rather than as a stable absolute or essence.

The New Historicist Critique of Facts and the Contemporary Controversy about Facts

In recent years, well after the advent of new historicism, the question of what makes a fact has attracted public debate and prompted rethinking about the new historicist critique of facts. When we bring that debate into dialogue with new historicism, then together they suggest not that facts are irrelevant but instead that we cannot just make facts up. Even if we fool some people, we gain no reasonable credibility by supposing that we can invent our own facts, free from evidence and the frank consideration of bias. Instead, we need evidence to make facts credible, and—as historicism can teach us—we gain from considering the variety of possible kinds of evidence and the assortment of arguments for and against possible facts. Facts gain their status as facts after interpretation, not before interpretation. We can achieve consensus about some facts more than about others. The degree of consensus, based on evidence and argument, can then influence how we distinguish fake facts and false facts from facts we can trust and build on.

With the new historicists, then, the previous two generations of literary studies come full circle. The new critics called for close attention to the text rather than to history or the social world. With structuralism and deconstruction, critics developed increasingly sophisticated methods to study texts closely. But many critics missed the social dimension that the new critics tried to move away from. New historicists, therefore, drawing on the increasingly prominent Marxist ideas discussed in Chapter 8, try to restore literature to its social history while retaining the tools of deconstruction and poststructuralism that can help us see social history in its multifarious intricacy.

The critics most identified as founding figures of new historicism are Louis Montrose and especially Stephen Greenblatt (Figure 9.1). Greenblatt coined the term *new historicism*, but he used it casually and never liked it as the name of a critical method. He prefers to call the method *cultural poetics*, drawing on the structuralist sense of *poetics* as the study of a larger system (not necessarily a poetic system). Greenblatt's work first attracted wide interest with a book called *Renaissance Self-Fashioning: From More to Shakespeare* (1980). (*More* refers to Thomas More, the British Renaissance politician and writer.) In that book, Greenblatt provides subtly literary and historicist readings of a series of British Renaissance writers, focusing on how their culture shaped their sense of selfhood or subjectivity. People who know little or nothing about new historicism or Greenblatt's book have supposed that Greenblatt's expression "self-fashioning" refers to how the self fashions itself. Their misunderstanding of Greenblatt turns his historicist and partly Marxist, Foucauldian method upside down (on Foucault, see later in this chapter), converting it into a routine bourgeois celebration of capitalist individuality, thus missing the point. Greenblatt explains that he started to write about how the self fashions itself, but ended up writing much more about how the self is fashioned by, is almost passive before, broader cultural forces.

Sometimes, Greenblatt and other new historicists who followed in his wake wrote about historical matters at length before they began to discuss a literary text, which dramatized the way that their approach differed from earlier, less historicist criticism. They often began an article or book chapter with a provocative anecdote based on an obscure but startling historical source. In Greenblatt's most influential works, *Renaissance Self-Fashioning* and *Shakespearean Negotiations* (1988), that strategy showcased the turn to history and playfully jabbed at the routines of the usual old historicist criticism.

Figure 9.1 Stephen Greenblatt (1943–).

To skeptics' eyes, the history overwhelmed the literary interpretation, and the dramatic anecdotes tested readers' patience by showing off the critics' historicist erudition without giving enough attention to the literary texts. But for readers who have the patience to read through to the end or who appreciate Greenblatt's historicist curiosities and his skill at making unexpected and revealing cultural connections, Greenblatt eventually gets to the relation between the history and the literature. He tries to sort out what he calls "the circulation of social energy," the way that literature comes not only from individual authors but also from the cultural controversies of an age, with the controversies provoking the literature and the literature interpreting the controversies, in a continuous cycle of exchange and influence.

Some critics have complained that in Greenblatt's interpretations, the literature ends up confirming the dominant ideologies rather than contesting them, and sometimes those critics complain that new historicism as a whole, following Greenblatt's example, underestimates the capacity for literature to change the world. In Marxist terms (as reviewed in Chapter 8), they find that Greenblatt and his new historicist colleagues put too much weight on ideology, interpellation, and even false consciousness and not enough weight on relative autonomy, agency, and intervention. If so, however, that balance (or imbalance) owes to Greenblatt's own predilections, not to anything necessarily inherent in new historicist principles.

Over time, as new historicism grew more routine, lost its new-ness, and evolved simply into historicism, Greenblatt's idiosyncrasies, however interesting, came to matter less than the general principle that literature and history shape each other, as opposed to the old-fashioned habit of seeing literature as a passive reflection of history. After all, if we care about literature, then it might seem odd to see it, even implicitly, as merely passive, merely reflecting other things through what new historicists sometimes call the *reflection model* of literary criticism. If literature only reflected the rest of the world, then we would have no reason to read literature. On the other hand, if it did not reflect the rest of the world at all, then it would have no capacity to comment on the world. We value literature and other aes-thetic productions in part for their nuanced (Marxists might say their dialectical) combination of reflecting and rethinking the rest of the world. New historicism has tried to craft a model for criticism that takes that combination of passive reflection and active rethinking into account, both in literary art and in the art of criticism.

HOW TO INTERPRET: HISTORICIST EXAMPLES

Shakespeare's comedies, for example, and other comic dramas of Shakespeare's time and for many years afterward typically end with many of the characters falling in love and marrying. The term *comedy* referred not to humor, as it does today, but to a happy ending. And with the naturalization of heterosexuality, a happy ending tended to mean marriage between female and male characters. Sometimes, most famously in Shakespeare's tragedy *Romeo and Juliet*, the charac-ters fall in love and marry at a young age.

But historian Lawrence Stone's landmark *The Family, Sex, and Marriage in England, 1500–1800* (1977) argues that marriages in Re-naissance England typically came comparatively late; that parents, kin, or friends typically arranged the marriages; and that they ar-ranged marriages not for love but for economic reasons. The upper and middling classes often sent their infants to wet nurses, and chil-dren usually left their parents to work as servants or apprentices, or to go to school. Parents and children often died young (compared to our own time), and living arrangements for all classes were crowded and lacked privacy. For all these reasons, Stone argues, sexual and emotional attachments minimized warmth and intimacy.

For a historicist literary critic, then, Stone's argument raises prob-lems, because the history and the plays do not match. The mismatch throws up a roadblock for old (or traditional) historicist criticism especially, because traditional historicism relies on the reflection model, and in this case the literature does not reflect the history. (At least the literature does not reflect the history if Stone has the history right. Some historians dispute Stone's findings.) But because new historicism challenges the reflection model's implication that literature passively reproduces its surrounding culture, Stone's findings might offer an opportunity for new historicist literary criticism.

New historicists could argue, for example, that the difference between the plays and the cultural pattern suggests that the plays talk back to the cultural pattern (exercising relative autonomy and agency, making an intervention). Perhaps the plays seek an escape from the expected pattern, or perhaps they parody it or experiment by exploring alternatives. Or, by a model that sees less disruption of and more compliance with the dominant expectations, comic drama portrays a fantasy world that has little to do with what actually goes on in daily life and therefore cannot much disrupt or pressure daily life. Or more than one of those models applies at the same time, potentially in conflict with each other and underlining the internal contradictions within comic drama's relation to its culture and to the dominant ideologies of its culture.

We might see those competing forces as balancing each other out, almost in a social version of new critical balance. Or we might see them in poststructuralist disequilibrium, with the resistance to the dominant ideologies overwhelming the simultaneous urge to comply with those dominant ideologies, or with the urge to comply overwhelming the resistance. Our choices from such a wide palette of options would probably depend on how we observe and interpret a host of individual details about cultural history, the language and the performance traditions of the actual plays, and the dialogue between the plays and the history.

For another example, let us consider a historicist reading of William Wordsworth's 1798 "Lines Composed a Few Miles above Tintern Abbey" proposed by Marjorie Levinson, who concentrates especially on the opening lines:

> Five years have past; five summers, with the length
> Of five long winters! and again I hear
> These waters, rolling from their mountain-springs
> With a soft inland murmur. — Once again
> Do I behold these steep and lofty cliffs,
> That on a wild secluded scene impress

Thoughts of more deep seclusion; and connect
The landscape with the quiet of the sky.
The day is come when I again repose
Here, under this dark sycamore, and view   10
These plots of cottage-ground, these orchard-tufts,
Which at this season, with their unripe fruits,
Are clad in one green hue, and lose themselves
'Mid groves and copses. Once again I see
These hedge-rows, hardly hedge-rows, little lines
Of sportive wood run wild: these pastoral farms,
Green to the very door; and wreaths of smoke
Sent up, in silence, from among the trees!
With some uncertain notice, as might seem
Of vagrant dwellers in the houseless woods,   20
Or of some Hermit's cave, where by his fire
The Hermit sits alone.
These beauteous forms . . .
                    (Wordsworth 163–164)

Rewriting the tradition of reading Wordsworth and Romantic poetry as communing with nature, Levinson argues that "the primary poetic action" of this poem "is the suppression of the social" (Levinson 37). She sees Wordsworth as fleeing to nature not so much to reach nature as to escape the social. For Levinson, Wordsworth's poem keeps trying to get away from what it gazes at, starting with the opening leap past spring and fall, as if summer and a long winter could make a year by themselves. The setting of "Tintern Abbey," it turns out, was anything but "wild" and "secluded" (line 6). The abbey was crowded with tourists like Wordsworth, guidebooks in hand, and with beggars seeking alms from the tourists (see Figure 9.2). Nearby, the town of Tintern had an ironworks busy supplying the war against France and polluting the river beside the abbey.

Here as in much of Great Britain, the growth of enclosures—that is, the fencing of communally farmed property so that only a few owners had access to it—had dramatically changed the local economy, taking the means of support from ordinary people whose poverty the war deepened even more. The picturesque hedge-rows were the fences that deepened the poverty that in turn crowded the abbey with beggars, so by figuring some of the causes of poverty as "lines/Of sportive wood run wild" (lines 15–16), Wordsworth masks the hedges' concrete social meaning, transforming them into geometric abstractions of playful organic greenery. The small farms were indeed "Green to the very door" (line 17), because, after common lands were hedged off, the farmers had only their own garden plots to plant and needed to use every inch. Again, Wordsworth covers the social, historical, and economic details under a mask of greenery and natural beauty.

"Wreaths of smoke" (line 17) float up from the woods because impoverished people burned trees to eke out what little living they could by making charcoal for the ironworks. Thus, the "houseless" vagrants (line 20) are not merely the ghostly, spiritualized Nature of a lyrical simile. They are actual people who have no home because of their poverty. By transforming the vagrants (plural) yet more into a mystifying hermit (singular), Wordsworth transforms the suffering of many—a political and cultural crisis—into the tourist-poet's private, apolitical vision. As Levinson notes, "hermits choose their poverty; vagrants suffer it" (Levinson 43).

In this reading, the social, cultural world is not absent from the poem, but the poem tries to make it disappear into the "beauteous forms" (line 22)—like the abstract lines of hedge-rows—of this characteristically Romantic nature poem. Trying to push out the social and cultural makes possible an exaltation of the poet's supposedly private imagination communing with nature. But the poem's nature

Figure 9.2 *Part of Tintern Abbey, Monmouthshire, 1810,* by I. W. Barrett.

is itself culture, because it is the cultural construction of the poem's effort to repress the social. The point is not that Wordsworth skips past history and poverty. The point is that both the grubby poverty that Wordsworth's lyrical idealizing masks and the lyrical idealizing itself are part of the same historical landscape.

In that way, nothing is outside history. The historical, social world helps shape the poem and its ideology of nature, and the poem, against its own denials, speaks with sadness and fear about the devastation of the social, historical world. If we read those denials, then we can reread the poem's vision of nature and nature poetry as a plea (in Althusser's terms) for an imaginary relation to the real conditions of environmental and economic devastation.

Perhaps these new historicist alternatives to the reflection model end up relying on the reflection model all over again, because they still show the literature responding to the history. But they replace direct reflection with indirect reflection, with mediated reflection. From that perspective, new historicism does not replace the reflection model so much as it sophisticates the model. Regardless, it gives critics a new set of questions, a set of questions that continues the dialogue between more pessimistic and more optimistic models of Marxist interpretation, as we reviewed them in Chapter 8.

As historicism has grown more familiar in literary studies, some critics, especially in Renaissance studies, have called for *presentism*. Traditionally, to call a critic a presentist was a put-down. It accused the critic of distorting literature from the past by relying on models from the present. For example, in the pejorative sense of the term, a presentist might miss the point by calling Chaucer a feminist or by seeing an environmentalist sensibility in *Moby-Dick*'s portrayal of whale hunting or a gay sensibility in its comical same-sex bed scene. On the other hand, scholars who now advocate presentism might well want to know about the relation between Chaucer and feminism or between *Moby-Dick* and gay studies or environmentalism. They argue that we can never know the past in itself. We can only view the past through the lens of the present. Therefore, they believe, to disavow our interests in the present would distort our view of the past more than to own up to our interests frankly.

In that way, presentism can offer a strategy for doing historicism better, with an alertness to how our view of history depends on our position in the present. Or it can make a deliberate strategy out of keeping a measured distance from the past and asking not what happened then, but how what happened then looks through the lens of our interests now, or how what happened then speaks to what is happening now. Instead of trying to reconstruct an Elizabethan performance of *Hamlet*, a presentist stage production might ask how to perform or interpret *Hamlet* for our own time. Whichever of these strategies a presentist or historicist chooses, they all trouble the binary opposition between the present and the past, in different ways encouraging us to study each in relation to the other.

But studying history is not as easy as it may sound. Some of the early new historicists, English professors and graduate students still learning how to work with history, were accused of relying on Lawrence Stone's work too heavily or relying on this or that other small array of secondary historical scholarship. Over the years, in the wake of new historicism, historicist critics have grown into better historians, but the intense historical study that goes with historicist criticism is a challenge in itself. To ask critics to learn and research everything we expect from a literary critic *plus* everything we expect from a historian is asking a lot. Historicism, to put it plainly, is hard work.

We might also wonder how new historicism can translate into the classroom. Many students do not know much history. Some students even turn to literature in part to get away from studying history. Would historicist teaching require literature students to read less literature so that they can read more history? Or would the history help bring the literature to life, intensifying the students' ability to appreciate and engage with the literature? There is no one-size-fits-all answer to these questions, but they hint at the obstacles and the excitements in historicist criticism and teaching.

MICHEL FOUCAULT

New historicists drew heavily on the writings of the poststructuralist philosopher Michel Foucault, a major figure often grouped with Roland Barthes, Jacques Derrida, and Jacques Lacan to represent the first and leading wave of poststructuralist (and more or less Parisian) innovators. Foucault's writings, which we have already begun to address in Chapter 7, bring a wide and changing range of methods to a wide range of topics, far more than we can address here, but we can pick out a few concepts that have carried notable influence in literary and cultural studies.

Knowledge, power, and discourse. Foucault wrote about the relation between power and knowledge. He argued that we internalize patterns of expectation from the surrounding culture, absorbing the culture's expectations so much that we take them for granted and suppose that they come from our own thinking. Typically, we think of knowledge as responsive to something outside itself. In that model, if a person has knowledge, that knowledge is knowledge of an essence exterior to the person. Foucault argued almost the opposite: that power constructs what we recognize as knowledge. He saw knowledge, therefore, as mediated by history, rather than as pure knowledge of unmediated raw truth. Foucault called this kind of knowledge **discourse.**

In Foucault's sense of the term, *a discourse is a practice that produces what it purports to describe.* A discourse is a common pattern of culturally internalized expectation rather than the supposedly pure or essential truth that people traditionally mean by the term *knowledge.* When Foucault used the term *discourse,* he did not exactly mean languages or systems of representation, the related sense of the term *discourse* that is its other meaning in structuralism and post-structuralism (as we have seen in earlier chapters). He meant something closer to the Marxist notion of ideology that we reviewed in Chapter 8. But Foucault was suspicious of Marxism, because he did not believe in the Marxist sense of truth that Althusser called "real conditions." He also saw Marxism as clinging to a suspect model of economic determinism, whereas discourses do not necessarily come from economics.

For example (as we have seen in Chapter 7), we can recognize discourses of gender, internalized patterns of cultural expectation about femininity and masculinity that, as Judith Butler has argued, construct through repetition what they purport to know. People may

---

Foucault's Model of Power and Knowledge

Traditional model: Knowledge produces power

- power suppresses
- power coerces

Foucault's model: Power produces knowledge (as discourse)

- power regulates, disciplines, polices, surveils
- power leads us to internalize it

suppose that women move, talk, and dress in a certain variety of ways and men move, talk, and dress in a different variety of ways, but the discourse of gender (including the ways that people move, talk, and dress) constructs that knowledge through repeated actions and expectations. If people did not repeat that discourse in their actions and expectations, then they would not continue to believe in it and see it as knowledge. And indeed, we do not repeat that discourse perfectly and at all times, and to the extent that we do not repeat that discourse we open a path for alternative, less dominant modes of understanding gender. In that way, discourses are not absolute, but nevertheless they wield great power. The discourse of gender does not describe gender, as we might think before Foucault, as if gender were there prior to the discourse. Instead, it produces the gender that it purports to describe. Perhaps you can see similarities between Foucault's sense of discourse as producing, rather than merely describing, and Derrida's sense that language and systems of representation generate so much momentum that the signifiers spin free from any particular signifieds.

Foucault worked out these ideas by studying institutions, such as insane asylums, medical clinics, and prisons, institutions that regulate behavior socially and psychologically through discourses of madness, illness, and punishment. In *Discipline and Punish: The Birth of the Prison* (1975), Foucault proposed that the Panopticon, a prison designed (and never built) by the English philosopher Jeremy Bentham (1748–1832), offers a model of modern culture (Figure 9.3). Bentham designed the Panopticon with prison cells circling around a guard tower so that a guard in the tower can watch each prisoner, but the prisoners cannot tell when a guard watches them. Therefore, Bentham reasoned, prisoners, knowing that a guard might be watching at any time, would protect themselves by policing their own behavior, whether or not a guard is actually watching. Indeed, the prison would not need a guard to watch all the time, because prisoners would internalize the rules that the guard enforces, and so the prisoners would police themselves.

To Foucault, modern society works like the Panopticon. To stay with the earlier example of gender and to use the terms that Foucault has provided critical theory and cultural studies, our discourses of gender *regulate, discipline, police,* and *surveil* (as in keeping under surveillance) behavior and beliefs, producing and reproducing stereotypical ideas of gender. People internalize those ideas so deeply that no one else has to make people believe or live by those ideas, because people surveil themselves (they police, discipline, regulate themselves), making sure that they abide by the dominant discourses of gender. We live now in a world of video cameras, to the point that most of us, most of the time, become our own video cameras watching and policing ourselves.

You can probably think of ways of dressing, walking, talking, or gesturing that signify femininity or masculinity and that many people absorb so thoroughly that they police themselves, restricting potential impulses to act in what the dominant discourse paints as the wrong way. To Foucault, such self-disciplining works more powerfully than coercion. (If you recall Chapter 8, then you might hear Foucault's ideas echoing or at least paralleling Gramsci's notion of the state versus civil society or Althusser's notion of RSAs versus ISAs.)

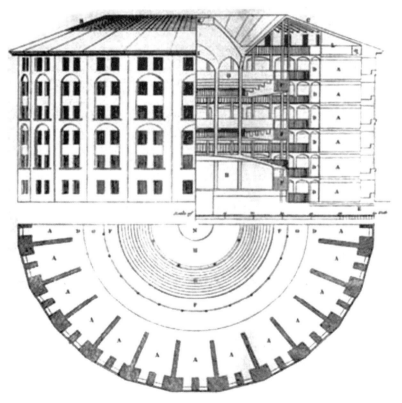

Figure 9.3 Jeremy Bentham's design for the Panopticon, 1791.

Knowledge itself, then, to Foucault (such as knowledge of gender expectations), is a means of surveillance, regulation, and discipline, a discourse that produces what it purports to describe. In this model, the subject is not a person or individual, a knowing, self-understanding agent of free will. Instead, the subject is a place where discourses come together.

Similarly, in *The History of Sexuality, Volume 1: The Will to Knowledge* (1976), Foucault (as we began to see in Chapter 7) discusses the discourse of sexuality as a means of power and social regulation. As people internalize the discourse of sexuality, it regulates and administers people's lives. He criticizes what he calls "the repressive hypothesis," the Freudian notion that we suffer from repressing our sexuality. He argues that sexuality, in the era of supposed repression, is anything but repressed. With the massive medical and educational discourse about sexuality, it is a central obsession, and the discourse of sexuality, the will to knowledge of sexuality, emerges as a power to regulate sexuality, not to repress it. It regulates sexuality in part by identifying certain sexual behaviors as "other," especially homosexuality. Thus, to Foucault power produces discourse rather than repressing it. Instead of asking the traditional questions about who has power or what people want to do with power, Foucault asks how power constructs subjects, making subjects effects of power. Foucault proposes that before modernity, a variety of sexual acts were recognized. Still, those acts did not determine identities as homosexual or heterosexual. But the modern discourse of sexuality, Foucault argues, constructs subjects as queer or straight according to their behavior, thus converting behavior into identity.

Biopolitics and biopower. Later in his career, beginning with the last section of *The History of Sexuality, Volume 1*, Foucault urged attention to what he called biopolitics and biopower. As discipline and punishment work repressively, to restrict life, biopower works to optimize life. As Foucault's earlier discussion of discipline focused on individual bodies, his discussion of biopolitics focused on populations. The biopolitics of state surveys, regulations, and legislation builds a technology of power for governing large groups of people through managing healthcare, insurance, agriculture and food, social security and pensions, sexuality, reproduction, housing, migration, zoning, the keeping of statistics about populations, and so on. While biopolitics seeks to foster health and longevity and govern the mechanics of birth and mortality, it is not neutral. On the contrary, it can favor particular styles of living and sexuality as well as a world of state racism where "the race that holds power and is entitled to define the norm" wages war against people it sees as deviating from that norm and threatening what it sees as "the biological heritage" (Foucault 61).

Foucault and resistance. Foucault's readers have varied in how much potential they see Foucault allowing for resistance to the power of dominant discourses. They vary in part according to which works of Foucault they concentrate on and perhaps according to what they want to see Foucault as saying. Sometimes it seems that Foucault sees power as so pervasive that we have little chance to resist it. At times, nevertheless, he sees power as generating its own resistance, because any discourse of power—such as the dominant discourses of sexuality or gender—will necessarily be imperfect and incomplete. People do not always dress, walk, talk, and gesture the way that the discourse of gender tells them to. And they do not always repress their sexuality the way that the discourse of sexuality tells them to. Sometimes, Foucault sees power as generating resistance merely to squelch that resistance, but at other times he sees the resistance as opening a potential for change, though he does not develop that sense of resistance in much detail. We can line up these two opposite views of power and resistance (or of Foucault's ideas about power and resistance) with the more pessimistic and more optimistic Marxist models reviewed in Chapter 8, the models that offer, pessimistically, ideology, interpellation, and false consciousness or, optimistically, relative autonomy, agency, and intervention.

Indeed, despite Foucault's suspicion of Marxism, his influence on literary and cultural criticism sometimes merges with or parallels the influence of Marxism on literary and cultural criticism. Foucault's ideas, for example, influenced Greenblatt when Foucault visited the University of California at Berkeley as Greenblatt and others there worked out the ideas that led to new historicism. Those who look skeptically on what they see as Greenblatt's habit of underestimating resistance to dominant ideologies sometimes match that reading of Greenblatt with a similar reading of Foucault. By contrast, the belief that we can resist dominant ideologies and powerful discourses tended to draw on the more optimistic version of Marxist thinking that often identified less with new historicism and more with cultural studies.

CULTURAL STUDIES

The term **cultural studies** can confuse people, because it sounds so general, and many critics who know little about the term's history use it in a general way to refer to any study of culture or to any study of aesthetic production (film, art, literature, music, and so on) that goes beyond the study of form to include study of the surrounding culture. But the term *cultural studies* has a specific meaning and history, for it refers to the cultural studies movement associated with the Centre for Contemporary Cultural Studies at the University of Birmingham in Great Britain. It can also include the heritage of weaving together literary studies with the study of popular culture, cultural history, Marxism, and the working class that emerged through the writing of Raymond Williams, a practice that Williams called **cultural materialism.** Cultural studies and cultural materialism developed along similar paths, though at first cultural materialism, like the new historicism, gave more attention to literary history, often including Shakespeare. Indeed, cultural materialists succeeded in bringing their ideas to a wide audience in part because, led especially by Jonathan Dollimore and Alan Sinfield, they wrote provocatively about Shakespeare, the most widely studied English-language writer. I will use the term *cultural studies* broadly, allowing it to include cultural materialism, its close cousin.

Founded by Richard Hoggart and later directed by Stuart Hall (Figure 9.4), the Centre for Contemporary Cultural Studies developed cultural studies into what we might describe as an effort to bring Marxism together with poststructuralism, psychoanalysis, and—eventually—feminism for the study of contemporary popular culture. As we might expect, not all critics influenced by Marxism appreciated the idea of bringing Marxism together with poststructuralism, because, from a Marxist materialist perspective, poststructuralism can seem to sidestep material culture in favor of language and "discourse." But thanks partly to the influence of cultural studies, the growth and evolution of contemporary Marxism changed poststructuralism, leading it away from the socially disconnected language play of early deconstruction to make it engage deeply with politics and material culture, even when it understands material culture as a form of language or discourse. Students from many countries traveled to study at Birmingham and then often returned to their home countries, spreading the ideas and methods of cultural studies and the influence of Hall's intellectual leadership. (On Hall, see also Chapters 4, 10, and 11.) A Jamaican who moved to Britain at the age of nineteen, Hall played an active role in the politics of the British left, advocating nuclear disarmament and critiquing the right-wing policies of Prime Minister Margaret Thatcher.

In line with the interest that cultural studies takes in popular culture, Hall saw a need for the left to understand why the right appealed to the popular electorate, a need that has continued to evolve as we witness a resurgence of the right across much of the world,

Figure 9.4 Stuart Hall (1932–2014).

including the United States, the United Kingdom, India, Brazil, the Philippines, and much of the European Union. From a left position, as we have seen, when the general populace elects a right-wing government, they vote against their own interests. The left, therefore, needs to interpret the working class's readiness to elect right-wing politicians against the left's expectation that the working class would lead resistance to the dominant, right-wing hegemony. (Here, as through much of this chapter, I am drawing on the Marxist concepts and terms outlined in Chapter 8.) For that reason, cultural studies scholars investigate how dominant ideologies tend to reproduce themselves through interpellation, so that working-class youth, for example, aspire to working-class jobs like the jobs of their family and friends, instead of seeking revolutionary change.

Led in part by Hall, cultural studies scholars eventually began to integrate the study of race with the study of class, a crucial expansion. (See the discussion of race and class in Chapter 8.) We cannot understand the new rise of the right without facing how some on the right feel threatened by such developments as the election of Barack Obama and the rise of a multiracial electorate, as well as by continued immigration to the United States from Central America and Mexico and increased immigration to Europe from Africa, the Middle East, and South Asia.

Dominant, residual, and emergent. Cultural studies scholars sometimes draw on Raymond Williams's terms **dominant, residual,** and **emergent.** The dominant describes the leading cultural forces of any given time. The residual describes older, potentially declining forces, and the emergent describes newer, potentially rising forces. Williams's sense of competing directions working at the same time in the same culture coincides with a deconstructive sense of multiple forces and internal contradictions in any particular cultural pattern or activity. The concept of the dominant also draws on Gramsci's notion of hegemony (see Chapter 8 on Marxism). Dominance is never total or absolute. The dominant never dominates everything. Therefore, when we refer to the dominant we refer not to absolute control but instead to an ongoing process that needs continuous work to sustain itself. Imperfections within the dominant open the possibility that it will give way to other forces. In that sense, the dominant, the residual, and the emergent are not utterly separate from each other. The dominant of any time incorporates into itself residual forces from previous dominants, often changing them while also sustaining them and using them to sustain its own dominance. In that sense, the dominant, residual, and emergent are not separate stages leading inevitably in a certain direction. Instead they represent structures of ongoing exchange.

Emergent forces may oppose dominant forces, but dominant forces may also preserve themselves by incorporating emergent forces, as when politicians take up the rhetoric of those who oppose them and use it to sustain their own influence. Thus when the right asserts its own religious freedom and civil rights as a logic for restricting queer access to healthcare and social services, drawing on and recoding older rhetorics of freedom and rights, we see the dominant incorporating older, residual ideas to consolidate its own threatened authority. Similarly, when white nationalists say that white lives matter, they try (probably less effectively) to incorporate and recode emergent anti-racist rhetoric to make it support dominant and residual racist assumptions. In neither of these cases does any one idea hold a monopoly on contemporary opinion. Instead, the concepts of dominant, residual, and emergent, and their intricate intertwining, give us a vocabulary to interpret continually changing cultural forces.

Cultural studies and relative autonomy. As they studied popular culture, such as music, TV, movies, and magazines, cultural studies scholars often came to see a degree of relative autonomy in popular culture. Instead of looking down on popular culture and seeing it as separate from and inferior to the elite culture of canonical literature typically studied in colleges and universities, cultural studies scholars came to respect its intellectual, aesthetic, and even political seriousness. They often study what they call *subcultures*, such as youth culture, immigrant culture, Black British culture, working-class culture, or smaller groups that fit within or combine such categories or that gather around a specific kind of music (for example, Black British dance hall reggae), a set of magazines (for example, preteen girls' magazines), a specific TV show (for example, *Star Trek* and "Trekkies," *Game of Thrones*), or any other genre of popular culture, from advertising to shopping malls, from Donald Trump rallies to Instapoetry.

Because cultural studies critics focus on popular culture, some critics see cultural studies as ignoring aesthetics. Some critics even praise what they see as cultural studies' frequent neglect of aesthetics, seeing aesthetics as elitist, while others lament the lower profile of aesthetics in cultural studies. Still others see the enthusiasm for popular culture as itself a form of respecting the aesthetics of popular culture instead of looking down on it, the way that pre-cultural studies scholars often looked down on popular culture as less serious.

By taking the people and pleasures of popular culture seriously rather than scornfully, cultural studies scholars shifted the study of popular culture from the study of how its fans are dupes of the broader cultural hegemony to studying how they use popular culture to speak back to and perhaps even resist or begin to resist the expectations of dominant ideologies, such as consumerism, sexism, racism, capitalism, class elitism, and so on. In that way, cultural studies scholars came to identify with the more optimistic pole of the continuum between pessimistic Marxism, which believes that dominant ideologies are too powerful to allow much resistance to them, and optimistic Marxism, which sees more opportunity to crack the shell of interpellation and resist dominant ideologies. Over the years, so many cultural studies projects focused on the resistant side of popular culture that eventually the readiness of cultural studies scholars to find relative autonomy and resistance in popular culture came to seem rote and predictable rather than carefully thought through. In turn, then, scholars responded by moving away from rote optimism and developing an increasingly nuanced sense of the relation between popular culture's compliance with dominant ideologies and its resistance to dominant ideologies.

For example, if we return to Danielle, the hypothetical thirteen-year-old girl from Chapter 8 who listens to misogynist hip-hop, we can see how cultural studies draws on Marxism to interpret popular culture and subcultures, such as youth and music cultures, with a nuanced respect for the routines of ordinary people and ordinary life, taking seriously the ability of emergent subcultures to resist and make trouble for dominant ideologies or at least to begin to question them. The reading of Danielle in Chapter 8, though included under Marxism, comes from cultural studies. It draws on the ability of cultural studies scholars to take popular culture and its participants seriously and to recognize the genuine thinking that goes on in popular culture, including the potential resistance in cultural activities that previous scholars saw as ignorant, duped compliance with consumerism and triviality.

HOW TO INTERPRET: A CULTURAL STUDIES EXAMPLE

Cultural studies and literature. At first, cultural studies, apart from its cultural materialist component, did not usually address literature, still less elite (or "literary") literature, as opposed to the literature of popular culture. Literature scholars now draw on cultural studies, however, and integrate it with literary studies. Whether drawing on Foucault, on cultural studies, or simply on related trends in literary criticism, they often read literary writing in relation to other cultural activities, including both popular and elite culture, and usually without the sense, once routine but now usually seen as dated, that "literary" writing is inherently superior to popular culture. "Literary" writing may often make for better "literary" literature, in the cultural context of what we expect from "literary" art, but it is not inherently, essentially better for all purposes. For many readers, moods, or purposes, the writings of Dan Brown, Charlaine Harris, or Stephen King, or the latest online chatter tracking a celebrity or a sports team, serve better than the writings of T. S. Eliot, James Joyce, or John Keats. Indeed, the methods of interpreting literature that this book describes can usually work equally well for interpreting popular culture, and the methods that cultural studies scholars bring to popular culture can usually work equally well for interpreting literature.

We can also read literature and popular culture together. In the wake of cultural studies, new historicism, and Foucault, even literary critics who interpret older writing will often look to the popular culture of an earlier age. Or if they study a time more or less before popular culture, they will still look at literature as part of a wide range of cultural history and expression. If they draw on the new historicist critique of the reflection model or the cultural studies alertness to agency in cultural expression, then literary critics will not read literature simply as reflecting cultural history. Instead, they will read literature as part of the culture, in some ways passively reflecting it and in some ways speaking back to it, from within it, and helping to change it or contributing to a broader array of cultural conversations that, collectively, can begin to change it.

A *cultural studies approach to Shakespeare's Sonnet 130*. Cultural change, however, is hard to measure, and it is even harder to pick out the exact agents that lead to change. If a feisty sonnet criticizes a dominant ideology or discourse, how can we tell that it has cultural agency? Shakespeare's Sonnet 130, for example, concludes by insisting on the speaker's love for his mistress, after beginning with these famous lines:

> My mistress' eyes are nothing like the sun;
> Coral is far more red than her lips' red;
> If snow be white, why then her breasts are dun;
> If hairs be wires, black wires grow on her head.
>   (Shakespeare 1867)

We could say that the speaker's insistence on his love for a woman who does not fit the stereotypical patterns (or discourses) of western European beauty resists an ethnocentric model (a discourse) of beauty and feminine value, or of abusive masculine objectification of feminine beauty, and that therefore this poem makes an intervention, shows a degree of relative autonomy, or exercises resistant agency.

That is a plausible argument, and I find it convincing. But by drawing on the strategies of cultural studies and historicism, we can push the argument much further, so that I can only give a taste of the possibilities in the short space available here. For another scholar might argue that the sonnet's resistance to stereotypically Western forms of feminine beauty is so conventionalized that it does not really offer a protest. For there were other poems like Sonnet 130. They reversed a standard pattern of poems, sometimes identified with the Italian poet Petrarch, that formulaically romanticized the beauty of a beloved woman. Poems like Sonnet 130 that reversed that pattern are called anti-Petrarchan. Therefore, we might argue, Sonnet 130 does more to repeat a familiar literary form than to protest a discourse or a social ideology.

That would suggest the kind of formalist argument that tends to read form as if its art insulated it from the social connections that historicist and cultural studies scholars insist on, so we might respond by saying that such insulation is not possible or that the mere existence of a conventionalized, oft-repeated form shows not a lack of resistance in anti-Petrarchan poetry but rather a breadth of resistance calling out for such forms as anti-Petrarchan sonnets to give it expression.

Still, a skeptic might respond by saying that it seems fanciful to find cultural protest in this sonnet if there is no evidence that readers in Shakespeare's time interpreted the sonnet that way, especially if we think of ourselves as historicist and cultural studies critics. Indeed, historicist and cultural studies critics often must rely on how they think that readers might or could have responded, especially when there is no direct evidence from outside the text about how actual readers responded.

That reliance on speculation raises a variety of questions. It could make us shrug our shoulders and give up on historicism. Or it could send us to archival research. Maybe, for example, we can find responses that readers wrote in the margins of a literary text, or comments in letters or diaries, or, for more recent times, book reviews, blogs, or social media that give readers' opinions about a literary work. Or, though we might not find responses to a particular text, such as Shakespeare's Sonnet 130, from the time when it was written, we might still find discussions of ideas like those in Shakespeare's sonnet—perhaps even in other sonnets or in responses to other sonnets, or in images such as that in Figure 9.5. Or, drawing on cultural studies' interest in contemporary culture, we could, like a presentist, study how the sonnet works in our own time, with or without supposing an analogy between how it works in our own time and how it worked in the poet's time. We could set up focus groups or surveys, or we could read students' papers, observe class discussions, or survey published criticism.

At the least, we need not give up on the fragile possibility of supposing ways that readers might have responded, based on the possibilities implied in the text itself in relation to our historicist understanding of the surrounding culture, because the skills of close reading that the new critics taught us can also prove suggestive for cultural interpretation. Even when we have a record of responses from actual readers, whether historical readers or contemporary readers, we might say—drawing on psychoanalysis and deconstruction—that what those readers say about their responses is itself only their own interpretation of their responses. Readers are not fully conscious of their own responses, and any textualization of their response—a remark scribbled in a margin, a comment in a letter or diary or blog, a book review, class discussion, student paper, or work of professional literary criticism—is itself a text as subject to multiple readings as the literary text itself. In many ways, therefore, the record of an actual

Figure 9.5 A visual version of anti-Petrarchan satire. When a woman has eyes like suns, cheeks like roses, teeth like pearls, and breasts like globes, she may end up looking less than lovely. From John Davies' translation of Charles Sorel's *The Extravagent Shepherd, or, The History of the Shepherd Lysis*, 1654. Second edition, 1660.

response does not necessarily give us a better overall picture of people's responses than we can derive from educated speculation about how readers *might* respond. (For more on readers' responses, see Chapter 11.)

CULTURAL STUDIES, HISTORICISM, AND LITERATURE

By bringing Marxism together with structuralism, deconstruction, psychoanalysis, and other movements in contemporary critical theory, cultural studies developed along a parallel track with new historicism, despite differences between the two groups. Cultural studies, a predominantly British movement, tended to address contemporary popular culture, and new historicism, a predominantly American movement, tended to address literature from the past. Drawing on an optimistic strain of Marxism, as we have seen, cultural studies tended to take notice of the possibility for agency, relative autonomy, and resistance to dominant ideologies, whereas new historicism, drawing on a more pessimistic strain of Marxism and on Foucault, often noticed ways that dominant ideologies or discourses overwhelmed the possibility for resistance, or allowed resistance but used the resistance to prop up the dominant ideologies by showing how they can crush the resistance. In short, by returning to the continuum reviewed in Chapter 8 between, at one pole, more optimistic Marxist notions of resistance that put weight on relative autonomy, agency, and intervention and, at the other pole, more pessimistic notions of resistance that put weight on ideology, interpellation, and false consciousness, we can say that new historicism tended to land on the pessimistic pole and cultural studies on the optimistic pole (Table 9.1).

In the 1980s, as new historicism and cultural studies rose to prominence, some commentators tried to inflate these differences among allies and paint new historicism and cultural studies as great antagonists. But as each group rose to prominence, its advocates also read the work of the other group, and each learned from the other and evolved to the point that the supposedly vast difference between the two groups faded. Cultural studies scholars did not often take up literary studies, and there was never much demand for them to do so, for there is no shortage of literary scholars or literary scholarship. But literary scholars on both sides of the Atlantic and in many countries increasingly study popular culture, including popular literature, often relating popular culture to elite literature in the same ways that they relate history to elite literature. Meanwhile, cultural studies scholars, as we have seen, grew suspicious that their tendency to see possibilities for resistance had calcified into a habit rather than a thought-through

Table 9.1 Cultural Studies vs. New Historicism

CULTURAL STUDIES	NEW HISTORICISM
contemporary	historical
popular culture	elite literary culture
more optimistic about resistance	more pessimistic about resistance
British	American

practice, while historicist literary scholars moved beyond new historicists' tendency to underestimate cultural agency and relative autonomy. The two movements learned from each other and, eventually, blended together more than they retained their differences.

To suggest, briefly, how things stand in light of this dialogue and partial blending of historicism (no longer new) and cultural studies, let us return to Dorothy Parker's "A Telephone Call," discussed in Chapter 6 on feminism, and Kate Chopin's "The Story of an Hour," discussed in Chapter 8 on Marxism. We might see "A Telephone Call" as compliant with the ideologies (or discourses) of gender that it portrays or as resisting those ideologies by mocking its character's compliance with them. We might see "The Story of an Hour" as mocking and punishing Louise's independence by killing her off or as sympathetically identifying with her and showing how sadly an unequal system of marriage constrains her.

Regardless, it would not make for a satisfying or even a convincing literary critical argument to say that these stories could be one thing or could be the opposite thing and then shrug our shoulders and leave it at that without daring a more decisive interpretation. Deconstructively, we already know that the stories could be, and are, more than one thing. But we can also see, deconstructively, that those opposite pessimistic and optimistic readings do not balance each other out in stable equilibrium, like a new critical paradox. They do not even have the same cultural consequences across the varying spectrum of cultural settings. For example, in Dorothy Parker's "New York to Detroit," a story similar to "A Telephone Call," the lonely woman finally calls her absent lover and hints that she is pregnant. The pessimistic and optimistic possibilities of these stories, then, carry a different weight in a setting that makes abortion or, for "The Story of an Hour," divorce legal or socially acceptable and a setting that makes abortion or divorce illegal or socially unacceptable. In that way, cultural settings and cultural history play an integral role in literary interpretation.

Our interpretations, therefore, will do well to refuse a timid formalist balance that merely says that it could be this or it could be that. We will do better as interpreters when we stand for something that we care about and believe in as we interpret how the combination of competing possibilities plays out in the material circumstances of actual historical and cultural conditions that we care about as readers and critics.

That is not easy, for, as we have seen from the Marxist critique of ideology, we do not choose what we care about all by ourselves.

A vast range of conscious and unconscious cultural forces and discourses shapes or helps shape our choices. And so as we ask ourselves what we care about most, we have to think critically about what drives our choices, but we can never fully answer that question. And sooner or later, however much our choices might be pushed along by forces beyond ourselves, we still have to choose. Historicist and cultural studies criticism, typically in combination with the other methods of criticism discussed in this book, offers us a chance to put our chosen commitments to work by thinking through the relation between literature and the historical and cultural conflicts and changes that we care about deeply.

FURTHER READING

Baudrillard, Jean. *Jean Baudrillard: Selected Writings*. Ed. Mark Poster. Stanford, CA: Stanford University Press, 1988.

Bérubé, Michael. *Public Access: Literary Theory and American Cultural Politics*. London: Verso, 1994.

Cisney, Vernon W., and Nicolae Morar, eds. *Biopower: Foucault and Beyond*. Chicago: University of Chicago Press, 2016.

Clifford, James. *Predicament of Culture: Twentieth-Century Ethnography, Literature, and Art*. Cambridge, MA: Harvard University Press, 1988.

Dollimore, Jonathan, and Alan Sinfield, eds. *Political Shakespeare: Essays in Cultural Materialism*. 2nd ed. Ithaca, NY: Cornell University Press, 1994.

During, Simon, ed. *The Cultural Studies Reader*. 2nd ed. London: Routledge, 1999.

Fiske, John. *Reading the Popular*. 2nd ed. New York: Routledge, 2011.

———. *Understanding the Popular*. 2nd ed. London: Routledge, 2010.

Foucault, Michel. *Discipline and Punish: The Birth of the Prison*. Trans. Alan Sheridan. New York: Pantheon, 1978.

———. *The History of Sexuality: An Introduction, Volume 1*. Trans. Robert Hurley. New York: Random House, 1978.

Frith, Simon. *Sound Effects: Youth, Leisure, and the Politics of Rock 'n' Roll*. New York: Pantheon Books, 1981.

———. *Taking Popular Music Seriously: Selected Essays*. Aldershot: Ashgate, 2007.

Frow, John, and Meaghan Morris, eds. *Australian Cultural Studies: A Reader*. Urbana: University of Illinois Press, 1993.

Gallagher, Catherine, and Stephen Greenblatt. *Practicing New Historicism*. Chicago: University of Chicago Press, 2000.

Gilroy, Paul. *"There Ain't No Black in the Union Jack": The Cultural Politics of Race and Nation*. 2nd ed. Chicago: University of Chicago Press, 1991.

Grady, Hugh, and Terence Hawkes, eds. *Presentist Shakespeares*. London: Routledge, 2007.

Greenblatt, Stephen Jay. *Renaissance Self-Fashioning: From More to Shakespeare.* Chicago: University of Chicago Press, 1980.

———. *Shakespearean Negotiations: The Circulation of Social Energy in Renaissance England.* Berkeley: University of California Press, 1988.

Grossberg, Lawrence. *Bringing It All Back Home: Essays on Cultural Studies.* Durham, NC: Duke University Press, 1997.

———. *We Gotta Get Out of This Place: Popular Conservatism and Postmodern Culture.* New York: Routledge, 1992.

Grossberg, Lawrence, Cary Nelson, and Paula A. Treichler, eds. *Cultural Studies.* New York: Routledge, 1992.

Hall, Stuart, and Tony Jefferson, eds. *Resistance through Rituals: Youth Subcultures in Post-War Britain.* 2nd ed. London: Routledge, 2006.

Hebdige, Dick. *Subculture: The Meaning of Style.* Rev. ed. London: Routledge, 2003.

hooks, bell. *Outlaw Culture: Resisting Representations.* New York: Routledge, 1994.

———. *Teaching to Transgress: Education as the Practice of Freedom.* New York: Routledge, 1994.

———. *Where We Stand: Class Matters.* New York: Routledge, 2000.

Levinson, Marjorie. *Wordsworth's Great Period Poems: Four Essays.* Cambridge: Cambridge University Press, 1986.

McRobbie, Angela. *The Aftermath of Feminism: Gender, Culture and Social Change.* Los Angeles: SAGE, 2009.

———. *Feminism and Youth Culture.* 2nd ed. London: Routledge, 2000.

Montrose, Louis Adrian. *The Purpose of Playing: Shakespeare and the Cultural Politics of the Elizabethan Theatre.* Chicago: University of Chicago Press, 1996.

Morris, Meaghan. *Pirate's Fiancée: Feminism, Reading, Postmodernism.* London: Verso, 1988.

Rose, Tricia. *Black Noise: Rap Music and Black Culture in Contemporary America.* Hanover, NH: Wesleyan University Press, 1994.

———. *The Hip Hop Wars: What We Talk about When We Talk about Hip Hop—and Why It Matters.* New York: BasicCivitas, 2008.

Ross, Andrew. *No Respect: Intellectuals and Popular Culture.* New York: Routledge, 1989.

Sinfield, Alan. *Faultlines: Cultural Materialism and the Politics of Dissident Reading.* Berkeley: University of California Press, 1992.

———. *Literature, Politics, and Culture in Postwar Britain.* Oxford: Blackwell, 1989.

Stallybrass, Peter, and Allon White. *The Politics and Poetics of Transgression.* London: Methuen, 1986.

Veeser, H. Aram, ed. *The New Historicism.* London: Routledge, 1989.

Williams, Raymond. *The Country and the City.* New York: Oxford University Press, 1973.

———. *Culture and Society, 1780–1950.* London: Chatto & Windus, 1958.

———. *The Long Revolution.* London: Chatto & Windus, 1961.

✻ 10 ✻

Postcolonial and Race Studies

In the middle of the twentieth century, the world turned a somersault. A small number of nations had colonized a huge proportion of the world's land and population. Roughly one out of every five people lived in British India alone, and the Soviet Union and China were expanding and consolidating their power. But as most of Latin America had wrested independence from Spain and Portugal in the early nineteenth century, so in the middle of the twentieth century most of Africa, the Caribbean, and South Asia, and many peoples in the Pacific and the Middle East, broke free from the rule of colonial powers in a wave of change that raised anticolonialist hopes and promised to reshape the world's hierarchies of power. Hopes soared again late in the twentieth century when Eastern Europe broke off from Soviet control. But in many ways, colonialism turned out to be more entrenched than anticolonialists anticipated or hoped.

Postcolonialism thus has a long history, but postcolonial studies, especially Anglo-American postcolonial literary studies, gathered force in the late 1970s, especially with Edward Said's *Orientalism* (1978) and then a series of influential articles by Gayatri Chakravorty Spivak and Homi K. Bhabha. These critics' work, and the work their ideas responded to and helped provoke, spoke to a powerful sense of need as readers faced up to changes in world politics and the growing recognition of English as a language of international literature and international daily life. Postcolonial studies emerged as a driving force in literary studies and helped reshape scholarship and teaching across the humanities and social sciences.

At its peak, the British Empire ruled roughly one quarter of the earth's land and population. Economically and culturally, British power fed off British conquests. But until the last few decades, the study of British history and especially British literature typically paid little attention to colonialism. We can understand why, because, in many ways, colonialism was so brutal that if the conquering peoples owned up to it, that might have led them to reject colonialism and give up the privileges of power. In that way, Westerners had a stake, however unconscious, in not owning up to colonialism, and certainly in not thinking about it critically. Today, postcolonial studies offers the possibility—not yet fulfilled—of making literary study as international as literature itself, and so it holds a powerful appeal for readers who care about the fate of the world and its writing.

Because of its attention to racial and national politics, postcolonial studies has also held special appeal for students, readers, and critics interested in the study of race and in the study of racial, ethnic, and national minorities, including, in the United States, African American studies, Latina/Latino studies, Asian American studies, and American Indian studies, and including, internationally, Black studies, transnational studies, indigenous studies, comparative literature, and the emerging field of world literature. Scholars in all these areas often see analogies and overlapping questions between their own concerns and the concerns of postcolonial studies. While this book's sections on postcolonialism and race studies can work as separate chapters, and some readers may choose to read them that way, I believe each section gains from a modest alliance, a compromise between reading postcolonial and race studies as independent topics and reading them as overlapping topics that inflect, internationalize, and localize each other.

POSTCOLONIALISM

The term *postcolonial* has grown routine, yet it has also led to confusion and debate. Scholars of postcolonialism often write about the colonial as well as or instead of the postcolonial, and in many ways we still live in colonial times, not postcolonial times. The term's suggestion of kinship with poststructuralism, corroborated by the poststructuralist approaches of the most prominent postcolonial theorists, such as Said, Spivak, and Bhabha, attracts suspicion from scholars who want more certainty than they see poststructuralism likely to encourage. Nevertheless, despite its distortions and deceptiveness, the term has emerged as a convenient label for the study of colonialism, postcolonialism, and, more broadly, cultural and political relations between more powerful and less powerful nations and peoples.

The different kinds of colonies. Postcolonial literary studies considers writing from colonizing peoples, colonized peoples, and—especially in the twenty-first century—formerly colonized peoples. Scholars sometimes describe the colonizing nations as "metropolitan" and sometimes divide the colonies into two different kinds (each with its own array of variations): **settler colonies** and **occupation colonies.** (Occupation colonies are sometimes called *exploitation colonies* or *colonies of conquest.*) In occupation colonies, such as colonial India and Nigeria, the colonists remain a small proportion of the population. Typically, they leave their metropolitan homes to do their work exploiting the colony, and then they return home and other colonizers replace them. In settler colonies, such as Australia, New Zealand, Canada, and the United States, the colonizers move in permanently, and they or their descendants often grow far more numerous than the people they colonize, whose numbers the colonizers often reduce by disease and by abuses that sometimes reach the level of genocide. Sometimes the settlers forcibly or culturally limit outnumbered indigenous peoples to specific areas where, surrounded by settlers, they live in **internal colonies,** such as Indian reservations or reserves, South African Bantustans, and, by loose analogy, urban ghettos.

Scholars have debated whether to include settler colonies in postcolonial studies at all. The settlers often act like occupiers and identify with their metropolitan homelands, yet they also develop a sense of difference from or even resentment of their homelands. Sometimes, as often in the United States, they even lose their awareness of being settlers, act as if the indigenous peoples have disappeared, and see immigrants like their own ancestors as invading interlopers.

Regardless, the division into two groups, settler colonies and occupation colonies, can fog differences between different examples in the same group. And some examples, such as Ireland, Algeria, Kenya, Hawai'i, and South Africa, do not fit clearly into either group. In the Caribbean the two patterns combine, as the colonists decimated the native peoples, replaced them with and absorbed them into forcibly imported populations of enslaved laborers, and then acted much like exploitation colonists. The distinctions among different kinds of colonies thus remain up for debate, and they probably serve us best if we question them and keep them provisional.

Following the independence of India and Pakistan (including what is now Bangladesh) in 1947, the wave of newly independent nations inspired excitement and hope across South Asia, Southeast Asia, the Pacific, Africa, and the Middle East. Some countries had to fight the colonial powers before achieving independence, but most won independence peacefully. Some countries went on to set up successful democracies, while others met a more checkered fate, shifting back and forth between elected and imposed governments.

In many countries, local oligarchs and dictators betrayed the promise of independence by exploiting the divisions and disarray left by colonialism. Such leaders reproduce many of the abuses of colonialism, including the concentration of capital and resources in a few hands, undemocratic government, ethnic and racial demagoguery, the exploitation of labor and the environment, the displacement of local populations, and restrictions on speech and civil liberties. Under their leadership, postcolonialism transforms into **neocolonialism.** Neocolonialism updates the ravages of colonialism, merely splitting the profits between the local oligarchs and the colonial powers, now represented not only by colonialist governments but also by colonialist, international corporations, often turning the rage for "globalization" into colonialism under another name.

Hybridity. All these shifts in politics and economics, including the cosmetic adjustments that change little beyond the color of some of those who reap the profits, underline that colonialism is a matter of how people think as well as a matter of military power. The shifts of recent history leave the world not so much divided in two between colonizers and colonized as (in postcolonialist lingo) **hybrid.** Cultural hybridity comes from the way that colonized people and colonizers have taken on many of each other's ways of living and thinking. Many colonizing peoples moved to the lands they colonized. And millions of people from colonized and formerly colonized countries, under the pressure of war, forced displacement, or economic disaster or in search of economic and educational opportunities or change, have migrated to the metropole and to other formerly colonized countries.

With enormous (in postcolonialist lingo) *migrant, diasporic,* or *exiled* populations, with the mixing of peoples and cultures, with global trade and communication, and with disputes over whether and how much to welcome migrants, the metropolitan countries and the colonized countries have both changed. Historically, the metropolitan countries have tended to deny the ways that international dialogue, migrant populations, the descendants of migrants, and the commerce between cultures have changed the metropole.

They also often see the changes in colonized nations and populations as peculiar, amusing, or threatening mixtures that compromise the authenticity of supposedly exotic locales, as if historical change were a feature of the metropole but not of the rest of the world. More recently, amidst a reaction against migration from Africa and the Middle East to Europe, from the European continent to the United Kingdom, and from Mexico and Central America to the United States, many people in metropolitan countries have responded with a fear that migration may bring too much cultural change.

Stuart Hall, who (as we saw in the previous chapter) left Jamaica to live in England, described how hybridity is not so new as many skeptics about immigration may suppose. It threads its way through the definitional features and daily routines of contemporary life, despite the cultural clichés and denials that often pressure us to overlook it:

> People like me who came to England in the 1950s have been there for centuries; symbolically, we have been there for centuries. I was coming home. I am the sugar at the bottom of the English cup of tea. I am the sweet tooth, the sugar plantations that rotted generations of English children's teeth. There are thousands of others beside me that are, you know, the cup of tea itself. Because they don't grow it in Lancashire, you know. Not a single tea plantation exists within the United Kingdom. This is the symbolization of English identity—I mean, what does anybody in the world know about an English person except that they can't get through the day without a cup of tea?
>
> Where does it come from? Ceylon—Sri Lanka, India. That is the outside history that is inside the history of the English. There is no English history without that other history. The notion that identity has to do with people that look the same, feel the same, call themselves the same, is nonsense. As a process, as a narrative, as a discourse, it is always told from the position of the Other. (Hall, "Old and New" 48–49)

English prosperity, Hall notes, was founded on colonialism, including the Jamaican sugar plantations worked by his enslaved ancestors. The anchoring ritual of daily English life grounds English culture in the colonialism that filled the teacups of England with South Asian tea and Caribbean sugar. Those British people who would define contemporary Britain as definitionally white can do so only at the cost of denying the hybridity and colonialism that gave them the culture they brag about and the power to pretend it can exclude so much of what makes it possible. Much as the colonialists and racists imagine that their identity depends on a shared appearance, it depends instead on a difference and variety that they deny. The so-called Other whom they seek to exclude lies deeply and definitionally within them, and no less so because the racists and colonialists deny it. We all live in a hybrid world.

Postcolonialism, transnationalism, globalization. With rapid globalization, cultural critics often call attention to the ways that contemporary international culture, politics, and economics have taken on an increasingly corporate dimension. Giant transnational corporations re-enact the colonialism of old under a mask of, at best, half-truths about mutual economic development. With frequently exploitive wages, terrible working conditions (especially for women), ferocious environmental devastation (for more on transnational environmental devastation, see Chapter 12), and collusion with corrupt and undemocratic governments, contemporary transnational corporate globalization often takes more than it brings or shares. By the twenty-first century, with the movement of migrant, exiled, and diasporic populations and the surging power of multinational and now transnational corporations, transnationalism and globalization have emerged as the contemporary inheritors of postcolonialism. Many critics now move back and forth among the terms *postcolonialism, transnationalism,* and *globalization,* sometimes magnifying their varying nuances and other times using them almost interchangeably, while other critics keep the term *postcolonialism* at the forefront because of its franker invocation of politics and imbalances of power, and because it connects to the history of colonial and postcolonial resistance and writing, a history that we may now, in brief, review.

Négritude. In the 1930s, a group of French-speaking black poets and intellectuals in Paris, inspired partly by the American Harlem Renaissance, put together a literary and political movement that they called **Négritude.** Led by the Senegalese Léopold Senghor and the Martinican Aimé Césaire, the Négritude writers called for pride in blackness. They believed that black people, whether from Africa or the African diaspora, share a "collective personality" that differs radically from the European colonizers. Senghor went on to become the first president of Senegal, and Césaire served many years as mayor of Fort de France, the capital of Martinique. When Martinique became a French province, he served as the island's representative in the French National Assembly. The European colonizers saw the people they colonized as barbaric, but the writers of Négritude reversed that view and saw the European colonizers as the true barbarians.

The Nigerian playwright and Nobel Prize laureate Wole Soyinka criticized what he saw as a defensiveness in the Négritude movement's assertion of black pride. Controversially, he responded to Négritude by declaring, "A tiger does not proclaim his tigritude, he pounces" (quoted in Jahn 265; see also Soyinka 126–139).

   Fanon. Among critics of Négritude, the Martinican psychiatrist Frantz Fanon (Figure 10.1) stands out. Fanon was one of the most provocative, influential theorists and practitioners of anticolonial resistance. After fighting with the Free French Forces against the Nazis in World War II and then studying medicine and psychiatry in France, Fanon sought work in Africa and was appointed to direct an Algerian psychiatric hospital. In 1954, he joined the National Liberation Front to fight for Algerian independence from France. In an essay called "The Fact of Blackness," Fanon wrote with lyrical astonishment about the dehumanizing pain of racial labeling and generalizing, whether by outsiders, such as when whites label blacks, or by insiders, such as when the poets of Négritude labeled blacks. Having moved to France, he described how it felt when people reduced him to nothing more than a derogatory slur or a racial label, as when a child, seeing Fanon, said to its mother "Look, a Negro!" (Fanon, *Black Skin* 109).

   A student and friend of Césaire, Fanon sympathized with the Négritude movement, understanding how racist colonialism could

Figure 10.1 Frantz Fanon (1925–1961).

provoke a prideful counterreaction, especially after colonialism had gone so far to strip colonized peoples, including blacks, of their sense of racial self-respect and a proud history. Still, while Fanon valued the pride rekindled by Négritude, he objected to what he saw as its romantic oversimplifications. He argued that when colonized intellectuals visit with the people, too often they return with "mummified fragments" (Fanon, *Wretched of the Earth* 160), the "sterile clichés" of "customs, traditions, and costumes" in "a banal quest for the exotic" (Fanon, *Wretched of the Earth* 158). In Fanon's eyes, the black or Arab intellectual trying to act like one of the people ends up acting like the white racist cliché of a black or an Arab. Négritude, Pan-Africanism, and similar transnational movements, he feared, depended on a romantic delusion of sameness that threatened to mask the variety of African and black peoples. Fanon believed that in the guise of rejecting colonialist prejudice, the poets and philosophers of Négritude reinvigorated the same stereotypes that the colonizers believed in, except that the Négritude movement celebrated a supposed sensuality and communalism that colonizers saw as depraved and uncivilized.

The colonizers taught native peoples to believe in and internalize the colonizers' racist sense of native peoples' inferiority. In response, Fanon argued that anticolonial violence can cleanse native peoples of their fear and self-doubt. Because colonialism was violent, he believed that it would take violence to overthrow colonialism. He did not believe that the colonial powers would grant independence. Independence, according to Fanon, must be won. When the colonial powers tried to sit down with the colonized elite and negotiate independence, he believed that the elite represented their own interests, betraying the masses and positioning themselves to rule the common people as the colonizers had ruled them. Fanon warned that betrayals from the native elite, together with the false pride of Négritude and similar movements, would allow formerly colonized peoples, led by Europeanized native intellectuals, corrupt capitalists, and dictators, to sustain the exploitations of colonialism through a self-colonizing neocolonialism.

In that way, and as a psychiatrist, Fanon attended to the psychological condition of internalized racism that allowed colonized peoples to perpetuate the colonialist and racist myths of their inferiority. He understood why, in reaction against colonialism, colonized peoples often sought to romanticize their precolonial history and civilization and their shared racial heritage. After all, the colonizers taught them that they were inferior and had no history or civilization. But he also saw distortions in such romanticizing dreams and believed that the precolonial past could never be recovered, because colonized cultures—like all cultures—change continuously. Fanon called for the Négritude movement and other romanticizing visions celebrating a glorious past and collective consciousness to serve as a bridge to a revolutionary practice that would build a wide range of individual postcolonial nations.

Language and the decolonization of the mind. Pursuing the call for decolonization not only of the political system but also of the mind, Kenyan novelist Ngũgĩ wa Thiong'o (Figure 10.2), noting the close relation between language and thought, argues that African writers should stop writing in the European languages (such as English, French, and Portuguese) that the colonizers forced on the peoples they colonized. Instead, he proposes, they should write in their own African languages. Ngũgĩ himself stopped writing novels in English and began to write in Gikuyu, allowing his novels to reach a larger audience among his own people, though he also translates or has others translate his novels into English.

Not everyone has accepted Ngũgĩ's argument. Many African or other native writers cannot write in a native language. Some prefer English, French, or Portuguese because it can reach a larger audience, including a larger audience of Africans. And some, notably the Nigerian novelist Chinua Achebe (Figure 10.3), have pointed out that the

Figure 10.2 Ngũgĩ wa Thiong'o (1938–).

Figure 10.3 Chinua Achebe (1930–2013).

language they write in is not the same as the language of the coloniz-ers. Achebe writes not in British English but in African English, just as many native writers across the world write in their own version of what was once a colonizing language. Sometimes, it is the language or one of the languages of their schooling or their daily lives and the language of the people around them. They have made it their own language.

FROM ORIENTALISM TO DECONSTRUCTION: EDWARD SAID, HOMI BHABHA, AND GAYATRI CHAKRAVORTY SPIVAK

Said. In literary studies, the boom in postcolonial criticism began with Edward Said's *Orientalism* (1978). Drawing on the ideas of Michel Foucault (see Chapter 9), the Palestinian American Said

(Figure 10.4; pronounced with two syllables, *Sah-eed*) argued that the West has constructed a **colonial discourse** (in the Foucauldian sense of the term *discourse*) that produces the ideas about the Orient—the East—that the discourse purports to describe. Said called that colonial discourse **Orientalism**. Said does not mean the "Orient" in the usual sense the term carries today, to refer to East Asia. Instead, he uses it in an older sense to refer to the Indian subcontinent and especially to the Islamic Middle East, though his ideas can be and have been applied to all colonial discourse, including discourse about East Asia, sub-Saharan Africa, racial minorities in the West, and the rest of the colonized world.

In Said's model, and beginning especially in the nineteenth century, Western discourse about the East (travel accounts, journalism, scholarship, literary and political writing, studies of religion and language) constructed the East as sensual, lazy, exotic, irrational, cruel, promiscuous, seductive, inscrutable, dishonest, mystical, superstitious, primitive, ruled by emotion, a sink of despotism at the margins of the world where all people are alike and where their actions are determined by the national or racial category they belong to ("the Arabs," "the natives"). Said argued that descriptions of the East in these terms generated a discourse that produced and then continued to reproduce the East in such terms, and that has continued to reproduce the East and the colonized or formerly colonized world in such terms up to the present day. In constructing the East, Orientalist discourse also constructed a West that was everything the East was not: rational, hardworking, kind, democratic, moral, modern, progressive, technological, individualist, and the center of the world, the norm against which everything else was a deviation.

Figure 10.4 Edward Said (1935–2003).

The binary opposition that Said observed between East and West maps onto a parallel discourse of gender. Orientalist discourse finds qualities in the East that overlap with the qualities that misogynist discourse finds in the feminine (women as supposedly irrational, emotional, promiscuous, seductive, dishonest, lazy). And the qualities it sees in the West overlap with the qualities that it sees in the masculine (men as supposedly rational, dependable, hardworking, and strong). In that sense, colonialism often feminizes the colonized, partly in an effort to masculinize itself. Said argued that the West constructed the East by unconsciously taking qualities that the West feared in itself and projecting them onto the East, allowing Westerners to suppose that the West does not have those qualities and that those qualities define the East, separating it from the West. In that way, Westerners can imagine the East as an Other to the West's self.

To postcolonial scholars, the Orientalism that Said described continues to shape economic, political, and military relations between the Anglo-American West and the East, including the Islamic Middle East. More broadly, it shapes relations between the colonialist or neocolonialist world and the colonized or formerly colonized world. In the process, it shapes each side's inability to understand or think through the perspectives of the other side. Culturally, the binary opposition between colonizer and colonized reproduces itself by allowing the West to treat its own ways of thinking as universal truths. The ruling assumption is that since the colonizing powers had the means of conquering the rest of the world, the colonizing cultures are therefore superior and the colonized cultures inferior, as if the means of conquest were a measure of all other values. Aesthetically and literarily, the colonizing world treats its own standards for art and literature as if they were universal and natural rather than culturally specific and constructed, keeping metropolitan cultures from seeing the value and specificity of art, literature, and ways of thinking in colonized cultures.

Later postcolonial critics, while finding Said's account broadly convincing, often see it as overly binarized, too confidently separating the discourses of the East and the West without attending to the cultural or even deconstructive blur between cultures and the internal differences within cultures, including differences of class and gender. After all, Westerners, even colonizers, sometimes recognize difference and variety within the East as well as within their own countries. While the binary opposition between colonizers and colonized that Said's *Orientalism* exposed has shaped the questions and issues of later postcolonial criticism, the discussion of that binary opposition has often questioned its rigidity. Such questions typically arise either from a historicist sense of cultural complexity or from a characteristically deconstructionist impulse to break down binaries in favor of multiplicity.

Bhabha. In that vein, Bhabha and Spivak take a more deconstructive perspective than Said. Their highly theorized, densely jargoned, arcane writings have provoked a storm of interest for the challenges they pose and a storm of resentment for what some readers see as pretentious and impenetrable elitism.

Homi Bhabha (Figure 10.5; not to be confused with the famous physicist of the same name) joins the critique of Said's *Orientalism* as too committed to a binary opposition between colonizer and colonized. Drawing on language and ideas from structuralism, deconstruction, psychoanalysis, and Foucault, Bhabha asks us to consider the psychological ambivalence, the struggle of opposite and contradictory feelings, in the colonized or formerly colonized world and in colonial and postcolonial discourse. He describes the colonized and colonizing worlds as **hybrid,** versus Said's sense of one culture thinking about its opposite culture. The term *hybrid,* popularized by Bhabha, Stuart Hall, and others, has emerged, as we have seen, as a synonym for cultural multiplicity, though to some critics (myself included), its history as a term for crossbreeding two different species can carry inappropriately biological connotations and seem to reinstall the binary opposition that the term supposedly undermines. Regardless, the cultural multiplicity suggested by the term expresses a sense of continuous cultural change across history that colonialists and some anticolonial movements might seem to deny.

From Fanon's perspective, for example, the movements celebrating a collective consciousness or a return to a precolonial past overlook the hybridity or cross-cultural multiplicity of contemporary culture. They merely put a better-intentioned spin on the colonialist sense that colonized peoples are locked in an unchanging past and usually in a distorted vision of that past as well, as in the stereotypes of Africans (jungle, spear, etc.), American Indians (feathered war bonnet, face paint, etc.), and Arabs (scimitar, camel, etc.). Just as Westerners no longer typically ride a horse or carry a flintlock, though some Westerners do, especially at ceremonial times, so Africans, American Indians, and Arabs live in a multicultural modernity that

Figure 10.5 Homi K. Bhabha (1949–).

often looks like contemporary London, Paris, or New York. And the multicultural modernity of Nairobi, Window Rock (the capitol of the Navajo Nation), and Beirut or of Mumbai (formerly called Bombay), Jakarta, Manila, Seoul, Mexico City, San Juan, and Kingston often *is* the multicultural modernity of London, Paris, and New York, because the same people, goods, and corporations routinely migrate across political and cultural borders.

Rather than seeing borders as dividing utterly different peoples, we might therefore think of borders—such as the southern and northern borders of the United States and the borders between nations of the European Union—as porous transit points that sift and sort people as much as they separate them. A large proportion of the world's population now lives in more than one supposedly but not actually separate culture or lives in a country or region other than where they or some of their near ancestors were born. People sustain and change the cultures they bring with them, and they sustain and change the cultures where they live, so that, as we have seen, the supposedly separate cultures are no longer separate or distinct (if they ever were). Instead, they are hybrid and multiple.

Nevertheless, the pressure to essentialize identity invites us to deny the hybridity around us and within us. Such denial often takes the form of literary and cultural stereotypes, from the warlike images of spear, war bonnet, and scimitar that a conquering culture imposes, ironically, on those it conquers, to the full panoply of racial, gender, regional, and national stereotypes, including those that Said exposed as produced by the colonial discourse that purports to describe them. Against our familiar way of critiquing stereotypes, Bhabha argues, deconstructively, that the problem with stereotypes is not their inaccuracy but instead their fixity, their denial of the play of signifiers. Perhaps that amounts to the same thing. But for Bhabha the point lies in the way that the fixity of stereotypes denies variation and change, as if variety and history were the privilege of those who impose stereotypes but are not available for those who have stereotypes imposed on them.

Bhabha tries to shift the critique of stereotype from saying that one image is positive and another negative to the work of looking at the ambivalent process of stereotyping, the way that stereotypes deny something about the self while they assert something about the other. In that sense, Bhabha's challenge echoes the feminist critique of "images-of-women" feminism (as discussed in Chapter 6). He sees stereotypes not so much as false as he sees them as projections of what the stereotyping culture fears about itself onto an "other" that it can delude itself into supposing is separate from the stereotyping self. (In that sense, Bhabha echoes Said's argument about Orientalism, but Bhabha intensifies the psychoanalytic lingo of projection, introjection, ambivalence, and displacement.)

He also sees the discourse of critiquing stereotypes, in its ambivalent effort to fix (meaning, to stabilize) representation, as characteristic of literary realism's denial of desires and cultures that it typically runs away from representing, despite realism's devotion to presenting the truth. Supposedly realistic novels such as André Gide's *The Immoralist*; W. Somerset Maugham's *The Moon and Sixpence*; E. M. Forster's *A Passage to India*; Richard Wright's *Native Son*; Alan Paton's *Cry, the Beloved Country*; and Philip Roth's *Goodbye, Columbus* work hard to undermine stereotypes. But even as they undermine some stereotypes, they still trade on other stereotypes of gender, sexual orientation, race, religion, ethnicity, or nationality. The usual objection calls the stereotypes unrealistic because they are inaccurate. But from Bhabha's perspective, the problem lies less in the misleading inaccuracy than in what the desire to represent fixed, static patterns says about the representing cultures and about readers who go along, passively taking the static patterns for granted.

Bhabha describes cultural ambivalence as dramatized in what he calls **mimicry.** Inevitably, in a world of cultural mixing and differences of power, colonized people often end up mimicking their colonizers, adopting the colonizers' language, educational systems, governmental systems (parliament or congress, courts, constitution, laws), clothing, music, and so on. While some might see such mimicry as a form of internalized colonization or self-colonization, as in Ngũgĩ's critique of African writing in European languages, Bhabha calls attention to the way that the colonized's mimicry of the colonizers can express the colonized's ambivalence and, in turn, can provoke ambivalence and doubt in the colonizers.

When the colonizers gaze in the mirror of the colonized's mimicry, the image they see looks, as Bhabha puts it, *"almost the same, but not quite."* The blend of repetition and difference can threaten the colonizers' sense of their own power and superiority. It can even threaten their sense of racial privilege when they begin to recognize that the mimicry is also, as Bhabha puts it, *"almost the same but not white"* (Bhabha 86, 89). The signifiers slip far enough away from what they supposedly signify that they tilt the mimicry into menacing mockery. The colonizers may suppose that their surveillance of the colonized, in Foucauldian terms, disciplines the colonized. But when the colonizers gaze at the colonized and see the mimicking colonized's displacement of the colonizers' gaze turned back on the colonizers, it alienates the colonizers from their confidence in their own essence, thus destabilizing colonialism itself.

The colonized mimic the colonizers, as Bhabha argues. On the other hand, though Bhabha does not say so, the colonizers can also mimic the colonized—and they do. Almost any example we might give will spark controversy and disagreement, and, because the binary opposition between colonized and colonizer has multiplied so profusely, some examples can raise questions about who, if anyone, is or resembles the colonized and who, if anyone, is or resembles the colonizers. White musicians have often imitated the music of black musicians, and historically many white musicians, like colonialists, manipulated contracts so that the white imitators and not the black composers got the profits. This is not to say that white imitations or variations on music composed by blacks are necessarily a bad thing, but it is to say that they have an ugly history of abuse. Similarly, the world music movement could be read as mimicry, as could tanning parlors, or the practice of curling, straightening, or otherwise arranging hair in ways that make it look more like the hair that, however simplistically, many people associate with another race than what they think of as their own race, or whites imitating clothing styles or speech patterns that they associate, however stereotypically, with blacks, or the scandal over college "ghetto parties" where white students dress up like stereotypes of African Americans, or "taco and tequila" parties where they dress up like stereotypes of Mexicans. On my own campus, until recently, and amidst enormous controversy, a white student dressed up like a stereotype of an American Indian and performed a calisthenic "dance" at halftime of football and basketball games, to the cheers of a roaring crowd and the horror of most Indian students and faculty. Different people will often interpret provocative examples like these in different ways, and many of our interpretations will vary with the context, with whether one group acts in some way like another group out of envy, respect, scorn, or mockery. Even then we will often debate whether imitations intended as respectful can nevertheless come across—given the intentional fallacy—as disrespectful.

Neither side, colonizers or colonized—if we can still speak, for convenience, of two sides and a binary opposition, amidst the circulation of so much deconstructive imitation and instability—can hold a monopoly on mockery. And neither side can hold a monopoly on instability or on the capacity to expose the other side's instability. The two directions of mimicry, however, do not disrupt in the same ways. When less powerful people mimic more powerful people, they can menace the power structure, as Bhabha argues. But when more powerful people mimic less powerful people, they can reinforce the power structure. Even so, when colonizing people mimic colonized people, the mimicry can also suggest the colonizers' vulnerability, expressed as a desire for what they also suppress, both when that means suppressing other people and when it means suppressing something within themselves. That sense of ambivalent vulnerability and desire makes mimicry a potent force in any cultural repetition, lying in wait to shake up dominant discourses and ideologies.

Imperialist nostalgia. The anthropologist Renato Rosaldo noted that colonizing peoples often mourn for the past of the colonized cultures they have tried to destroy. He called the colonizers' sentimental respect for a colonized culture **imperialist nostalgia.** It allows the colonizers to define their own culture through progress and change while fencing progress and change off from the colonized culture. Imperialist nostalgia, Rosaldo writes, "makes racial domination appear innocent and pure" by making the colonizers think that they respect what they have tried to destroy (Rosaldo 68). We can see imperialist nostalgia in movies and novels about the American West that memorialize American Indians into a frozen past, a brief moment—usually from the nineteenth century—that the colonizers hold up to represent what Indians always were and what they supposedly should be still, whether in movies and novels or in the stereotypical feathered headdresses of sports mascots and children's play. We can see it as well, Rosaldo notes, in such fiction and films as *A Passage to India, Out of Africa,* and *The Gods Must Be Crazy.* Change, the colonizing peoples think, is for "us." Any hint of change in "them" must be denied, because it threatens to slide into mimicry. It threatens the binary opposition that allows colonizers to see themselves as essentially different from the people they colonize, thus allowing the colonizers to justify their conquests.

Spivak. Gayatri Chakravorty Spivak (Figure 10.6) first attracted wide notice by translating into English Derrida's most influential book, *Of Grammatology.* Her own work brings deconstruction together with feminism, Marxism, and postcolonial theory, and her interest in feminism and gender helped expand and deepen postcolonial criticism. Spivak notes that imperialism is central to British history and culture, and yet the study of British literature (before the growth of postcolonial studies) largely ignored it, colluding in the ideological suppression of one of the motors that drive British culture. She contends that to study the role of imperialism in the literature of colonizing countries can help make visible the **worlding** of the so-called Third World. By that she means that it is not enough to see Third World writing as a separate thing out on the margins of metropolitan culture. Instead, given the hybridity and interconnectedness of cultures, the Third World is part of the metropolitan world, just as the metropolitan world is part of the Third World.

Spivak has chided early Anglo-American feminist literary criticism for concentrating on how female characters heroically boost their subjectivity, their sense of individual personhood. In effect, she criticizes

Figure 10.6 Gayatri Chakravorty Spivak (1942–).

"images-of-women" feminism (see Chapter 6) for a narcissistic obsession with the individualism of "strong women" and an obliviousness to imperialism and colonialism, an obliviousness that Spivak's work helps to change. Here it may help to quote Spivak and then work carefully through the argument in her quoted words. To Spivak, the "feminist individualist heroine" offers "an allegory of the general epistemic violence of imperialism, the construction of a self-immolating subject for the glorification of the social mission of the colonizer" (Spivak, "Three Women's Texts and a Critique of Imperialism" 251). That is, she sees the ideology of individualism, including bourgeois feminist individualism, as part of the suppressed logic of colonialism. She sees it as something to be criticized and not, as traditional feminists supposed, as something to be sought and celebrated. For metropolitan women, bourgeois individualism offers a false freedom earned partly on the backs of women and men in the Third World, whose labor and subjugation pays for metropolitan privilege.

To *immolate* means to sacrifice, especially by burning. Self-immolating, therefore, meets self-sacrificing. It means suicidal sacrifice for a larger ideal, especially suicide by fire, a form of suicide that—as we will soon see—has special resonance for the history of Hindu India. To Spivak's thinking, metropolitan women see Third World women as disrespectful of themselves, as "self-immolating," as compared to metropolitan women, who are in love with their own newly achieved feminist self-hood. By seeing Third World women as persecuted and as submitting to their own persecution ("self-immolating"), metropolitan feminists put themselves in a self-glorifying position of superiority that allows them to tell Third World women how to do things better. By telling Third World women to respect themselves more and strive for feminist individualism, the metropolitan women take on a "social mission" that, to Spivak, exposes the colonizers' sexist and colonialist delusion of their own superiority over the people whose labor makes the colonizers' privilege possible.

In this context, Spivak's influential article "Can the Subaltern Speak?" (1985) raises reverberating questions for postcolonial theory, feminist theory, and race, minority, or *subaltern* studies. But Spivak's writing is notoriously dense, and "Can the Subaltern Speak?," like much of her writing, often verges on the unreadable. Because the article's key argument is so provocative, however, I will try to summarize it.

To understand Spivak's argument, you need to know that the term *subaltern*, which she takes from Antonio Gramsci, refers to people with less power. (For Gramsci, see Chapter 8.) Spivak's examples of subalterns are women, Indians (South Asian Indians), and Indian women in particular. You also need to know about the history of "sati," the controversial Hindu practice of widow burning. (Sometimes spelled suttee, it rhymes with "What, me?")

British colonialists had their ways of rationalizing the British empire. They often saw themselves not just as conquerors but as good liberal conquerors. As supposedly good conquerors, they often sought to let Indians rule themselves according to Indian practices. But the British ran into a problem following that principle when it came to sati. On the one hand, their liberalism told them not to interfere with Indian practices. On the other hand, it also told them that widow burning was abhorrent and had to be halted. The conflict seemed irresolvable. Their solution was to say that widows could be burned only if they first agreed to be burned.

To complicate matters, the literal meaning of "sati" is not "widow burning" but "good wife." To some Hindus, for a widow to be a good wife meant that she must want to be burned. You can imagine the dilemma, then, in the British colonial authorities asking a woman to say that she did not want to be a sati, since a widow and others could see that as meaning that she did not want to be a good wife. By contrast, the British and many Hindus who opposed sati argued that to be a good wife did not require widows to commit fiery suicide.

All this raises thorny issues for a postcolonialist, Derridean, Marxist feminist like Spivak. When a widow says that yes, she wants to be burned (to self-immolate), who is speaking? Is she choosing for herself, Spivak asks, or is that impossible, because she has been interpellated into a misogynist set of expectations for feminine behavior? Is she speaking for herself, or has she been so absorbed into patriarchal culture that she speaks for the patriarchy, even if she believes that she speaks for herself? Can we even tell whether it is one or the other, and, if so, how can we tell? Can people who oppose or support sati speak for the sati better than she speaks for herself?

As a Derridean, Spivak is skeptical of what she sees as the romanticizing notion that anyone can voice an inner, true, and complete self, an essence. As a Marxist, she believes that we often exaggerate our individuality and do not realize how much we speak for larger, often oppressive ideologies—like sexism and patriarchy—that we have been interpellated into accepting as truth. As a feminist, she suspects that women who say they want to be burned to death because their husband has died are speaking for the patriarchy, not for themselves, even if they think that they speak for themselves. And yet as a feminist, she also wants to take seriously what women say and think. She fears that it is terribly presumptuous to tell a woman that what you say you think is not really what you think but is only what the patriarchy wants you to think. Putting all this together, Spivak finds the question of whether the subaltern can speak for herself or even for a larger subaltern group, such as women or colonized Indians or Indian women, an aporia. As you may recall from Chapter 4, Derrida uses the term *aporia* for an undecidable impasse, a question that we cannot answer.

Yet Spivak's question about whether the subaltern can speak is enormously urgent. Let us think about its implications by looking at some places where the question might turn up. Think of the innumerable times you have heard someone (perhaps yourself) say something like: I want to study African American literature (or queer studies or women's literature or some particular subaltern topic) so that I can see what African Americans (or women or Asian American women or Latinas and Latinos) *really think*, so that I can hear their true voice. You have probably heard politicians and cultural commentators say they want to find out what a given group of people really thinks, want to hear the voice of the people or of some particular group of people. But you may also notice that some people from a given group—say, African American women—will say one thing, and others will say something else, sometimes something dramatically different. Which of them speaks in the true voice of African American women? Spivak's argument suggests that there is no one true voice, no essence, of African American women or Indian women or any subaltern group (or any group at all) and that whenever we say there is, we demeaningly oversimplify and essentialize Indian women, African American women, or whatever group we are trying to describe.

As you can imagine, Spivak's approach has set off a good deal of controversy. It challenges ideas that many people take for granted, unsettling common assumptions in minority studies, postcolonial studies, and women's studies. On the other hand, many people in minority studies, postcolonial studies, and women's studies welcome Spivak's nonessentialist approach. They see it as helping us do minority studies, postcolonial studies, and women's studies by helping us respect the variety of opinions and voices in any group. It can make us more alert to how, when we think that people speak for a particular group, or when people claim to speak for a particular group, or even when they claim to speak for themselves, they may be speaking for another group whose interests they have been interpellated into mistaking for their own.

Spivak does not answer "No" to the question "Can the subaltern speak?" She does not argue that subalterns cannot speak. She sees the question as open, continuous, and unanswerable. After all, she says in a later piece, she is a subaltern and she speaks perfectly well (Spivak, *Outside* 59). (People who dislike her prose style might say that she doesn't speak so well after all.) But at the end of her article, in a regrettable moment that caused widespread confusion, she says, "The subaltern cannot speak" (Spivak, "Can the Subaltern Speak?" 130). People who follow her argument have always understood that she did not mean that sentence as a conclusion and that, in context, that sentence only names a tempting conclusion she is not ready to accept. But other people who succumbed to the near-impenetrability of Spivak's prose seized on that one sentence, took it out of context, and used it to represent the whole argument. (Does all this, ironically, back up Spivak's point that we cannot necessarily take people's words as representing their true belief?) Thus, some critics attacked Spivak for saying that subalterns cannot speak, wondering how she could possibly say that, as a speaking subaltern herself. In the latest version of her article, Spivak regrets that she ever wrote that sentence, clarifying that she did not mean it as a conclusion (Spivak, *Critique* 308).

Spivak's argument encourages us not to oversimplify the opinions and writing of individual speakers and writers or of groups of people. It encourages us to see the range of views in any group and even within a single person. Deconstructively, Spivak's argument can also help make us more alert to the internal contradictions in any speaking, writing, set of opinions, individual, or group of people, for it reminds us that even when we think we speak for ourselves, we might be a mouthpiece for ideas that come from somewhere else. In that way it challenges the generalizations we make or witness day after day—the claims that this group of people believes this or that group believes something else, that this group is like that or that group is like this. But like Bhabha's argument about ambivalence, Spivak leaves us hanging. Rather than telling us that people do speak for themselves or that they only think they speak for themselves while they actually speak for ideas imposed on them, she audaciously casts aside essentialist conclusions about individuals and groups and leaves the question both urgent and unanswerable.

Known for her resistance to essentialism, Spivak has also invited cultural critics, who usually look skeptically at essentialism, to experiment by making their resistance to essentialism more flexible. In a world that often takes essentialist beliefs for granted, she notes that essentialist arguments sometimes inspire people to seek political change, including people who would not find inspiration in the nonessentialist arguments of literary and cultural critics. In some of her writings, Spivak suggests that in such circumstances it might not betray our principles to try out essentialist claims, in a temporary way, to help inspire change for the better. She calls that short-term essentialism **strategic essentialism** (Spivak, *In Other Worlds* 202–215; *Outside* 3–10). While Spivak never makes much of this argument and has not even stuck to it, others—eager to license essentialism—have seized on the idea of strategic essentialism.

The question might hinge on whether an expression of strategic essentialism does more harm in the long run than good in the short run. If we say, for example, that children tend to be worse off in households headed by women, do we do more good by encouraging fathers to stay with the mothers of their children or more harm by suggesting that households must have a head, that only one person can be the head, and that it is best for men and not women to be that one person, and suggesting as well (indirectly) that women need to pair off with men, that heterosexual couples are preferable to same-sex couples, and that lesbians and single women make bad mothers?

Similar questions arise in the controversy over racial gerrymandering (separating electoral districts based on race), profiling for security at airports (who "looks" like a terrorist?), or making claims about literary style according to gender, race, or nationality (do female and male writers, or German and Korean writers, or indigenous and European writers, have distinct styles?). To some critics and theorists, such questions—or questions about other essentialist claims designed to encourage people to improve their lives—lead to yet another aporia. Many other critics and theorists, however, believe that essentialist claims can help out in practical ways that matter more than the sometimes demeaning implications that essentialist claims can carry. Still, others argue that the demeaning implications magnify over time and end up hurting people more than they help people.

Some readers resent the high-theoretical approach of Bhabha, Spivak, and the many less well-known critics who roughly work in or follow their manner. Critics who think that Spivak believes that the subaltern cannot speak wonder how she could let her deconstructive sense of play lead her away from practical politics, but Spivak pays considerable attention to practical politics, far more than Bhabha. Bhabha's critics, especially, sometimes prefer less abstract talk of ambivalence and mimicry and more attention to material politics. It is one thing to destabilize colonialism by a little mimicry that exposes colonial ambivalence and another thing to destabilize it by blowing up a bridge or, without violence, by nationalizing the assets of colonialist foreign corporations, unionizing exploited laborers, building schools and hospitals, electing leaders, or redistributing land monopolized by colonialist and neocolonialist overlords. Skeptics sometimes see Bhabha and Spivak, both originally from India, as betraying their postcolonial status and perspective by studying and teaching in Britain (Bhabha) and the United States (Spivak, and now also Bhabha). Or at least they resent that Western critics have celebrated postcolonial critics who live in the West, not in the East.

Some critics also resent that Bhabha, Spivak, and many other postcolonial critics rely on what skeptics describe as European theory. Such doubts oversimplify the picture. Derrida, to take just one notable example of a European theorist whose work influenced Bhabha and Spivak, was African as well as European. Born and raised in Algeria, not Paris, he dedicated his career to overturning the truisms of European philosophy. While he did not develop his ideas independently of European thinking and cultural practices, it would turn his writing inside out to reduce it to a representative product of European thought and culture. Spivak draws on Indian bodies of thought as well as on figures like Derrida, Marx, and Freud, and she insists that no one has the right to limit what ideas she can think with. "Only the elite playing at self-marginalization," Spivak argues, "can afford the impossible luxury of turning their backs on" what she calls "the usefulness of First World male thinkers" (Spivak, "Can the Subaltern Speak?" 121).

Spivak and others have especially encouraged postcolonial thinkers to bring feminism to postcolonialism. Some postcolonial cultural critics, determined to address Third World cultures respectfully, close their eyes to Third World misogyny or even defend it as part of local cultural practices. From such a perspective, outsiders and feminists are asked to refrain from criticizing not only historical practices that abuse women, such as sati, but also such locally common contemporary practices as domestic violence, rape, limited rights to own property, limited educational opportunity, lack of voting rights, restrictions on the right to work outside the home, restrictions on dress or on movement in public spaces, female genital mutilation (even the various names for that practice provoke controversy), and restrictions on choice about whether to marry or when or whom to marry. Such requests to hold off criticism come from a fear that misogynist practices like these might be misconstrued as specific to the colonized world or to one particular colonized people. Westerners often call attention to misogynist practices in the Third World to prop up colonialist fantasies about the supposedly primitive practices of colonized peoples. By publicizing misogynist practices in the Third World, people from the colonizing metropole can keep themselves from seeing their own culture's abuse of women, and they can keep themselves from seeing, as well, how colonization has encouraged the abuse of women.

Nevertheless (and to be open about my own perspective), to refrain from criticizing such abuses is to suppress the variety in the history and traditions of the so-called Third World, for just as such practices have their supporters among colonized peoples, so they also have their opponents among colonized peoples. An unwillingness to criticize Third World practices essentializes formerly colonized cultures as unchanging and internally consistent, condescending to the Third World as an exotic, precious land fenced off from cultural debate, a land where neocolonialist demagogues can twist postcolonialism into an excuse for naturalizing and essentializing the abuse of women. Instead of separating feminism from postcolonial studies, as if they were opposites, many feminists argue that it is dangerous to pursue postcolonial studies and postcolonial politics without feminism. Often, they argue, with Spivak, that feminism and postcolonialism must depend on each other if they want to pursue their mutual commitments to recognition and justice.

HOW TO INTERPRET: A POSTCOLONIAL STUDIES EXAMPLE

In *Avatar*, to take, for now, just one example (and I am writing before *Avatar 2* and the other sequels have been released), a group of Americans sets up a mining colony with a private army on the moon of a distant planet. They find a vast deposit of the valuable mineral unobtanium on lands where there lives an indigenous, more or less humanoid species called the Na'vi. They also bring scientists, led by Grace Augustine, who study the moon's people and plants by lying in a trance inside coffin-like machines that connect them with avatars, Na'vi bodies bred from their own human DNA mixed with Na'vi DNA. In effect, the human scientists log in to other bodies (as in William Gibson's novel *Neuromancer*) and become, for the length of their trances, earthlings inside the huge blue bodies of Na'vi. Jake Sully, a white American who uses a wheelchair, enjoys his transformation into an avatar body, but soon Jake gets lost in the woods. Neytiri, a Na'vi, comes to Jake's rescue. At first she scorns his ignorance, but then she teaches him the language and ways of her people. Meanwhile, after failing to convince the Na'vi to give up the land where they live, the colonists attack and nearly win before the Na'vi, now led by Jake, defeat them.

Though the Na'vi have a language, in a figurative sense they cannot speak. For it turns out that they need a white, colonialist American man to speak for them. In his absorption into his avatar, the disabled white American man lives out a fantasy of able-bodied magnificence. And his fantasy is also a fantasy for much of the film's audience. Huge, rippling with his new blue muscles, and more limber than a cat, he gets his legs back, and his sex life, and he gets to play the hero and the king. Here, unlike in Bhabha's model, the colonizers, through their avatars, mimic the colonized. In a classic colonialist fantasy of mimicry, of going native and playing Indian, whites get to take the human resources of a colonized culture, much as they mine its mineral resources. (For more on the fantasy of going native and playing Indian, see the scholarly studies by Philip Joseph Deloria and Shari M. Huhndorf.) In this case, Jake gets the thrill of "going in," as Grace puts it when she takes on her avatar's body. But the outsider white who goes native by dressing, talking, or rapping like the stereotype of another race retains the ability to go back out. For many whites, it seems like fun to play at being black or brown, red or yellow (or blue), so long as they don't get stuck with it.

Such play contributes to the colonialist pattern of taking colonized people less seriously, even seeing them as children who need the protection—or control—of parental colonizers. For though the Na'vi are another species, they are also black and brown earthlings. They blend African features into their blue faces, and black, Latina and Latino, and American Indian actors wearing a hybrid blue blend of African American, African, and American Indian hairstyles voice the leading Na'vi characters. The Na'vi also reenact classic movie stereotypes of scowling Africans and American Indians surrounding their captives and yipping and whooping. *Avatar* joins a long tradition of novels, stories, and movies from *The Last of the Mohicans*, *The Man Who Would Be King*, and *Heart of Darkness* to *Tarzan* and *Dances with Wolves* where white men try to escape their failures or discover or reassure themselves by putting on the mask or behavior of nonwhites. The removable mask allows white readers and viewers to enjoy their chocolate cake while holding on to the safety of white privilege.

The indigenous culture is so much simpler than the colonizers' culture that Jake can parachute in (so to speak) to another world and learn its culture, its language (or learn it fairly well, though at a climactic moment he diplomatically asks his rival to translate for him), its repertoire of bodily movement and possibility, and all the ways of its woods—in a few months. It is as if a freshman from Peoria who rockets to a college in another solar system could pass for a native and end up as campus president, star athlete, and king of the planet before the first semester ends. Jake not only learns the Na'vi culture, he also learns it better than they know it themselves, so well that he can marry the chief's daughter, as he calls Neytiri, and take over. White men can do that kind of thing, versus the indigenous Neytiri, who despite her early magnificence eventually gets reduced to the Pocahontas stereotype, the Indian princess who validates her colonizer by loving him, by serving his colonialist, masculine narcissism and bowing to his power. While Neytiri's skills and panache threaten to overwhelm the desire to keep her fixed and controllable, she subordinates her own knowledge and leadership to the white man she once condescended to. Indeed, the natives love the slumming white man so much that they verify his fantasy by adopting him (as in so many colonialist fantasies), thus justifying *his* presumption as *their* fantasy, not just his. Much as they resist colonization, therefore, really they want it. Because they want it, colonization can seem like a good thing, if the colonizers do it with friendly condescension instead of with war. The Na'vi do not want to lead themselves, because the quick-study colonizer, especially the liberal kind who makes colonialist presumption and imperialist nostalgia seem caring, can lead them better. He can speak for and to the subalterns better than they can speak for or to themselves.

Their wish to have him speak for them never gets presented as a troubling weakness. In one sense, the Na'vi are not weak at all. They are perfect, so perfect that they have no disagreements among themselves (natives are too simple for that) other than about how to treat the invaders. Nothing can be more interesting about an indigenous culture, the film implies, than what its people think of the invaders, at least for the audience whom the invaders in so many ways stand in for. We see no signs of crime among the Na'vi, no ethical challenges, environmental problems, disease, population growth, economic conflicts, or class divisions. Though they have no classes, they have an inherited nobility, as colonizers typically suppose that indigenous peoples inherit their leaders, rather than choosing them. For colonizers to recognize that indigenous peoples (or species) might go through a deliberate political process would lead them to see the colonized as mimicking the colonizers. That kind of mimicry, the kind that Bhabha writes about, would threaten the colonizers' sense of their own superiority. In the same light, the bad colonizers, with their private army, cannot imagine that the Na'vi might organize and defend themselves and the land they live on well enough to defeat the colonizers. From the colonizers' eyes, that too would look like mimicry.

When the good colonizers mimic the Na'vi, transforming themselves through avatars, the Na'vi offer the troubled conquerors a perfect, gorgeous fantasy island of escape. It is a land without disagreement or disability, where all is static until the colonizers come like Columbus and make history begin in what Jake calls "a fresh start on a new world." But it is never a new world, a place without history, where only the colonizing voice can speak, unless you see only through the eyes of the colonizers who justify their invasion by denying the history and cultural depth of the people they colonize.

Already, in this beginning of a reading, you can see how postcolonial studies can overlap with race studies.

RACE STUDIES

As postcolonial studies has grown, so has the study of race and ethnicity, which both draws on and contributes to postcolonial studies. The study of race and ethnicity comes under many names and in many varieties. In its more specific dimensions, it overlaps with area studies, such as South Asian studies, African studies, Latin American studies, and Pacific studies, and in the United States it overlaps with such fields as Asian American studies, Latina/o studies, American Indian studies, Hawaiian studies, indigenous studies, whiteness studies, and, the most established of these undertakings, African American studies. In its broader dimensions, the study of race and ethnicity is sometimes simply called *race studies* or *ethnic studies*. In contemporary practice, it also includes what has come to be called *critical race studies* or *critical race theory*, which considers these topics in light of the many ways of thinking addressed in this book. Each of these movements has its own nuanced and elaborate history, and often a far longer history than postcolonial studies. Rather than trying to recount those many long histories here, then, I will review patterns of thought and directions of inquiry in contemporary critical race theory that have done the most to draw on and contribute to postcolonial, literary, and cultural studies.

Race, representation, and form. Critical writing about literature by white writers pays attention to the aesthetics and form of the writing much more often than critical writing about literature by writers of color. Many critics of color have lamented that difference, but it continues. When writers are not white, many readers see the primary role of their writing as the representation of race. When writers are white, many readers see the primary role of their writing as telling a story, using interesting or beautiful language and form, or representing more or less any topic the writers choose. Most writers of color, like many other writers, want readers to pay attention to how their writing represents race, but they do not always or necessarily see racial representation as the be-all and end-all of everything they write. They may even feel a pressure that white writers do not feel to live up to readers' expectations about what the writers are supposed to think about race, even though, of course, writers of color think a great variety of different things about race and everything else, and, like white writers, they do not think about race all the time.

As often as critics lament the funneling of writing by writers of color into its representation of race, that funneling shows little sign of diminishing. And there is certainly nothing wrong with writing about racial representation and with interpreting how writing represents race. But we have a bigger, more challenging, and more rewarding project before us if we allow our interpretation of literature by writers of color to include everything that we include when we interpret literature by any writers. If we limit the interpretation of writing by writers of color to the interpretation of race, then we misrepresent what it means to live with, write in, and represent racialized life and art.

Race, racial mixing, and cultural identity. Our ongoing cultural obsession with race persists despite, and partly because of, a widespread perplexity over the definition of race. Race itself, and the particular identity groups that we racialize, do not fit into singular, all-encompassing essentialist definitions. Indeed, contemporary studies of race, region, and ethnicity, like feminism and queer studies, often join with postcolonial studies to rethink essentialist assumptions about identity, history, politics, and literature.

In United States Latinx and Chicanx studies, the political and cultural border between Mexico and the United States has emerged as a figure of the irrepressible yet contested mobility of Latina/Latino peoples and cultures. In the influential *Borderlands/La Frontera: The New Mestiza* (1987, 1999) Gloria Anzaldúa (Figure 10.7) evokes the **borderlands** in her bilingual title and through a feminist and queer blend of autobiography, history, and advocacy, written in a mixture of prose and poetry. Writing in English, Spanish, Spanglish, and Nahuatl, Anzaldúa insists on a mixing of national, racial, sexual, and gendered cultures and identities, including Mexican, Chicana, Indian, mestiza (racially "mixed"), lesbian, working-class, and Tejana. She argues that colonialist and patriarchal assumptions have tried to deny the mixing that shapes identity. As Anzaldúa sees it, colonialist, patriarchal thinking has tried to use the border to suppress the mixing of identities. But instead of suppressing the mixture of identities, the porous border ends up contributing to and representing the mixture of identities. Anzaldúa calls for crossing the borders of multiple identities instead of supposing that different identities can stay on different sides of an imposed and unsustainable dividing line.

Anzaldúa helped popularize the notion of **mestizaje,** or racial mixing, as a representative figure for Latina/Latino peoples and cultures. The term *mestizaje* has a diverse history. Its connotations vary across the many different countries of Latin America, where it can sometimes suggest romantic and patriarchal celebrations of a mythically unified national identity. But for Latinas and Latinos in the

Figure 10.7 Gloria Anzaldúa
(1942–2004).

United States, Anzaldúa helped reshape the term to figure resistance
to assimilation and to figure pride in the mobility and multiplicity of
identity, both politically and artistically.

Similarly, Caribbean writers and cultural critics have theorized
métissage (mixing, or **creolization**), led especially by the Martinican
writer Edouard Glissant, a student of Césaire and associate of Fanon.
Glissant described what he called *antillanité* (after the Antilles, the
Caribbean islands), translated from French into English as "Caribbeanness." Acknowledging the influence of Césaire's belief in a singular
black identity based in Africa, Glissant set his vision of Caribbean
culture and art in a multiplicity that defies Négritude through the
Caribbean model of many cultures, languages, and peoples mixed
together. He saw Caribbean peoples, with their mixture of African,
French, English, Spanish, indigenous, and South Asian origins, as
producing a *métissage* that never settles into what he saw as the stable
sameness of Négritude or of conventional European models of identity. For Glissant, *antillanité* and *métissage* represent a *"poétique de la
relation,"* rendered in English as a "cross-cultural poetics," based in
a continuous changing within and between languages, such as the
Creole French of Martinique and the European French also spoken in
Martinique. While *antillanité* and *métissage* represent roughly the same
thing as hybridity or borderlands, borders take a distinct form in the
Caribbean, with its island nations and their partly parallel histories,
and with Martinique and Guadeloupe now recognized as provinces
of France. Hybridity can suggest a completed combination of separate histories, whereas for Glissant, *antillanité* and *métissage* suggest a
combination that produces something different from its contributing
parts, fluidly recombining in a process of continuous change.

Glissant did not set creolized cultures against noncreolized or "pure" cultures. He did not see creolization as a way to glorify the Caribbean world compared to the rest of the world. For all peoples, he argued, are cross-cultural. Instead, he posed creolization against the idea that cultures ground their identity on an inherited and unique history and then hold to that identity without change, exiling people who do not live up to the inherited model. "To assert peoples are creolized, that creolization has value," he argued, "is to deconstruct in this way the category of 'creolized' that is considered as halfway between two 'pure' extremes." He objected, for example, to the category of "Colored" (multiracial) in apartheid South Africa, calling it "barbaric . . . that this intermediary category has been officially recognized." "Composite peoples," Glissant believed, cannot "deny or mask their hybrid composition, nor sublimate it in the notion of a mythical pedigree, . . . because they do not need the myth of pure lineage" (Glissant 140–141). Glissant's work helped inspire the next generation of Martinican writers, notably Patrick Chamoiseau, to call on *Créolité* (creolization) as a figure for Caribbean language and literature.

Yet another similar pattern of thinking has emerged in the discussion of American Indian literature, where the Anishinaabe (Ojibwe, Chippewa) writer Gerald Vizenor has tried to undermine notions of racial purity and fixed, stable ideas of Indianness by seeing the performance of Indian identity as under pressure to live up to the colonialist culture's cliché fantasies of Indianness: the stoic wooden Indian, the savage warrior in a feathered headdress, the romantic Indian princess, the natural ecologist, and so on. Vizenor refers to such fixed beliefs about Indianness as "terminal creeds," and he makes fun of their power over people's imaginations.

Instead of essentializing racial or genetic purity, Vizenor values tribal history and heritage. Thinking through humor and satire, Vizenor models many of his writings on the irrepressible playfulness of tribal trickster stories, and he revalorizes sometimes-derogatory terms like *mixedblood* as models for the unpredictable combinations of ideas and histories in contemporary "postindian" life and writing. For Vizenor the terms *mixedblood* and *crossblood*—his rewriting of mixed blood or half-breed—evoke a cultural, not a biological identity, though for some later critics the terms carry uncomfortably biological connotations. Some critics also fear that Vizenor's skepticism about stable identities can threaten indigenous sovereignty and practical, tribally rooted politics. To Vizenor, however, the terms *mixedblood* and *crossblood* represent not a biological essence passively received by those who carry it but instead a cultural heritage that Indian peoples pass to each other across a long and steadily changing history of cultural exchange and conflict.

Notions such as the borderlands, the new mestiza, Caribbeanness, *métissage*, creolization, Créolité, and trickster mixedbloods echo the model of double-consciousness that W. E. B. Du Bois (pronounced *dew BOYS*) chose to describe African Americans in *The Souls of Black Folk* (1903). In Du Bois's famous words,

> The Negro is a sort of seventh son, born with a veil, and gifted with second-sight in this American world,—a world which yields him no true self-consciousness, but only lets him see himself through the revelation of the other world. It is a peculiar sensation, this double-consciousness, this sense of always looking at one's self through the eyes of others, of measuring one's soul by the tape of a world that looks on in amused contempt and pity. One ever feels his twoness,—an American, a Negro; two souls, two thoughts, two unreconciled strivings; two warring ideals in one dark body, whose dogged strength alone keeps it from being torn asunder. (Du Bois 16–17)

When Du Bois describes black Americans as "gifted with second-sight," he suggests that black Americans, and we might say by implication other minorities, have had to learn how the majority sees them. In Lacanian terms, when they look at themselves in the mirroring reflection of the culture around them, then their imaginary relation to their own reflection, their comfort with themselves, keeps getting interrupted by a symbolic tap on the shoulder. That tap comes from their awareness of a difference between how they see themselves and how others see them, or even just how others might see them. Thus, those in the minority have the gift of two perspectives. And they also have the burden of two perspectives.

Du Bois's words can help relieve that burdensome pressure by exposing its causes and logic. At the same time, they can suggest a muted, sympathetic self-criticism. They can help caution us against the temptation that some critics feel to celebrate the mixing of cultures and races, as if more conspicuously mixed people were somehow better than less conspicuously mixed people. As Glissant takes pains to argue, that would miss the point. *Métissage* does not mean that mixed people are better than unmixed people. It means that everyone is mixed and that we do better to acknowledge the ceaseless mixing than to fantasize that any one people somehow is or should be pure and separate from other peoples.

As every person and group is mixed, and no one group is better or purer than other groups, there is no wisdom in conceptualizing more conspicuously mixed people as pitiable, walking battlegrounds for psychic and cultural warfare, as biological embodiments of the "two unreconciled strivings" and "two warring ideals" that Du Bois lamented. Glissant, Anzaldúa, and Vizenor warn us against getting stuck in such ways of conceptualizing mixed identities as inevitably tortured, and they help point us to a more relaxed recognition of the ordinariness of cultural multiplicity.

Indigenous peoples. Scholars of indigenous studies often note with dismay that postcolonial studies and race and ethnicity studies usually ignore or give little heed to indigenous peoples, even though indigenous peoples are central to their concerns. From the perspective of indigenous peoples, we still live in colonial times, not postcolonial times, and so indigenous studies has much to contribute to postcolonial studies, in the sense that postcolonial studies includes the study of past and present colonialism. Increasingly, indigenous studies scholars address the problem of internalized colonization, or self-colonization, what Ngũgĩ calls "the colonization of the mind." That is to say that though indigenous and other colonized peoples have often resisted the colonizers, they have also often had to go along with the colonizers, and as a consequence they have often absorbed colonialist values as their own. "It is the final triumph of a system of domination," Ngũgĩ notes, "when the dominated start singing its virtues" (Ngũgĩ, *Decolonising* 20). Indigenous studies scholars, therefore, increasingly seek out strategies of decolonization.

The Maori scholar Linda Tuhiwai Smith, for example, writes about the ways that researchers studying indigenous peoples often focus on the researchers' needs, not on the needs of the colonized, indigenous peoples. Much as colonizers exploit colonized and indigenous peoples and their natural resources for the colonizers' own purposes, so researchers studying indigenous peoples often treat the people they study like natural resources waiting to be exploited. Researchers typically ask what indigenous people can do for them, not what they can do for the indigenous people they study. In *Decolonizing Methodologies: Research and Indigenous Peoples* (1999), Smith proposes strategies for indigenous peoples to help shape their own futures by decolonizing the ways they think about themselves and the ways that they work with professionals who study them, both outside researchers and indigenous researchers. Some scholars and indigenous leaders believe that all research about an indigenous community should first receive approval from the community. Other scholars see that expectation as infringing on the academic and intellectual freedom of the researchers. They challenge the ability of a given group of community members, even elected officials, to speak for the community at large. Such debates have revolved around social science research, which can have large and direct social consequences—helpful or damaging—for indigenous communities.

It is harder to anticipate how such debates will shape out in the humanities. Euro-American poets and novelists, for example, working without a community's permission, have often rewritten sacred indigenous ceremonies as poetry, or mined them as atmosphere for fiction. From one perspective, such writers are following their creative imagination and showing their appreciation for native cultures. From another perspective, they are treating indigenous rituals as "material" for their own purposes, much as other people have stolen indigenous natural resources and artifacts or have stolen or occupied indigenous lands. Should a tribal poet or a poet from outside the tribal community need to receive permission to write a poem about a flower that grows on tribal land? Probably not. But what if the poem describes a custom? What if it describes a sacred ceremony that depends on specialized knowledge, perhaps knowledge that, according to custom and belief, would be compromised if outsiders learn about it or commercialize it?

Such questions partly have to do with the vexed issue of indigenous sovereignty. When people have survived a history of direct and indirect genocide, had their lands stolen, their governments thrown out, their customs demeaned and pushed aside, their children taken away, their languages and religious ceremonies banned, and their cultures trivialized as the playthings and entertainment of the colonizing culture (think cowboys and Indians in toy stores and on the screen or Indian sports mascots like the Cleveland Indians' "Chief Wahoo"), they sometimes take a special interest in asserting their right to run their own lives, including their governments, lands, schools, religious practices, laws, courts, and so on. What, then, about their intellectual life, art, and literature and about the intellectual life, art, and literature of people from the colonizers' world when they visit or trespass on indigenous lands or use indigenous cultures for their own purposes? When indigenous peoples claim political sovereignty, can they also claim what Osage scholar Robert Warrior has called "intellectual sovereignty"? Perhaps different questions of this kind call for different answers. Indigenous and anticolonialist scholars now often raise such questions, and the responses to many of the questions are still emerging and hard to codify.

In part because of their political sovereignty, many indigenous people do not think of their native or indigenous identity as a race. American Indians, to take one example, have something that other racialized peoples in the United States lack: political independence (however vexed in its complicated relation to federal and state law), with their own lands and nations (also known as tribes). Each American Indian nation has its own land, political system, laws, and courts, including laws about who qualifies as a citizen of the nation. At this writing, there are over 570 federally recognized Indian nations, or tribes, in the United States (plus state-recognized tribes, and other tribes seeking recognition). Different Indian nations have varying degrees of common ancestry among themselves and with other Indian nations, but they each have their own nationality. No other peoples or races in the United States have their own lands and nations. That makes American Indians different from every other identity group in the United States.

Critical race theory. All these notions contribute to or overlap with critical race theory. Critical race theory emerged in legal studies in the 1970s and 1980s as an outgrowth of and response to critical legal studies, a left-influenced rethinking of rights discourse. To critical legal scholars, the institutions of law are not neutral, as they believe that liberals have traditionally supposed. The discourse of rights is not something that simply needs opening up to all populations. Instead, critical legal scholars see the discourse of law and rights as committed to upholding traditional power relations, even if indirectly. For example, a traditionally liberal, rights-based perspective might say that all people should have the right to own a radio or TV station or contribute as much as they like to a political candidate. By contrast, a position more skeptical of rights-based thinking might say that we need to put limits on rights, in this case the right to own multiple media outlets or contribute to political candidates, or else the wealthy will buy up radio and TV stations and politicians until they own nearly all the mass media and the politicians, allowing a wealthy few to shut down the wide range of expression that politics and the media have the potential to encourage.

Building from such perspectives, Derrick Bell, a founding figure of critical race theory, argued that in the United States white jurists and leaders began to support civil rights not so much from a commitment to people of color as from a desire to protect entrenched white interests. For example, in the famous 1954 *Brown v. Board of Education* case that declared racial segregation illegal in public schools, the United States Supreme Court palliated restive African Americans and burnished the United States' image for the Cold War, but the court did little to enforce desegregation. The segregation of schools not only continued but actually increased. Bell argued that such decisions, justified on the ground of abstract rights rather than actual power relations, end up propping up rather than weakening white privilege. According to critical race theory, then, racism is not merely a removable blemish on an otherwise sound system. It is integral to the system itself. And those in power will rarely join in changing the system unless (in what critical race theorists call *interest convergence*) they see change as serving their own interests.

In this view, power relations produce racial difference. Hegemonic power relations (see Chapter 8 on Marxism) would have us believe that racial difference comes from biology, but the biology of race is a cultural fiction. As a hegemonic cultural fiction, the idea that race is biological is so deeply entrenched that most people take it for granted as unquestioned fact. But biologists say the opposite. Biologists say that there are no genes for race and that people of "different" races usually have more in common genetically than people of the "same" race. The markers of race, such as skin color and hair texture, have a visual convenience but otherwise hold little biological meaning compared to other genetic variables. Historical and cultural conventions attribute vast significance to those markers, but nothing requires us to see them as so meaningful. Still, the superficial markers of race offer a convenient tool for colonialism and racism, which desperately seek to naturalize abusive power relations, leading us to think that we discover profound, timeless differences between peoples while keeping us from seeing that, in many ways, colonialism and racism have imposed and constructed those differences.

Following this logic that sees race as a construction rather than an essence, critical race theory, whether in legal studies, the social sciences, or the humanities, pays special heed to rethinking race as a cultural category rather than a biological category. With its history of critiquing rights discourse, including the discourse of civil rights, critical race studies invites us to include but also to move beyond the politics of recognition and inclusion or the mere exposure of inequity and oppression, the traditional goals of civil rights advocates. For example, critical race scholars question what they call **race-blind racism** (or *color-blind racism, race-neutral racism, or implicit bias*.) A rights discourse may suppose that we can decide policy most fairly by ignoring race and basing policy on other concerns, such as merit. But from the perspective of critical race theory, racial prejudice is always already embedded in the system, so that to be blind to race is to allow deeply ingrained racism to continue unchallenged.

Even supposedly neutral notions such as merit are not always neutral, for they often carry within them racial preconceptions that favor certain kinds of merit over other kinds. The advocates of racial neutrality can see the same behavior from people of different races and judge its merit differently. Or they can see members of a racial group they do not belong to as, for example, too quiet or too vocal or keeping too much to themselves or mixing too much with others (prejudice often comes in contradictory, opposite forms), while seeing what they think are their own ways as a universal, merit-based norm rather than a cultural pattern. In short, because racism has a bad rep, it often appears in masked form, sometimes (but not always) masked even to the people who practice it. If they recognized it as racism, or thought that others would recognize it as racism, they would more likely change it or stop it.

The mask of neutrality conceals beliefs and acts that have racist consequences, sometimes called *disparate impact* or *adverse impact*. The controversial study of *disparate impact* can help uncover the implicit bias in race-blind racism. If a policy does not mention race but statistics show that it hurts a large proportion of people in one race and helps or does not hurt a large proportion of people in another race, then it has a disparate, adverse impact. Those who designed the policy may not have intentionally acted with racist motives. Or they may have, while trying to make it sound as if they did not. Either way, their policy, though ostensibly race-blind, has racist consequences. For example, there are debates about whether it is fair to require government-issued ID cards for voters or set minimum height requirements for police officers. Such policies lead to a disparate impact not necessarily for any given person, but nevertheless for large groups of people according to their race, given that people of color often have less access to government-issued ID cards and that some racial groups trend shorter and others trend taller. Defenders of the policies say they do not mention race and therefore are race-blind or race-neutral. Critics say that their race-blindness is a form of race-blind racism.

Such considerations can have everything to do with how we interpret literary characters or variations in literary style. Japanese-influenced literary understatement in such writers as the Americans

Hisaye Yamamoto and Julie Otsuka and the Canadian Joy Kogawa, for example, while not representative of all Asian American and Asian Canadian writers (far from it), can get misread as blandness or as feminine timidity, whereas understatement in the prose of Ernest Hemingway can seem to evoke a profoundly understated universal insight into human character and the subtly suggestive power of literary language. That is why race-blindness can let unwitting racism and implicit bias slide in, and why claims for objectivity, however well meant, can end up reinforcing white privilege. Cultural institutions, therefore, such as the legal system and the systems of literary taste, may see themselves as objective, but they routinely include unwitting, implicit bias. As Fanon put it, "For the colonized, objectivity is always directed against him" (Fanon, *Les damnés* 38; my translation).

The concept of white privilege has received more attention in public discussion recently. Some white people push back against it, because they recall the hardships they have suffered and think that therefore they have no advantages. But the concept of white privilege does not mean that white people never face hardship. It means that such hardships as they may face do not come from other people's responses to their whiteness.

Whiteness studies and racialization. In the process of reevaluating how the dominant culture presupposes its own ways as timeless and universal, critical race studies has taken up the study of whiteness, often impelled by African American scholars and other scholars of color. Just as the broad category of race takes on new dimensions once we think of it as a construction rather than an essence, so any particular race takes on new dimensions when looked at with an awareness of its constructedness. Historians, sometimes influenced by deconstruction and poststructuralism, have asked how whites became white, a question that would make no sense if whiteness were an unchanging essence.

From the perspective of whiteness studies, whiteness is a position of power masked as a position of biology. For example, in a controversial and influential argument, historians such as Noel Ignatiev have claimed that Americans did not initially see Irish immigrants as white people, and indeed often saw them in the same degrading way that racists saw African Americans. Irish Americans then became white by joining whites in looking down on African Americans. Sadly, the process of looking down on African Americans became a ladder that European immigrants climbed to reach the social and racial position of white privilege. In that way, European immigrants and their descendants exploited the visual markers of difference be-tween African and white Americans.

Inspired in part by the novelist Toni Morrison's *Playing in the Dark: Whiteness and the Literary Imagination* (1992), whiteness stud-ies undermines the cultural habit of seeing whiteness as a natural and universal standard from which everything else is a deviation. Whiteness studies notes the many differences among white people and the pressure that whites often feel or cultivate to suppress their differences so as to construct an imaginary unity among whites that makes it possible for whites to exclude nonwhites.

At the same time, whiteness studies carries its own dangers. After all, scholars and students of literature have been studying whiteness for a long time, without calling it whiteness. Wherever race may seem absent—perhaps in novels by Jane Austen and Henry James, in poems by Alexander Pope and Emily Dickinson, in films by Alfred Hitchcock and stories by Edgar Allan Poe—it is nevertheless always there. Scholars and students might not recognize race when it comes masked in the false neutrality of invisible whiteness, but the study of whiteness and race is one of the unspoken topics of the study of writing by white writers, just as the study of blackness is one of the frequently spoken topics of the study of writing by black writers. The danger looms, then, that whiteness studies can slide into the same old thing under an updated name. But that might not happen if white-ness gets seen as a constructed position of privilege and power that, like a colonizing culture, can trade on power and on false notions of universality to sustain its power.

Still, the idea that whiteness is a construction may not seem ter-ribly threatening to white people, whose position of power is secure enough for them to continue enjoying its privileges. But the idea that racial categories are culturally constructed can seem threatening to some people of color if, out of newness to poststructuralism, they mis-construe the deconstruction of race to mean that race in general or any particular race does not exist. But as many scholars of color, along with Euro-American scholars, have pointed out, to say that race or any particular race is not a biological or essential category does not mean that race does not exist. Instead, it changes our understanding of how race exists. It changes race from something biological and es-sential to something historical.

In that sense, the idea that racial categories are constructed can help us resist racist ideas, understand race itself, and understand in-dividual races. For example, it can help us recognize the wide range of ways of being black for black cultures across Africa and across the African diaspora as well as within any individual black person. That, in turn, can help individual black people resist essentializing pressures to conform to one particular model of blackness rather than other models that they may prefer. It can help us understand how "black" in Great Britain can refer to people with African ancestors and to people with South Asian ancestors, while "black" in the United States refers only to people with sub-Saharan African ancestors. Similarly, the notion of race as a construction can help us understand Anzaldúa's ideas about the borderlands, and it can help us understand the international and cross-border alliances and histories that have yoked so many different peoples together under the umbrella concept of "Asian American."

Many critics try to get at the way race is an ongoing process and construction by referring, at least some of the time, to racialized peoples or groups rather than to races. The term **racialization** suggests something that is done to people, while the term *race* can suggest, by contrast, something that people simply are. *Racialization* indicates that we too often see racialized people through the lens of preconceptions and cultural patterns about race, as if race were a stable fact and not a continually shifting and provisional construction. Because of racialization, individual people can get defined, as Fanon lamented, by preconceptions about a group they belong to, making it harder for others and even for the individuals themselves to see their individuality. In turn, because racialization masks individuals, it also risks distorting the groups they belong to, reducing each group to uniformity and stereotype by erasing the variations across the group.

Racial appropriation. The topic of racial appropriation raises so many searching questions that here I will focus as much on provoking questions as on suggesting possible responses to those questions.

When I teach a play, I invite students to read the text as a script for performance. Like a musical score, the script or text of a play makes possible an enormous variety of different performances. To help students imagine and understand performance, we sometimes act out parts of the play in class. My classes follow an open-casting policy, meaning that any student can play any role, regardless of how they or others might understand the roles as able-bodied or disabled or matching any particular race, gender, nationality, sexuality, or age. Sometimes students come up with fun, provocative ways of playing against type or playing within type in a satirically exaggerated way. A classroom performance speaks to the performers themselves as the primary audience. What about a public performance in the theater, TV, or film? A public performance speaks less to the performers and more to the audiences. Most public performances directly or implicitly match roles to performers through such identity categories as race, ability, gender, age, and so on. When the part and the performer do not match racially, some people find it liberating and some find it a racially abusive appropriation or mimicry. Controversy flared up over Broadway shows, for example, when a white actor was cast for a Eurasian part in *Miss Saigon*, and when performers of color played white "Founding Fathers" and their families in *Hamilton*.

Are there characters in fiction, drama, or film whose race makes no difference to the character's identity? If so, then does casting such a part with a white performer, or having a story describe a character as white, or not describe a character's race at all, sustain that neutrality, or not? Does casting or describing such characters as a race other than white undermine racial neutrality? Why or why not? How might such questions vary according to who lives in the geographical and cultural area of the performance?

What might we gain or lose if films, TV shows, music videos, and plays cast without regard to identity categories, or cast in opposition to identity categories? In racial terms, what consequences might follow if white performers could play any part? If performers of color could play any part? What opportunities would open or close, and for whom? What cultural connotations might get elaborated, mimicked, or masked? Should costuming (clothing, hair, makeup) express race? What about accents, vocabulary, styles of speech or bodily movement, or styles of sport or dance? What happens when characters or performers play within or outside of stereotypes? How do you respond when people say that playing outside of specific cultural patterns tramples over the representation of specific cultures? How do you respond when people say that playing within specific cultural patterns reduces people to those patterns?

If a white person writes or acts the part of a character of color, is that the same as when a person of color writes or acts the part of a white person, or not? How does it compare to writing or acting across gender, or without gender, or across different models of gender? How do you interpret the skepticism that arose about *Atypical* when the lead part—a teenager on the autism spectrum—went to an actor who is not on the spectrum? (The producers responded in the next season by casting performers on the spectrum to play additional parts both on and off the spectrum.) What happens when you reshuffle the possibilities? How, for example, does an Asian performer playing a white role, or a previously white role, compare to an Asian performer playing a Native American role? Or playing a Latina or Latino role? Or to a Latina, Latino, or Native American playing an Asian role? Does it matter if a performer of Japanese ancestry plays the part of a character of Chinese ancestry, or if a Puerto Rican performer plays a Mexican or Chicana/o role? What about characters or performers with multiple ancestries? What might happen in a play like Caryl Churchill's *Cloud 9*, where, between the acts, the stage directions tell the actresses and actors to switch parts across races, accents, nationalities, ages, genders, and sexualities?

The film *Get Out* satirizes the long history, in effect a horror story, of nonblacks abusively appropriating black people and black culture, along with stereotypical racist fantasies of black hyper-sexuality. Such abuses fit into a long tradition. In the enormously popular nineteenth-century minstrel shows, white performers dressed up in blackface makeup and performed grotesquely stereotypical impersonations of black musicians. Eric Lott's influential study of minstrelsy, aptly titled *Love and Theft*, describes blackface minstrelsy as "less a sign of absolute white power and control than of panic, anxiety, terror, and pleasure" (6–7), driven "by envy as well as repulsion, sympathetic identification as well as fear" (9). Playing off Laura Mulvey's description of the male gaze in film (reviewed in Chapter 6), Lott describes the white desire to stare at blacks, and to stare at white performances of blackness, as "the 'pale gaze'—a ferocious investment in demystifying and domesticating black power in white fantasy by projecting vulgar black types [performed by whites] as spectacular objects of white men's looking . . . in relation to an objectified and sexualized black body, and it was often conjoined to a sense of terror" (157–158). What makes more powerful people want to share, steal, or gaze at the culture of less powerful people, or at fantasy performances of that culture? How do such appropriations help serve the emotions of the more powerful? What consequences can they lead to for the emotions of the less powerful?

We see a contemporary variation on the same pattern today when nonblacks masquerade as blacks online through stolen avatar photos and false names, or by directly saying they are black. Such *digital blackface* also includes the widespread pattern of nonblacks repeatedly expressing their emotions through reaction GIFs that portray the reactions of black people. When lifted from their original context and posted over and over, such GIFs risk reducing black people to racist clichés of emotional exuberance.

How, then, can we tell the difference between abusive cultural exchanges and respectful cultural exchanges? Given the long history of racial appropriation when white musicians perform music composed by blacks and reap all or nearly all the profits, does that mean that white or other nonblack musicians should never perform black-composed music? Hardly anyone would make that claim. How then does that history of racist appropriation condition what white or other nonblack musicians should or should not do when they play black-composed music? What about when black musicians perform white-composed music? Superficially, the two directions may sound symmetrical, but the history of abuse makes them asymmetrical. How do such terms as black music or white music oversimplify the mashup of musical traditions? When do we get something useful from such terms, even if they oversimplify? How do questions about what musicians do in relation to the racist history of musical appropriation compare to questions about what listeners do? What other examples of racial appropriation can you think of, respectful or disrespectful?

Tracking a specific tradition: African American writing and Signifyin(g). Because race is a cultural category, it has a cultural history, and scholars can trace the cultural history of racial and ethnic groups and the ways they express that history in literature. In that spirit, in 1926 Langston Hughes argued against fellow African American writer George S. Schuyler's contention that "Negro" American writing was like other American writing and not distinctively African American. Hughes believed, by contrast, that the best aspirations of "Negro" writers require a specifically African American art. Later critics took up Hughes's challenge and called for a specifically African American criticism describing what they see as the specificity of African American writing and culture. For example, Houston A. Baker, Henry Louis Gates, and Hortense J. Spillers have proposed cultural histories, traditions, and rhetorical patterns from African, African diasporic, and African American culture that shape the continuing history of African American literature. Spillers plots African American cultural studies and structures of gender through an intricate web of poststructuralism and psychoanalysis. In "Mama's Baby, Papa's Maybe: An American Grammar Book," for example, she argues that because slavery devalued black motherhood and fatherhood, African Americans had to construct alternative models of masculinity, femininity, and gender.

Baker uncovers what he calls a "vernacular theory," finding patterns in African American literature that emerge from the blues and its grounding in economic strife. Gates, like Baker, proposes a "vernacular theory" of African American literature. He finds a tradition of theorizing in black speech and oral storytelling. Gates studies West African trickster traditions of "double-voiced discourse"—figurative language—and finds that African Americans have shaped and reshaped those traditions through the oral practice of signifying, or—as Gates more playfully evokes the spoken word—Signifyin(g).

For Gates, Signifyin(g) suggests not only the ceaseless proliferation of signifiers in Derrida's expansion of Saussure's ideas but also an African American tradition of language play through repetition with difference. Through repeating the language of both African Americans and non-African Americans—yet repeating it with a difference—African American speech often delights in figurative language, sometimes in a playfully competitive way and sometimes as an homage to community and tradition. Gates sees examples of such Signifyin(g) and repetition with a difference in everyday talk and in art that ranges from playing the dozens (the game where people trade witty, jocular insults about each other's mother) to jazz musicians playing each other's standards, not for "critique and difference," but for "unity and resemblance" (Gates xxvii). He also sees it in the way that African American novelists signify on their mainstream literary predecessors, on African American oral traditions, and on the Signifyin(g) of earlier African American novels, thus signifying an African American literary tradition.

For example, Gates argues that in her novel *Their Eyes Were Watching God*, Zora Neale Hurston mixes the English of traditional novelists with the English associated with African American speech, often twining the two together in free indirect discourse, a form that, as we saw in Chapter 3, mixes the language of an exterior narrator and an interior character. In that way, Hurston signifies on the mainstream tradition of self-consciously focalizing narration represented, for example, by Henry James. At the same time, in a double voicing that signifies on Du Bois's theory of double-consciousness, Hurston's free indirect discourse also signifies on the controversial tradition of African American writers, such as Paul Laurence Dunbar, writing in language associated with specially African American speech. Then, over a generation later, Gates argues, in *The Color Purple* Alice Walker—who did much to return attention to Hurston's forgotten writing—signifies on Hurston by having her characters *write* in a language that echoes the way Hurston's characters *speak*. The ongoing dialogue of books talking to other books and talking about talk as

Figure 10.8 Beyonce and Jay-Z in the Louvre, Signifyin(g) on Leonardo Da Vinci's Mona Lisa in *Apes***t*.

well as about books builds what Gates calls "the black tradition's own theory of itself" (Gates xxiii).

In a 1934 article called "Characteristics of Negro Expression," Hurston had already written about a frequent "will to adorn" in African American language, including a delight in imitation and mimicry as art forms. The same signifying tradition replays in Beyoncé and Jay-Z's *Apes**t*, which sets black music and dance against the suddenly passive backdrop of the history of elite Western art on display in the premier palace of European art history, the Louvre in Paris (Figure 10.8). Beyoncé and Jay-Z offer up repetition with a difference, signifying on elite art history by revoicing it, making it reappear for a huge audience while also reinventing it by centering a blackness that the European tradition has depended on but suppressed. In the process, they honor the past, critique it and change it, and make it their own.

HOW TO INTERPRET: POSTCOLONIAL AND RACE STUDIES EXAMPLES

Hemingway's famous stories "The Snows of Kilimanjaro" and "The Short Happy Life of Francis Macomber" take for granted a colonialist way of thinking. They purport to portray what they call "Africa," as if their little space in British-ruled Kenya could represent the vast variety of peoples and places from Casablanca to Nairobi, Addis Ababa to Accra, and Cairo to Cape Town. The whites on safari in Hemingway's stories depend utterly on their black servants, but the stories reduce their servants to the background, to exotic local color, like part of the scenery. Now and then the servants step forth from the shadows, but only to receive a command from the great white hunters who cannot admit that they depend on Africans. The white hunters call their Kenyan servants "boy," with the usual contortions of colonizers trying to prop up their power and masculinity by feminizing and infantilizing the colonized. Colonizers often think of the colonized as children and think of themselves as parents. That protects them from seeing the colonized as peers and justifies the way the colonizers take charge, as if they conquered, ruled, and dominated economically out of the kindness of their hearts and for the good of the colonized. Conveniently for colonialist fantasy, the colonized Kenyans in Hemingway's stories never talk back, and they never have their interiority represented or even acknowledged, beyond a vague romanticizing sense that they know the secrets of the bush, secrets that the great white hunters know too but that tenderfoot white tourists like the Macombers must have explained to them. Thus, when a "boy" driving the white hunters' car brings the car to a halt, the story erases his agency by saying "The car stopped" (Hemingway 14), as if the driver had nothing to do with it and the car stopped itself.

Hemingway published those stories in 1936, two years before the birth of Ngũgĩ wa Thiong'o, black Kenya's first novelist. Ngũgĩ's first novel, *Weep Not, Child* (1964), offers another perspective. It is not entirely an opposite portrait, because Ngũgĩ especially concerns himself with internalized colonialism and neocolonialism, and thus many of Ngũgĩ's African characters naturalize European power as much as do Hemingway's white characters. In the opening pages of *Weep Not, Child*, the young boy Njoroge, who wants desperately to go to school and perhaps eventually to study overseas, talks with his older brother, trying to understand the local white settler who has taken over their family's land. "I wonder why he left England, the home of learning, and came here. He must be foolish," Njoroge says. "I don't know," his brother replies. "You cannot understand a white man" (Ngũgĩ 23). Not surprisingly, Ngũgĩ takes for granted the black interiority that is unimaginable to Hemingway. But while Hemingway's white characters do not think to speculate about black interiority, Ngũgĩ's black characters think hard about white interiority, though they do not claim to understand it. Indeed, because they are subject to white rulers, they have little choice but to think about it. They cannot afford the denial of the other that the white settlers luxuriate in and that the white settlers depend on to uphold and justify their colonialism.

Nevertheless, Njoroge has absorbed the colonialist belief system that makes a European education seem superior to a Kenyan education. And in material ways, it is superior, because the exchange between cultures, the worlding of Kenya as shaped by colonialism, makes the colonizers' knowledge hold special value for the colonized, even apart from the way that internalized colonialism exaggerates that value. Yet even as Njoroge admires white knowledge, he also looks at it with comical but insightful skepticism. To Njoroge, only a fool would leave the England that Njoroge aspires to and trade it for the Kenya that Njoroge wants to escape. He cannot understand what Kenya has for the white man, whose ancestors lived on another land, because, as a young boy, he does not understand the economics of colonialism. Even so, Ngũgĩ implies, Njoroge understands more than he realizes when he decides that the project of colonialism must be foolish.

The movie *Dirty Pretty Things* (2002) shows colonialism and neo-colonialism as they continue to evolve, this time in the London metropole, now worlded by immigrants from across the globe, whose mere presence reshapes empire and challenges the idea of borders. Or maybe their presence does not reshape and change so much after all, for neocolonialism does not do much to transform colonialism. Okwe, a Nigerian doctor and undocumented immigrant, works in London by day as a taxi driver and by night as a hotel clerk. As he stares down into a hotel toilet that overflows because someone has stuffed it with a human heart, and as we stare back up at Okwe through a camera that looks from the perspective of the heart in the toilet, *Dirty Pretty Things* gives new meaning to the expression "heart of darkness," a colonialist phrase for Africa, a phrase made unforgettable by Joseph Conrad, another immigrant, who wrote in Britain at the peak of colonialism.

In this heart of darkness of nighttime London, undocumented immigrants sell their organs to a documented immigrant who sells them to a Briton. In return, the undocumented immigrants get forged documents. Their organs and prostituted bodies become objects and metaphors of colonialist appropriation, the new exploited natural resources of neocolonialism. The immigrants participate, however reluctantly, in their own colonization by agreeing to sell their organs, as well as by submitting to the sexual abuse that other immigrants—a South Asian sweatshop boss and the movie's villain, "Sneaky" the Spanish organ merchant—charge to keep from turning them in to the authorities. The movie itself self-colonizes, and tries to colonize its audience, through a tawdry resort to frozen stereotype in its only extended portrayal of a black woman, Juliette. Surprise of surprises, Juliette turns out to be the familiar whore that Western movies have such difficulty escaping when they imagine black women. In yet another nonsurprise, Juliette is—if you'll excuse the expression—a whore with a heart.

When Okwe, Juliette, and the sexually abused Turkish hotel maid Senay turn the tables on Sneaky the organ merchant by drugging him to cut out and sell his kidney, the British organ buyer gets suspicious. Used to dealing with Sneaky, not Okwe, he asks, "How come I've never seen you people before?" Okwe responds, in a set piece for the movie, "Because we are the people you do not see. We are the ones who drive your cabs. We clean your rooms. And suck your cocks." The last sentence throws in a dash of half-gratuitous sex for the trailer to help market the film. Abusive and self-colonizing though that may be, it can also draw the neocolonialist market to see a movie that chastises neocolonialism.

In some ways, in the eyes of the colonizers, the immigrants of London are not all that different from the nearly invisible African "boys" of Hemingway's stories. They are the workers—here represented by taxi drivers, maids, and sex workers—whose colonized labor makes the empire possible. Yet the colonizers suppose that the colonialist world is self-supporting and that its international workforce does not exist. Or at least, when they can no longer suppose that, they try to keep supposing it, in the form of immigration restrictions and enforcement. Meanwhile, desperate to escape the corrupt neocolonialism that Okwe runs from in Nigeria, the worlded refugees of colonized and formerly colonized lands join with the colonizers in the London metropole. Together, they break the binary opposition between colonizer and colonized, and, with whatever anguish, the colonized and formerly colonized find themselves complicit in their own continuing colonization. It may sometimes be a pretty thing, with the colonialist exoticizing of the colonial world and with the colonized people's attraction to the enticements of the West, but it is also a dirty thing.

Let us take one more example. In Nella Larsen's 1929 Harlem Renaissance novel *Passing*, Irene and Brian Redfield talk about Irene's friend Clare while they eat breakfast served by their maid "Zulena, a small mahogany-coloured creature" (184). Irene and Clare, child-hood friends, are both light-skinned African Americans, but years ago Clare left her friends to pass for white. She used her new assump-tion of whiteness to marry a virulently racist but wealthy white man. Years later, she suddenly wants to sneak back to the world of African Americans, now and then, so long as she can get away without her husband's knowledge. Irene wonders why Clare would want to return to the company of African Americans, knowing how her husband thinks. "'It's always that way,'" Brian says.

> "Never known it to fail. . . . They always come back. I've seen it happen time and time again."
> "But why?" Irene wanted to know. "Why?"
> "If I knew that, I'd know what race is."
> "But wouldn't you think that having got the thing, or things, they were after, and at such a risk, they'd be satisfied? Or afraid?"
> "Yes," Brian agreed, "you certainly would think so. But, the fact re-mains, they aren't. . . ."
> "Well, Clare can just count me out. I've no intention of being the link between her and her poorer darker brethren." (185)

Clare and Irene's ability to pass for white, unlike Zulena and Brian, throws a wrench in the essentialist, binary opposition between white and black, and a wrench in the essentialist presumption that one set of characteristics can define black people, who appear here in mul-tiple colors and class positions: the "mahogany" servant Zulena, the prosperous Redfields, one of them light and the other dark, and the light and now extremely wealthy Clare. The very concept of passing may seem to unravel the capacity to define blackness, whiteness, and race. Even Brian, a physician, a medical professional, admits that he does not know how to define race. At the same time, nevertheless, the capacity to pass from one side to the other of a racial divide shows that regardless of the biological irrelevance of race, the surrounding social world has constructed a binary opposition between two groups of people defined by their histories rather than by their bodies.

Clare's movement from white back to black echoes the novel's white cultural tourists who visit Harlem at night, as Irene describes it, "'to see Negroes . . . , to gaze on these great and near great while they gaze on the Negroes'" (198). They revel in a blackness they ex-oticize at night, and then they return to the white world by day. They treat blacks and black culture, including the artistic imagination of Harlem music and dance, as a fashionable toy to appropriate for their entertainment without having to live the hardship and racial prejudice that permeate much of daily African American life. When Clare, after joining the white world, returns to the black world by night, she seems to have absorbed the white world's exoticizing view of blackness. In that way—and far beyond essentialist understandings of race—her very determination to recover her blackness also expresses and corroborates her new whiteness.

But Clare's movement from white to black is not symmetrical with her movement from black to white. When she moves from black to white, she does not appropriate whiteness in the same loaded way that she, like the white tourists, later tries to appropriate blackness. The power difference between the two groups tilts what might otherwise seem symmetrical. Clare's appropriation of whiteness does not condescend to whiteness. It does not exoticize whiteness. It profits off whiteness, but it does so personally, not as part of a broader pattern that keeps whites as a group from gaining economically. When the appropriation of whiteness and the appropriation of blackness differ, the difference shows us how much lies at stake in the abusive appropriation of blackness.

Passing has often received criticism for focusing on upper-class black characters, as if to write about such characters necessarily means to ignore or scorn other blacks. Similarly, the poetry of Larsen's Harlem Renaissance contemporary Langston Hughes often received criticism for focusing on lower-class black characters, as if to write about lower-class black characters necessarily means to ignore or scorn blacks who are not lower-class. Many readers somehow assume that to portray certain kinds of black characters means to suggest that those characters represent the sum total of what all blacks are or should be. Once we call out that assumption, its silliness stands out, but so long as it remains unspoken it drives many readers to impose narrow expectations on the work of racialized writers, expectations that they would not impose on white writers. Writing by racialized writers often gets reduced to what it represents, and by a terribly constricted vision of what its representation can mean. Writers of color get damned if they represent one way, and damned just the same if they represent another way. And as we saw earlier, those narrow models of racial representation often push out readers and critics' attention to literary form.

Many readers, including professional critics, refer to Irene as the narrator of *Passing*. But *Passing* has no internal narrator, no character narrator. It is written in the third person, not the first person. Irene, as we can tell from our study of narration in Chapter 3, is a focalizer, not a narrator, and often the narration highlights her focalizing by rendering it in free indirect discourse. Thus when the narration describes Zulena as "a small mahogany-coloured creature," it may seem hard to tell whether the air of arch superiority comes directly from the anonymous exterior narrator or indirectly from Irene herself, mediated through the external narrator in free indirect discourse. As we read on in the novel and interpret Irene, noticing, for example, that she mocks Clare's exoticizing by insinuating that Clare sees other blacks as "her poorer darker brethren," we may find ourselves more inclined to attribute the condescension to Irene. In that way, the form of free indirect discourse invites us to speculate and interpret, and at the same time shows us that we need to differentiate between the different modes of blackness represented by the condescending, uptight Irene, the compliant Zulena, and the exoticizing Clare.

More elaborately, we can also read free indirect discourse in this passage from the early scene where Irene sees Clare for the first time in many years, without either of them yet recognizing the other.

> Again she looked up, and for a moment her brown eyes politely returned the stare of the other's black ones, which never for an instant fell or wavered. Irene made a little mental shrug. Oh well, let her look! She tried to treat the woman and her watching with indifference, but she couldn't. All her efforts to ignore her, it, were futile. She stole another glance. Still looking. What strange languorous eyes she had! (149–150)

Here the narration works through the third person, but as each woman stares at the other, the description through Irene's staring at Clare directs us to look through Irene's eyes, like the shot/reverse shot that structures visual focalization in film (see again Chapter 3). The choppy shifting between longer and shorter sentences, the talky "Oh well," exclamation points, and sentence fragment ("Still looking") together tell us, without quotation marks, that the narration has absorbed Irene's thoughts into its ongoing flow. Yet the writing remains in the third person, telling us that it has dived into the peculiar mix, definitional of free indirect discourse, of looking, at the same time, through the eyes of an internal focalizer (Irene) and through the more abstract eyes of the anonymous external narrator. The undefinable betweenness of free indirect discourse evokes, all at once, Clare and Irene's partial but incomplete recognition of each other, their dawning but incomplete recognition of each other's blackness in an environment (a hoity-toity restaurant) that codes them as white, and their unacknowledged erotic attraction to each other amidst their daily, conventionally heterosexual lives. In short, the form of the novel, a form that many critics ignore or misread in their zeal to focus exclusively on cultural representation, has everything to do with its cultural representation and, we might argue, even deepens that cultural representation beyond what conventional exposition might provide. The undefinable in-betweenness and doubleness of the form bespeaks all at once the persistence of African American specificity and racial difference amidst the undefinability of race. When Brian admits that he does not "know what race is" while at the same time insisting that race continues to pull at Clare, he ends up defining race—in its undefinability—more than he knows.

POSTCOLONIAL AND RACE STUDIES AND LITERARY STUDIES

Race studies has influenced literary studies by inviting readers to expand beyond white-written works and to read race in nonessentialist ways. By unveiling the central role of race, it has given critics ways to understand power relations across literary history. In that light, critical race theory, as a more specific dimension of race studies, contributes to the nonessentialist momentum of race studies, encouraging critics to think about racial difference as rooted in the distribution of power, much like colonialism.

Meanwhile, postcolonial studies, combined with race studies, has also changed literary studies. It has led to a growing movement for the study of world literature, opening beyond the limits of any one language, even when readers rely on translations. In English departments, we increasingly read writing from formerly colonized countries beyond Great Britain, Ireland, and the United States. We continue to read Shakespeare, Jane Austen, and Virginia Woolf, for example, but we also read Achebe, Ngũgĩ, Soyinka, Jean Rhys, V. S. Naipaul, R. K. Narayan, Anita Desai, Buchi Emecheta, Salman Rushdie, and many other writers from formerly colonized lands.

Moreover, postcolonial studies has changed the way that we read British, Irish, and American writing. In an economy and cultural life that depend on colonial and neocolonial exploitation, colonialism is woven through the literary self-portrait of imperialist nations, sometimes explicitly, as in Conrad's *Heart of Darkness*, and sometimes surreptitiously. In the wake of postcolonial studies, Shakespeare's *The Tempest*, for example, often emerges as a parable of the colonized and the colonizer. For contemporary criticism, *The Tempest*'s Prospero and Miranda often represent the characteristically masculine and feminine roles of European colonizers. Ariel stands in for the colonized elite, and Caliban dramatizes the fate of the colonized masses. In Austen's *Mansfield Park*, Said argues, Sir Thomas Bertram's rule at home follows principles of order that echo and, by implication, partly depend on his rule over his barely mentioned sugar plantations in Antigua (in the Caribbean). From that observation, Said argues that Austen's refined novel and its social world depend on the unmentioned but sordid economics and cultural violence of slavery and colonialism. Similarly, Spivak—and many critics following her—interpret Charlotte Brontë's *Jane Eyre* (as we saw in Chapter 6) as resting on and struggling to deny its Jamaican Creole backstory. Achebe himself has famously proposed an African postcolonial rereading of Conrad's *Heart of Darkness*. He recognizes that Conrad's novel bemoans colonial violence. Even so, Achebe argues, *Heart of Darkness* reduces African people to a foil for the horrors that Europeans fear in themselves. Conrad and his European characters cannot see Africans as fully-fledged people with their own languages, cultures, thinking, and psychological interiority. Rather than seeing Africans as people, Conrad sees them as a stage for a drama about Europeans.

In these ways, whether or not literary writing dwells explicitly on colonialism and racial conflict, it often depends on them, for colonialism and racial conflict are part of the economic and cultural foundation of Europe, the United States, and the many lands that they have conquered militarily, politically, or economically. From Shakespeare and his predecessors to the present, colonialism and racial conflict have helped to shape English-language culture and literature.

FURTHER READING

Achebe, Chinua. "An Image of Africa: Racism in Conrad's *Heart of Darkness*." 1977. In *Hopes and Impediments: Selected Essays, 1965–1987*. London: Heinemann, 1988: 1–20.

Anzaldúa, Gloria. *Borderlands/La Frontera: The New Mestiza*. 2nd ed. San Francisco: Aunt Lute Books, 1999.

Ashcroft, Bill, Gareth Griffiths, and Helen Tiffin, eds. *The Post-Colonial Studies Reader*. 2nd ed. London: Routledge, 2006.

Baker, Houston A. Jr. *Blues, Ideology, and Afro-American Literature: A Vernacular Theory*. Chicago: University of Chicago Press, 1984.

Bernabé, Jean, Patrick Chamoiseau, and Raphaël Confiant. *Eloge de la créolite*. Paris: Gallimard, 1989.

Bhabha, Homi K. *The Location of Culture*. London: Routledge, 1994.

Byrd, Jodi A. *The Transit of Empire: Indigenous Critiques of Colonialism*. Minneapolis: University of Minnesota Press, 2011.

Calderon, Hector, and José David Saldívar, eds. *Criticism in the Borderlands: Studies in Chicano Literature, Culture, and Ideology*. Durham, NC: Duke University Press, 1991.

Césaire, Aimé. *Discourse on Colonialism*. 1950. Trans. Joan Pinkham. New York: Monthly Review Press, 1972.

Chatterjee, Partha. *The Nation and Its Fragments: Colonial and Postcolonial Histories*. Princeton, NJ: Princeton University Press, 1993.

Coulthard, Glen. *Red Skin, White Masks: Rejecting the Colonial Politics of Recognition*. Minneapolis: University of Minnesota Press, 2014.

Crenshaw, Kimberlé, et al., eds. *Critical Race Theory: The Key Writings That Formed the Movement*. New York: New Press, 1995.

Delgado, Richard, and Jean Stefancic. *Critical Race Theory: An Introduction*. 3rd ed. New York: New York University Press, 2017.

Fanon, Frantz. *Black Skin, White Masks*. 1952. Trans. Charles Lam Markmann. New York: Grove Press, 1967.

——. *The Wretched of the Earth*. 1963. Trans. Richard Philcox. New York: Grove, 2004.

Gates, Henry Louis Jr., ed. *"Race," Writing, and Difference*. Chicago: University of Chicago Press, 1986.

——. *The Signifying Monkey: A Theory of African-American Literary Criticism*. New York: Oxford University Press, 1988.

Gilroy, Paul. *The Black Atlantic: Modernity and Double Consciousness*. Cambridge, MA: Harvard University Press, 1993.

Glissant, Edouard. *Caribbean Discourse: Selected Essays*. Trans. J. Michael Dash. Charlottesville: University Press of Virginia, 1989.

Hall, Stuart. *The Fateful Triangle: Race, Ethnicity, Nation*. Ed. Kobena Mercer. Cambridge, MA: Harvard University Press, 2017.

Hill, Mike, ed. *Whiteness: A Critical Reader*. New York: New York University Press, 1997.

hooks, bell. *Black Looks: Race and Representation*. Boston: South End Press, 1992.

——. *Yearning: Race, Gender, and Cultural Politics*. Boston: South End Press, 1990.

Huhndorf, Shari M. *Mapping the Americas: The Transnational Politics of Contemporary Native Culture*. Ithaca, NY: Cornell University Press, 2009.

Kauanui, J. Kēhaulani. *Paradoxes of Hawaiian Sovereignty: Land, Sex, and the Colonial Politics of State Nationalism*. Durham, NC: Duke University Press, 2018.

Lewis, Reina, and Sara Mills, eds. *Feminist Postcolonial Theory: A Reader*. Edinburgh: Edinburgh University Press, 2003.

Loomba, Ania. *Colonialism/Postcolonialism*. 3rd ed. London: Routledge, 2015.

Lott, Eric. *Love and Theft: Blackface Minstrelsy and the American Working Class*. New York: Oxford University Press, 1993.

Lowe, Lisa. *Immigrant Acts: On Asian American Cultural Politics*. Durham, NC: Duke University Press, 1996.

Lyons, Scott Richard. *X-Marks: Native Signatures of Assent*. Minneapolis: University of Minnesota Press, 2010.

McClintock, Anne. *Imperial Leather: Race, Gender, and Sexuality in the Colonial Contest*. New York: Routledge, 1993.

Morris, Rosalind C., ed. *Can the Subaltern Speak? Reflections on the History of an Idea*. New York: Columbia University Press, 2010.

Morrison, Toni. *Playing in the Dark: Whiteness and the Literary Imagination*. Cambridge, MA: Harvard University Press, 1992.

Napier, Winston, ed. *African American Literary Theory: A Reader*. New York: New York University Press, 2000.

Ngũgĩ wa Thiong'o. *Decolonising the Mind: The Politics of Language in African Literature*. London: James Currey, 1986.

Omi, Michael, and Howard Winant. *Racial Formation in the United States: From the 1960s to the 1990s*. 3rd ed. New York: Routledge, 2015.

Said, Edward W. *Culture and Imperialism*. New York: Knopf, 1993.

———. *Orientalism*. New York: Pantheon Books, 1978.

———. *The World, the Text, and the Critic*. Cambridge, MA: Harvard University Press, 1983.

Saldívar, José David. *Border Matters: Remapping American Cultural Studies*. Berkeley: University of California Press, 1997.

Smith, Linda Tuhiwai. *Decolonizing Methodologies: Research and Indigenous Peoples*. London: Zed Books, 1999.

Spillers, Hortense J. *Black, White, and in Color: Essays on American Literature and Culture*. Chicago: University of Chicago Press, 2003.

Spivak, Gayatri Chakravorty. "Can the Subaltern Speak? Speculations on Widow-Sacrifice." *Wedge* 7/8 (Winter/Spring 1985): 120–130. Longer version in *Marxism and the Interpretation of Culture*. Ed. Laurence Grossberg and Cary Nelson. Urbana: University of Illinois Press, 1985: 271–313.

———. *A Critique of Postcolonial Reason: Toward a History of the Vanishing Present*. Cambridge, MA: Harvard University Press, 1999.

———. *In Other Worlds: Essays in Cultural Politics*. London: Methuen, 1987.

———. *Outside in the Teaching Machine*. New York: Routledge, 1993.

———. *The Post-Colonial Critic: Interviews, Strategies, Dialogues*. Ed. Sarah Harasym. London: Routledge, 1990.

———. "Three Women's Texts and a Critique of Imperialism." *Critical Inquiry* 12 (Autumn 1985): 243–261.

Strain, Heather, dir. *Race: The Power of an Illusion*. California Newsreel, 2003. DVD.

Vizenor, Gerald. *Fugitive Poses: Native American Indian Scenes of Absence and Presence*. Lincoln: University of Nebraska Press, 1998.

Vizenor, Gerald. *Manifest Manners: Postindian Warriors of Survivance*. Hanover, NH: University Press of New England, 1994.

Williams, Patrick, and Laura Chrisman, eds. *Colonial Discourse and Post-Colonial Theory: A Reader*. New York: Columbia University Press, 1994.

Wu, Jean Yu-wen Shen, and Thomas C. Chen, eds. *Asian American Studies Now: A Critical Reader*. New Brunswick, NJ: Rutgers University Press, 2010.

Young, Robert J. C. *White Mythologies: Writing History and the West*. 2nd ed. London: Routledge, 2004.

✳ 11 ✳

Reader Response

In the late 1960s and the 1970s, a good deal of excitement arose about *reader-response criticism* and *reader-response theory*. The idea of basing our critical perspective on what reader-response critics usually call "the reader" held a special appeal to critics and has continued to hold a special appeal to students, because most of us feel intensely aware of ourselves as readers, and so reader-response criticism can seem to speak directly to who we are and what we do.

Nevertheless, the hodgepodge of formalist, philosophical, psychological, and historicist activities loosely netted together under the label of *reader-response criticism* (and similar terms) have little to do with each other beyond their interest in "the reader," in readers in general, or in actual historical readers. We might go so far as to say that there is no separate category of "reader-response criticism," because all criticism is reader-response criticism. As critics have increasingly sensed that all criticism is reader-response criticism, the once seemingly sharp cutting edge of reader-response criticism and theory has blunted over the years, and its influence has faded. It seems helpful, therefore, to integrate reader-response criticism into all the other kinds of criticism that we do, and I have tried to live up to that goal throughout this book. For that reason, as we study reader-response criticism directly in this chapter, we can also use it to pull together and review the rest of the book.

Because readers are audiences, the study of readers can consider audiences of any kind, including viewers of film, drama, and sports; listeners to music or conversation; and readers of sonnets, novels, tweets, text messages, or websites. We can thus see reader-response criticism at work in the discussion of how readers project unity onto a text in Chapter 2, on new criticism. We also see versions of reader-response criticism in the discussion of how audiences read situation comedies, detective novels, and other genres in Chapter 3, on structuralism; in deconstructionist double readings of a text in Chapter 4, on deconstruction; in Lacan's view of how we project our own desires onto the space of the other in Chapter 5, on psychoanalysis; in how film spectators view action adventure films with women leads or view female characters as erotic objects in Chapter 6, on feminism, and in the way that racial conflict can generate oppositional, critical, spectators, also in Chapter 6. Chapter 7, on queer studies, considers how we read the varying performance of gender, and it sees homosexual panic as certain readers' response to the discourse of homophobia. Reader response continues to influence key concepts in Chapter 8, on Marxism, in the discussion of how a text can interpellate readers or—as Brecht argued—how a performance can jar readers out of their interpellations, and in Chapter 9, on historicism and cultural studies, in the discussion of how fans interpret popular culture and readers approach a Shakespeare sonnet. In Chapter 10, on postcolonialism and race studies, we can see mimicry and the construction of race as sociocultural forms of reader response. Even apart from its blending with so many other methods, however, reader-response criticism in itself has struck a nerve and raised fascinating, fundamental questions about how we read and what reading is in the first place. For that reason, it deserves separate treatment as well as integration into the rest of this book.

Reader-response critics oppose themselves to the new criticism. As we saw in Chapter 2, the new critics believed in interpreting a literary text as a relatively intrinsic object, minimizing the history and culture that surround a text. Working from that principle, William K. Wimsatt and Monroe C. Beardsley decided that to interpret the meaning of a text based on our affective response to the text is a fallacy, an error in interpretive logic. The entire concept of reader-response criticism and theory opposes itself to Wimsatt and Beardsley's dismissal of affective responses. But if we reject Wimsatt and Beardsley's principle and declare that interpretation based on responses is not fallacious, then we can oppose our way of interpreting to their theory but not really to their methods, because even Wimsatt and Beardsley and the other new critics, in interpreting a text, are responding to it. They may believe that their interpretations reveal the intrinsic meaning of a text,

Reader, Writer, Text, and Context

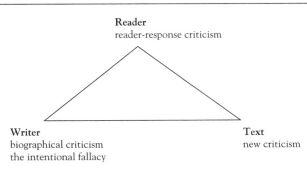

Reader
reader-response criticism

Writer
biographical criticism
the intentional fallacy

Text
new criticism

Biographical criticism and the intentional fallacy focus on the writer, new criticism on the text, and reader-response criticism on the reader (Figure 11.1).

Outside the triangle lies the context. The later methods of criticism discussed in this book sometimes pay considerable attention to the context, whether or not they also pay considerable attention to the reader, the writer, and the text.

but they still derive their sense of intrinsic meaning from their own responses. They may include other readers' responses as well, but even then they depend on their responses to the other responses. There is no escape from readers' responses. It is, so to speak, responses all the way down. Every method in this book is a reader-response method, whether or not it focuses on that dimension of its own method. If there is anything specific to reader-response criticism, then, it is not the use of readers' responses. It is the focus on the use of readers' responses. And that focus raises a host of provocative questions that continue to attract interest even while the vogue has diminished for reader-response criticism as a separate method.

IDEAL, IMPLIED, AND ACTUAL READERS

The brief flame of the vogue for reader-response criticism first burned brightly in the early work of Stanley Fish, who set his procedure directly against new criticism and the new critical critique of the affective fallacy by calling it *affective stylistics*. He concentrated on following the zigs and zags of the reader's response as it unrolls sequentially, word by word, while the reader reads a text. The text raises certain expectations in the reader and then frustrates or fulfills those expectations as it proceeds along. For example, Virginia Woolf's novel *Mrs. Dalloway* begins with the following one-sentence paragraph: "Mrs. Dalloway said she would buy the flowers herself." That sentence raises a variety of expectations from readers. We expect that as we read on, we will find more about who Mrs. Dalloway is, whom she says this to, why she might or—perhaps still more—might not buy them herself, and why she or someone else wants flowers in the first place. Something is up, we expect, and we expect to find out what. How and when we find the answers to those questions and even whether we find them will influence our gradually building understanding and interpretation of the novel. We might even expect that as the novel goes on, its opening words will end up carrying extra importance.

The ideal reader. Fish's reader is not just any reader, however, but an "informed reader" or even, because informed, an "ideal reader." The **ideal reader** is not the sort who says go hang Mrs. Dalloway and her flowers and has no patience for an opening sentence that does not explain itself. Instead, the ideal reader responds to challenges and mysteries with relish.

Especially when we have trouble understanding a text, we can ask what kind of ideal reader it seems to address. Perhaps we do not understand the poem or the movie, but then we can ask who would understand it. What does the poem or movie do to construct—that is, to prepare and shape—its ideal reader? Were there ideal readers for this text when it first appeared? Are there now? Over the course of time, what might have changed the ideal readers of a particular text? As the movie or poem or novel moves from its beginning to its ending, does it do anything to change its readers? To educate them? To teach them how to read? By asking such questions, even when we find a text difficult to understand, we can use that difficulty to produce understandings that we might not have anticipated.

Fish tends to take the ideal reader in a more limited way. He ends up basing his suppositions about how ideal readers respond on his own understanding of how he himself responds. Regardless, the key thing is the reader's response, so that the meaning of a text lies not in what readers find in a text, as if it existed there before and independently of a reading. Instead, the meaning lies in what readers do as they read.

The implied reader. Similarly, the German critic Wolfgang Iser, drawing on German phenomenological philosophy, follows the way a text sets up an **implied reader.** As we read a text, we can sort out implicit assumptions that it makes about its readers, what they know and believe or do not know and believe. But a text always remains incomplete, especially while readers find themselves in the middle of its sequence of words and implications. In that way, a text sets up "gaps," inviting readers to fill in the gaps and inviting readers then to compare how they fill in the gaps to the way that the text itself eventually fills or does not fill in the same gaps.

For both Fish and Iser, reading a text is a continuous dialogue between expectations that a text provokes in the reader and how readers respond to those expectations. Readers respond by forming hypotheses about the text and then testing those hypotheses against the continuing sequence of text. In a more extreme reader-response model there is no text except in the mind of the reader, for we only know a text by how readers respond to it. But for Fish and Iser, as well as for Louise Rosenblatt, an earlier critic who describes reading as an ongoing transaction between the text and the reader working together, the text guides readers' responses. In that way, reading enacts a continuous dialogue between the shifting directions of a text and the shifting responses of a reader. The meaning of a text, then, comes not from the text alone (as the new critics thought) or from the reader alone, but from the two together.

Actual readers. Less influentially than Fish and Iser, the work of Norman Holland and David Bleich has called attention to the psychological process of readers. Both Holland and Bleich study actual readers, as opposed to the hypothetical ideal and implied readers of Fish and Iser. Holland draws on *ego psychology*, a mostly American branch of psychoanalysis that, in literary and cultural criticism, has never achieved anything like the prominence of more deconstructive psychoanalytic approaches. From the perspective of more contemporary deconstructive psychoanalytic criticism, ego psychology suggests too confident a sense of a singular, stable subject, a secure self or ego, which probably accounts for the limited interest that Holland's work has attracted except as a representative example of psychologically based reader-response criticism. Holland supposes that each reader forms a particular ego or "primary identity" based on early childhood and then projects the concerns of that identity onto a literary text. In his model, the text almost disappears in favor of different readers' more or less idiosyncratic responses to the text.

Bleich takes Holland's model to its logical conclusion by calling forthrightly for a full-scale focus on the readers' subjectivity, calling for readers to write out their responses, grounding their view of a text in the ways that it connects to their personal experience. For Bleich, more objective interpretations of a text merely mask interpretations that grow out of our personal quirks and histories. Bleich's method may tell us a great deal about individual readers, but it does not try to tell us much about the texts they read. It might not even tell us much about readers, for if we follow its logic, then when we read about readers' responses, we project our own personal interests onto our reading of the other readers, making them yet another text that all but disappears under the veil of our own subjective concerns. The method has a logic to it, therefore, but not a very communal logic.

STRUCTURALIST MODELS OF READING AND COMMUNICATION

Jakobson's model of communication. Structuralists and historicists, along with the later work of Fish, have taken reader-response criticism in more communal directions. In a classic structuralist article, Roman Jakobson proposed a basic model of communication that helped bring attention to the role of readers in a larger arc of connected structures. For Jakobson, any communication has six components: "The ADDRESSER sends a MESSAGE to the ADDRESSEE. To be operative the message requires a CONTEXT referred to . . . , seizable by the addressee, and either verbal or capable of being verbalized; a CODE fully, or at least partially, common to the addresser and addressee (or in other words, to the encoder and decoder of the message); and, finally, a CONTACT, a physical channel and psychological connection between the addresser and the addressee, enabling both of them to enter and stay in communication" (Jakobson 353).

CONTEXT

ADDRESSER .... MESSAGE .... ADDRESSEE

CONTACT

CODE

(Jakobson 353)

All communications include all six components, but different kinds of communications give different weight to different components.

- Communication focused on the addressee, which Jakobson calls the *conative* function, takes it purest form in imperatives ("Do it!"—meaning "*You* do it!") and vocatives. Vocatives are expressions that directly speak to the addressee, such as "O Romeo, Romeo" (Shakespeare 1114), "O ye" in "O ye of little faith" (Matthew 8.26), and "Reader" in "Reader, I married him" from Charlotte Brontë's *Jane Eyre* (Brontë 454). The addressee is the reader and hence the center of interest for reader-response criticism, but all six functions are tied to each other and attract their own interest, inflecting how we understand the addressee/reader.

REFERENTIAL

EMOTIVE   POETIC   CONATIVE
                       PHATIC

         METALINGUAL

                                   (Jakobson 357)

- Declarative sentences focus on the *referential* function. They refer to the context, the world around us, as when I say, "Outside my window, it is raining."
- The *emotive* or expressive function concentrates on the addresser expressing an attitude or emotion. At its purest, in interjections—"Ouch!"—the emotive function puts little weight on the referential function (the context it refers to) and has little in the way of developed syntax. In such cases, instead of fitting into the syntax of a sentence, interjections are themselves what Jakobson calls "equivalents of sentences" (354). For example, "Ouch!", translated into a sentence, means "It hurts!"
- *Phatic* messages focus on the contact between the addresser and the addressee. They try to begin the communication or to continue it, break it off, or test it. Examples include "Hello," "How you doing?," "Uh-huh," "Goodbye," "Can you hear me?," "Do you hear that static?"
- *Metalingual* communication is language about language, about the code we use to communicate. Linguistics is a metalanguage. Any time we ask for a definition, we use metalanguage, even in ordinary communication. Examples include "What do you mean?" and "Can you say that another way?"

- For Jakobson (and this is his greatest interest), communication that focuses on the message itself concentrates on the *poetic* function. The poetic function includes poetry and any other language that attends to aesthetics, to artfulness, such as (in varying ways and degrees) the overlapping categories of hip-hop lyrics, rhyme, alliteration, wit, lyrical narrative, political slogans, and proverbs ("A friend in need is a friend indeed").

Jakobson's model has helped anchor the study of many features of communication, not only about readers. For our purposes here, it encourages us to consider how readers fit into the overall structure of communication, including literature and film.

The narratee. In the structuralist tradition that Jakobson helped bring to literary criticism, the narratologist Gerald Prince proposed a model for readers within narrative, that is to say, not readers of narrative but readers represented by a narrative, fictional readers rather than real readers. Prince called the fictional reader in narrative the **narratee.** He saw the narratee as one pole of a structuralist binary opposition between narrators and narratees. That is, a fictional narrator narrates (or speaks) to a fictional narratee. When the speakers of Elizabeth Barrett Browning's and Shakespeare's sonnets say "How do I love thee? Let me count the ways" and "Shall I compare thee to a summer's day? / Thou art more lovely and more temperate," they are interior narrators (or speakers) who narrate (speak) to their beloveds, and their beloveds are interior narratees (Browning 237, Shakespeare 1846). In an epistolary novel (a novel made up of letters between the characters), like Samuel Richardson's *Pamela* and *Clarissa* or Chaderlos de Laclos's *Les Liaisons Dangereuses*, the interior narrators and narratees often switch roles back and forth, writing letters to other characters, and reading letters from other characters.

When Jane Eyre says, "Reader, I married him," she envisions an exterior narratee for her story. In that case, the fictional narratee lines up closely with the actual reader, but they do not have to be the same. Some narrators, as in Joseph Conrad's *Heart of Darkness* or Philip Roth's *Portnoy's Complaint*, for example, narrate to narratees in the fictional setting. In *Heart of Darkness*, Marlowe tells his story to other men who sit and listen. They are fictional metonymies of readers, but they are not actual readers. Similarly, Portnoy tells his story to his psychoanalyst. Some narratees play a key role in the story, such as the king who listens to Scheherazade in *A Thousand and One*

Nights and will kill her if she does not tell a story lively enough to keep his interest. In many a novel, such as Henry James's *The Turn of the Screw*, the narrator writes for fictional narratees who might read the story later but who—like Marlowe's friends, Portnoy's psychoanalyst, or King Shahryar in *A Thousand and One Nights*—are not actual readers. Just as the narrator, even an implied exterior narrator, as we saw in Chapter 3, is a construct that is not the same as the author but is in some ways like the author, so the narratee, even an implied exterior narratee who does not actually appear in the story, is not the same as the reader but is in some ways like the reader.

Encoding and decoding. In another influential structuralist model (Figure 11.2), the cultural studies scholar Stuart Hall (whose work we looked at in Chapters 4, 9, and 10) has reconsidered Jakobson's model of addresser (or sender), message, and addressee (or receiver). Hall observes that a communication system is not perfectly efficient. It is asymmetrical; what gets sent is not the same as what gets received. When people send a message they encode it, and the encoding shapes the message, because the message gets mediated, influenced, by the encoders' discourses, ideologies, and technologies. When people receive a message, they decode it. And the decoding, like the encoding, shapes the message, because it too is mediated by discourses, ideologies, and technologies. Readers, viewers, and listeners are decoders. Hall uses the example of a television news program, though he could

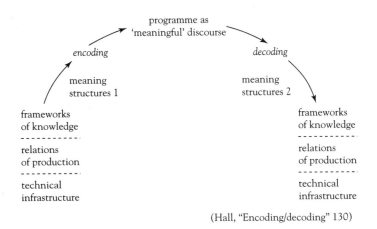

(Hall, "Encoding/decoding" 130)

Figure 11.2 Stuart Hall's model of encoding and decoding.

just as well take examples from other kinds of messages, such as a song, a poem, a novel, or a movie.

For example, when a novel or a newscast ignores a male character's or a male political candidate's clothing or family status and defines a female character or candidate by her clothing or family status, or defines a nonwhite character or public figure through race but does not define a white character or public figure through race, then some of the decoders might notice the discrepancy and object to it. In such a case, those decoders process the message in a different way from the encoders.

Many considerations influence the encoding. A network might encourage its staff to present the news in an objective manner or in a politically partisan manner. The newscast must be brief, and it typically favors stories and approaches that can be filmed. In the same way, the conventions of poetry encourage messages (poems) that come in a brief format, often, at least before modern poetry, in meter and rhyme. The conventions also shape the poem-message through the quasi-interruption and pacing of line breaks. Similarly, the decoders'—the readers'—knowledge and understanding of the patterns and conventions of newscasts or poems influence the decoding. Thus, the message changes according to each moment of encoding and, on the other side of the process, each moment of decoding. For the message is never the signified itself, stable and secure. It is always a discourse of signifiers in process.

Hall then loosely divides decodings (readers' responses) into three different kinds: *dominant-hegemonic* (drawing on Gramsci's notion of hegemony, introduced in Chapter 8 on Marxism), *negotiated*, and *oppositional*. Decoders in the dominant-hegemonic position accept the ideological assumptions of the encoders and thus accept the message more or less as the encoders would like. Decoders in the negotiated position accept some of the encoders' ideological assumptions but oppose others. As they process the message—the newscast or novel—they negotiate a compromise between the encoders' assumptions and other assumptions that differ from the encoders' assumptions. And decoders in the oppositional position reinterpret the message through the filter of ideological assumptions that oppose the assumptions of the encoders, in the way, for example, that right-wing decoders read the messages (newscasts, poems, novels, movies, slogans) of left wingers and that left wingers read the messages of right wingers. (For bell hooks' similar concept of oppositional spectators, see Chapter 6.)

You may have noted, dear readers and decoders (whether dominant-hegemonic, negotiated, or oppositional), that I often write *readers*, in the plural, when I might have written *reader*, in the singular. I would like to suggest that it usually helps to think of readers in the plural, because—explicitly or implicitly—reader-response criticism usually considers more than one reader. Thinking about readers in the plural helps us get beyond the idiosyncrasy of a possibly unrepresentative reader (except when that is our special interest) and concentrate more broadly on the social process that many readers share. By drawing on Marxism, Hall's description of three broad kinds of readers helps us consider reading as a social process.

AESTHETIC JUDGMENT, INTERPRETIVE COMMUNITIES, AND RESISTING READERS

Aesthetic judgment. Similarly, critics who theorize what has come to be called the canon, the standard set of literature that critics and teachers typically study and teach, have noticed how the canon changes over time as the readers who construct it change over time. We have already seen, in Chapter 6 on feminism, that feminist critics changed the canon by inviting us to set aside patriarchal filters of reading and open our minds more to literature written by women and to literature that thinks about women respectfully. We noted as well that critics who study a variety of minority literatures have, like feminist critics, led the still ongoing process of reshaping the canon.

In that context, critics have also rethought our understanding of how readers determine aesthetic judgments. Barbara Herrnstein Smith observes that we have traditionally thought of aesthetic taste as an absolute. In that model, a work of art is either good art, or it is not good art. But Smith and others have noted that the idea of what is good or not good varies with the reader or group of readers and even, for any one reader, varies from reading to reading. With each reading, we see different things and interpret in different ways. Aesthetic taste, Smith argues, is therefore *contingent*, meaning that it varies as the conditions of reading vary.

A great many influences shape those conditions. Hall's three kinds of readers, for example, will likely produce different versions of aesthetic taste, leading them to different conclusions about the value of some of the poems, movies, or stories that they watch and read. Similarly, as we saw in Chapter 8, Pierre Bourdieu argues that aesthetic taste tends to vary with the social position of readers and audiences.

Thus while we sometimes achieve a relative consensus about aesthetic taste, we never achieve a complete consensus. Our opinions vary as widely as our lives and the personal and social circumstances that shape our lives. Again, that is not to say there are no continuities. Some songs, paintings, or poems attract larger followings, and some attract smaller followings. Some attract larger followings among some groups and smaller followings among other groups. In all these ways, as Smith argues, aesthetic taste is variable and contingent, not a stable and absolute essence.

Interpretive communities. In a similar vein, in his later work Fish (Figure 11.3) proposes that our readings of literary texts depend not so much on what the texts say in some intrinsic or absolute way as they depend, contingently, on what he calls **interpretive communities.** Interpretive communities have their own interpretive strategies and conventions. Critics like to think that they propose original interpretations, but from the perspective of Fish's model of interpretive communities, the very idea of originality is part of the anything-but-original form that interpretive communities dictate for our interpretations. When the expectations of the interpretive community require critics to claim

Figure 11.3 Stanley Fish (1938–) reading.

originality, then the process of claiming originality is itself an un-original act, a rote submission to preexisting conventions of interpretation. After all, to claim originality, critics and students go through the same unoriginal motions that others who claim originality have already gone through before. That is, they say how previous critics got it wrong or neglected to account for this or that, and how their own approach will show something that previous critics missed. And then the next critic will do the same thing to them, repeating the same formula of what Fish sees as a bogus originality. Fish's model has much in common with the structuralist notion that language produces the world it describes rather than merely reflecting that world.

Though we might see Fish's model as a critique of interpretive communities, he does not see it that way. He sees it as describing a routine part of the way things work. When we judge the quality of our interpretations, Fish contends, we are not judging their degree of truth about the text so much as their ability to understand the protocols of our interpretive communities. Nevertheless, Fish's model gets astutely at the numbing, thumb-twiddling routine of much professional and daily life. It can also help students understand that whether or not they write insightful interpretations for their classes, they need to learn the form of writing insightful interpretations. If they learn the form, that will go a long way to carrying the day, whether or not their interpretations have all that much insight.

To Fish's critics, his view of interpretive communities gives us little reason to care, little reason to favor one interpretation over another, if they both live up to the expectations of an interpretive community. But if you care about feminism, for example, or about aesthetic ingenuity, then you might give special value to a feminist interpretation or an interpretation that has an eye for aesthetic playfulness. While Fish could respond that such caring only defines your interpretive community, the broader interpretive community of literary and cultural criticism does not always pay heed to questions of aesthetics and certainly has not usually favored feminism. Indeed, interpretive communities have often sought to push feminism away. Fish acknowledges differences within interpretive communities. He sees arguing over differences as itself one of the principles of the broader interpretive community. But to most other critics' way of thinking, interpretive communities are less stable entities than Fish's model allows for, and the things we care about most often come at least partly from motives that the uninspiring model of interpretive communities cannot capture.

In a structuralist mode that can bear comparison to Fish's sense of interpretive communities, Jonathan Culler, as we have seen in Chapter 3, argues that readers bring a specific competence to the process of reading specific genres of literature. Readers who are not competent in the rules of reading a novel, for example, could mistake a novel for a history or a biography, just as a reader not competent in colloquial speech will misunderstand such expressions as "Hold your horses" and "Don't lose your head." For Culler, then, the goal of structuralist interpretation, or structuralist poetics, is not to interpret an individual literary text but instead to describe the competence that readers depend on and expect for any particular genre, from sonnets to film noir, from stage comedies to high school movies or detective novels.

More skeptical poststructuralists respond by asking, "What if two readers disagree over the competence required to read a particular genre? Whose competence is the right competence?" As Culler himself recognizes in his later, deconstructive writing, where he asks what it would mean to read specifically as a woman, different readers and different groups of readers—we might even say different interpretive communities—bring different perspectives. From a deconstructive position, attuned to multiple possibilities, reading as a woman (or as any particular kind of reader) can include a variety of different and even contradictory responses. For example, women readers who have been interpellated into patriarchal assumptions (that is, who have come to take patriarchal assumptions for granted) will understand reading as a woman in different ways from women who read as feminists.

Resisting readers. While Culler tracks the variety of strategies that women readers might follow, Judith Fetterley calls for a specifically feminist approach to reader-response criticism. A key though often-underrecognized contributor to the early years of feminist criticism, Fetterley proposes, in *The Resisting Reader: A Feminist Approach to American Fiction* (1978), that critics traditionally did not see how the most frequently studied American writing takes patriarchal assumptions for granted, as if making everything hinge on how a story turns out for its male characters, whatever the cost to its female characters, were the natural and universal way to read. Fetterley seeks a reader-response criticism that does not merely trace a neutral process of reading the formalist strategies of a literary text. For in a patriarchal setting, strategies that present themselves as neutral have a way of ending up as patriarchal. Such strategies ask even women readers to read as if they were patriarchal men.

Instead, Fetterley asks critics to challenge patriarchal ideology by seeing how it shapes characters and readers. She invites critics to see how literary texts and literary criticism can join with patriarchal assumptions or can expose them and criticize them, like the oppositional readers described by Hall, the critical spectators described by hooks (Chapter 6), and the disidentifying spectators described by Muñoz (Chapter 7). To Fetterley, classic American fiction and much of the criticism of that fiction, from Washington Irving's "Rip Van Winkle," Nathaniel Hawthorne's "The Birthmark," and Ernest Hemingway's A *Farewell to Arms* to Norman Mailer's An *American Dream*, see women and women characters as problems, unless they die. If we allow such guiding patterns and beliefs to fade into the unnoticed wallpaper in the literary background, then they hurt readers, especially women readers. Her approach has much in common with Althusser's description of the way that ideology recruits subjects to go along with the system that hurts them (as we saw in Chapter 8). But Fetterley insists that through feminist reading we can recognize patriarchal ideology, and she believes that by recognizing patriarchal ideology we can begin to change it.

RECEPTION THEORY AND RECEPTION HISTORY

Reception theory. In more explicitly historicist terms than Fish or Iser, and in terms that can fit with Fetterley's call to change our way of reading, the phenomenological critic Hans Robert Jauss, the leading figure in a German version of reader-response theory known as *reception aesthetics* or *reception theory*, has called for interpreting the history of the ways people read a literary work by studying the **horizon of expectations** that surrounds that work. Jauss asks what was possible for writers to expect when and where a work was written, and he compares that range of possible expectations to the range of possible expectations for a work's readers, both when the work was written and as those expectations change over time.

Carson McCullers's novel *The Heart Is a Lonely Hunter*, for example, trades on the expectations that readers in 1940 brought to a potentially popular new novel. Though from the perspective of today's horizon of expectations, McCullers's novel seems fascinated with unfulfilled, even unrecognized queer sexualities, there is little address to queer concerns in recorded responses from the novel's first readers or even from the next generation of readers. In the 1960s, high school English teachers frequently assigned *The Heart Is a*

Lonely Hunter, even though those same teachers would not think of bringing, or at least would not dare to bring, queer questions explicitly into the high school classroom, if for no other reason than fear for their jobs in a queer-hostile world. Given the horizon of expectations in the 1940s, McCullers could closet the novel's queerness, making it at once highly visible and highly invisible, according to different readers' varying familiarity with horizons of expectations that included or excluded queerness. Today, the horizon of queer expectations has enlarged, and though the novel has no unequivocal gay or lesbian acts or characters, its queerness seems poignantly visible.

Similarly, when I first taught Hemingway's *The Sun Also Rises* and referred to the scene in Chapter 3 where Brett arrives at a bar with a group of gay friends, students insisted that they remembered no such scene. Or if any students did notice it, they felt that they needed to keep silent. When I then pointed the scene out, the vocal students expressed shock that Hemingway could write with what they saw as such subtlety, that he could signal gayness with clarity and yet code it in ways that kept them from noticing it, that left them trapped in their naturalization of heterosexuality. Today, the horizon of expectations has changed. The words on the page are the same, but their meaning has shifted, for the same passage needs no explanation. Students pick up on it so easily that the same words that my earlier students found subtle now look heavy-handed.

Reception history. Inspired partly by German reception theory, Anglo-American critics developed what they call **reception history.** Reception history studies the history of how readers respond to a given film or literary work, writer, or movement in literature or film. It is not easy to uncover the reception history of older works in their own time. Few of Chaucer's or Shakespeare's contemporaries wrote down their responses. Even if they did write them down, in most cases what they wrote probably did not survive. We can more easily study the history of responses to Chaucer or Shakespeare in later times as well as study the responses to later works. With the growth of the printing press, the emergence of newspapers, magazines, and book reviews, the increasing proliferation and survival of books that readers have scribbled on, and eventually with the proliferation of letters, searchable databases, Internet search engines, book apps, and social media, critics can uncover a vast history of responses to literature and film by actual readers and audiences, as opposed to the hypothetical and abstract readers of most reader-response theory. Critics can even follow how responses to a work have changed as each new wave of critical theory discussed in this book emerges and joins the conversation.

Sometimes scholars compare the reception of different works or writers. Michael Bérubé has compared the reception of the white novelist Thomas Pynchon, who tried to hide from the public yet achieved enormous fame with the publication of his novel *Gravity's Rainbow*, to the reception of the brilliant African American poet Melvin Tolson, who did everything he could think of to build his reputation and yet was forgotten as remarkably as Pynchon was lionized. Jacqueline Bobo has studied African American women's responses to films about black women, such as *The Color Purple* and *Daughters of the Dust*. Besides the reception histories of individual films, writers, or books, some scholars take a more cultural studies or sociohistorical approach. Janice Radway, for example, joined a group of women romance readers and wrote about their patterns of reading the way an anthropologist might write an ethnography based on participant observation. Her work contributed to the growth of audience studies in cultural studies, as in the cultural studies interpretations of popular culture and its fans discussed in Chapter 9. Similarly, but more historically, Elizabeth McHenry has researched the history of African American readers by studying African American literary societies in the nineteenth and early twentieth centuries.

Work such as Bobo's and McHenry's can help deter critics from the common practice of assuming, without realizing it, that readers are white, in a world where cultural ideologies of race encourage people to naturalize whiteness much as they naturalize heterosexuality. Similarly, works such as Fetterley's, Radway's, and Bobo's speak critically to the unconscious but common assumption that readers are men or are students and academics. As we study the history of readers and reading, therefore, we do well to keep in mind the multiplicity of readers and the ways that each writer's audience differs from the audience of another writer.

PARANOID, SUSPICIOUS, AND SYMPTOMATIC READING VERSUS SURFACE READING

Some recent critics have invited us to rethink how we understand the strategies and goals of critical reading itself. Eve Kosofsky Sedgwick has characterized the dominant practice of critical interpretation as too committed to what she calls *paranoid reading*, as too caught up in what the philosopher Paul Ricoeur dubbed *the hermeneutics of suspicion.* (In this context, the term *hermeneutics* refers to strategies of interpretation. For more on Sedgwick, see Chapter 7.) In a similar argument, Stephen Best and Sharon Marcus have criticized a style of interpretation sometimes called *symptomatic reading.* Drawing especially from psychoanalytic and Marxist criticism, Sedgwick, Best, and Marcus see contemporary critics as trying to put themselves in a superior position above the works that they interpret. For example, they question the way that many critics interpret a text by looking for symptoms, the way a psychoanalyst interprets a person, as if critics can understand a text but a text cannot understand itself. In that sense, Sedgwick argues that contemporary critics have grown too wary and suspicious of the texts that they interpret. They have succumbed to thinking that a critic should triumph over a text by digging up and exposing its supposedly dangerous, repressed meaning.

For Sedgwick, contemporary criticism too often celebrates its own supposed insight into dangerous social assumptions that critics see as motivating the works they interpret. She argues that we already know the disturbing things about literature and culture that critics congratulate themselves for revealing: "Why bother," she asks, "exposing the ruses of power in a country where, at any given moment, 40 percent of young black men are enrolled in the penal system?" "The paranoid trust in exposure seemingly depends," she argues, "on an infinite reservoir of naïveté in those who make up the audience for these unveilings." In this way, Sedgwick sees critics as too quick to suppose that readers of literature are dupes of the unconscious and oppressive social assumptions that Marxists call ideology and false consciousness. (For Louis Althusser's Marxist understanding of ideology and false consciousness, see Chapter 8.) Such critics suppose that readers do not understand the social problems they see around them. Sedgwick has tired of critics rediscovering, over and over again, ideas that many critics take for granted and yet suppose that other readers do not understand: "How television-starved would someone have to be," she asks, "to find it shocking that ideologies contradict themselves, that simulacra don't have originals, or that gender representations are artificial?" (18–19).

On the other hand, we might argue that for most of the population, the tragedy of so many black men locked in the penal system remains out of sight and anything but obvious, and therefore, like so many other things that literary and cultural critics try to expose, desperately worth exposing. Often, we *are* dupes of false consciousness. We often go along casually with ideological, unconscious social assumptions that work against our own interests. And often, we do read ideological assumptions as uncontradictory essences, and we mistake the simulated representations and lies that we see in the mass media for reified truths. For those reasons, readers and critics may reasonably find value in criticism that exposes our ideological assumptions. Even Sedgwick says that she does not want to get rid of what she calls paranoid reading. She confesses to practicing it herself. But she fears that we have let it slide into a stale pattern that keeps us from thinking of alternatives. Sedgwick urges us to bring "reparative" ways of reading into our critical repertoire, giving more attention to the pleasure and aesthetics of reading, focusing less on rejecting cultural injustice and more on finding possibilities for reform.

Similarly, when Best and Marcus say they have grown tired of *symptomatic reading*, they refer to interpretation that treats a text as a series of symptoms expressing something deeper and buried. Like Sedgwick, they identify symptomatic reading with criticism influenced by psychoanalysis and the Marxist critique of ideology, especially from Althusser and Fredric Jameson. They question Jameson's idea that a text has a political unconscious, a set of social and political assumptions that it remains unaware of, and they question his belief that the goal of criticism is to expose those assumptions as wrong. (For more on Jameson, see Chapter 8.) Also like Sedgwick, Best and Marcus believe that we no longer need critics to expose deeply buried, terrible social secrets such as government corruption and racism. They argue that contemporary technology already exposes the social abuses that once remained hidden. They do not oppose symptomatic reading, but they call for us to focus as well on what they call *surface reading*.

Under the rubric of surface reading Best and Marcus include a great many critical practices. They ask us to study what people do with literature apart from reading it (buy it, sell it, show off with it, and so on). They ask us to study the language of literature, savor the emotions that it provokes, take what it says at face value, see how literature describes itself, ask what patterns one work shares with another (narratologically, or in theme or genre), or draw on "distant reading" or "data mining" to see what patterns computer-mediated searches can find across many different literary works or within individual works.

Best and Marcus's critique of reading in depth and advocacy of surface reading has attracted both interest and skepticism. It seems unwise for them to trust contemporary technology to take care of exposing terrible social abuses. No doubt technology—such as cell-phone video cameras and social media—helps expose abuses, but it can also help commit, hide, and defend abuses. Nor did contemporary technology invent the process of exposing social abuses and corruption. There have always been exposés, and yet we always need more exposés. It is also hard to tell how much contemporary technology helps us interpret depths and how much it traps us in interpreting surfaces. Indeed, we might wonder about the binary opposition between depth reading and surface reading. Any good reading looks at surfaces, and any good surface reading looks at depths. Even the alternatives to depth criticism that Best and Marcus propose seem to have as much to do with depths as they do with surfaces.

Many critics, therefore, even if they take inspiration from Best and Marcus's encouragement of new models of reading, resist the idea that to interpret beyond the surface necessarily means to interpret in a paranoid, suspicious, or symptomatic way. Rita Felski, for example, appreciates the critique of suspicious, symptomatic readings that give way to rote predictability, but she objects to the way that the term *paranoid* can pathologize critical interpretation. Felski observes that as a style of interpreting the world around us, suspicious interpretation has a much longer and wider history than we can find in literary criticism. She reminds us, as well, that the hermeneutics of suspicion can lead not only to political insights but also to aesthetic pleasure. At its best, Felski says, the hermeneutics of suspicion brings "a jolt in perspective that allows previously unsuspected layers of meaning to come into view" (109). Suspicious interpretation can offer great pleasure as a test of our wits and skills. Suspicious readers often turn their critical scrutiny on literary works that fascinate them. They "inhabit the text, come to know it thoroughly, explore its every nook and cranny, in order to draw out its hidden secrets . . . , and suspicion turns out not to be so very far removed from love" (112–113). Felski risks returning us to the platitudes about the value and pleasure of critical thinking that Sedgwick, Best, and Marcus try to shake us out of. But Sedgwick, Best, and Marcus end up calling for the same renewed attention to the aesthetic pleasure of reading that Felski calls for, except that Felski suggests that they underestimate the aesthetic pleasure of suspicious reading. We might even say that the aesthetic pleasure in their suspicious readings of suspicious reading accounts for much of the attention that their provocative arguments have attracted. In these ways, the dialogue among Sedgwick, Best, Marcus, Felski, and others can pleasurably defamiliarize our understanding of critical reading, helping us think through our practices with a more nuanced, self-questioning interpretation of the challenges that our critical habits, motives, and pleasures can mask or inspire.

READERS AND NEW TECHNOLOGIES

The impulse to generalize about large bodies of literature or writing, in contrast to close reading of individual texts, has received a huge boost from computers, which draw on *data mining* to expand the resources for **distant reading**. Scholars can search the increasingly massive databases of writing and find patterns not observable by unaided human eyes. Instead of reading twenty novels or a hundred poems and generalizing, through subjective impressions, about the history of "the novel" or "poetry" in, say, the nineteenth century, literary historians who practice distant reading can read (or "read") thousands, hundreds of thousands, or millions of texts from a particular genre, time, or span of times, searching for consistent or changing patterns of language, genre, emotional expression, gender, time, geography, money, anything that scholarly ingenuity, combined with statistics, computational analysis, and programming, can help us ask about, investigate, count—and then, through counting, interpret.

As the electronics and computer revolution has accelerated, media studies scholars such as Henry Jenkins have expanded their study of the audiences for popular culture. Building on the participatory process of reading described by Fish and Iser, Jenkins describes how fans of popular culture—Trekkies, for instance, or fans of the TV show *Supernatural*—"poach" on popular media to build vast subcultures of fandom and fanfiction. Fanfic subcultures continue to multiply, for example, expanding to toys like GI Joe and Transformers and boy bands like One Direction. For Jenkins, as for other cultural studies media scholars, consumers of popular culture rarely fit the model of consumers as passive dupes, a model that earlier scholars sometimes took for granted. Consumers participate in the culture they consume, and their participation changes what they consume.

The participation of audiences and the marketing strategies of corporations make multiple media converge. *Harry Potter*, for example, began as a novel, but it turned into a massive multimedia constellation of novels, films, and video games; authorized and unauthorized websites, blogs, and books; action figures and other toys; reading groups; classes; sports (Muggle Quidditch); and theme parks. Readers respond and participate in an enormous variety of ways across the cornucopia of Harry Potter reading, play, fantasy, writing, and watching. The electronic dimension of reader response is growing so rapidly that any account of it will soon look quaintly out of date.

Indeed, David Gauntlett has called for a Media Studies 2.0, playing off the interactivity that defines what has come to be called Web 2.0. He wants the study of media participation to move from seeing audiences and readers as receivers and instead to seeing them as partners who share in producing what they receive. Readers collaborate to write Wikipedia and other wikis. They respond to their reading by posting, tweeting, and retweeting on Instagram, Facebook, and Twitter. They review books, films, and other products online. They say what they "like." They sample and remix music and play interactive video games. They screen phone calls and Photoshop memes. They publish their own blogs, websites, and videos, and they respond to or link to other people's blogs, websites, and videos. They chat. They use the reply function. They save movies, TV shows, and podcasts to watch or listen to later. They join online polls and petitions and dress up at fan conventions.

Questions arise, then, about exactly what and how much the new technologies change. Are teenagers on their laptops and phones as influential producers of contemporary culture as corporate executives? Sometimes they are, but not typically. Does the new omnipresence of cameras protect people around the world from political repression and crime? Sometimes, but again, not always. Perhaps we risk overestimating the changes brought on by the revolution in computers and electronics. Readers have always responded actively to their reading, as the plots of novels themselves have dramatized from Miguel de Cervantes's *Don Quixote* to Gustave Flaubert's *Madame Bovary*, Ray Bradbury's *Fahrenheit 451*, and A. S. Byatt's *Possession*. Audiences rioted at a performance of Shakespeare's *Coriolanus* in Paris in 1934 and at a performance of J. M. Synge's *The Playboy of the Western World* in Dublin in 1907. The poems of Robert Browning grew so popular in the late nineteenth century that hundreds of small towns set up their own Browning Societies. In response to the novel and stage versions of *Uncle Tom's Cabin*, many audience members and readers decided to oppose slavery and, in Great Britain, kept their leaders from joining the United States' Civil War on the side of the Confederacy. Readers of Goethe's 1774 *The Sorrows of Young Werther* responded with "Werther fever." Young men dressed like Werther and then, sometimes, identifying with the literary character far too much (warning: spoiler alert), they even shot themselves. These are extreme examples, but there is nothing new about participatory readers responding to their reading with energy and passion.

In some ways, then, the electronics and computer revolution changes the media while it continues the same process of participatory reading and critical spectatorship that literary and film critics began to write about decades ago. But in other ways, perhaps the changes in media cross a threshold that transforms participatory reading itself and transforms audiences as well. As we move increasingly into an electronic world, leaving print and paper behind or taking them with us, the study of readers' responses offers challenges that we can only begin to anticipate.

Let us return, then, to the idea that texts do not make meaning by themselves. Readers make meaning. Scholars disagree about whether readers make meaning in collaboration with texts, such that texts shape and limit how readers can interpret them, or whether, as the tree might not fall in the forest if no one hears or sees it, readers bear sole responsibility for their interpretations. Either way, reading is not merely passive. Just as we discussed critical spectators in our consideration of feminist film theory and popular culture, so readers are spectators and, like all audiences, read with varying degrees of passivity and criticism. One goal of this book is to encourage our dialogue about how, as readers, we can respond less passively and more critically.

FURTHER READING

Anker, Elizabeth S., and Rita Felski, eds. *Critique and Postcritique*. Durham, NC: Duke University Press, 2017.

Bérubé, Michael. *Marginal Forces/Cultural Centers: Tolson, Pynchon, and the Politics of the Canon*. Ithaca, NY: Cornell University Press, 1992.

Best, Stephen, and Sharon Marcus. "Surface Reading: An Introduction." *Representations* 108.1 (Fall 2009): 1–21.

Bleich, David. *Readings and Feelings: An Introduction to Subjective Criticism*. Urbana, IL: National Council of Teachers of English, 1975.

———. *Subjective Criticism*. Baltimore: Johns Hopkins University Press, 1978.

Bobo, Jacqueline. *Black Women as Cultural Readers*. New York: Columbia University Press, 1995.

Bode, Katherine. *A World of Fiction: Digital Collections and the Future of Literary History*. Ann Arbor: University of Michigan Press, 2018.

Eco, Umberto. *The Role of the Reader: Explorations in the Semiotics of Texts*. Bloomington: Indiana University Press, 1978.

Felski, Rita. *The Limits of Critique*. Chicago: University of Chicago Press, 2015.

Fetterley, Judith. *The Resisting Reader: A Feminist Approach to American Fiction.* Bloomington: Indiana University Press, 1978.

Fish, Stanley. *Is There a Text in This Class? The Authority of Interpretive Communities.* Cambridge, MA: Harvard University Press, 1980.

————. *Surprised by Sin: The Reader in "Paradise Lost."* 2nd ed. Cambridge, MA: Harvard University Press, 1998.

Flynn, Elizabeth A., and Patrocinio P. Schweickart, eds. *Gender and Reading: Essays on Readers, Texts, and Contexts.* Baltimore: Johns Hopkins University Press, 1986.

Freund, Elizabeth. *The Return of the Reader: Reader-Response Criticism.* London: Methuen, 1987.

Gauntlett, David. "Media Studies 2.0." http://davidgauntlett.com/digital-media/from-the-archives-media-studies-2-0/.

Holland, Norman N. *5 Readers Reading.* New Haven, CT: Yale University Press, 1975.

————. *The Dynamics of Literary Response.* New York: Oxford University Press, 1968.

Holub, Robert C. *Reception Theory: A Critical Introduction.* London: Methuen, 1984.

Iser, Wolfgang. *The Act of Reading: A Theory of Aesthetic Response.* Baltimore: Johns Hopkins University Press, 1978.

————. *The Implied Reader: Patters of Communication in Prose Fiction from Bunyan to Beckett.* Baltimore: Johns Hopkins University Press, 1974.

Jauss, Hans Robert. *Toward an Aesthetic of Reception.* Trans. Timothy Bahti. Minneapolis: University of Minnesota Press, 1982.

Jenkins, Henry. *Convergence Culture: Where Old and New Media Collide.* 2nd ed. New York: New York University Press, 2008.

————. *Textual Poachers: Television Fans and Participatory Culture.* New York: Routledge, 1992.

Larsen, Katherine, and Lynn S. Zubernis. *Fangasm: Supernatural Fangirls.* Iowa City: University of Iowa Press, 2013.

Mailloux, Steven. *Interpretive Conventions: The Reader in the Study of American Fiction.* Ithaca, NY: Cornell University Press, 1982.

McHenry, Elizabeth. *Forgotten Readers: Recovering the Lost History of African-American Literary Societies.* Durham, NC: Duke University Press, 2002.

Moretti, Franco. *Distant Reading.* Brooklyn: Verso, 2013.

Piper, Andrew. *Enumerations: Data and Literary Study.* Chicago: University of Chicago Press, 2018.

Radway, Janice A. *Reading the Romance: Women, Patriarchy, and Popular Literature.* 2nd ed. Chapel Hill: University of North Carolina Press, 1991.

Rosenblatt, Louise M. *The Reader, the Text, the Poem: The Transactional Theory of the Literary Work.* Carbondale: Southern Illinois University Press, 1978.

Sedgwick, Eve Kosofsky. "Paranoid Reading and Reparative Reading; or, You're So Paranoid, You Probably Think This Introduction Is about You." In *Novel*

Gazing: Queer Readings in Fiction. Ed. Sedgwick. Durham, NC: Duke University Press, 1997: 1–37.

Smith, Barbara Herrnstein. *Contingencies of Value: Alternative Perspectives for Critical Theory.* Cambridge, MA: Harvard University Press, 1988.

Suleiman, Susan, and Inge Crosman, eds. *The Reader in the Text: Essays on Audience and Interpretation.* Princeton, NJ: Princeton University Press, 1980.

Tompkins, Jane P., ed. *Reader-Response Criticism: From Formalism to Post-Structuralism.* Baltimore: Johns Hopkins University Press, 1980.

Underwood, Ted. *Distant Horizons: Digital Evidence and Literary Change.* Chicago: University of Chicago Press, 2019.

Zunshine, Lisa. *Why We Read Fiction: A Theory of Mind and the Novel.* Columbus: Ohio State University Press, 2006.

✳ 12 ✲

Recent and Emerging Developments: Environmental Criticism and Disability Studies

This closing chapter attempts to review some recent and emerging developments, but it does not try to take up every latest thing. Here I attempt the more modest task of addressing key areas of inquiry that have settled into prominence without yet reaching the point where a great majority of critics see them as crucial for critical thinking at large. As snapshots of rapidly developing conversations, the reviews of ecocriticism and disability studies in this concluding chapter will not go into the same detail as the other chapters. The goal is simply to offer an accessibly but not cryptically short impression of how critics and theorists are shaping and reshaping emerging new curiosities and challenges.

I might have chosen other areas besides environmental criticism and disability studies. Readers interested in recent and emerging developments may also want to explore, for example, affect studies, trauma studies, performance studies, print culture and the history of the book, studies of literature and aging, food studies, and studies in the humanities and science or in cognitive science and neuroscience. This book does not try to cover everything, nor should it. But I believe that readers will find a great deal of interest in ecocriticism and disability studies both in themselves and in what they can represent about the possibility for continued critical questioning.

ENVIRONMENTAL CRITICISM

Ecocriticism, which has gradually expanded into environmental criticism, may matter more than any other critical method. Still, many people don't want to hear about it. They figure we can put off worrying about the environment until later. But later may be too late.

The exposé of pesticides and industrial deception in Rachel Carson's 1962 *Silent Spring* shook up environmental complacency and helped inspire a new ecological politics. The conservationist movement began before *Silent Spring,* but before Carson it had less sense of crisis. Even for many years after *Silent Spring,* though, literary criticism usually favored apolitical interpretation, as the earlier chapters of this book indicate. Eventually, beginning in the early 1990s, as literary criticism reacted against its apolitical history, many critics working from diverse directions—notably Lawrence Buell in the United States and Jonathan Bate in Great Britain—put together a new movement that grew out of the new ecological activism and came to be known as ecocriticism.

Literary and cultural critics' responses to ecological activism and ecocriticism have therefore proceeded along two tracks. One track sees ecological issues as trivial or as stuff for policy wonks, of little interest for aesthetics or for literary and cultural criticism. The other track sees reimagining our world in more ecologically sustainable ways as the most urgent, dramatic, and all-encompassing challenge we face. For those reasons, at the same time as we have witnessed a huge growth in ecocritical thinking, ecocriticism has remained something of an enclave, something that many critics believe they can leave to others and do not need to integrate into their own thinking. In a book like this, ecocriticism could easily receive a full chapter (as it is now the focus of many books, journals, articles, and courses), and yet it has not yet reached the breadth of recognition that makes ecocritical thinking routine for critics in general.

One of the leading early ecocritics, Cheryll Glotfelty, offers a widely quoted definition: "Simply put, ecocriticism is the study of the relationship between language and the physical environment. Just as feminist criticism examines language and literature from a gender-conscious perspective, and Marxist criticism brings an awareness of modes of production and economic class to its reading of texts, ecocriticism takes an earth-centered approach to literary studies" (xviii). Glotfelty's definition leaves room for many approaches. Instead of presenting ecocriticism as one approach, I will try to summarize it historically by reviewing a series of key binary oppositions that have shaped debates in ecological activism and ecocriticism.

We can associate much early ecocriticism with one or more of the following interests:

- a focus on writing directly about nature;
- a focus on nature writing from Great Britain and the United States;
- an often reverential focus on nature writing by idolized white male writers;
- an indifference to or suspicion of critical theory, especially poststructuralism;
- ecofeminist approaches, sometimes in the manner of second-wave feminism;
- a focus on ecology, understood as the study of natural balance in distinct, stable ecosystems;
- a focus on the local, including specific ecosystems, usually far from cities.

More recent ecocriticism often takes contrasting approaches to these same interests, generating a series of conversations and debates that shape an ongoing dialogue. Here I will review ecocriticism by looking at the conversations and debates between earlier and more recent approaches. Sometimes contemporary ecocritics reject the earlier approaches, while other times they bring newer and older approaches together.

Nature and nature writing. Early ecocriticism typically turned its attention to nature writing, usually to nonfiction prose that addresses the wilderness, the woods, or large mammals. Favorite writers included Henry David Thoreau, John Burroughs, John Muir, Mary Austin, Aldo Leopold, Rachel Carson, Edward Abbey, Annie Dillard, Terry Tempest Williams, and Barry Lopez, or, in poetry, William Wordsworth and Gary Snyder. Most of these writers are white American men. In ecocritical interpretations of such writing, nature came to seem like a binary opposition to human culture, and human culture came to seem like a force that contaminated or destroyed nature. Ecocriticism often took the form, then, of glorying in nature, celebrating its freedom from culture, lamenting how culture contaminates nature, or exposing the scandal of pollution, of culture's destruction of nature.

For such critics, nature often seemed like a bedrock of the knowable and absolute. It was the once-sure thing now terribly at risk of disappearing before the corruption of human indifference and hostility. As structuralism and deconstruction turned literary and cultural criticism to a focus on language and representation (see Chapters 3 and 4), ecocritics sometimes aligned themselves with more traditional critics who believed that a focus on language threatened their sense of the concreteness of actual life and the actual world we live in. Structuralism and poststructuralism, to some ecocritics, thus came to seem like part of the overcivilized indifference that collaborated with or encouraged destruction of the natural world.

But more recent ecocriticism tends not to suppose that we can access nature as a concrete and securely known thing independently of the constructions of language and representation that mediate our perception of nature. The concept of nature is cultural, and the concept of culture is natural. There is wilderness in civilization, and there is certainly civilization in wilderness. That is to say, when we see or hear a tree fall in the forest, we see, hear, and understand the tree and its falling according to our varying cultural perspectives and methods of interpretation.

For example, ecocritics have usually looked critically on the common human and literary habit of **anthropomorphism,** the practice of attributing human qualities to nonhuman entities, as when we describe a cheerful robin, an angry storm, or furious rapids. On the one hand, such descriptions can make powerful metaphors. On the other hand, as the Victorian art critic John Ruskin famously complained in his critique of what he called the *pathetic fallacy,* they can misrepresent the described object. If we pause to think about them, they can end up sounding maudlin or silly. They can appeal to a superficial and humanly self-serving way of misinterpreting the world around us. (In Ruskin's older sense of the term, *pathetic* means something that incites the emotions, and fallacy, as we saw in Chapter 2, refers to something false.) We may find value in the human connection implied by anthropomorphic description, and even Ruskin was not hostile to all uses of the pathetic fallacy. But more typically, critics see anthropomorphic description as falsely imposing a human frame of thought that blocks us from recognizing the specificity of the nonhuman. We may intend anthropomorphic language as a description of nature, but it can keep us from seeing the nature that we use it to describe.

In literature, anthropomorphism can get hard to interpret because we have grown so used to it that we often do not consider the possibility of looking at it critically. Anthropomorphism gets especially tricky when writers use it ironically. Critics of the poetry of Robert Frost, for example, argue that Frost's poems use anthropomorphism to mock, rather than to endorse, the anthropomorphizing characters' naïve misunderstanding of nature. In Frost's sonnet "Design" (1922), the speaker finds a white spider on a white flower holding a white moth. When he feels terrified that the convergence of three white objects looks "Like . . . a witches' broth," a broth that "steered" them together into an oppressively uniform "design of darkness," his terror tells us a good deal about him, and about the human desire to anthropomorphize, to project human-like will onto the natural world. But it tells us little about the spider, the flower, or the moth. Or at least it tells us little about any will that they share with each other or with people, as opposed to the pitiless converging of chance that allows a white spider to eat an unsuspecting white moth on an indifferent white flower, ironically a kind of flower called a "heal-all" (Frost 275). The urge to interpret, to anthropomorphize, coincidence is so strong that it is hard not to wonder if the spider *knew* that by climbing onto a white flower it might camouflage itself and so catch a wary victim that would otherwise avoid it. And yet the speaker's uncontrollable desire to inflate the unlikely possibility of spidery calculation into a grand plan of an evil universe exposes the poem's ironic, horrified glee at our desire to project our own fears onto the emotional blankness of a steely nature.

In the long run, if we break the habit of anthropomorphism, then we can look anew and see much more of nature. For that reason and many others, critics now bring a much wider sense of what we see when we look at nature, the human, and the environment. We now read a wider range of writers and writings, internationally as well as by class, gender, race, genre, and style. The deconstructive suspicion of binary oppositions has also led to a suspicion of the binary opposition between nature and culture. The built world is as much a part of our environment as the traditionally conceived natural world. The natural world, as ecological activism has helped us recognize, does not exist apart from the human world. Pesticides, garbage, and human-induced global warming, for example, reach everywhere. Any time we observe even the most isolated parts of nature, our presence helps shape the nature that our idealism may delude us into thinking is separate. The critique of anthropomorphism, in other words, does not mean that we can perceive a nature free of the human. Instead, it underlines the stakes, responsibilities, and modesties that we need to recognize as we confront the relation between the natural and the human, between nonhuman nature and human nature.

As animals ourselves, we are part of nature. Therefore, contemporary ecocriticism, now sometimes going under the terms *environmental criticism* or *literature and the environment,* is as likely to study the urban world and the international, postcolonial, and transnational world as the woods or the wilderness. Impelled by the **environmental justice** movement, which notes, for example, how toxic waste tends to end up near the poor and in or near neighborhoods where most residents are people of color rather than in white, prosperous neighborhoods, contemporary ecocriticism also calls attention to social imbalances of power along racial, economic, and national lines.

Deep ecology. **Deep ecology** is more a philosophical orientation than a biological argument. Sometimes, it also takes on a spiritual dimension. Deep ecologists believe in respecting the inherent value of nature as much as the value of the human. They see traditional environmentalists as too focused on *managing* nature for the benefit of humans, whereas deep ecologists value nature, by ethical choice, for its own sake. They believe that humans should change radically, simplifying human life to adapt to nature. Noting how the growth of the human population brings destruction to the natural world, deep ecologists argue, like many other environmentalists, for limiting human population growth. The ethical force of deep ecology's respect for nature and the frank rhetorical power of the expression "deep ecology" have helped keep deep ecology highly visible in ecological thinking. Even so, when confronted with the choice we must sometimes make between nonhuman life and human life, most advocates of deep ecology make the same choice to favor human life as other ecologists and nonecologists.

Ecofeminism. Ecofeminism has run in tandem with these other developments while also bringing its own motives and concerns. Ecofeminists see how patriarchal thinking often associates nature with women and associates culture—civilization—with men, thus linking the exploitive domination of nature with the exploitative domination of women. Ecofeminists have critiqued a wide set of verbal, cultural, and literary metaphors that often drive the plot as well as the language of literature, feminizing or maternalizing land and landscape as spaces for men to own, rape, exploit, and control. Such metaphors extend across many lands and regions. They have loomed especially large, as Annette Kolodny has shown, in the westward movement of American literature and culture into what patriarchal settler colonialists often imagined as a feminine "virgin land" yearning for masculine conquest and exploitation.

As ecocriticism came together in the same years as second-wave feminism reached prominence, one strain of ecofeminism drew on the second-wave feminist sense of a universally shared, essentialist identity for women. (On second- and third-wave feminism, see Chapter 6.) For ecofeminists of this strain, concepts like Mother Earth and Mother Nature seem ennobling. Some second-wave-style ecofeminists link women and their menstrual cycle to the natural cycle of the moon and link women's ecological sensibility to mythical earth goddesses. Celebrating a distinctively women's nature, they see feminine cooperation and nurturing as better than the competitiveness and individuality that they associate with men and with men's ways of thinking, or at least with typically masculine ways of thinking, which have led to patriarchal abuses of women and nature.

Such approaches are anathema to later, third-wave, and more deconstructive feminists, who object to what they see as sweeping, condescending, essentialist generalizations, such as claims that women are inherently more cooperative and sympathetic than men. Third-wave feminists reject stable binary oppositions such as women versus men and nature versus culture. Instead, they see continuous movement and multiplicity, which means that they see many different kinds of women (and many different kinds of men). Most contemporary ecofeminists want nothing to do with a belief in earth goddesses. While they may critique the history of patriarchal abuses of women and nature, they do not see men as inevitably and only patriarchal or women as always and completely free from absorbing patriarchal ways of thinking. They see second-wave feminist versions of ecofeminism as romanticizing the link between women and nature and as unwittingly accepting the old patriarchal prejudices about reasonable men driven by intellect, and about emotional women left to the mercy of their bodies, and as supposing that those prejudices get better if we relabel them as feminist.

Contemporary ecofeminists are more likely to critique ideologies of nature that imagine humans as outside of nature and as looking at nature in something like the way that Laura Mulvey has argued that patriarchal audiences of film gaze at women on the screen, as if women were passive objects with no agency of their own and no ability to construct their own gaze. (On Mulvey's theory of visual pleasure, see Chapter 6.) In the same way, the argument goes, the patriarchal, anti-ecological gaze at nature presupposes a passive natural world with no agency of its own and no ability to do its own gazing or to gaze back.

Instead of romanticizing women as necessarily kinder to the environment than men, contemporary ecofeminists, like contemporary feminists in general, understand that women can absorb patriarchal and anti-ecological ideologies, even if, overall, they also believe that women tend more often than men to offer alternatives to those ideologies. Therefore, contemporary ecofeminists recognize women's agency and invite women to continue to grow in their agency. They want women of all classes, races, regions, and ethnicities to have the same power that men have to determine environmental policy.

Powerful but cliché ideologies often come in contradictory opposites. On the one hand, therefore, ecofeminists reject the interpretation of nature as essentially feminine or of women as essentially natural. On the other hand, they also reject the opposite mythology of nature as a heroic preserve of masculine adventure and discovery in opposition to a supposedly dull, unheroic, overcivilized world of feminine, interior domesticity. In short, like many other critics, ecofeminists see humans as too quick to project a nature that reflects their own ideology. In particular, they critique the patriarchal ideology that feminizes nature, naturalizes the feminine, and reduces both to their exploitable use value for men.

Ecocriticism, ecology, and the new ecology. Traditionally, ecocritics understand ecology as the study of natural balance and distinct **ecosystems.** They understand ecosystems as self-regulating and self-repairing. In this model, ecosystems typically progress through a succession of stages to what ecologists call a *climax community*, where the different species live and die together in balanced harmony and equilibrium. After a forest fire, for example, the burned area, if left undisturbed, grows back through a succession of stages until it returns to a mature forest. Such a view sees humans as prone to interfering with natural ecosystems, if not outright destroying them, but it also envisions an alternative human possibility of reconstructing human practices and civilization to live in harmony with natural ecological equilibrium.

Contemporary, revisionist ecocriticism now sometimes rejects this vision of equilibrium, balance, and harmony, aligning itself instead with newer models of ecology known variously as the new ecology or as disequilibrium ecology, postequilibrium ecology, or dynamic ecology. The difference between the old ecology and the new ecology echoes the difference between structuralism and poststructuralism. I am not suggesting that the movement from structuralism to poststructuralism caused its parallel movement in the science of ecology, but only that it may help us understand the two inclinations if we see their parallel sources in linked but competing habits of human thought. In both cases, the later movement exaggerates the tendency of the earlier movement to presuppose a rigid model of fixed, stable systems in balanced equilibrium, but the contrast between old and new models helps dramatize the new revisionist model of unstable processes in disequilibrium and continuous flux.

Traditional ecologists sometimes overestimated the stability of succession in the stages leading to climax communities. The word *stage* implies too much of a one-directional movement, and the word *climax* suggests too much finality. Traditional ecologists also sometimes underestimated the key qualifications that I have described two paragraphs earlier with the term "typically" and the phrase "if left undisturbed." In mirror image, new ecologists underestimate the sense of change in the movement from stage to stage and underestimate the recognition in the expressions "typically" and "*if* left undisturbed." Regardless, the new ecologists powerfully shifted the discussion, especially outside scientific ecology and in popular and ecocritical cultural interpretation, by recognizing the oversimplification in the model of natural harmony and balance, an oversimplification that has often driven popular discussion and cultural criticism.

The new ecology carries profound implications for interpreting relations between people and nature. By recognizing the continuous process of natural change, rather than romanticizing ahistorical stasis and equilibrium, it moves us away from an artificial binary opposition between the natural and the human. It takes us away from idealizing an impossible, irrecoverable state of harmony and equilibrium free from human participation. While literary writing and film, for example, may continue to fantasize an idealized natural world, the ideologies underlying such a fantasy can distract us from the inevitably human dimension, the construction in literary and artistic representations of our environment and, more largely, in any perception of our environment. As we have seen, humans are not outside observers locked in a separating gaze at an ideal, agentless, or merely exploitable natural other. Humans are—we are—animals. We are part of nature. Rather than excusing us from responsibility for our relations with the rest of nature, our position as animals within nature structures our relation to the rest of nature and to each other.

Animal studies. Indeed, the distinct and rapidly growing field of *animal studies* overlaps with and plays an increasing role in ecocriticism. Like ecocriticism, animal studies draws on a huge variety of fields, including zoology, politics, literature, law, philosophy, art history, and more. It has a long history, with notable moments including Jeremy Bentham's argument in the eighteenth century for better treatment of animals (for more on Bentham, see Chapter 9); Peter Singer's influential *Animal Liberation* (1975), which coined the term *speciesism* by analogy with racism and sexism; and more contemporary work by Donna Haraway, Jacques Derrida, and Giorgio Agamben. But no brief discussion or list can get across animal studies' range of fields and perspectives. More modestly, I hope here simply to begin to suggest some of the deeply challenging questions that animal studies scholars ponder.

Animal studies draws on questions of epistemology (the theory and study of knowledge), asking what animals are, and how the study of animals can shape our knowledge of human animals. And it draws on questions of ethics, asking how humans should treat, represent, and learn from animals. Should nonhuman animals have the same rights as human animals? And if we answer yes, or to the extent that we answer yes, then how much do we recognize animals' rights because we identify with nonhuman animals, and how much because we respect and value their difference from human animals? What are the ethics of eating or declining to eat animals, or supporting or opposing scientific experimentation on animals, or industrial farming? How do we judge or interpret the conflict, or decide what to do in response, when one animal competes with the group? Or when the individual animal or the group competes with a different species? Or competes with nonanimal dimensions of nature, such as a river, a lake, a tree, a forest, or a meadow? Should we cull or hunt individual animals to help the herd? Or its prey? Or its ecosystem?

How do animals think, and how do they feel emotions, in their own terms or compared to humans? How do we distort our understanding of animals by representing them in anthropomorphic terms? What are the consequences and ethics of animal metaphors in human language and literature (dog-eat-dog, fishy, horsing around, cat fighting, brute, loony, bird-brain, bug, and so on)? Should we find more interest or value in the large, seemingly charismatic animals so often favored in nature writing, from whales to wolves, than in small, seemingly un-charismatic animals, from worms to lice to snail darters? Sometimes we see anthropomorphically, attributing human characteristics to animals, and sometimes we see zoomorphically, attributing animal characteristics to humans. Both practices raise ethical questions, and both practices challenge the stability and reliability of the binary opposition between human and nonhuman animals.

Globalization and environmental justice. While early ecocriticism usually focused on writing about specific ecosystems and on writing by the relatively prosperous, later ecocriticism, including some of the same critics, often expands the field's geographical and cultural range. Thus, as new ecologists question the stability and separateness of ecosystems, and as critics in general respond to increasing globalization, so ecocriticism increasingly turns to the transnational, globalized interconnectedness of the environment. Ecocritics such as Ursula K. Heise and Rob Nixon have called attention to literature that, by form and argument, dramatizes the environmental stakes of postcolonial politics, transnationalism, and contemporary deterritorialization and cosmopolitanism.

Modernization and globalization reshape space and empty out the local. National and transnational currencies replace local exchanges. Commerce adopts nationally or internationally standardized procedures. The site of government moves far away. The clothes you wear as you read this, and the food that gives you the energy to read, almost always come from far away. Many of the dangers in the food you eat and the air you breathe also come from far away, and when they don't, then they come from local production to feed faraway places or, in the case, for example, of electrical production, to help you consume products from faraway places. Meanwhile, chains, malls, and strip malls make every place the same place. In much of the industrialized world, what little remains in the sense of the local now comes through going to your neighborhood chain store or chain restaurant at your neighborhood strip mall, run with reassuring anonymity and an international currency, such as the dollar or the euro. There you buy products manufactured far away by corporations that export jobs from your region or nation to faraway places with deplorable working conditions, shifting much of the remaining employment in the metropolitan local to standardized, low-wage service jobs, such as the jobs in the chains where you buy standardized consumer products, made to seem individualized by coming in a smartly labeled, predetermined palette of colors and flavors. When you move or travel—and you *will* move and travel—then you reproduce the same false sense of the local in another place that is reassuringly, and terrifyingly, the same place.

Even for those people who, unlike most of the people reading this book, will not move and will not travel much, the traditional sense of place is emptied out by the standardization that produces the interchangeable placeless places for the movers and the travelers. Those who live away, at least for now, from metropolitan networks of postcolonial transience and forced migration find themselves more than ever caught in monoculture economies that depend on zigzagging, transnational, and First World markets. Meanwhile, reckless misuse of resources is changing the climate, so that cultures around the world will soon have to change dramatically, and vast spaces of the island and coastal local will simply disappear.

Because environmental thinking, as we have seen, has typically invested deeply in the local, the loss of the local changes or expands the object of environmental thinking to the global. Or it changes the remaining local, including sometimes the national, the sovereign, or the indigenous, from a point of retreat or escape to a base of defense against the exploitatively global. Indeed, the tradition of understanding the local as an empty place for retreat and escape can unwittingly reduce it to a vacation playground for the prosperous. In that way, nature writing sometimes blots out the people who own or live in more populated spaces, and also risks denying the poor and denying indigenous peoples. However unwittingly, nature writing of that kind collaborates with settler colonialism. (On settler colonialism, see Chapter 10.) But if we rewrite the local and the transnational or global as mutually interconnected, then we change our understanding of environmental, ecocritical scale and change our sense of the relation between nature and the politics of poverty.

Ramachandra Guha and Juan Martínez-Alier, among others, have decried the tendency of some Western ecological activists to join with colonizing ideologies and impose their vision of conservation on Third World spaces without consulting or taking seriously, for example, South Asian or African needs or preferences. Sometimes Western media and Western ecological activists can see Western environmentalism but cannot see what Guha and Martínez-Alier have called the **environmentalism of the poor.** In the same way, the **environmental justice** movement calls attention to the history of environmental activism's ability to see ecological issues in rural and wilderness spaces and difficulty seeing ecological issues in urban spaces and the spaces of people of color. Guha and Martínez-Alier describe the difference as "full-stomach" versus "empty-belly" environmentalism (xxi). A truly international ecological movement and ecocriticism needs to pay attention, Rob Nixon argues, to what he calls, in the title of his book, *Slow Violence and the Environmentalism of the Poor.*

Nixon's concept of slow violence poses a challenge for writers, filmmakers, and the mass media. We know, he argues, how to make images and tell stories about disasters that flash before us in a moment: the falling towers on 9/11, a battle, a train wreck, an explosion, a hurricane, or a murder. Therefore, we recognize such events and take them seriously. But we do not know how to tell the story of environmental devastation, which often comes in the form of slow violence, building up gradually over generations. We struggle to find ways to tell the story of the "elusive violence of delayed effects," because we know how to portray "spectacular" time better than we know how to portray "unspectacular time" (Nixon 3, 6). Thus, we struggle to show the high drama in the story of climate change or the acceleration of species loss. Toxic buildup, radiation poisoning, and air and water pollution sicken and kill many more people than more familiar, more easily portrayed disasters, yet because they move so slowly, sickening and killing us one by one instead of all at once, we do not know how to write them or image them. And all those devastations disproportionally hit the poor. Our media and our writers dramatize the environmental suffering of the prosperous and leave comparatively untold the environmental suffering of the poor—and the environmental activism of the poor.

The nonhuman. While the environmental justice movement and the literary and cultural criticism it spawned focus on broadening our attention to the human consequences of environmental change, another movement in cultural and environmental criticism turns our attention to the nonhuman. In recent years critical interest in the nonhuman has gathered force from a wide variety of different but overlapping directions and labels, including the new materialism, the posthuman, thing theory, and object-oriented ontology as well as animal studies, and, more recently, what has come to be called critical plant studies.

Humans tend to underestimate how comprehensively we live with the vegetal world. We wear plants. We live inside things made from plants. We lie, sit, stand, or walk on plants. Our energy comes through eating plants. Even when we eat animals instead of plants, those animals depend on eating plants or eating other animals that eat plants. We also use plants to heal us, to decorate our skin and our indoor and outdoor surroundings, and to populate our art, film, and literature. The page you touch as you read these words, like the pages of most of the history of writing, was made from plants. We have built our civilizations so thoroughly through the cultivation of plants that we might think of them as cultivating us as much as us cultivating them. In those contexts, critical plant studies asks how plants respond to their surrounding environment, how they feel and think, how humans and human literature and other cultural representations think about vegetal life, understand plants, misunderstand them, use them and abuse them, and exalt them or try to reduce them to their use value for humans.

In the humanities, the growing study of the material world takes inspiration from a fatigue with what some critics read as too much abstraction in the structuralist- and deconstructive-inspired focus on social construction, discourse, and textuality. It responds as well to a haunting doubt about the dematerializing life of our increasingly digitized world. At the same time, the touchable, often hold-in-your-hand instruments of dematerializing digitization loom largely as *things* in our digitized daily lives. And the interest in things and their agency also gains force from the fear of a world increasingly populated and run by drones, robots, artificial intelligence, and algorithms, and from the ecological recognition that humanity is destroying the things around us and within us.

Much of the study of the nonhuman, from whatever perspective, has to do with shrinking our sense of humans as exceptions, as distinctive and special. After all, the surrounding world, organic and inorganic, continues inside us as well as outside us. We swallow it, breathe it in, and absorb it through the surfaces of our bodies. The boundary between the human and the nonhuman therefore depends on a falsifying binary opposition. As I write these words, I am eating plants. Those plants are now part of me, and I am part of them. The study of the nonhuman thus opposes itself to *anthropocentrism*, thinking that centers on humans and human perspectives. (Anthropocentrism is related to but not the same as anthropomorphism, discussed earlier.)

The philosophical movement dubbed *object-oriented ontology*, propelled by Graham Harman and Levi Bryant, contemplates the independent existence of objects, apart from any reliance on human perception of them, including objects that range variously from rocks and trees to storms and global warming. It tries to separate objects from their captivity in the human needs and desires that we project onto them. Bill Brown, pursuing what he calls *thing theory*, distinguishes between objects and things. To Brown, objects become things when they exceed their mere physicality and take on resonant meaning, which exposes the thingness in the mere object. Similarly, Jane Bennett calls our attention to the vibrancy of things. Instead of seeing objects and things as passive, she sees them as active agents. Omega-3 fatty acids, for example, can influence our moods. Trash in the landfills, forgotten and out of sight, spews deadly chemicals and dangerous methane. When we see the liveliness of an object, such as litter, a toy, or a gadget, she suggests, the object transforms into a thing and we see its thing-power. By neglecting the selfhood, will, and agency of matter, Bennett argues, our anthropocentric perspectives stoke human pride and feed "earth-destroying fantasies of conquest and consumption" (ix). She believes that by recognizing the liveliness of matter, of the stuff both outside and inside our bodies, we can achieve a more environmental ethic, because we will no longer see ourselves as fundamentally different from the rest of the world that we live in. We will no longer look at the world as subjects looking at objects once we realize that we ourselves are also objects and that the objects we look at are also subjects, are also our kin and ourselves.

Questions for ecocriticism. Let us conclude with some of the questions that ecocritics have typically asked. (The following questions takes their inspiration from a longer list of ecocritical questions proposed by SueEllen Campbell.) What does a given work of literature, film, or other cultural representation show of the nonhuman world? What does it show and not show of the relation between the nonhuman and the human? How and when do the narrators, focalizers, and other characters participate or not participate in the environment they observe or live in? Does anything nonhuman—natural or built, a river, storm, mountain, car, neighborhood, street, apartment, room, animal, farm, tool, object of furniture or art—act as a character acts? For works not directly about nature or the environment, what changes if the critic's approach brings nature or the environment from the background to the foreground, from the setting to the center, from an incidental position to the position of a major (if still nonhuman) character?

Does the work anthropomorphize places, plants, or animals? How does it understand or value animals? "As stimulus-response machines? As products of evolution, fighting to survive? As objects of our scientific inquiry? As servants to humans, or as imitation humans?" Does it "see animals as beings equal in value to humans, partly like us and partly different" (Campbell 216–217)? Or does it see animals as beings of less value than humans? How does it understand or value plants? Does it see plants only through what they do for humans? Does it see plants as inert or passive, or does it see plants as agents?

What does the work show and not show of environmental history? How does it show the boundaries of the places it describes, and what makes or unmakes those boundaries, and how does it show the relations between places, including local, national, and international places? How does it show changes over time and environmentally, and what human or nonhuman forces produce those changes? What political assumptions or consequences underlie the work's environmental representations and assumptions? Is it nostalgic? What is its "attitude toward contemporary life—globalization, multinational corporations, sport-utility vehicles, virtual reality, shopping malls, agribusiness, consumer capitalism," and so on, or "its attitude toward the comparable issues of its own time?" (Campbell 218). Does the work's portrayal of nature or the environment, or its assumptions or beliefs about the relation between people and their environment, connect to imbalances of social power or to variations and cultural assumptions in relation to economics, class, race, gender, sexuality, disability, ethnicity, or nationality?

DISABILITY STUDIES

We are bodies and minds. Over the last few decades, disability studies has led many literary and cultural critics, with increasing momentum, to rethink bodies and to rethink minds: all minds, and all bodies, and sometimes the idea that we can draw a sharp distinction between minds and bodies.

Models of disability. As we have seen in Chapter 7, Eve Kosofsky Sedgwick observed that attitudes to queerness follow two competing models, a minoritizing model that sees queerness as a special condition of a limited population, and a universalizing model that sees queerness as something that everyone participates in. A parallel set of minoritizing and universalizing models shapes much of the thinking in disability studies. On the one hand, sometimes disability studies addresses the distinct conditions of a limited population. That is a minoritizing model. On the other hand, at other times disability studies goes against the minoritizing model by exposing how more or less everyone has been, is, and/or will be disabled. That is a universalizing model.

In a related but different binary opposition, disability activists and disability studies often seek to replace a *medical model* of disability with a *social model*. The medical model is about the disabled person. The social model is about the social world that constructs a person as disabled. For example, we might ask where a disability lies, in the person in a wheelchair, or in the system that relies on stairs that a person in a wheelchair cannot climb. Still more, the same stairs that provide an obstacle to wheelchairs may work better than a ramp for someone who is blind. Different people, and different disabilities, lead to differing needs and preferences. Especially, then, in the context of changing paradigms of architecture and new technologies, we might argue that the social system constructs the definition of disability and constructs the binary opposition between disability and ability. If, or to the extent that, the obstacle lies in the architectural environment, then the social environment constructs the disability rather than merely responding to or finding the disability, and therefore disabilities are social constructions. By that argument, if you can't get up the stairs, we should blame the social and architectural system. We shouldn't blame you. If we change the system, then you can get to where the stairs go with no difficulty.

The growth of the social model has played a crucial role in disability activism, helping to lead, in the 1990s, for example, to the Americans with Disability Act in the United States and the Disability Discrimination Acts in Australia and the United Kingdom. On the other hand, the social constructionist or so-called social model carries its own problems. It can seem to diminish recognition and understanding of the obstacles and material pain that some disabled people face, and such diminishing can undermine the distinct cultures that have grown up through alliances among disabled people. It can also make light of the complications that sometimes riddle disabled life, such as—to name just a few examples—the complications of relying on attendants, of diminished privacy, or of disturbing stigmas and what those stigmas can lead to socially and personally.

Some scholars have compared the stigmas against people with disabilities to the stigmas against women, queer people, or people of color. Rosemary Garland-Thomson calls for an intersectional merging of disability studies and feminist studies. After all, she notes, both attend to such topics as reproductive technology, bodily variation, inequity, the ethics of care, medicalization, narrow and hierarchical models of normalcy, the social construction of identity, and the social integration of diverse groups of people. To take just one example, feminist studies and disability studies critique how women and people with disabilities can feel pressured to match culturally imposed models of bodily presentation.

Garland-Thomson also notes that people with invisible disabilities, like queer people, must decide whether to pass for nondisabled or to come out of the closet. Drawing on Adrienne Rich's critique of compulsory heterosexuality (see Chapter 7), Robert McRuer connects disability to queerness and critiques what he calls compulsory able-bodiedness. As the concept of straight depends on the concept of queer, so the concept of able-bodied depends on the concept of disabled, including when people suppose that they can forget about or ignore disability or queerness or brush them to the side.

Writing about disability and race, ethnicity, and blackness, Chris Bell observed how disability studies scholars, until recently all white, routinely refer to the position of blacks and the civil rights movement as a model for the position of people with disabilities and for disability activism. Yet the same scholars typically ignore black people with disabilities, or at best they suppose that black people with disabilities face the same conditions as white people with disabilities. Bell called for more attention to the variety of racial and ethnic positions among the disabled as well as the overlapping variety of positions among people of color. (Compare the discussion of intersectionality in Chapter 6.) Bell also pointed out that the disabilities of African Americans, such as Harriet Tubman (epilepsy) and Emmett Till (polio left him with a stutter), get written out of history in favor of seeing blacks as black alone. While early disability studies tended to take for granted, without thinking about it, that disabled people are straight and white, the force of arguments like Garland-Thomson's, McRuer's and Bell's increasingly leads to the recognition that without the inclusiveness that disability studies, by definition, tries to embody, it cannot live up to its goals of respecting people with disabilities.

In these various ways, disability studies criticism, responding to the international, rapidly growing disability rights movement, calls for critical perspectives that draw on and encourage respect for disabled people, much as criticism that grows out of race studies, feminist studies, queer studies, and postcolonial studies calls for respecting groups of people who historically have less power. And disability studies calls as well for respecting the variety within each group. But it is not always clear which practices best respect disabled people, or how such practices vary from person to person and group to group, and sometimes the practices we might advocate come woven with unexpected contradictions.

Government surveys in the United Kingdom and the United States show about 19% of the population as disabled. The numbers increase with age, ranging from 6% for children to about half of those 65 and older, and over 70% for those 80 and older (Brault 4–5, "Family Resources Survey" 79). That is a far higher proportion of the population than any one of the racial minorities, whose cultures and literatures have attracted far more acknowledgment and study. But for disabilities, such numbers vary depending on what we count as disability. Do we include intellectual as well as physical disabilities? What about people who depend on eyeglasses (which more than doubles the overall numbers)? Do we include Deaf people (a question that has attracted considerable controversy)? Most of the able-bodied are simply, as disability activists have put it, temporarily able-bodied. They move in and out of disability as they move in and out of illness or injury. And as the percentages noted here indicate, most people live with increasing disabilities as they approach the end of their lives, all the more noticeably now that we have an increasingly older population, which also increases the number of caregivers.

Historically, the dominant cultural pattern sees the disabled, if it sees the disabled at all, as Other, as something to be covered up, fascinated with, or both. Yet as the patterns noted here also show, the conceptual conflict between a minoritizing and a universalizing model is a conflict between the actual self and the potential self, and a conflict between the self that has been, is, or will be disabled, and the mythologized cultural Other.

The conflict between a minoritizing and a universalizing model is also psychological and political. To see the disabled as Other is to deny the disabled as self. In the minoritizing model, disability may seem like a deficit, like a medical problem or impairment. But it may also offer a motive for cultural and political identification, pride, and alliance among those with the same disability or among the disabled in general. The alliance across disabilities can expand identifications and political power. Or, like the universalizing model, it can diminish the distinctive identities, lives, activities, and cultural expression of any particular disability.

Deaf activists, for example (and here I follow the practice of capitalizing the D for the cultural or linguistic group and not capitalizing it for the physical circumstance of not hearing), call for seeing Deaf language and culture as the expression of an identity rather than as a

The Language of Disability

By analogy with the terms *racism* and *racist,* and *sexism* and *sexist,* disability activism has given us the terms *ableism* and *ableist* for prejudice against disabled people. Such terms help us recognize prejudice where we might not have recognized it before.

In the same way, the term *disability* can help us recognize and think about disability where we might not have recognized or thought about it before. Today, the term *disability* tends to encompass both physical and intellectual disabilities. Intellectual disabilities include a variety of categories not always linked together and not always considered disabilities, including mental disabilities, general learning disabilities, specific learning disabilities, acquired brain injuries, and neurodegenerative diseases. Increasingly, the term *mental retardation* has given way to the term *general learning disability.* Neurodegenerative diseases include Alzheimer's, Parkinson's, and Huntington's, and they often come with dementia. Writing about the language for mental disability, Margaret Price observes that no terms are neutral, and that a partial list of current terms "includes *psychiatric disability, mental illness, cognitive disability, intellectual disability, mental health service user* (or *consumer*), *neurodiversity, psychiatric system survivor, crazy,* and *mad*" (298).

Indeed, terminology can get complicated. Among English-language speakers, for example, there is controversy over the call from some disability activists for *person-first* language, that is, for language that refers to a person before referring to a disability, such as "a person with Down syndrome," versus language that puts the disability first, such as "an autistic person." Those who favor person-first language argue that it focuses on the person instead of defining the person by a disability. Opponents of person-first language argue that it diminishes a disability and diminishes disability culture, making a disability something to hide. Sometimes, they also argue that certain disabilities are indeed integral to who someone is, and are not just an add-on. Many people feel strongly about this debate or about other evolving changes in the language surrounding disability.

The very word *disability* has tended to replace words like *crip-ple*. It moves away from pejorative terms (freak, monster, gimp, dummy), but it still relies on a negative. Some disability activists have tried to recuperate *cripple*, changing its force by owning it or even by reshaping it as *crip*. Terms have changed and will continue to evolve, as language always changes, sometimes amidst strong feelings or debates.

problem. After all, those who are not deaf are left out of Deaf culture, so that while we may see deaf people as disabled, we can just as well see hearing people as disabled. Such an approach has led to conflict over the advisability of, for example, cochlear implants. Disabled people do not always want a "cure." Disputes arise over the conflict between pride in disabled people and culture versus adaptation to the surrounding, dominant culture. At the same time, in the deconstructive paradoxes of daily politics, sometimes these seeming opposites can inhabit each other, so that people can feel pride in the culture of adaptation as well as pride in the current culture and expression of people with disabilities—a culture that includes adaptation. Either way, people have to make practical decisions about how to live and what to advocate.

Disability and literary history. We may still be in the relatively early stages of figuring out how these questions play out when we bring disability studies to the interpretation of literature, film, and culture. As in the early stages of feminist criticism or the criticism of literature by or about racial and ethnic minorities, readers and critics often take an interest in literary history. They wonder how disabled writers and characters have fared over the centuries. In that light, as we saw in the discussion of "images-of-women" feminist criticism in Chapter 6, a focus on judging the accuracy or cultural responsibility of images of the disabled can loom large.

Because a desire to suppress recognition of disability has often blended with a continuing fascination for disability, the literary history turns out to be tricky. Readers sometimes begin by supposing that few disabled writers have won much recognition. But since disability is paradoxically both a minority and a more or less universal characteristic, it turns out that we have had many acclaimed disabled writers, though literary history has not usually focused on their disability. Lists of names tend to oversimplify, reducing writers to the characteristic they are listed for. Lists must also leave out many more writers than they include. But they can help make a history concrete, so at the risk of oversimplification and excess brevity, we might mention, just as examples, such celebrated writers (with their disabilities in parentheses, when they are not well known) as John Milton, Alexander Pope, Lord Byron, Walt Whitman (progressive paralysis), Bernard Shaw (probably ADHD), W. B. Yeats and F. Scott Fitzgerald (probably dyslexia), Flannery O'Connor, Sylvia Plath, and Octavia Butler (dyslexia), among many others. In a more receptive world, disabled writers and their reputations would likely flourish more often, including such writers as Harriet Martineau and Constance Fenimore Woolson, nineteenth-century Deaf writers who have lately attracted an increased readership, and others who, with constrained educations or unreceptive audiences, never became the writers they could have become.

Disabled characters populate literary history as well, in works ranging from (again, just to name a few examples) Shakespeare's *Richard III*, Milton's *Samson Agonistes*, and Swift's *Gulliver's Travels* to Shelley's *Frankenstein*, Melville's *Moby-Dick*, Faulkner's *The Sound and the Fury*, Carson McCullers's *The Heart Is a Lonely Hunter*, Sylvia Plath's *The Bell Jar*, Tony Kushner's *Angels in America*, Kazuo Ishiguro's *Never Let Me Go*, and so on. Most people can probably think of many films that dramatize disability, classics such as *City Lights*, *The Best Years of Our Lives*, *The Three Faces of Eve*, *The Miracle Worker*, *A Patch of Blue*, *My Left Foot*, and so on, as well as films made from the novels and plays named here and, more recently, such acclaimed twenty-first-century films and TV shows as *Memento*, *A Beautiful Mind*, *Avatar*, *Silver Linings Playbook*, *Rust and Bone*, *Game of Thrones*, *Atypical*, and again, on and on.

In *Rust and Bone* (widely acclaimed, though in the United States not widely shown), audiences have tended to focus on Stéphanie's acquired disability (Figure 12.1). We watch the dramatic accident when she loses her lower legs to an orca whale (echoing *Moby-Dick*), and then we watch her adjust to living with a changed style of mobility. At the same time, her lover Ali, a powerful fighter who easily carries Stéphanie where her wheelchair won't go and who seems equal to any physical challenge, mirrors Stéphanie's physical disability in his own mental disability. For Ali has difficulty managing his temper and sustaining a consistent connection to those he loves. As Stéphanie's pitying gaze at herself magnifies her vision of her new, easily visible disability, Ali has trouble seeing his long-standing but less immediately visible disability. Similarly, responses to the film have focused on her disability and overlooked his disability. The mirror reflection between characters and between more visible and less visible disabilities exposes how some abilities and disabilities can magnify or shrink according to how we understand them, or how we don't understand them. It can remind us to think about both visible and invisible disabilities. Depending on how we think about disability and ability, therefore, we might find more disabilities in literature, film, and beyond than we typically expect, and we might find a greater variety of abilities and disabilities.

Stereotypes. As we saw in the discussion of images-of-women feminist criticism in Chapter 6, a focus on characters can lead to a focus on stereotypes and a call for strong, appealing, nonstereotypical characters. The stereotypes in literature, perhaps especially in mass-marketed film, often run in the same directions as troubling stereotypes in the culture at large. One stereotype defines people and characters with disabilities entirely through their disability, both in their own thoughts and in their role in a literary plot. Another stereotype defines the disabled, dehumanizingly, as nonsexual. Yet another stereotype reduces people and characters with disabilities to the inspiration they provide others simply by living their daily lives, as if nondisabled people did not also design the world around them to fit their own circumstances. On the opposite side of the stereotype

Figure 12.1 Stéphanie and Ali (Marion Cotillard and Matthias Schoenaerts) head to the beach to go for a swim in *Rust and Bone.*

from what some critics and disability activists call "inspiration porn," another stereotype reduces any deviation from the role of inspiration to an ungrateful wallowing in bitterness.

The critique of demeaning stereotypes, like early feminist images-of-women criticism, thus provides considerable insight, and yet it risks confining writers by telling them what to write. It can bank too heavily on the assumption that there is only one way to understand the real and so only one correct way to represent a particular group, such as women, immigrants, a racialized group, or people with disabilities, and so it can reduce our ability to see, for example, how such groups vary and overlap intersectionally. As Samantha Dawn Schalk has argued, it therefore risks cutting out from our consideration the vast possibilities for representing disabilities in writing—such as speculative fiction—that invests less in conventional models of character and realism. The critique of demeaning stereotypes can also scold writers who dwell on disabled suffering and press them to err in the opposite direction by dwelling on inspiring role models. In that way, it risks replacing one stereotype with another stereotype, an overcompensating, more sentimental stereotype of strong characters who overcome terrible obstacles and triumph heroically. The call for realistic characters thus conflicts with the call for strong characters because—realistically—disabled people, like everyone else, are not always strong.

When disabled characters are neither inspirational nor bitter, they often appear, like many queer characters or characters of color, as sidekicks, decoration, or excuses for a little quirky variety. Some critics, therefore, have complained that disability often gets ignored or pushed, like the sidekicks, to the margin. In effect, they argue that it gets overly minoritized.

Without diminishing that argument, I would also argue that in another sense the typical portrayal of disability clashes with a minoritizing view. To see that clash, we might recollect Toni Morrison's argument in *Playing in the Dark: Whiteness and the Literary Imagination*. Against the view that American literature has underrepresented African Americans, Morrison argues (see Chapter 10) that from another angle we can see white American literature as obsessed with defining Americanness through its relation to African Americans. Of course, for the representation of disability, even in the United States, Americanness is not the issue. Instead, the issue is the definition of what gets constructed as normal. We do not construct the normal and then, later, construct the disabled. We construct the normal *through* constructing the disabled. We construct the (supposed or idealized) self through constructing the other. Morrison argues that African Americans have a pervasive presence in American literature beyond their position as minorities, because African Americans provide a use value for the dominant sense of white Americanness. In the same way, disabled people go beyond minority status by providing a use value for a fearful sense of instability in the supposedly normal. For example, when able-bodied people stereotype people with disabilities as bitter or self-pitying, the able-bodied people try to separate themselves from their own fears about themselves by projecting what they fear about themselves onto the disabled other. In such ways, the able use the disabled to deny the vulnerability of the able and to construct the able sense of self as normal.

Binary oppositions of disability. Disability studies often draws on the cultural patterns of binary oppositions that at the same time both stand out and come apart, mutually inhabiting each other: self/other, us/them, minoritizing/universalizing, disabled/able, disabled/normal, normal/abnormal, victim/agent, socially constructed/medical, congenital/acquired, temporary/permanent, visible/invisible, metaphorical/lived, physical/mental, the contrast between different disabilities/ the alliance between different disabilities. We can read social, political, and literary representation and understanding through the criss-crossing grid of these prolific but unstable binary oppositions.

One of the most incisive and influential arguments about disability in literature comes in a landmark article by David T. Mitchell. Mitchell sees narrative as a prosthesis driven by a desire for compensation, implicitly like the desire that impels some disabled people to use a prosthesis, such as a synthetic limb or organ, a wheelchair, a cane, or electronic or computerized assistance. He argues that narrative feeds on the extraordinary, and that "difference demands display" (22). The disability that drives narrative, he continues, makes a disabled character stand out as different or unique, suppressing the possibility for the disabled character to identify or ally with other disabled people as members of a group with a shared interest. Mitchell also praises the way that disability can serve as a metaphor for something else, including "social and individual collapse" (16). Finally, he says, the literary disabled character typically gets either "left behind or punished" (23).

We can reread and magnify Mitchell's arguments through the grid of binary oppositions around the concept of disability. On the one hand, disability may seem like something extraordinary that provokes a will for compensation. Such a view of disability fits the minoritizing model. On the other hand, in the universalizing model, part of the definition of disability includes the possibility of seeing disability as ordinary. Rather than being special—inspirational or bitter, worthy of abhorrence or pity—disabled people and characters live their ordinary lives with the circumstances dealt them, just like anyone else. And, as we have noted, more or less everyone else will sooner or later find themselves disabled. Even so, Mitchell is surely right to observe that cultural preconceptions drive many works of film and literature to leave behind or punish disabled characters. One exception may come in the inspirational characters, who often survive and thrive, when they don't die nobly. Surely Mitchell is also right to observe that disability often works metaphorically.

Disability and metaphor. Sometimes, nevertheless, metaphors of disability cause problems. They convert disability to its use value, rather than accepting disability for itself. Once, for example, as I prepared to teach *Moby-Dick*, before the advent of disability studies, I found myself planning to tell students that when Ahab (the whaling captain who loses his leg to the teeth of the whale named Moby Dick) keeps his cabin blinds shut ("the old man's bolted door . . . with fixed blinds inserted," Chapter 123), his closed blinds suggest his limited vision of the world around him. I also prepared to say that Ahab's chomped-off leg, which limits his mobility, metaphorically reveals his obstinate inflexibility, like the fixed blinds. I didn't see these as major insights, since any reader already knows that Ahab is inflexible and often uses his ability to understand some things to mask his inability to understand other things. But I still planned to burden my students with these pitifully uninspired observations.

Then it dawned on me that one of my students was blind, and another had an arm that ended above the elbow. Suddenly, I felt clueless. The blind student didn't lack insight into the world around her, and the one-armed student didn't lack intellectual flexibility—quite the contrary, as it happened, in both cases, though I hope I would have had the sense to recognize my cluelessness even if they were intellectually ordinary students. I hesitated to give up the insights that I felt too proud of, but gradually I realized that they added up to very little. They taught us how to read like a certain model of an English professor, a model that I was horrified to see I had partly come to embody. Such "insights" relied on a trivializing version of new critical metaphor and symbolism. They reduced literary interpretation to a game of find-the-symbol. As a critical reader of new criticism,

I had already started to look at that game with suspicion. After I thought about my two students and realized the silliness of my paltry insights, the realization led me to critique the very concept of literary metaphor.

We all recognize that writing often signifies, or metaphorizes, a firm mind by a firm chin, or moral weakness by a weak chin, and so on. Maybe learning to recognize such metaphors helps us interpret the intent of writers who buy into or trade on those prejudices. But as R. J. Palacio's novel *Wonder* can remind us, if we actually interpret people that way, then we would terribly misread—misinterpret—our world and its people. Metaphor is a great literary resource, but a dawning sense of disability studies began to teach me that literary metaphor can also be dangerous. It can trade simplistically on what Mitchell and Sharon L. Snyder, criticizing literary metaphors of disability, call "the metaphoric opportunism of literature as a form of public slander" (18).

Althusser's interpretation of ideology, as reviewed in Chapter 8, suggests that metaphor weaves into ideology. We may make our metaphors—sometimes, more or less—but mostly we find them instead of making them. And we find them in the ideologies that already surround us, including ideologies woven into disturbing preconceptions about disability. Thus we have such metaphorical expressions as spineless, blind to, dumb, lame, deaf to, and so on, which have drawn criticism from disability activists and from the interest that disability studies takes in language. Even if we decide to hold on to some of those metaphors or others like them—because, perhaps, we value the way they make us face the actual conditions of living with disabilities—we may find ourselves rethinking metaphor, linguistic, and literary representation.

Voices, bodies, and minds. Disability studies shares with race and gender studies a commitment to recovering past voices and making space for new voices, in this case the voices of disabled people. Indeed, disability activism and disability studies depend centrally on the voices and imaginations of people with disabilities, voices that, as we have noted, have not always found the receptiveness or attention that they deserve. Given the topic of disability studies, its interest in the "voices" of the disabled may come as no surprise. But habits die hard, and so the cultural habit of underestimating or overlooking the ideas and writing of people with disabilities has a stubbornness that makes it helpful to remind ourselves to listen to and read the voices of the disabled—spoken, signed, written, typed, drawn, and so on.

And yet we may learn to listen and read better if we keep in mind the cautions that, as we saw in Chapter 10, Gayatri Spivak has raised by asking the provocative, controversial question, "Can the subaltern speak?" For not all disabled writers rely on a literal voice or think or write with the same ideas or perspectives. Inevitably, some disagree with each other. And that's often a good thing. A disabled person lives amidst ideology, like anyone else. Therefore, it is possible for a disabled person to think or write in ways that work against the interest of the disabled, simply because that person lives at risk of absorbing (being interpellated into) the ableist ideas and prejudices in the world around us. We may even disagree among ourselves about what practices and beliefs work for or against the interest of people with disabilities. Moreover, depending on the people, contexts, and disabilities, the same ideas can work for or against disabled people or different groups of disabled people.

By drawing on Spivak's caution, we can turn to the writing of disabled people in an unromanticizing way that does not assume that we will find one defining voice, one experience, and one way of thinking that defines all disabled people across the variety of disabilities and without differences among writers, times, cultures, or even within a single writer. Disabled voices, as well, inevitably share some perspectives with nondisabled voices. Again, we need to draw on both the minoritizing and the universalizing dimensions of disability and ability, and indeed of identity in general, if we want to interpret and value the imaginations of disabled people with the respect, insight, and open-mindedness that disability activism and disability studies demand and deserve.

Some disability studies scholars see the body as definingly central to disability and to disability studies. Sometimes, such scholars look with skepticism at the prominence that literary studies, influenced by structuralism, deconstruction, and Foucauldian notions of discourse, often gives to language and representation. They fear that the focus on discourse, language, and representation turns us away from the materiality of bodies, disability, and corporeal experience, including, as we have noted, pain and the practicalities of living with impairment. But they may overlook that in structuralism and poststructuralism, discourse, language, and representation are themselves both material and the medium of corporeal representation. Their sense that bodies can provide the signified without the signifier invests in the belief in a prediscursive materiality that Derrida critiques as a belief in the metaphysics of presence (see Chapter 4). But even

Derrida recognizes the persistence of such beliefs. And the sense of concreteness that such beliefs provide continues to anchor much of the activism and sense of identity that motivate disability studies.

At the same time, we associate many disabilities more with the mind than with the body. And after all, everyone, not just disabled people, has a body. We risk causing new problems if we see disabled people as more bodied than nondisabled people. Disability does not bring disabled people more of a body than able-bodied people have, but the able-bodied and the disabled bring different signifiers of their corporeality. To the extent that we have defined our culture's dominant ideas of corporeality through an illusion that supposes we can think about able bodies apart from thinking about disabled bodies, disability studies helps us redefine what it means to have a body. And because disability comes in intellectual as well as in physical forms, disability studies also helps us redefine what it means to have a mind. In light of disability studies, then, no one should continue to imagine mind and body or ability and disability as stable binary oppositions that separate their defining opposites from each other.

A FUTURE FOR CRITICAL THEORY

In the years when critical theory moved to the center of literary studies and provoked a good deal of skeptical resistance, the scholars, teachers, and journalists who resisted critical theory sometimes saw it as dangerous. They argued that critical theory made literature and literary study too abstract. And the abstraction of critical theory, they believed, made it less relevant to students and other readers and more distant from students' and readers' everyday lives. By now you can see, I hope, that critical theory can work in exactly the opposite way. It can make the study of literature more concrete, because critical theory is about the connections between literature and our everyday lives. Critical theory makes literary study more relevant to our lives, not less relevant.

As our lives change and the generations shift, so do the strategies of interpretation that we bring to interpreting literature and culture. Readers can keep up with the changes simply by continuing to read and perhaps by talking over their interests with other readers. Taking a course can help, but keeping up does not require taking a course. I never had the chance to take a critical theory course, and most of what I have written about in this book I learned after I finished taking courses. Much of it did not even exist yet while I was taking courses. I had to teach myself. You can teach yourself, too.

It might help us understand change if we try to anticipate the future based on what we know about the present. We might guess, for example, that the increasing interest in studying culture will continue to split literary studies into those who care little about aesthetics and art or care little about cultural representation and those who (like myself) persist in merging the study of form and aesthetics with the study of culture. But we cannot count on our predictions for the future. We can, however, choose to help make that future by engaging with it, by continuing to read and question.

To encourage your continuing reading and questioning, you might go back and review a part of this book that caught your interest and then read some of the critical writings that it discusses. If we ever suppose that we have already learned what critical theory has to teach us, then we will stop learning. But if we keep reading and questioning, then we will adapt to the future and help shape that future.

FURTHER READING

Environmental Criticism

Alaimo, Stacy. *Exposed: Environmental Politics and Pleasures in Posthuman Times.* Minneapolis: University of Minnesota Press, 2016.

Bate, Jonathan. *The Song of the Earth.* Cambridge, MA: Harvard University Press, 2000.

Bennett, Jane. *Vibrant Matter: A Political Ecology of Things.* Durham, NC: Duke University Press, 2010.

Braidotti, Rosi. *The Posthuman.* Cambridge: Polity Press, 2013.

Brown, Bill. *Other Things.* Chicago: University of Chicago Press, 2015.

———. *A Sense of Things: The Object Matter of American Literature.* Chicago: University of Chicago Press, 2003.

Buell, Lawrence. *The Environmental Imagination: Thoreau, Nature Writing, and the Formation of American Culture.* Cambridge, MA: Harvard University Press, 1995.

———. *The Future of Environmental Criticism: Environmental Crisis and Literary Imagination.* Malden, MA: Blackwell, 2005.

———. *Writing for an Endangered World: Literature, Culture, and Environment in the U.S. and Beyond.* Cambridge, MA: Harvard University Press, 2001.

Garrard, Greg. *Ecocriticism.* 2nd ed. Abingdon: Routledge, 2012.

Guha, Ramachandra, and Juan Martínez-Alier. *Varieties of Environmentalism: Essays North and South.* London: Earthscan, 1997.

Haraway, Donna J. *Manifestly Haraway*. Minneapolis: University of Minnesota Press, 2016.

———. *When Species Meet*. Minneapolis: University of Minnesota Press, 2008.

Heise, Ursula K. *Sense of Place and Sense of Planet: The Environmental Imagination of the Global*. New York: Oxford University Press, 2008.

Hiltner, Ken, ed. *Ecocriticism: The Essential Reader*. London: Routledge, 2015.

Kohn, Eduardo. *How Forests Think: Toward an Anthropology beyond the Human*. Berkeley: University of California Press, 2013.

Kolodny, Annette. *The Lay of the Land: Metaphor as Experience and History in American Life and Letters*. Chapel Hill: University of North Carolina Press, 1975.

Laist, Randy, ed. *Plants and Literature: Essays in Critical Plant Studies*. New York: Editions Rodopi, 2013.

Marder, Michael. *Plant-Thinking: A Philosophy of Vegetal Life*. New York: Columbia University Press, 2013.

Nixon, Rob. *Slow Violence and the Environmentalism of the Poor*. Cambridge, MA: Harvard University Press, 2011.

Phillips, Dana. *The Truth of Ecology: Nature, Culture, and Literature in America*. New York: Oxford University Press, 2003.

Singer, Peter. *Animal Liberation: The Definitive Classic of the Animal Movement*. Fortieth Anniversary Edition. New York: Open Road, 2015.

Disability Studies

Bartlett, Jennifer, Sheila Black, and Michael Northern, eds. *Beauty Is a Verb: The New Poetry of Disability*. El Paso, TX: Cinco Puntos Press, 2011.

Bauman, Dirksen, Heidi Rose, and Jennifer Nelson, eds. *Signing the Body Poetic: Essays on American Sign Language Literature*. Berkeley: University of California Press, 2006.

Bell, Christopher M., ed. *Blackness and Disability: Critical Examinations and Cultural Interventions*. East Lansing: Michigan State University Press, 2011.

Davis, Lennard J. *Bending over Backwards: Disability, Dismodernism, and Other Difficult Positions*. New York: New York University Press, 2002.

———. *Enforcing Normalcy: Disability, Deafness, and the Body*. London: Verso, 1995.

———, ed. *The Disability Studies Reader*. 5th ed. New York: Routledge, 2017.

Garland-Thomson, Rosemarie. *Extraordinary Bodies: Figuring Physical Disability in American Culture and Literature*. New York: Columbia University Press, 1997.

———. "Integrating Disability, Transforming Feminist Theory." In *Feminist Disability Studies*. Ed. Kim Q. Hall. Bloomington: Indiana University Press, 2011: 13–44.

———. *Staring: How We Look*. New York: Oxford University Press, 2009.

McRuer, Robert. *Crip Theory: Cultural Signs of Queerness and Disability*. New York: New York University Press, 2004.

Mitchell, David T., and Sharon L. Snyder. *Narrative Prosthesis: Disability and the Dependencies of Discourse.* Ann Arbor: University of Michigan Press, 2000.

Schalk, Samantha Dawn. *Bodyminds Reimagined: (Dis)ability, Race, and Gender in Black Women's Speculative Fiction.* Durham, NC: Duke University Press, 2018.

Snyder, Sharon L., Brenda Jo Brueggemann, and Rosemarie Garland-Thomson, eds. *Disability Studies: Enabling the Humanities.* New York: MLA, 2002.

TERMS FOR POETIC FORM

Here readers will find a beginning list of basic terms for discussing poetic form. For more information and examples, readers may look up any of these or related terms online and consult published guidebooks. There are many good guidebooks to poetic terms as well as, more broadly, to literary terms in general. I especially recommend William Harmon and Hugh Holman, *A Handbook to Literature*. Serious students may wish to own it. Serious students of poetry may wish to consult or own the *Princeton Encyclopedia of Poetry and Poetics*. My favorite book of poetic terms is John Hollander's *Rhyme's Reason*, which brilliantly defines each term in language that acts out the term it defines. While I highly recommend it, some readers find it too witty.

THE SOUND PATTERNS OF WORDS

rhyme: when words begin with different sounds and end with the same sound. Examples: wow and cow, dog and slog, honey and funny, cupcake and milkshake, hip-hop and flip-flop.

alliteration: sounds repeated at the beginnings of nearby words: loud lass, cute cat, green grows the grass. (Note: there is no alliteration in *certain curtain* or *with whom* or *Go George!*, because those words do not begin with the same *sounds*, even though they begin with the same letters.)

assonance: vowel sounds repeated in the middles of words: hope grows cold slowly.

onomatopoeia: language that mimics the sound it describes, like *quack* for the sound of a duck, or, more subtly, the *stl* sound in the phrase *whistling wind*.

THE RHYTHM OF LINES

meter: the rhythmical pattern of stressed and unstressed—accented and unaccented—syllables in a line of poetry.

measure: the same as meter.

foot: the basic unit of meter, usually with two or three syllables, one of them stressed.

scanning or **scansion**: to scan a line or poem is to observe and mark its metrical pattern (its pattern of meter).

iambic and **iamb**: an iamb is a foot of 2 syllables, the first syllable unstressed and the second syllable stressed. Iambic meter consists of a series of iambs. It is the most common meter in English. Examples of iambs: hurray, José, today, Japan, review, "To be or not to be" (from Shakespeare's *Hamlet*), "My Life had stood - a Loaded Gun -" (from Emily Dickinson).

trochaic and **trochee**: a trochee is a foot of 2 syllables, the first syllable stressed and the second syllable unstressed. Trochaic meter consists of a series of trochees. Examples of trochees: Twitter, Facebook, Google, Kathy, Brian, Johnson, tip-top, hip-hop, China, London, Boston, "Once upon a midnight dreary, while I pondered, weak and weary" (from Edgar Allan Poe's "The Raven").

anapestic and **anapest**: an anapest is a foot of 3 syllables, the first 2 syllables unstressed and the third syllable stressed. Anapestic meter consists of a series of anapests. Examples of anapests: in the blink of an eye, in the fullness of time, "And the eyes of the sleepers waxed deadly and chill" (from Lord Byron's "The Destruction of Sennacherib"), "Can the warrior forget how sublimely you rose?" (From Jane Johnston Schoolcraft's "Invocation to my Maternal Grand-father").

dactylic and **dactyl**: a dactyl is a foot of 3 syllables, the first syllable stressed and the last 2 syllables unstressed. Dactylic meter consists of a series of dactyls. Examples of dactyls: Mexico, Canada, Pakistan, India, Washington, Katherine, Mulligan, volleyball, poetry, higgledy-piggledy, "Cannon to right of them / Cannon to left of them" (from Alfred, Lord Tennyson's "The Charge of the Light Brigade").

spondaic and **spondee**: a spondee is a foot of 2 syllables, both of them stressed. An individual spondee is fairly unusual. A series of spondees falling into a regular spondaic meter is extremely unusual. Examples of spondees: Go! Go!, Yes, now!, Help! Help!, "Howl, howl, howl, howl!" (from Shakespeare's *King Lear*).

dimeter: a dimeter line has 2 feet.

trimeter: a trimeter line has 3 feet.

tetrameter: a tetrameter line has 4 feet.

pentameter: a pentameter line has 5 feet.

hexameter (or Alexandrine): a hexameter line has 6 feet.

hendecasyllabic: an iambic pentameter line with an extra unstressed syllable at the end (*hen* means eleven). Example: "Yet in these thoughts myself almost despising" (from Shakespeare's Sonnet 29).

end-rhyme: rhyme at the end of a line.

internal rhyme: rhyme in the middle of a line (before the end of the line).

end-stressed rhyme (more traditionally, in a sexist usage, called masculine rhyme): end-rhyme with a stress on the last syllable. Example: talk / walk.

end-unstressed rhyme (more traditionally, in a sexist usage, called feminine rhyme): end-rhyme with the last syllable unstressed. Example: talking / walking.

off-rhyme, near rhyme, half rhyme, slant rhyme, eye-rhyme: when words nearly rhyme without fully rhyming, or appear to rhyme by their spelling but do not actually rhyme. Examples: hush / push, ball / bull, friend / mined, girl / goal, boy / buy.

caesura: a strong pause in the middle of a line, signaled by punctuation—such as a period, question mark, exclamation point, semi-colon (;), or colon (:)—that requires a stronger pause than a comma.

end-stop: when a line ends with a pause enforced by punctuation at the end of the line.

enjambment: when a line has no pause or punctuation at the end, so that the last word of the line leads directly into the first word of the next line.

THE PATTERN OF STANZAS OR GROUPS OF LINES

stanza: a group of poetic lines, usually separated from other stanzas by a blank line (or sometimes by indenting the beginning of the stanza).

couplet: a 2-line stanza, or—as at the end of a Shakespearean sonnet, a pair of rhymed lines.

tercet: a 3-line stanza.

quatrain: a 4-line stanza, or a 4-line section of a sonnet.

sestet: a 6-line stanza, or a 6-line section of a sonnet.

octet or octave: an 8-line stanza, or an 8-line section of a sonnet.

ballad form (ballad stanza, ballad meter): a ballad has iambic quatrains with a tetrameter (4-foot) line, then a trimeter (3-foot) line, then another tetrameter line followed again by another trimeter line (4 feet, 3 feet, 4 feet, 3 feet). Also known as hymn meter, because hymns typically follow the same pattern.

sonnet, including Shakespearean (or English) sonnets and Petrarchan (or Italian) sonnets: sonnets have 14 lines in iambic pentameter. A Shakespearean sonnet has three quatrains followed by a couplet (4-4-4-2), with the rhyme scheme abab cdcd efef gg. A Petrarchan sonnet has an octave and then a sestet (8-6). The octave rhymes abbaabba, while the sestet can follow a variety of rhyme schemes. Poets (sonneteers) often work variations on these two basic patterns. (Spenserian sonnets, a less common form, have a rhyme scheme of abab bcbc cdcd ee.)

blank verse: unrhymed lines of iambic pentameter (common for extremely long poems, where rhyme might get tiring, such as John Milton's *Paradise Lost* or William Wordsworth's *The Prelude*).

free verse: poetry without regular rhyme or meter.

⚘ Works Cited ⚘

"Actress' Abortion Written into TV Show." *The Onion*, March 13, 2007. http://www.theonion.com/articles/actress-abortion-written-into-tv-show,2166/.

Adichie, Chimamanda Ngozi. *We Should All Be Feminists*. New York: Anchor, 2014.

Althusser, Louis. "Ideology and Ideological State Apparatuses (Notes towards an Investigation)." In *Lenin and Philosophy and Other Essays*. Trans. Ben Brewster. New York: Monthly Review Press, 1971: 127–186.

Aristotle. *Poetics*. Trans. S. H. Butcher. New York: Hill and Wang, 1961.

Austen, Jane. *Persuasion*. 1817. Ed. James Kinsley. New York: Oxford University Press, 2004.

Austen, Jane. *Pride and Prejudice*. 1813. Ed. James Kinsley. New York: Oxford University Press, 2008.

Austen, Jane. *Sense and Sensibility*. 1811. Ed. James Kinsley. New York: Oxford University Press, 2004.

Barthes, Roland. "The Death of the Author." In *Image-Music-Text*. Selected and trans. Stephen Heath. New York: Hill and Wang, 1977: 142–148.

Beauvoir, Simone de. *The Second Sex*. Trans. Constance Borde and Sheila Malovany-Chevallier. New York: Random House, 2010.

Bechdel, Alison. *Dykes to Watch Out For*. Ithaca, NY: Firebrand Books, 1986.

Bennett, Jane. *Vibrant Matter: A Political Ecology of Things*. Durham, NC: Duke University Press, 2010.

Bhabha, Homi K. *The Location of Culture*. London: Routledge, 1994.

The Bible: Authorized King James Version. Ed. Robert Carroll and Stephen Prickett. Oxford: Oxford University Press, 2008.

Booth, Wayne. *The Rhetoric of Fiction*. Chicago: University of Chicago Press, 1961.

Brault, Matthew W. "Americans with Disabilities: 2010." US Department of Commerce. Economics and Statistics Administration. United States Census Bureau, 2012.

Brontë, Charlotte. *Jane Eyre*. 1847. London: Oxford University Press, 1973.

Brooks, Cleanth. *The Well Wrought Urn: Studies in the Structure of Poetry*. New York: Reynal & Hitchcock, 1947.

Browning, Elizabeth Barrett. *Selected Poems*. Ed. Margaret Forster. Baltimore: Johns Hopkins University Press, 1988.

Campbell, SueEllen. "Asking Ecocritical Questions." In *Teaching North American Environmental Literature*. Ed. Laird Christensen, Mark C. Long, and Fred Waage. New York: MLA, 2008: 215–222.

Chopin, Kate. *The Complete Works of Kate Chopin*. Ed. Per Seyersted. Baton Rouge: Louisiana State University Press, 1969.

Cixous, Hélène. "The Laugh of the Medusa." In *New French Feminisms: An Anthology*. Ed. Elaine Marks and Isabelle de Courtivron. Amherst: University of Massachusetts Press, 1980: 245–264.

Coleridge, Samuel Taylor. *Biographia Literaria or Biographical Sketches of My Literary Life and Opinions*. Ed. James Engell and W. Jackson Bate. 2 vols. Princeton, NJ: Princeton University Press, 1983.

Crenshaw, Kimberlé. "Demarginalizing the Intersection of Race and Sex: A Black Feminist Critique of Antidiscrimination Doctrine, Feminist Theory and Antiracist Politics." *University of Chicago Legal Forum* (1989): 139–167.

Crenshaw, Kimberlé. "Mapping the Margins: Intersectionality, Identity Politics, and Violence against Women of Color." *Stanford Law Review* 43.6 (July 1991): 1241–1299.

Deloria, Philip Joseph. *Playing Indian*. New Haven, CT: Yale University Press, 1998.

de Man, Paul. "Semiology and Rhetoric." *Allegories of Reading: Figural Language in Rousseau, Nietzsche, Rilke, and Proust*. New Haven, CT: Yale University Press, 1979.

Derrida, Jacques. "Différance." *Margins of Philosophy*. Trans. Alan Bass. Chicago: University of Chicago Press, 1982.

Dickinson, Emily. *The Poems of Emily Dickinson: Reading Edition*. Ed. R. W. Franklin. Cambridge, MA: Harvard University Press, 1999.

Donne, John. *The Complete English Poems*. Ed. C. J. Patrides and Robin Hamilton. 2nd ed. London: Dent, 1994.

Doyle, Arthur Conan. "The Adventure of Charles Augustus Milverton." 1904. In *The Return of Sherlock Holmes*. Ed. Richard Lancelyn Green. Oxford: Oxford University Press, 1993: 157–175.

Du Bois, W. E. Burghardt. *The Souls of Black Folk*. 1903. New York: Fawcett, 1961.

Duggan, Lisa. "Queering the State." *Social Text* 39 (1994): 1–14.

Eagleton, Terry. *Literary Theory*. Minneapolis: University of Minnesota Press, 1983.

"Family Resources Survey: United Kingdom, 2010/11." London: Department for Work and Pensions, 2012. https://www.gov.uk/government/uploads/system/uploads/attachment_data/file/222839/frs_2010_11_report.pdf.

Fanon, Frantz. *Black Skin, White Masks*. Trans. Charles Lam Markmann. New York: Grove, 1967.

Fanon, Frantz. *Les damnés de la terre*. Paris: François Maspero, 1976.

Fanon, Frantz. *The Wretched of the Earth.* Trans. Richard Philcox. New York: Grove, 2004.

Faulkner, William. *As I Lay Dying.* 1930. New York: Vintage International, 1990.

Faulkner, William. *Light in August.* 1932. New York: Vintage International, 1990.

Felski, Rita. *The Limits of Critique.* Chicago: University of Chicago Press, 2015.

Foucault, Michel. *The History of Sexuality, Volume I.* Trans. Robert Hurley. New York: Vintage, 1978.

Foucault, Michel. *"Society Must Be Defended": Lectures at the Collège de France, 1975–1976.* Ed. Mauro Bertani and Alessandro Fontana. Trans. David Macy. New York: Picador, 2003.

Freud, Sigmund. *The Interpretation of Dreams (First Part).* Vol. 4. *The Standard Edition of the Complete Psychological Works of Sigmund Freud.* Ed. and trans. James Strachey. London: Hogarth Press, 1955.

Frost, Robert. *Robert Frost: Collected Poems, Prose, and Plays.* Ed. Richard Poirier and Mark Richardson. New York: Library of America, 1995.

Gates, Henry Louis, Jr. *The Signifying Monkey: A Theory of African-American Literary Criticism.* New York: Oxford University Press, 1988.

Glissant, Edouard. *Caribbean Discourse: Selected Essays.* Trans. J. Michael Dash. Charlottesville: University Press of Virginia, 1989.

Guha, Ramachandra, and Juan Martínez-Alier. *Varieties of Environmentalism: Essays North and South.* London: Earthscan, 1997.

Hall, Stuart. "Cultural Identity and Cinematic Representation." *Framework* 36 (1989): 68–81.

Hall, Stuart. "Encoding/decoding." In *Culture, Media, Language: Working Papers in Cultural Studies, 1971–1979.* Ed. Stuart Hall et al. London: Hutchinson, 1980: 128–138.

Hall, Stuart."Old and New Identities, Old and New Ethnicities." In *Culture, Globalization and the World System: Contemporary Conditions for the Representation of Ethnicity.* Ed. Anthony D. King. Minneapolis: University of Minnesota Press, 1997: 41–68.

Hemingway, Ernest. *The Short Stories of Ernest Hemingway.* New York: Scribner, 1938.

Huhndorf, Shari M. *Going Native: Indians in the American Cultural Imagination.* Ithaca, NY: Cornell University Press, 2001.

Irigaray, Luce. *This Sex Which Is Not One.* Trans. Catherine Porter with Carolyn Burke. Ithaca, NY: Cornell University Press, 1985.

Jahn, Janheinz. *Neo-African Literature: A History of Black Writing.* 1966. Trans. Oliver Coburn and Ursula Lehrburger. New York: Grove Press, 1968.

Jakobson, Roman. "Closing Statement: Linguistics and Poetics." In *Style in Language.* Ed. Thomas A. Sebeok. Cambridge, MA: MIT Press, 1960: 350–377.

Jameson, Fredric. *The Political Unconscious: Narrative as a Socially Symbolic Act.* Ithaca, NY: Cornell University Press, 1981.

Lacan, Jacques. *Ecrits: A Selection.* Trans. Alan Sheridan. New York: Norton, 1977.

Lacan, Jacques. *The Four Fundamental Concepts of Psycho-Analysis*. Ed. Jacques-Alain Miller. Trans. Alan Sheridan. London: Hogarth Press, 1977.

Laqueur, Thomas. *Making Sex: Body and Gender from the Greeks to Freud*. Cambridge, MA: Harvard University Press, 1990.

Larsen, Nella. *"Quicksand" and "Passing."* Ed. Deborah E. McDowell. New Brunswick, NJ: Rutgers University Press, 1986.

Levinson, Marjorie. *Wordsworth's Great Period Poems: Four Essays*. Cambridge: Cambridge University Press, 1986.

Marx, Karl. *A Contribution to the Critique of Political Economy*. Trans. N. I. Stone. 2nd ed. Chicago: Charles H. Kerr, 1904.

Melville, Herman. *Moby Dick*. 1851. Ed. Tony Tanner. Oxford: Oxford University Press, 1988.

Mitchell, David T. "Narrative Prosthesis and the Materiality of Metaphor." In *Disability Studies: Enabling the Humanities*. Ed. Sharon L. Snyder, Brenda Jo Brueggemann, and Rosemarie Garland-Thomson. New York: MLA, 2002: 15–30.

Mitchell, David T., and Sharon L. Snyder. *Narrative Prosthesis: Disability and the Dependencies of Discourse*. Ann Arbor: University of Michigan Press, 2000.

Mos Def. "Hip Hop." *Black on Both Sides*. Priority Records, 1999. CD.

Mulvey, Laura. "Visual Pleasure and Narrative Cinema." In *Visual and Other Pleasures*. Bloomington: Indiana University Press, 1989: 14–26.

Ngũgĩ, James. [Ngũgĩ wa Thiong'o.] *Weep Not, Child*. 1964. New York: Collier Books, 1969.

Ngũgĩ wa Thiong'o. *Decolonising the Mind: The Politics of Language in African Literature*. London: James Currey, 1986.

Nixon, Rob. *Slow Violence and the Environmentalism of the Poor*. Cambridge, MA: Harvard University Press, 2011.

Plato. *The Dialogues of Plato*. Trans. B. Jowett. 4th ed. 4 vols. Oxford: Oxford University Press, 1953.

Pound, Ezra. *Selected Poems*. New York: New Directions, 1949.

Price, Margaret. "Defining Mental Disability." In *The Disability Studies Reader*. Ed. Lennard J. Davis. 4th ed. New York: Routledge, 2013: 298–307.

Proulx, Annie. "Brokeback Mountain." In *Close Range: Wyoming Stories*. New York: Scribner, 1999: 253–285.

Rich, Adrienne. "Compulsory Heterosexuality and Lesbian Existence." *Signs* 5.4 (Summer 1980): 631–660.

Robinson, Edwin Arlington. *Selected Poems of Edwin Arlington Robinson*. Ed. Morton Dauwen Zabel. New York: Collier, 1965.

Rosaldo, Renato. *Culture and Truth: The Remaking of Social Analysis*. 2nd ed. Boston: Beacon, 1993.

Rowling, J. K. *Harry Potter and the Chamber of Secrets*. New York: Arthur A. Levine Books, 1999.

Rubin, Gayle. "The Traffic in Women: Notes on the 'Political Economy' of Sex." In *Toward an Anthropology of Women*. Ed. Rayna R. Reiter. New York: Monthly Review Press, 1975: 157–210.

Saussure, Ferdinand de. *Course in General Linguistics*. Ed. Charles Bally and Albert Reidlinger. Trans. Wade Baskin. New York: Philosophical Library, 1959.

Sedgwick, Eve Kosofsky. "Paranoid Reading and Reparative Reading; or, You're So Paranoid, You Probably Think This Introduction Is about You." In *Novel Gazing: Queer Readings in Fiction*. Ed. Sedgwick. Durham, NC: Duke University Press, 1997: 1–37.

Shakespeare, William. *The Riverside Shakespeare*. Ed. G. Blakemore Evans et al. 2nd ed. Boston: Houghton, 1997.

Sisson, Gretchen and Katrina Kimport, "Telling Stories about Abortion: Abortion- Related Plots in American Film and Television, 1916–2013." *Contraception* 89 (2014): 413–418.

Soyinka, Wole. *Myth, Literature and the African World*. Cambridge: Cambridge University Press, 1976.

Spivak, Gayatri Chakravorty. "Can the Subaltern Speak? Speculations on Widow-Sacrifice." *Wedge* 7/8 (Winter/Spring 1985): 120–130. Longer version in *Marxism and the Interpretation of Culture*. Ed. Laurence Grossberg and Cary Nelson. Urbana: University of Illinois Press, 1985: 271–313.

Spivak, Gayatri Chakravorty. *A Critique of Postcolonial Reason: Toward a History of the Vanishing Present*. Cambridge, MA: Harvard University Press, 1999.

Spivak, Gayatri Chakravorty. *In Other Worlds*. New York: Methuen, 1987.

Spivak, Gayatri Chakravorty. *Outside in the Teaching Machine*. New York: Routledge, 1993.

Spivak, Gayatri Chakravorty. "Three Women's Texts and a Critique of Imperialism." *Critical Inquiry* 12 (Autumn 1985): 243–261.

Stevens, Wallace. *The Collected Poems of Wallace Stevens*. New York: Knopf, 1982.

Whitman, Walt. *Complete Poetry and Collected Prose*. Ed. Justin Kaplan. New York: Library of America, 1982.

Wordsworth, William. *Poetical Works*. Ed. Thomas Hutchinson and Ernest de Selincourt. Oxford: Oxford University Press, 1969.

Photographic Credits

Chapter 2: page 24, William R. Ferris Collection, Southern Folklife Collection, Wilson Library, University of North Carolina at Chapel Hill. **Chapter 3:** page 45, Ferdinand de Saussure (1857–1913). Courtesy of Library of Congress. **Chapter 4:** page 88, Jacques Derrida (1930–2004). Courtesy of University of California, Irvine; page 143, Photo by Giancarlo BOTTI/Gamma-Rapho via Getty Images. **Chapter 5:** page 121, courtesy of Library of Congress. Page 143, Photo by Laski Diffusion/Getty Images **Chapter 6:** page 166, Photo by Herve GLOAGUEN/Gamma-Rapho via Getty Images; page 177, Laura Mulvey (1941–). Courtesy of Laura Mulvey; page 184, Kimberlé Crenshaw (1959–), UCLA School of Law. **Chapter 7:** page 193, courtesy of Library of Congress; page 198, Photo by Paco Freire/SOPA Images/LightRocket via Getty Images; page 203, Michel Foucault (1926–1984), Courtesy of Bruce Jackson; page 205, Photo by Diana Davies, Manuscripts and Archvies Division, The New York Public Library; page 214, Eve Kosofsky Sedgwick (1950–2009). Duke University, 1997. **Chapter 8:** page 230, Karl Marx (1818–1883), London, 1861, Courtesy of International Institute of Social History; page 237, Antonio Gramsci (1891–1937), Photo by Laski Diffusion/Getty Images; page 241, Louis Althusser (1918–1990). **Chapter 9:** page 273, Stephen Greenblatt (1943–); page 277, Tintern Abbey, by Copley Fielding. From Thomas Roscoe, Wanderings and Excursions in South Wales, with the scenery of the River Wye, 1837. © The British Library Board; page 282, Jeremy Bentham's design for the Panopticon, 1791; page 286, Donald Maclellan/Hulton Archive/Getty Images; page 292, From Charles Sorel, The Extravagant Shepherd, or, The History of the Shepherd Lysis, 1654. Second edition, 1660. Courtesy of Rare Book and Manuscript Library, University of Illinois Library, University of Illinois at Urbana-Champaign. **Chapter 10:** page 303, Frantz Fanon (1925–1961); page 305, Ngũgĩ wa Thiong'o (1938–), Courtesy of Yale University; page 306, Chinua Achebe (1910–2013), Courtesy of Don Hamerman; page 307, Photo by Ulf Andersen/Getty Images; page 310, Honi K. Bhabha (1949–), Courtesy of Harvard University; page 315, Gayatri Chakravorty Spivak delivering her lecture Art and Democracy as part of Cork Caucus 2005, curated by Art/not art, Charles Esche and Annie Fletcher. Image courtesy of the National Sculpture Factory, Ireland. Photographer: Dara McGrath; page 327, Gloria Anzaldua, photo by Margaret Randall; page 342, Beyonce and Jay-Z, Apes***t. **Chapter 11:** page 365, Stanley Fish (1938–) reading, Ferdinand Hamburger Archives, Sheridan Libraries, Johns Hopkins University. **Chapter 12** page 401, Stéphanie and Ali (Marion Cotillard and Matthias Schoenaerts) head to the beach to go for a swim in *Rust and Bone*.

✦ Index ✦

Key terms appear in bold, along with the numbers for the pages that introduce and explain them.